Conceptions of the Absurd
From Surrealism to the Existential Thought of Chestov and Fondane

THE EUROPEAN HUMANITIES RESEARCH CENTRE

UNIVERSITY OF OXFORD

The European Humanities Research Centre of the University of Oxford organizes a range of academic activities, including conferences and workshops, and publishes scholarly works under its own imprint, LEGENDA. Within Oxford, the EHRC bridges, at the research level, the main humanities faculties: Modern Languages, English, Modern History, Literae Humaniores, Music and Theology. The Centre stimulates interdisciplinary research collaboration throughout these subject areas and provides an Oxford base for advanced researchers in the humanities.

The Centre's publications programme focuses on making available the results of advanced research in medieval and modern languages and related interdisciplinary areas. An Editorial Board, whose members are drawn from across the British university system, covers the principal European languages. Titles include works on French, German, Italian, Portuguese, Russian and Spanish literature. In addition, the EHRC co-publishes with the Society for French Studies, the British Comparative Literature Association and the Modern Humanities Research Association. The Centre also publishes *Oxford German Studies* and *Film Studies*, and has launched a Special Lecture Series under the LEGENDA imprint.

Enquiries about the Centre's publishing activities should be addressed to:
Professor Malcolm Bowie, Director

Further information:
Kareni Bannister, Senior Publications Officer
European Humanities Research Centre
University of Oxford
47 Wellington Square, Oxford OX1 2JF
enquiries@ehrc.ox.ac.uk
www.ehrc.ox.ac.uk

LEGENDA

European Humanities Research Centre
University of Oxford

Conceptions of the Absurd

From Surrealism to the Existential Thought of Chestov and Fondane

❖

RAMONA FOTIADE

LEGENDA
European Humanities Research Centre
University of Oxford
2001

Published by the
European Humanities Research Centre
of the University of Oxford
47 Wellington Square
Oxford OX1 2JF

LEGENDA is the publications imprint of the
European Humanities Research Centre

ISBN 1 900755 47 5

First published 2001

British Library Cataloguing in Publication Data
A CIP catalogue record for this book is available from the British Library

LEGENDA series designed by Cox Design Partnership, Witney, Oxon
Printed in Great Britain by
Information Press
Eynsham
Oxford OX8 1JJ

Copy-Editor: Dr Jeffrey Dean

CONTENTS

ACKNOWLEDGEMENTS

I am particularly grateful to Toby Garfitt for his advice and support throughout the years, as well as his invaluable help in reading and correcting the final draft of this volume. I would also like to thank Alan Montefiore, without whose continuing help and guidance my research project would not have been possible. Christina Howells and Michael Holland, who supervised this project when it was a thesis, as well as Rhiannon Goldthorpe and Leszek Kolakowski, who examined it, made useful suggestions and corrections with regard to matters of style and content. The following people were kind enough either to read parts of my work or to discuss ideas relating to it with me: Isaiah Berlin, Malcolm Bowie, Michael Inwood, Olivier Salazar-Ferrer, Alfons Grieder. I am also indebted to Jasper Griffin, who translated many passages from Greek and Latin. While my special acknowledgements and thanks go to each and every one of them, I am the only one responsible for any errors and infelicities in what follows.

The Grut Charitable Trust provided the material support for my research at Oxford University. The British Academy and the Department of French at Glasgow University gave me the opportunity to undertake extended research in Paris and to spend a period of study leave preparing the manuscript of this book for publication. Alice Laurent provided unlimited access to private archives and information on Chestov's life and work. Her generous help and support is much appreciated. Thanks are also due to Claire Paulhan and Jacqueline Artier, for allowing me to consult the archives of the Institut Mémoires de l'édition contemporaine and the Bibliothèque de la Sorbonne respectively.

Finally, I would like to thank my parents, and to pay homage to my father's published translations of Chestov's philosophical works and correspondence from the original Russian.

NOTE ON REFERENCES

Any emphasis (e.g. italicized words or passages) in quotations is original, unless otherwise stated.

Throughout the book, I have adopted the French transliteration of Léon Chestov's name. Occasionally, references to English critical studies on Chestov include a different transliteration: e.g. Louis S. Shein, *The Philosophy of Lev Shestov (1866–1938): A Russian Religious Existentialist* (Lewiston, ME: The Edwin Mellen Press, 1991).

INTRODUCTION

The twentieth century might, with hindsight, be described as the conflicting site of successive avant-garde waves that bear witness to the presence of a single unifying, pervasive concern with the Absurd. A surprising array of genres and a range of different types of intellectual or artistic endeavour have, at various times, been placed under the overarching denomination of the Absurd: for instance Dada and Surrealist experiments in art and literature or cinema, Ionesco's and Beckett's theatre, Camus's philosophy, Giacometti's sculptures, and so on. But the diversity of manifestations is perhaps less astonishing than the overall persistence of wilful attempts at questioning the validity of the classical rationalist discourse. This reaction to the perceived totalizing (totalitarian) aspirations of reason has generally been the object of studies devoted to the notion of irrationalism and to its extreme expression in madness. The significant recurrence of some forms of the absurd, such as the relationship between mental alienation and creativity, has often come to the attention of critics and philosophers, in its unnervingly elusive yet nagging provocation:

> La fréquence dans le monde moderne de ces œuvres qui éclatent dans la folie ne prouve rien sans doute sur la raison de ce monde, sur le sens de ces œuvres, ni même sur les rapports noués et dénoués entre le monde réel et les artistes qui ont produit les œuvres. Cette fréquence, pourtant, il faut la prendre au sérieux, comme l'insistance d'une question.[1]

Each time the question is voiced, the unsettling dissonance that is etymologically entwined with the absurd (Lat. *absurdum*, 'out of tune') can be heard as well. What is the absurd trying to say? Does it mean to say something about reason? How can it really *mean* anything? The sense of the apparent meaninglessness of individual existence, which derived as much from the increasing concern with human finitude as from the heightened awareness of a 'total crisis of civilization',[2] inspired a number of literary and philosophical interpretations of the absurd in the first half of the twentieth century.

This study aims to provide a coherent critical presentation of existential thought in the context of the philosophical and cultural debates of the 1920s and 1930s in France, with special reference to the Surrealist movement. While examining the ideas that constituted the line of thought elaborated by Léon Chestov (1866–1938) and Benjamin Fondane (1898–1944), I propose to show that, far from being an isolated or extraneous development in relation to the French intellectual milieu of the time, the existential project found support and illustration in the dissident views held by authors working on the boundaries of Surrealism (Antonin Artaud, Roger Gilbert-Lecomte, René Daumal). This particular approach highlights only one aspect of the revival of existential ideas in France during the inter-war period, and is inspired by Benjamin Fondane's critical response to the controversies and divisions inside the Surrealist movement, which can be said to reflect the wider confrontation between philosophical trends competing for supremacy in all other areas of French intellectual endeavour.

The message of the absurd is eminently multifarious and discordant. It actually emerges from a variety of sources, which accounts for its eclectic twentieth-century configuration. During the first decades of the century, the dramatic loss of faith in the progressive and purposeful character of history (as a result of the horrifying bloodshed of the First World War) brought about a resurgence of anti-rationalist conceptions. Added to this, the late-nineteenth-century idea of the death of God, and consequently the disappearance of the transcendent grounding of ethical and cognitive values, cancelled out established theological and moral arguments concerning the meaning of human existence. One can say that the full implications of Nietzsche's pronouncement in *The Gay Science* really came into their own during the First World War, as the magnitude of the destruction of human lives and the senseless atrocity of the trenches was beginning to sink in. But even without necessarily considering the collapse of Christian axiology in the light of Nietzsche's momentous reception in France at the turn of the century,[3] it is fair to argue that the decline of religious faith in modern times provoked much more than a crisis of classical metaphysical concepts; it led to the dissolution of the 'psychological matrix'[4] that accompanied man's theistic interpretation of the world. The sudden disclosure of a universe that seemed devoid of any pre-established meaning and constantly in need of being invested with human intentions and determinations in order to become meaningful highlighted the connection between man's new-found freedom and nothingness, between his unlimited choice and a 'vertigo of possibilities'.[5] Before becoming a favourite twentieth-century theme, nothingness figured extensively in Kierkegaard's influential analysis of anxiety in its relationship to freedom. Beyond the original theological argument in which Kierkegaard couched it, the notion of anxiety and the idea of man's confrontation with nothingness played a crucial part in the constitution of most subsequent interpretations of the absurd (from Heidegger to Sartre and Camus).

The emergence of the preoccupation with the absurd in the early twentieth century can also be associated with the steady rise of nihilism in Europe, from its origin in the influential generation of Russian intellectuals of the 1860s (preceded by Alexander Herzen, and including Chernyshevski, Dobrolyubov and Pisarev among others),[6] to its more recent illustration in avant-garde art and literature. One of the first philosophers who introduced this line of thought in France in the 1920s, and who moreover disclosed the subtle affinity between Russian nihilism and Nietzsche's philosophy, was Léon Chestov, a Russian emigré best known at the time for his influential comparative studies on Dostoevsky and Nietzsche, as well as on Tolstoy and Nietzsche.[7] As early as 1922–3, Chestov published a number of articles and philosophical essays in French translation,[8] which had a lasting impact on the generation of French writers and philosophers including Bataille and Gide, Malraux and Camus (to name but a few). Although less well-known than Nietzsche's first French biographer, Daniel Halévy, Chestov was equally instrumental in shaping Nietzsche's early reception in France. Some writers, such as Bataille, first came into contact with the German philosopher's thought by way of Chestov's critical interpretation.[9] Interestingly, this must also be the case for Dostoevsky's early reception in France if we are to judge by the available documentation, which often includes references to Chestov's works. Again, Bataille perhaps best captures Chestov's unique contribution to philosophical debates during the 1920s and 1930s, when he writes in an autobiographical note: 'Léon Chestov philosophait à partir de Dostoïevsky et de Nietzsche, ce qui me séduisait.'[10] But Bataille was only giving expression to a relatively widespread opinion concerning Chestov's non-systematic approach to philosophy. Jules de Gaultier,[11] as well as Boris de Schloezer (Chestov's translator and first critic in France) and later Camus,[12] referred directly or indirectly to the same peculiar blend of Russian and Nietzschean nihilism that intrigued and seduced Chestov's readers.

Among the young French intellectuals of the 1930s on whom Chestov's thought had a decisive impact, Camus remains the most prominent representative of the absurd in twentieth-century French literature and philosophy. Yet critics and historians have rarely pointed out the fact that Camus's *Mythe de Sisyphe* is a barely disguised polemical reply to Chestov's arguments on the absurd, and indirectly pays homage to most of the recurrent themes in the Russian philosopher's writing (the 'wall of evidence', the revolt against reason, the existential fight against Husserlian scientific rationalism, the affirmation of freedom and personal, subjective experience, and so on). Camus, not unlike Chestov before him, hesitated to speak of a 'philosophy of the absurd', and declared instead, in the opening paragraph of the *Mythe de Sisyphe*, his interest in a certain 'absurd sensibility': 'Les pages qui suivent traitent d'une sensibilité absurde qu'on peut trouver éparse dans le siècle — et non d'une philosophie absurde que notre temps, à proprement parler, n'a pas connue.'[13] In his book on Dostoevsky and Nietzsche, Chestov had used the phrase 'la philosophie de la tragédie' to define his own approach, and one can say that ever since the beginning of the twentieth century the absurd has been thematized in relation to (and sometimes as identical with) notions pertaining to tragedy, death, insanity, suffering and alienation. Camus interestingly suggests that his analysis in *Le Mythe de Sisyphe* will be guided by the 'pure' description of a *mal de l'esprit*.[14] But this vague, although persistent, mention of a spiritual *malaise* translates the same intuition (of an impending crisis) that the literary and artistic avant-garde movements of the turn of the century had brought to light. As one of the historians of the 1930s writes, regarding the emergence of a tragic conception of human existence:

> C'est aussi à partir des années 1930 qu'a commencé de s'exprimer dans toute la littérature européenne une vision de plus en plus tragique, de plus en plus désespérée de la condition de l'homme [...]. A cette mise en question du rationalisme dans la littérature depuis le début du siècle avait correspondu un mouvement analogue dans la réflexion philosophique.[15]

Chestov's existential critique of rationality sometimes seems to come surprisingly close to the nihilistic rejection of established aesthetic and ethical values that characterized the initial stance of Dada as well as the Surrealist avant-garde. In an article published in 1929, entitled 'Un philosophe tragique: Léon Chestov',[16] Benjamin Fondane explicitly comments on the complicity between Chestov's existential thought and the early orientation of avant-garde movements. Breton's famous dictum, 'Ni Dieu, ni maître', eloquently captures the spirit of widespread nihilistic rebellion that animated both the Dada and the Surrealist revolt against authority. In his *Entretiens*, Breton provided a most vivid description of the wartime confusion and brutal reversal of values, which characterized the generation of young people he belonged to:

> [...] vous connaissez cette nouvelle de Huysmans, un des chefs-d'œuvre du naturalisme, qui prend place dans *Les Soirées de Médan*. Eh bien, il suffirait de transposer cela quelque peu, de le maintenir un peu moins à ras de terre pour se faire une idée de l'*humeur* de certains gens dont j'étais, que la guerre de 1914 venait d'arracher à toutes leurs aspirations pour les précipiter dans un cloaque de sang, de sottise et de boue.[17]

However, Breton's statement indirectly highlights the fact that the war only acted as a powerful catalyst for tendencies that had already acquired more or less definite form in the art and literature of the *fin de siècle*. Breton's passionate, sarcastic paraphrase of Durtal's tirade from Huysmans's *Là-bas*[18] is just one of many striking examples of the Surrealist articulation of a transgressive discourse, an *au-delà de l'éthique*, inspired not so much by Nietzsche as by the decadent *fin-de-siècle* ideology. This affiliation becomes especially significant when one thinks of Breton's portrayal of Jacques Vaché as a kind of *Des Esseintes de l'action*.[19] Vaché exerted perhaps the most occult and long-lasting influence on Breton's understanding of revolt. It may suffice to recall here that Vaché's idea of humour, 'le sens de l'inutilité théâtrale (et sans joie) de tout', played a crucial part in the initial formulation of the Surrealist conception of the absurd. Alfred Jarry had preceded Vaché in this exploration *à rebours* of a paradoxically tragic sense of humour that illuminates the absurdity of the human condition. Jarry opened up the horizon of the theatrical and joyless futility of life under the implacable reign of death, which the First World War no less than the existential phenomenologies of human finitude (starting with Heidegger's *Sein-zum-Tode*) seemed bound to confirm. As one of the more recent critics of post-Jarry avant-garde writing has remarked: '*Ubu* ne conclut rien. *Ubu* n'inaugure rien non plus. N'engendre rien. N'annonce rien. Jarry trace un cercle où il promène ses acteurs et son public en rond. C'est ce chemin de ronde qui préfigure le siècle de l'Absurde qui va suivre.'[20]

In presenting Chestov's and Fondane's thought, the current study takes into account the two authors' consistent critique of both Husserlian and Hegelian phenomenologies, as well as their explicit attempt at distancing themselves from the philosophical conceptions elaborated by Heidegger, Jaspers, Sartre or Camus. A close examination of the French philosophical debates and the French reception of Chestov's and Fondane's works during the 1920s and 1930s has helped clarify the incomplete, and sometimes inaccurate, critical accounts of 'existential thought', as contrasted to better-known strands of Existentialism.

The term 'Existentialism' seems to have entered the French philosophical vocabulary towards the end of the 1930s, mostly in relation to Heidegger; it later gained precedence over words such as *existence* or *existentiel* (used as qualifiers in 'philosophie de l'existence' and 'philosophie existentielle'), which had been previously introduced with specific reference to Kierkegaard.[21] If Chestov and Fondane placed a special emphasis on the expression 'philosophie existentielle',[22] especially during the mid to late 1930s, this was a conscious attempt to distinguish more clearly their line of thought (as related to Kierkegaard's original use of the term 'existential') from the emerging German and French 'Existentialism' associated first with Heidegger and Jaspers and later with Sartre and Camus.

Chestov's article, 'Job ou Hegel? (A propos de la philosophie existentielle de Kierkegaard)',[23] published in 1935, anticipates his major study of Kierkegaard, *Kierkegaard et la philosophie existentielle*, published the following year, and explicitly insists on the difference between Kierkegaard's and Heidegger's philosophical conceptions. Chestov recalls the Husserlian phenomenological affiliation of Heidegger's ontological investigations, and contrasts Kierkegaard's non-systematic, subjective search for truth and certainty through faith with the systematic, speculative approach to truth and being, which goes back not only to Husserl's reclaimed Kantian heritage but also to Hegel's phenomenology, in opposition to which Kierkegaard defined his 'existential philosophy'.

Although in his first articles on philosophy Fondane avoids using any specific term to qualify Chestov's thought, and keeps to Chestov's phrase the 'philosophy of tragedy'[24] (as outlined in *La Philosophie de la tragédie: Dostoievski et Nietzsche*, 1926), from 1932 onwards, when he publishes his article on Heidegger and Dostoevsky, one can see a growing concern to clarify the distinction between Chestov's and

Heidegger's philosophical approaches. It is most probable that Fondane's deliberate decision to describe his own and Chestov's thought as 'philosophie existentielle'—a terminological choice that he amply elucidates and substantiates in at least three important philosophical studies written between 1936 and 1944[25]—emerged from an increasing need to define the 'existential' line of thought accurately and to distinguish it from rapidly proliferating variants of phenomenological or religious 'Existentialism'—from Heidegger, Jaspers, Sartre, Gabriel Marcel. In 1938, Fondane already considers the question of differentiating between 'existential philosophy' and Heidegger's ontology important enough to begin his presentation of Chestov by drawing attention to the confusion surrounding the term 'existential':

> Un critique allemand écrivait récemment que la philosophie de Léon Chestov commence justement là où celle de Heidegger finit: remarque d'autant plus pénétrante que l'auteur de *Sein und Zeit* et du *Kant*, passe pour être, lui aussi, un philosophe 'existentiel'; mais, pour cela même, sujette à malentendu. Il est vrai, qu'à la suite de Kierkegaard, Heidegger traite de l'angoisse, du néant, de l'être fini et délaissé, de la faute métaphysique dans l'être; mais [...] c'est à Kant que, finalement, il demande, en bon philosophe spéculatif, les moyens d'obtenir 'une lumière sur l'être'.[26]

Fondane, like Chestov, was well aware of the consequences of such misunderstandings, and explicitly addressed this problem in his later philosophical writings, in an attempt to preclude current and future critical misconstructions. Without anticipating the course of an argument that I intend to develop and substantiate in this study, what I want is to establish at this point is that, first, Chestov and Fondane deliberately and consistently described their thought as 'philosophie existentielle' or 'pensée existentielle'; and secondly, they shared a concern with accurately distinguishing the 'existential' line of thought from the emerging 'Existentialism' of the 1930s.

This study aims to restore Chestov's and Fondane's understanding of 'existential thought', in its interaction with the French intellectual milieu (in particular with the evolution of the Surrealist movement between 1928 and 1938), while paying special attention to the two authors' critique of Kantian, Husserlian and Hegelian arguments, as the most influential sources of philosophical investigations at the time. The restorative operation that I propose to undertake is not a historical reconstruction of either existential thought or Surrealism.

Relevant studies of literary history, surveys in the history of ideas, as well as available literary criticism, 'intellectual biographies' and other biographical material, constitute a useful, informative background, but not the focus of my argument. In relating Chestov's and Fondane's works to the controversies within and outside the boundaries of Surrealism, this study will bring out the distinctive features of 'existential thought' by comparing and contrasting them to the interpretation of philosophical and ideological issues that determined the split of the Surrealist movement and the emergence of alternative, dissident projects during a specific period of time. The method at work therefore combines the critical exposition of ideas with comparative analysis and aims to provide a theoretical and philosophical investigation rather than a mere historical account.

This particular approach determined the choice of a particular 'decade of controversy' (between 1928 and 1938) insofar as I decided to focus on the time when the interaction between existential thought and Surrealism was most relevant to the philosophical debates dominating the French intellectual milieu. Some preliminary remarks are needed in order to clarify the relevance of the two temporal reference points and the premiss of an argument that will hereafter assume rather than retrace the historical background briefly outlined and recalled here.

The evolution of Surrealism, from the days of its short-lived coexistence with the Dada movement to the so-called 'reasoning period', and the publication of the Second Manifesto in 1929, displays an inner tension between two major tendencies: on the one hand an anti-rationalist, individualistic revolt against secular and religious institutions, against moral and social constraints; on the other, an effort of integration in response to predominant scientific, cognitive and social theories of the time. The latter, prevailing tendency emerged from the attempt to validate on the one hand the results of early Surrealist experiments by relating them to a recognized theoretical foundation, and on the other the revolutionary aspirations of the movement by ensuring the effective transformation of reality, envisaged in its socio-political as much as in its aesthetic dimension. In this sense, psychoanalysis and Hegelian idealism provided the theoretical foundation required to validate the experiments with automatic writing, simulated madness or the investigation of dreams, whereas Marxist theory informed the Surrealist interpretation of revolution in terms of socio-political as well as aesthetic practice.

Fondane's critique of Surrealism, beginning with the articles published in 1927 and leading to the more substantial analyses included in *Rimbaud le voyou* (1933) and *Faux Traité d'esthétique: Essai sur la crise de réalité* (1938), focuses on the three main philosophical and theoretical sources that shaped the evolution of Surrealism: Hegelian idealism, Freudian psychoanalysis and Marxist historical materialism.[27] The publication of Fondane's *Faux Traité d'esthétique* in 1938 marks the culminating point of his debate with the Surrealist movement from the point of view of existential thought, which he starts to elaborate in 1929 in articles devoted on the one hand to Chestov and to comparative analyses of Chestov and Husserl or Heidegger and on the other to Chestov and Pascal, Kierkegaard, Nietzsche or Dostoevsky. Fondane's most significant philosophical work, *La Conscience malheureuse*, came out in 1936, two years before his final assessment of Surrealism.

By the time of the Second Surrealist Manifesto (1929), the original tension between anti-rationalistic individualism and the integrationist tendency—the appropriation of the rationale of scientific inquiry and the involvement in current social and political debates—had turned into an open confrontation, accompanied by violent recriminations and expulsions on charges of alleged aesthetic escapism levelled against members unwilling to engage in direct socio-political action. An eloquent illustration of this inner division can be found in the controversies surrounding Artaud's break with the Surrealist movement, or in Breton's initially ambivalent, then clearly antagonistic attitude toward writers gathered in alternative, non-affiliated groups such as *Discontinuité*[28] and *Le Grand Jeu*.[29] Both groups brought out their eponymous publications in 1928, a fateful time of effervescent activity on or outside the boundaries of the established Surrealist movement.[30] Literary critics, historians and bibliographers who have devoted their work to these two groups and to writers such as Fondane, Artaud, René Daumal and Roger Gilbert-Lecomte have uncovered a significant number of bio-bibliographical 'encounters' that justify the premiss of the comparative analysis which I undertake in this study. Insofar as the source of Breton's controversies with Artaud and *Le Grand Jeu* runs deeper than the question of immediate political and social engagements, my premiss is that Fondane's existential critique of Surrealism brings out the underlying conflict between divergent philosophical conceptions, in relation to which Artaud, Daumal and Gilbert-Lecomte also define their respective positions on the external frontiers of the Surrealist movement.

In 1984, Michel Carassou discovered and published Fondane's previously unknown 'Lettre ouverte à Antonin Artaud sur le Théâtre Alfred Jarry',[31] which indicates that Fondane saw all the performances of the Alfred Jarry Theatre (between 1927 and 1930), was in close contact with Artaud, and personally defended his project in 1928, during the famous scuffle with the Surrealists that interrupted the performance of Strindberg's *Songe*. The same year, Fondane contributed to the only issue of *Discontinuité*, and most probably came in contact with Daumal and Gilbert-Lecomte, during the events organized and attended by members of both alternative groups. Shortly before the publication of the two magazines, Arthur Adamov and Claude Sernet (Fondane's close friend) from *Discontinuité* had been involved along with Daumal in a theatre performance combined with a poetry reading at the *Studio des Ursulines*, and had published their poems in a 'programme of the Studio des Ursulines'.[32]

The historical and critical study devoted by Alain and Odette Virmaux (1981) to Roger Gilbert-Lecomte collected for the first time most of the existing information about the relationship between members of *Discontinuité* and *Le Grand Jeu*, as well as the relationship between *Le Grand Jeu* and Artaud.[33] The authors also mention the letter that Fondane[34] sent to Claude Sernet referring to his involvement in the confrontation between the supporters of *Le Grand Jeu* and the Surrealists at the *Maldoror* cabaret in 1930. Two years later, Daumal intended to invite Adamov to become part of *Le Grand Jeu*, while Artaud was considering the possibility of a joint theatrical project with Daumal, probably around 1932, when Jean Paulhan initiated several meetings between the leaders of *Le Grand Jeu* and Artaud.[35] Fondane openly expressed his special appreciation of *Le Grand Jeu* in his book on Rimbaud (1933), in which he critically distanced himself from the Surrealist movement.[36] The same year, Gilbert-Lecomte sent a letter of admiration to Fondane, with reference to his book of poems, *Ulysse*.[37] However, the most conspicuous event in this list of 'encounters' is the publication, in 1933, of a special issue, 'Cinéma 33', of the magazine *Cahiers Jaunes*, to which Fondane, Artaud, Daumal and Gilbert-Lecomte contributed (along with other members of *Le Grand Jeu*, as well as former members of *Discontinuité* such as Claude Sernet and Georges Neveux). The following year, Artaud published a very favourable review of Gilbert-Lecomte's book of poems, *La Vie, l'amour, la mort, le vide et le vent*, in *La Nouvelle Revue française*, which apparently ends the list of documented 'encounters'.[38]

To date, there has been no attempt to analyse from a philosophical perspective the complex interaction and exchange of ideas among these writers (Fondane, Daumal, Gilbert-Lecomte and Artaud) and the similarities evinced by their independently-pursued investigations. In most critical accounts, the obvious affiliation between Chestov's thought and that of his only disciple, Benjamin Fondane, has been dealt with as a self-contained aspect of studies devoted for the most part to the exclusive analysis of one of the two authors.[39] A consistent, integrated interpretation of their philosophical writings, which would bring out their understanding of existential thought by constantly presenting and corroborating Chestov's and Fondane's arguments, has rarely been attempted.[40] Moreover, the manner in which Fondane applied existential arguments to the critique of Surrealism, and to the examination of current philosophical debates in the French intellectual context of the 1920s and 1930s has never been related to the project elaborated by *Le Grand Jeu* (by Daumal and Gilbert-Lecomte), or to *Discontinuité*, or to Artaud's work. Valuable isolated attempts have been made to relate Fondane's critique of Surrealism to his existential thought[41] or to provide comparative accounts of Fondane's and Gilbert-Lecomte's ideas[42] or of Artaud's and Gilbert-Lecomte's projects[43] from a philosophical point of view. Separate philosophical interpretations of Fondane, Daumal and Artaud are also available.[44] Considering the current state of research, my intended approach seeks to uncover the subtle interaction and convergence of arguments that distinguish Chestov's and Fondane's thought from mainstream Surrealism, while relating it to the non-systematic philosophical projects elaborated in the writings of Daumal, Roger Gilbert-Lecomte and Artaud.

This study attempts to restore and examine the configuration of 'existential thought' by focusing on those issues in relation to which Chestov's and Fondane's delineation of their project in response to contemporary philosophical debates can be most adequately described. I have therefore structured my presentation into four main parts, corresponding to four areas of philosophical investigation: (1) consciousness, (2) subjectivity, (3) time and history, (4) ethics and freedom. The comparative analysis of different interpretations relating to each of these four areas makes possible not only the uncovering of the confrontation between existential thought and the predominant philosophical trends of the 1920s and 1930s but also that of the more specific situation of existential arguments in the context of the philosophical and ideological debates taking place within and without the boundaries of the Surrealist movement. The existential line of thought (mainly informed by Kierkegaard, Nietzsche and Dostoevsky, among acknowledged modern precursors) placed a special emphasis on contradiction and on negative and paradoxical forms of argumentation, and developed an anti-rationalist stance that can be said to characterize the early Dada and Surrealist avant-garde, while rejecting the idealistic, Hegelian-inspired project of late-1920s mainstream Surrealism. The present study examines the existential critique of Surrealism through a contrastive analysis of the existential and Surrealist interpretations of issues of consciousness, subjectivity, time and history, ethics and freedom. In presenting the line of argument that distinguishes existential thought from Husserlian phenomenology, as well as from later 'Existentialism' (especially with reference to Heidegger), I concentrate on elucidating the meaning and scope of the anti-rationalist notions and methods of investigation advanced by Chestov and Fondane (e.g. 'the fight against self-evidence', 'awakening', *creatio ex nihilo*, 'the second dimension of thought'), which have seldom been the object of consistent critical investigation.

The comparative analysis undertaken in this study provides a coherent account of Chestov's and Fondane's understanding of existential thought, while situating the distinctive arguments of their project more firmly in relation to debates whose influence on contemporary philosophical and cultural trends in France can only be appreciated with reference to the particular context of the 1920s and 1930s. The wider theoretical background of this analysis takes into consideration the conflict between the rationalist and anti-rationalist traditions in contemporary philosophical thought—between the line of thought leading from Kant and Hegel to Husserl, Freud and Marx on the one hand and the anti-rationalist position of non-systematic thinkers like Pascal, Kierkegaard, Nietzsche, Dostoevsky, on the other. This polarization corresponds to the symbolic conflict between Athens and Jerusalem as presented in Léon Chestov's last book, which reinterprets the Biblical or Judeo-Christian critique of rational knowledge from the point of view of a much-needed re-evaluation of the foundations of speculative, scientific knowledge.

Notes to Introduction

1. Michel Foucault, *L'Histoire de la folie à l'âge classique* (Paris: Gallimard, 1972), 555.
2. See e.g. Jean-Louis Loubet del Bayle, 'Une crise totale de civilisation', *Les Non-conformistes des années 30: Une tentative de renouvellement de la pensée politique française* (Paris: Éditions du Seuil, 1969), 248 ff.
3. As Douglas Smith argues in *Transvaluations: Nietzsche in France, 1872–1972* (Oxford: Clarendon Press, 1996), the early reception preceded the actual translation of Nietzsche's works, which began in the 1890s. Jacques Le Rider (*Nietzsche en France: De la fin du XIXe siècle au temps présent* (Paris: P.U.F., 1999), 92) situates the first translation in 1893, when Daniel Halévy and Robert Dreyfus's rendering of *Le Cas Wagner* came out in the ephemeral magazine *Le Banquet*. In 1902, Henri Albert published a volume of Nietzsche's collected works, *Pages choisies* (Paris: Mercure de France). One can really speak of the wider distribution of Nietzsche's writings, and of the considerable impact of his thought in France, only after the publication of the first translations.
4. William Barrett (*Irrational Man: A Study in Existential Philosophy* (London: Heineman, 1961), 21) comments on the waning of religion in terms of the breakdown of 'a solid psychological matrix surrounding the individual's life from birth to death, sanctifying and enclosing all its ordinary and extraordinary occasions in sacrament and ritual'.
5. Kierkegaard (*The Concept of Anxiety* (Princeton: Princeton University Press, 1980), 156) defines anxiety as the 'dizziness of freedom', when 'freedom looks down into its own possibility'.
6. For an informed presentation of Russian nihilism, see 'Part Two: Nihilism and the Absurd', James M. Edie (ed.), *New Essays in Phenomenology: Studies in the Philosophy of Experience* (Chicago: Quadrangle Books, 1969), 177–90.
7. Léon Chestov, *L'Idée du bien chez Tolstoï et Nietzsche: Philosophie et prédication*, trans. T. Beresovski-Chestov and Georges Bataille (Paris: Éditions du Siècle, 1925); *La philosophie de la tragédie: Dostoïevski et Nietzsche*, trans. Boris de Schloezer (Paris: Éditions de la Pléiade, 1926).
8. Léon Chestov, 'Dostoïevsky et la lutte contre les évidences', *La Nouvelle Revue française* 101 (Feb. 1922), 134–58; *Les Révélations de la mort: Dostoïevski–Tolstoï*, trans. & prefaced by Boris de Schloezer (Paris: Plon, 1923); *La Nuit de Gethsémani: Essai sur la philosophie de Pascal*, trans. Exempliarsky (Paris: Grasset, 1923).
9. Georges Bataille actually translated Chestov's study on Tolstoy and Nietzsche, which came out in 1925 (see n. 7 above). For Chestov's influence on Bataille, see Michel Surya's comprehensive study, *Georges Bataille: La Mort à l'œuvre* (Paris: Librairie Séguier, Éditions Garamont, Frédéric Birr, 1987), 67–74. Chestov's role in disseminating Nietzsche's philosophy in France is also more recently acknowledged by Jacques le Rider, *Nietzsche en France*, 133–4, 139, 141, 194.
10. Georges Bataille, *Œuvres complètes*, viii (Paris: NRF and Gallimard, 1976), 563.
11. One of the earliest commentators of Nietzsche's work in France, Jules de Gaultier introduced Chestov to most philosophical and literary circles in Paris and wrote the preface to the first edition of *L'Idée du bien chez Tolstoï et Nietzsche*, 1925.
12. An important critical study of Chestov, which informed Camus's interpretation

in *Le Mythe de Sisyphe*, was Rachel Bespaloff, 'Chestov devant Nietzsche', *Cheminements et carrefours* (Paris: Vrin, 1938). However, unlike Camus's analysis of Chestov, there is precious little reference to Russian writers (and no reference to Dostoevsky) in Bespaloff's article on Chestov.

13. Albert Camus, 'Un raisonnement absurde', *Le Mythe de Sisyphe*, in *Essais* (Paris: Gallimard, 1965), 97.
14. Ibid., 97.
15. Loubet del Bayle, *Les Non-conformistes des années 30*, 24.
16. Benjamin Fondane, 'Un philosophe tragique: Léon Chestov', *Europe* 19 (15 Jan. 1929), 142–50.
17. André Breton, *Entretiens 1913–1952* (Paris: NRF, 1952), 21.
18. 'Paraphrasant une tirade de Durtal, dans *Là-bas*, de Huysmans, et tout en spécifiant que je suis d'accord *dialectiquement* avec Durtal, je pense que le culte du Démon est moins insane que celui de Dieu. Le culte de Dieu purule et l'autre resplendit. Sinon, tous les gens qui implorent une divinité quelconque seraient déments! Il est fort probable que leurs élans vers l'au-delà du Bien coincident avec les tribulations enragées des sens, car la luxure est la goutte-mère du déisme'; André Breton, *Alentours III, Œuvres complètes*, i. 927. Cf. Huysmans's original text (*Là-bas* (Paris: Livre de poche, 1988), 289): 'les affiliés du Satanisme sont des mystiques d'un ordre immonde, mais ce sont des mystiques. Maintenant, il est fort probable que leurs élans vers l'au-dela du Mal coincïdent avec les tribulations enragées des sens, car la Luxure est la goutte-mère du Démonisme.'
19. Breton, *Entretiens*, 26.
20. Jean-Philippe deTonnac, *René Daumal l'archange* (Paris: Grasset, 1998), 26.
21. I am indebted to Toby Garfitt, who brought to my knowledge the following information on the introduction and early uses of 'Existentialism' and *existentiel*: (1) The earliest uses of 'Existentialism' in France can be traced back to articles published between 1936 and 1939 in *Recherches philosophiques*, *La Nouvelle Revue française* and *Revue internationale de philosophie*. In the 1937 session of the 'Société française de philosophie', occasional references to 'existentialisme' are greatly outnumbered by occurrences of terms such as 'philosophie existentielle' and 'philosophie de l'existence', which are especially used in relation to Kierkegaard and Nietzsche, often as part of an attempt to differentiate their thought from the later philosophies of Jaspers and Heidegger. See 'Subjectivité et transcendance (Séance du 4 déc. 1937)', *Bulletin de la Société française de philosophie* 37 (Oct.–Dec. 1937), 161–211. (2) The first dictionary that lists 'Existentialism' is the fifth edition of Lalande's *Vocabulaire technique et critique de la philosophie* (1947), which also dates Gabriel Marcel's and Jean Wahl's first use of *existence, existentiel* to 1925 and 1935 respectively. However, the entry devoted to 'Existentialism' also mentions that 'on applique ce nom aux idées de Jaspers, de Heidegger, de Chestov, quelquefois de Nietzsche. En France on cite surtout *L'Etre et le néant* (1943) de J.-P. Sartre.' This indicates that by the late 1940s the apparent convergence between existential philosophy and Existentialism already affected Chestov's reception in France. While at a superficial level it is true that both trends of thought are concerned with the question of 'existence', on a closer analysis one cannot fail to notice the discrepancy between the Existentialist phenomenological approach and the existential critique of phenomenology, which foregrounds Kierkegaard's and Nietzsche's controversial accounts of

morality and Christianity in order to arrive at a new understanding of 'faith' (the relationship between the living man and the 'living God'). From this point of view, neither Heidegger's nor Sartre's philosophy can be said to be 'existential'.

22. The original Russian versions of Chestov's writings, published in French translation beginning with 1922, indicate that the introduction of the phrase 'Ekzistentsialnaya filosofiya' (as distinct from 'Ekzistentsyalizm', never used by Chestov) dates from the mid- to late 1930s, a time when the French reception of both Heidegger's and Kierkegaard's works made necessary the clear distinction not only between two different terms but also between two divergent philosophical trends. It is also important to note here that Chestov's main French translator, Boris de Schloezer, was a close friend of the author and worked under the author's direct supervision. Together with Schloezer (who acted both as a translator and a commentator of Chestov from 1922), Benjamin Fondane played an invaluable role in disseminating Chestov's thought in France and dispelling conceptual confusions over the alleged affiliation or overlapping between 'existential philosophy' and Heideggerian ontology on the one hand and between 'existential philosophy' and Sartrian 'Existentialism' on the other.

23. Léon Chestov, 'Job ou Hegel (A propos de la philosophie existentielle de Kierkegaard)', *La Nouvelle Revue française* 240 (May 1935), 755–62. The first edition of Chestov's book on Kierkegaard came out in French translation: *Kierkegaard et la philosophie existentielle*, trans. Tatiana Rageot and Boris de Schloezer (Paris: 'Les Amis de Léon Chestov' and Vrin, 1936). The Russian edition, *Kirgegard i ekzistentsialnaya filosofiya*, was published afterwards, also in Paris (Dom Knigi and Sovremennya Zapisky, 1939).

24. See e.g. Benjamin Fondane, 'Un philosophe tragique: Léon Chestov', *Europe* 19 (Jan. 1929), 142–50, in which he speaks of 'une philosophie de la tragédie', or 'une philosophie qui demande d'être *vécue*, et non pas seulement professée' (149, 148).

25. Fondane elaborates on his and Chestov's understanding of existential thought in the preface and the first chapter of *La Conscience malheureuse* (Paris: Denoël & Steele, 1936), as well as in two later studies: 'Léon Chestov et la lutte contre les évidences', *La Revue philosophique de la France et de l'étranger* 124 (July/Aug. 1938), 13–50; 'Le Lundi existentiel et le dimanche de l'histoire', Jean Grenier (ed.), *L'Existence* (Paris: Gallimard, 1945), 25–53. It is significant to note that in 'Héraclite le Pauvre, ou Nécessité de Kierkegaard', *Cahiers du Sud* 177 (Nov. 1935), 757–70, which explicitly refers to and develops the comments that Chestov ('Job et Hegel') had made earlier the same year on Kierkegaard's 'existential philosophy', Fondane dates the reception of Kierkegaard in France to 1935: 'On publie des textes, des traductions et des commentaires', Fondane writes, and adds in a footnote: 'Œuvres originales présentées par les maisons Aubier, Alcan, Gallimard, Je Sers. Traductions d'essais publiés par Les Iles, Je Sers et le cahier de Foi et Vie'.

26. Fondane, 'Léon Chestov et la lutte contre les évidences', 13.

27. Fondane's early articles and letters relating to Surrealism have been collected by Michel Carassou, the editor of the recent edition of *Faux Traité d'esthétique* (Paris: Plasma, 1980), in a 'Dossier Benjamin Fondane et le Surréalisme' appended at the end of that volume (117–52). The earliest article dates back to 1925, but Fondane's most significant objections to Surrealism start to emerge in the articles

published in 1927: 'Louis Aragon ou le paysan de Paris', 'Les Surréalistes et la révolution', 'Lieux communs', *Faux Traité*, 125–9, 133–42.

28. The only issue of the eponymous magazine associated with the group documents Fondane's relationship with dissident Surrealist members or writers and artists working on the boundaries of Surrealism. The contributors of *Discontinuité* include Arthur Adamov, Claude Sernet, Monny de Boully, Jean Carrive, Fondane, Victor Brauner, Dida de Mayo, Georges Malkine and Man Ray. As I intend to argue, Fondane's critique of Surrealism finds support in the ideas expressed in the manifesto of this group, and in related programmatic articles published around the same time (1926–9) by the two editors, Arthur Adamov and Serge Victor Aranovitch.
29. The group was officially founded with the publication of the first issue of *Le Grand Jeu* (1928) and was dissolved in 1932. René Daumal and Roger Gilbert-Lecomte played the most significant part in defining the programme of this movement in relation to the influential philosophical and theoretical trends of the time (Hegelian idealism, Husserlian phenomenology, Freudian psychoanalysis, Marxism). Other contributors to *Le Grand Jeu* included Pierre Audard, Monny de Boully, Robert Desnos, André Masson, Mayo, Georges Ribemont-Dessaignes, André Rolland de Renéville, Roger Vailland and Roger Vitrac.
30. As one can see from the two preceding notes, expelled or disenchanted members of Surrealism such as Carrive, Desnos, Malkine, Masson, de Boully, Ribemont-Dessaignes and Vitrac start to contribute to *Discontinuité* and *Le Grand Jeu* between 1928 and 1930.
31. Michel Carassou, 'Fondane — Artaud, même combat!', *Europe* 667–8 (Nov.–Dec. 1984), 84–6. This short presentation of Fondane's relationship to Artaud introduces the letter in which Fondane discusses the aspects that unite his own aesthetic conception with Artaud's as opposed to the mainstream Surrealist position. A previously unknown direct meeting between Fondane and Artaud was brought to my knowledge by Jean Audard (former editor of both *Zarathoustra* and *Raison d'être*, 1928–30), who went to see Fondane in 1930 and then published an extract of his book on Rimbaud in *Raison d'être* 7 (July 1930), 16–20. This seems to indicate that Artaud not only received Fondane's letter on the Alfred Jarry Theatre (dating most probably from March 1930), but also answered the invitation contained in its last lines: 'Je vous attends de tous mes souhaits.'
32. See David Bradby, *Adamov*, Research Bibliographies & Checklists (London: Grant & Cutler, 1975).
33. Alain Virmaux and Odette Virmaux, *Roger Gilbert-Lecomte et le Grand Jeu* (Paris: Pierre Belfond, 1981), 82–3.
34. Benjamin Fondane, 'Lettre à Claude Sernet' [Paris, Feb. 1930], *Faux Traité d'esthétique*, 147–8. The letter is also mentioned in Virmaux and Virmaux, *Roger Gilbert-Lecomte*, 81.
35. The discussions concerning Daumal's intention to welcome Adamov as a member of *Le Grand Jeu* are documented by Gilbert-Lecomte's correspondence: see Letter to Daumal, 28 June 1932, *Correspondance* (Paris: Gallimard, 1971), 216–17. For references to Artaud's theatrical project with Daumal, and their meetings, see René Daumal, *Correspondance*, ii (Paris: Gallimard, 1993), 249, 280, 289–90.

36. Benjamin Fondane, *Rimbaud le Voyou* (Paris: Plasma, 1979; 1st edn Paris: Denoël & Steele, 1933), 160.
37. See 'Une lettre inédite de Roger Gilbert-Lecomte' (March 1933), *Cahiers du Sud* 377 (May–June 1964), 388–94, with a presentation by Claude Sernet. One should also mention here the surprising remark included in Daumal's *La Grande Beuverie* (Paris: Gallimard, 1938), 48: 'Ils me disent de lire Platon, les Oupanishads, Kierkegaard, Spinoza, Hegel, Benjamin Fondane, le Tao, Karl Marx et même la Bible'.
38. Antonin Artaud, 'La Vie, l'amour, la mort, le vide et le vent, par *Robert* [sic] *Gilbert Lecomte* (Cahiers Libres)', *La Nouvelle Revue française* (Dec. 1934), 925–7.
39. Most recent critics of Chestov mention Fondane either in passing or as a reference source for biographical and critical information; see Victoria Rooney, *Shestov's Religious Existentialism: A Critique* (Ph.D. thesis, Oxford University, 1990); Louis S. Shein, *The Philosophy of Lev Shestov (1866–1938): A Russian Religious Existentialist* (Lewiston, ME: Edwin Mellen Press, 1991); Andrius Valevicius, *Lev Shestov and his Times: Encounters with Brandes, Tolstoy, Dostoevsky, Chekhov, Ibsen, Nietzsche and Husserl* (New York: Peter Lang, 1993); José Maria Neto, *The Christianization of Pyrrhonism: Scepticism and Faith in Pascal, Kierkegaard, and Shestov* (Dordrecht: Kluwer, 1995). Apart from Natalie Baranoff-Chestov, *La Vie de Léon Chestov*, 2 vols., trans. Blanche Bronstein-Vinaver (Paris: Éditions de la Différence, 1991–3), Fondane's posthumously published *Rencontres avec Léon Chestov* (Paris: Plasma, 1982) has been an important, frequently-cited source of information on Chestov's life and work. Past and present criticism of Chestov does not provide a coherent account of Chestov's and Fondane's philosophies and does not attempt to relate their arguments. Critics of Chestov's work tend to have a superficial, incomplete knowledge of Fondane's work. Similarly, critics of Fondane's work tend to have a superficial knowledge of Chestov and to deal with the relationship between the two in self-contained chapters devoted either to Fondane's life and poetry (see John K. Hyde, *Benjamin Fondane: A Presentation of his Life and Work* (Geneva: Droz, 1971), 61–71; Monique Jutrin, *Benjamin Fondane, ou Le Périple d'Ulysse* (Paris: A.-G. Nizet, 1989), 43–56) or to Fondane's aesthetic conception (see Ann van Sevenant, *Il filosofo dei poeti: L'estetica di Benjamin Fondane* (Milan: Mimesis, 1994), 16–35). Van Sevenant is one of the very few critics who provide a brief outline of Chestov's and Fondane's thought. She chooses the term 'philosophy of existence' to describe their project, while failing to distinguish it from Heidegger's philosophy. Frank Bowman, 'Irredentist [*sic*] Existentialism: Fondane and Shestov', *Yale French Studies* 16 (Winter 1955–6), 111–17, starts from the fallacious, unsubstantiated premiss that Fondane and Chestov belong to the tradition of French and German Existentialism (illustrated by the author with references to Merleau-Ponty and Heidegger), then proceeds to analyse exclusively Fondane's writings. Bowman's occasional references to Chestov are unsupported by quotations from his work, and his account of Chestov's views is oversimplified.
40. To date, the best informed account of both Fondane's and Chestov's arguments can be found in Olivier Salazar-Ferrer, 'Benjamin Fondane le révolté', *Agone* 10 (1993), 45–69. For the only other integrated, consistent critical presentation of Chestov and Fondane see the chapter 'Le dialogue de l'urgence

(Chestov–Fondane)' in Bernard Chouraqui, *Le Scandale juif ou la subversion de la mort* (Hallier: Éditions Libres, 1979), 193–252.

41. See e.g. Michel Carassou, 'Benjamin Fondane du surréalisme à l'existentialisme', Anne Roche and Christian Tarting (eds.), *Des Années trente: groupes et ruptures* (Paris: CNRS, 1986), 249–56. Although Carassou uses the term 'existentialism' in his title, he consistently refers to 'existential philosophy' throughout his article.
42. See Leonard Schwartz, 'The Forgotten as Contemporary: Benjamin Fondane and Roger Gilbert-Lecomte', *The Literary Review* (Spring 1987), 465–7.
43. Phil Powrie, 'Film—Form—Mind: The Hegelian Follies of Roger Gilbert-Lecomte', *Quarterly Review of Film and Video* 12/4 (1991), 19–32.
44. Van Sevenant, *Il filosofo dei poeti*; Phil Powrie, *René Daumal: Étude d'une obsession* (Geneva: Droz, 1990); Camille Dumouillé, *Nietzsche et Artaud: Pour une éthique de la cruauté* (Paris: P.U.F., 1992); Jacques Derrida, 'La Parole soufflée' and 'Le Théâtre de la cruauté et la clôture de la représentation', *L'Écriture et la différence* (Paris: Éditions du Seuil, 1967), 253–92, 341–68.

CHAPTER 1

❖

Places in the Mind: Self-Evidence and Consciousness of Self

> Je pense à la vie. Tous les systèmes que je pourrai édifier n'égaleront jamais mes cris d'homme occupé à refaire sa vie
>
> ANTONIN ARTAUD, *Position de la chair*

> Il n'est pas dit que la folie ne doive jamais finir par avoir raison de la raison
>
> BENJAMIN FONDANE, *La Conscience malheureuse*

Some of the most significant arguments that define Chestov's and Fondane's view of existential thought, in opposition to systematic philosophy, can be said to have emerged from a critical re-examination of the Hegelian and Husserlian accounts of consciousness. More specifically, the existential critique was aimed against (1) Hegel's dialectical and historical interpretation of the stages in the evolution of Spirit (from consciousness to self-consciousness to Reason); (2) Husserl's theory of intentional consciousness, relating to his concept of 'self-evidence'. The Hegelian and Husserlian shared concern with a unifying account of human understanding prompted the existential polemical attempt to configure a non-unitary model of consciousness, based on irreconcilable contradiction and the notion of 'awakening'. In Chestov's and Fondane's writings, this notion functions within an argumentative framework that revives and further elaborates Plotinus' idea of the 'awakening to oneself', as well as Kierkegaard's critique of Hegel. Similarly, Chestov's constant emphasis on the 'fight against self-evidence' and the resulting 'absurd evidence' mobilizes a critical discourse directed against the Husserlian doctrine of 'self-evident' truth.

In this chapter I shall therefore investigate the key existential arguments relevant to issues of consciousness and truth ('self-consciousness' vs. 'awakening to oneself', 'self-evidence' vs. 'absurd evidence'), while considering the mainstream and dissident Surrealist reactions to phenomenological and psychoanalytical theories.

The understanding of consciousness that mainstream Surrealism reached in the late 1920s indicates a greater permeability to scientific and cognitive-philosophical ideas than the early anti-rationalistic, nihilistic stance would have led us to believe. The central role assigned to automatic writing and the Freudian-inspired exploration of dreams resulted in a decisive shift in the interpretation of the results of Surrealist experiments. Moving away from the radical destruction of rational thinking employed by Dada, Surrealism proposed a positive uncovering of 'the true functioning of thought'. Its definition as 'pure psychic automatism' opened the way to a doctrine that seemed gradually to incorporate the rationale of scientific thought in a 'pure chemical state',[1] while becoming more and more detached from the irrationality that Antonin Artaud, among others, initially associated with the movement. The Surrealist propensity towards the reconciliation of contraries led to the attempt to bring subjective psychological phenomena into the realm of verifiable, objective reality, which signals an effort of integration in response to the predominant scientific mentality of the time. This dialectical movement, and the subsequent appropriation of a Hegelian-inspired understanding of Spirit, departs from the existential notion of 'unhappy consciousness' informed by Kierkegaard's critique of the Hegelian system and grounded in a contradictory, paradoxical type of thinking.

Nothing made the distance between the Surrealist and the existential projects more apparent than the interpretation of madness with reference to consciousness and the problem of truth. The tenuous relationship between the search for the 'true functioning of thought' and the early Surrealist experiments with simulated mental alienation was resolved through an aestheticization of madness, which allowed for the assimilation of psychoanalytical and cognitive theories, while giving free play to an innocuous revolutionary practice in a sanitized mental and social environment. Conversely, the existential rejection of the classical account of madness as a deviation from normality, which needs to be brought back to the 'norm' of rational thought, led to an attempt to shatter the foundation of scientific knowledge through the subversive values of madness, disintegration and despair, placed over and above the endeavour to reconcile speculative and socio-political concerns.

Antonin Artaud initially credited the Surrealist movement with a unique ability to 'créer en nous des espaces à la vie, des espaces qui n'étaient pas et ne semblaient pas devoir trouver place dans l'espace'.[2] The places in the mind uncovered by experiments carried out within mainstream Surrealism and on its external frontiers not only failed to coincide, but actually emerged from radically opposed notions of consciousness, reality and experience. This difference in understanding the notion of consciousness in relation to experience will provide the basis for a comparative analysis carried out over to three main areas of debate: the existential 'fight against self-evidence'; 'awakening' and consciousness of self; intentionality vs. 'the absurd evidence'.

The Fight against Self-Evidence

The same year that the *Second Surrealist Manifesto* was published, Benjamin Fondane wrote an article in which he argued that the 'modern' or revolutionary movement of the time had unknowingly found its philosopher in the person of Léon Chestov.[3] However surprising, this statement corresponded to the diffuse yet consistent manifestation of a current of thought that both exceeded the framework of the Surrealist movement and mobilized its marginal or centrifugal forces around a different kind of engagement: 'la lutte contre les évidences'. The phrase was introduced into French writing by Chestov himself in 1922,[4] and was subsequently used by Fondane in his critique of Surrealism from the point of view of an ever-renewed questioning and destruction of the foundations and validity of rational, scientific knowledge.

Prior to Fondane's polemic with mainstream Surrealism, the 'fight against self-evidence' played a more specific role within the economy of existential thought. The arguments relating to this notion were in particular designed to counteract Husserl's theory of objectivity, based on the concept of 'self-evidence' and the thesis of the intentional constitution of data 'given' to consciousness (the so-called 'données de la conscience'). One of the problems that Husserlian phenomenology attempted to solve concerned the possibility of coming back to 'things-in-themselves' and reconsidering the status of objects given to consciousness in experience, in analogy with apodictically given ideal objects (e.g. logical and mathematical entities).[5] Chestov, as well as Fondane, argued against the universality of the phenomenological claim that data of experience can only be given in the form of their intentionally constituted objectivity.[6]

In a more general sense, associated with the wider scope of the existential critique of systematic philosophy, in Chestov's and Fondane's writings the 'fight against self-evidence' designates the anti-rationalist revolt against the necessary, apodictic principles of rational knowledge—against self-evident truths of fact (e.g. the laws of nature) or self-evident truths of reason (e.g. the fundamental principles of logic). As I intend to show in this chapter, the existential 'fight against self-evidence' focuses on (1) the rejection of both logical and natural necessity; (2) the confrontation within a particular, individual consciousness between self-evident truths and the so-called 'absurd evidence' of an alternative type of thinking. This ultimately amounts to an attempt to spell out the 'taboo' questions of rationalist philosophy, which Fondane explicitly addresses in the introduction to *La Conscience malheureuse*:

Des questions comme: 'qu'est-ce que la connaissance? d'où tient-elle son droit de juger et d'édicter des évidences,' [...] 'Le Savoir ne serait-il que vertu?' [...] (Nietzsche) menace, bien sûr, lui aussi, de 'malheur' celui qui aurait 'souillé sa probité intellectuelle'; mais il ne peut s'empêcher de nous avertir—*comme si quelque chose de plus haut que la 'probité intellectuelle' l'y poussait*—que le Savoir nous a arraché 'tout ce qui est consolant et saint, tout ce qui guérit, toute espérance' pour nous faire adorer 'la pierre, l'ineptie, la lourdeur et le destin'. [...] Que notre conscience soit malheureuse, est bien une de ces questions-là. Poser cette question—rien que la poser—c'est déjà affranchir la conscience, car elle est libre désormais, ne serait-ce que de lutter contre ce malheur qui l'informe et de s'en reconnaître distincte.[7]

The fight against self-evidence deliberately transgresses the limitations set by necessity to rational thought and the interdiction reiterated from Aristotle's imperative ἀνάγκη στῆναι (one must stop) to Kant's remarks about the 'absurd questions' that cover with shame those who ask them.[8] Fondane, like Chestov, discloses the ethical taboo lying under this appeal to shame and protecting the very foundation of Knowledge against the scrutiny of the obliterated principle of Life. The condition of rational man corresponds, in Chestov and Fondane, to that described in the book of Genesis after the Fall: the man who has tasted the Fruit of Knowledge cannot help thinking that the created world is imperfect, full of evil, precisely in so far as it is created—different in its essence from the eternal, ideal realm of reason. And this impression becomes confirmed by the apparently unsurpassable 'data of consciousness'.[9] Nothing can thereafter shatter the self-evidence of a logical judgement that seeks firm grounding in a more and more unified, purified field of consciousness, related to an increasingly rationalized field of experience. Chestov's critique of rational truth questioned the ontological status of ideal objects, in contrast to the being of existing individuals, while tracing this argument back to the famous polemic between Descartes and Leibniz about the 'creation of eternal truths'.[10] The possibility of 'created' rather than 'uncreated' truths of reason, submitted to the same law of γένεσις (creation) and φθορά (destruction) as individual living beings, emerges in contradiction to the so-called 'données de la conscience' and to their apparently non-temporal, autonomous character.

Breton himself referred the question of knowledge back to the book of Genesis ('Nous en sommes encore à lire les toutes premières page de la Genèse'), and seemed no less aware of the fatal danger posed by reason, in limiting the possibilities of thought and expression:

> Le péril où nous met la raison, au sens le plus général et le plus discutable du mot, en soumettant à ses dogmes irréversibles les ouvrages de l'esprit, en nous privant en fait de choisir le mode d'expression qui nous desserve le moins, ce péril, sans doute, est loin d'être écarté.[11]

However, Breton's idealistic belief in man's power to liberate or rather elevate himself above his contingent state, despite the Fall, endorsed rather than subverted the old rationalistic promise: 'Il ne tient peut-être qu'à nous de jeter sur les ruines de l'ancien monde les bases de notre nouveau paradis terrestre.'[12] It is significant to note here that the reference to the book of Genesis comes up in Breton's well-known 'Introduction au discours sur le peu de réalité', which according to Fondane could be said to provide the evidence for the prosecution in the 'procès intellectuel de l'art' opened by Roger Caillois.[13] In its search for the 'true functioning of thought', inspired by both psychoanalytical theory and Hegelian philosophy, Surrealism aimed to provoke a crisis in the traditional notion of reality and, more significantly, 'une crise de la conscience', as Breton emphatically stated in the Second Manifesto and later in *Qu'est-ce que le surréalisme?* (1934). However, Fondane argued that Surrealism only managed to reinforce 'la conscience honteuse du poète', the shameful awareness of a crisis reached when the poet himself questions the validity of his art from a scientific and philosophical point of view, making use of the exemplary instrument of knowledge—intelligence, '[cette] faculté dissolvante':

> Bien qu'acculé de force par la structure même de son acte [Fondane argues] à un domaine dont le moins que l'on puisse dire c'est qu'il est irrationnel et indéterminé, le poète s'est fait fort — afin de gagner un point d'appui reconnu indiscutable — d'exploiter cet irrationnel et indéterminé, qui lui sont échus en partage au moyen de techniques propres à le justifier et à justifier, du même coup, *l'exploitation rationnelle de l'irrationnel.*[14]

According to Fondane, the need to justify and objectively validate the results of Surrealist experiments and the very notions of 'super-reality', 'surrealist image', 'hazard', and so on signalled the attempted affiliation of the movement to the dominant scientific, rigorous mentality of the time. While declining to act as 'témoin à décharge au procès du monde réel', Breton pleaded for the 'état complet de distraction' that characterized the great scientist and the philosopher at work: Kant, Pasteur, Curie.[15] But should the poet adopt the impartial, indifferent view of reality, of existential, particular aspects, which defined the scientific and philosophical approach? This question resonates throughout Fondane's *Faux traité d'esthétique*, subtitled 'essai sur la crise de réalité':

> Faut-il penser que le rôle du poète n'est que de seconder le philosophe dans ses travaux d'usinage où le réel vivant se transforme constamment en réel chimique, en concepts intelligibles? qu'il s'accorde avec le philosophe pour oublier, ou négliger, la perte irremplaçable de substance qui s'est produite?.[16]

Fondane thus relates Breton's remarks from the 'Introduction au discours sur le peu de réalité' to a 'loss of substance' (to what might be described as the crisis of the substantialist view of reality, 'le réel vivant'), resulting from the endeavour to realign the Surrealist doctrine with the conceptual approach to psychoanalysis and Hegelian idealism.

In *Les Vases communicants* (1932), André Breton concludes his examination of dream and poetry with an unexpected reference to the biblical myth of the Fall of Man, which actually reaffirms Hegel's own interpretation of the fruits of the Tree of Knowledge as 'the principle of philosophy for all times':[17] 'Le poète à venir [...] tendra le fruit magnifique de l'arbre aux racines enchevêtrées et saura persuader ceux qui le goûtent qu'il n'a rien d'amer.'[18] The poet no less than the philosopher becomes convinced and able to persuade others that 'according to the old story of the Fall [...] the Serpent did not deceive man, for God says: "Behold, Adam has become as one of us; he knows good and evil"'.[19]

As Fondane argues in his *Faux Traité d'esthétique* (1938), the project of a 'paradis terrestre' revives the same old promise ('eritis sicut dei'), hailing the benefits of rational knowledge and ethics after the Fall. The extent to which this attitude towards knowledge permeates the Surrealist doctrine can be appreciated in relation to the so-called 'phase raisonnante', dating back to the ethical and political debates of 1925 and recalled by Breton in 1934, when he reconsiders the results of early experiments as mere 'matériaux à partir desquels tendait inéluctablement à se reposer, sous une forme toute nouvelle, le problème de la connaissance'.[20] Breton also noted once that the Kantian critique of pure reason and the need to clarify 'l'objectivité des données internes de la raison' still confronted contemporary scientists, such as Freud.[21] In *Légitime défense*, one of the first writings to come out of the reasoning phase, Breton briefly touches on the 'difficultés en apparence insurmontables d'objectivation des idées'.[22] The recurrent references to the 'problem of knowledge' and the question of objectivity usually introduce the Surrealist idea of a possible synthesis between opposite philosophical conceptions (e.g. 'raison' and 'déraison', 'savoir' and 'ignorance', reality and dream, etc.). This manner of posing the 'problem of knowledge' has very different aims from Chestov's and Fondane's radical questioning of 'knowledge as a problem', which starts from the premiss that the drive toward objectivity should be replaced by, rather than reconciled with, the subjective search for truth, and that truth itself emerges from individual revolt, a fight against one's own rationality.

The pathos of this subjective search for truth beyond rational certainty found one of its best expressions in Artaud's call for a 'libération totale de l'esprit' through that 'cri de l'esprit qui se retourne vers lui-même et est bien décidé à broyer désespérément ses entraves'. Artaud's violent incrimination of reason ('Nous souffrons d'une pourriture, de la pourriture de la raison'),[23] his 'cris d'homme occupé à refaire sa vie', reveal an understanding of revolt as the process by which reason is made to turn against itself and redeploy its violence against its own rigid structures. Even before his break with the

Surrealist movement, Artaud insisted on the subversive potential of the individual will ('une volonté de sens', 'une volonté de croyance'), which searches for new means of expression accessible only to the outcasts of logical, discursive thought:

Et toutefois entre les failles d'une pensée humainement mal construite, inégalement cristallisée, brille une volonté de sens. La volonté de mettre au jour les détours d'une chose encore mal faite, une volonté de croyance. Ici s'installe une certaine Foi, mais que les coprolaliques m'entendent, les aphasiques, et en général tous les discrédités des mots et du verbe, les parias de la Pensée. Je ne parle que pour ceux-là.[24]

The emphasis placed on individual will, as opposed to the limitations of logical judgement, uncovers one of the most important aspects of 'the fight against self-evidence'. Artaud explicitly relates the will to the notion of faith, and describes it as 'volonté de sens',[25] which in terms of the existential critique of rationality corresponds to the individual will to *create* meaning, and therefore to create an individual order of truth, beyond the limits of rational thought and beyond the equally restrictive rational speculation characterizing theological dogma. In *La Conscience malheureuse*, Fondane comments on the link between the fight against self-evidence and the will to suspend the given conditions of meaning and truth, which provokes 'une lutte à mort entre la vie et le savoir, entre l'être et le connaître, entre la "vérité" des évidences et la vérité de la foi'.[26]

A similar deployment of absolute negation can be found in many of the texts published by *Le Grand Jeu*, which define revolt in terms of 'un côté négatif de renoncements continuels'.[27] The fight against rational a priori and moral conventions is located at the level of individual consciousness and individual mind. The only genuine form of revolt is therefore the 'révolte de l'individu contre lui-même',[28] which accurately captures Chestov's and Fondane's understanding of the fight against self-evidence. It is in this sense that Fondane outlines the confrontation between two types of thinking, which takes place inside each individual:

En fait, la déchirure n'est pas seulement de l'homme à l'homme, mais dans l'homme même. Il y a un croyant dans le philosophe et un philosophe dans le croyant. [...] Tout porte à croire que (le principe de contradiction intérieure) est né par le même acte métaphysique qui — avant le temps — avait plongé l'homme — de par sa faute ou non — dans le monde déchiré des apparences. L'ennemi le plus terrible de l'homme, tout fait penser qu'il avait été placé dans l'homme même, et que la nécessité n'est que le négatif de la liberté.[29]

From the perspective of the fight against self-evidence, the most disturbing consequence of Breton's position as presented by Fondane was the Surrealist willingness to reconcile the notions of chance and necessity. Breton's understanding of 'le hasard objectif' reiterated rather than questioned the Freudian acquiescent view of natural and logical necessity in the transition between the unconscious and the conscious system:

L'ordre, la fin, dans la nature, ne se confondant pas objectivement avec ce qu'ils sont dans l'esprit de l'homme, il arrive cependant que la nécessité naturelle tombe d'accord avec la nécessité humaine d'une manière assez extraordinaire et agitante pour que les deux déterminations s'avèrent indiscernables. [...] *Le hasard serait la forme de manifestation de la nécessité extérieure qui se fraie un chemin dans l'inconscient humain* (pour tenter hardiment d'interpréter et de concilier sur ce point Engels et Freud).[30]

But, as Fondane argued, if the discovery of a super-reality was ever to succeed in liberating the human mind from the constraints of logical, speculative thinking, no change-effecting solution could possibly arise from either Hegelian idealism or Freudian psychoanalysis, let alone straightforward socio-political action. This view also characterized Antonin Artaud's understanding of revolt, which caused his rift with the Surrealist group. In his response to Breton's incrimination of non-Communist members of the group, Artaud insisted that the 'integral', effective revolution would have to be accomplished inside the mind of the individual subject:

Mais que me fait à moi toute la Révolution du monde si je sais demeurer éternellement douloureux et misérable au sein de mon propre charnier. Que chaque homme ne veuille rien considérer au delà de sa sensibilité profonde, de son moi intime, voilà pour moi le point de vue de la Révolution intégrale.[31]

If the Surrealist revolution ever promised to liberate man from his miserable condition, that could only have resulted, according to Artaud, from a fundamental change inside rather than outside the 'lieu mental' where the reign of Reason was perpetuated. Whereas Breton spoke of his 'faith' in automatic writing as a 'foi persistante dans l'automatisme comme sonde, comme espoir persistant dans la dialectique pour la résolution des antinomies qui accablent l'homme',[32] there is an altogether different notion of faith that Artaud and Roger Gilbert-Lecomte invoke in support of their views. The painful contradiction that they perceive between the necessities of nature and those of the self, the horrors of life that they cannot overcome through the sensuous enjoyment (*jouissance*) aimed at by the Surrealist liberation of unconscious desires, determines Artaud and Gilbert-Lecomte to place their hopes in the intervention of grace, in a faith leading to a transcendent, invisible order of things: 'On n'échappe à l'horreur de vivre que par une foi, une intuition, un instinct antique qu'il faut savoir retrouver au fond de soi-même. Sondez l'abîme qui est en vous.'[33] In the programmatic article defining the position of the newly-formed group *Le Grand Jeu*, the idea of chance occupies a central role, not in relation to some external necessity tuned to subjective, unconscious desires, but in the form of *grace*. Playing the great existential game implies both a one-off, lose-all-gain-all-gamble, and a constant renewal of such critical experience with each moment of life:

> *Le Grand Jeu* est irrémédiable; il ne se joue qu'une fois. Nous voulons le jouer à tous les instants de notre vie. C'est encore 'à qui perd gagne'. Car il s'agit de se perdre. Nous voulons gagner. Or, le Grand Jeu est un jeu de hasard, c'est-à-dire d'adresse, ou mieux de 'grâce': la grâce de Dieu, et la grâce des gestes.[34]

When Fondane referred to Breton as '[le] cartésien du miracle', he accurately identified the contradiction implicit in the Surrealist quest for purity and care for verification of the irrational and the indeterminate. This attitude is illustrated, for example, by Breton's sympathetic view of the 'revêrie scientifique' and his apology of the 'fièvre sacré' that related the 'inventeur du réflexe cutané planétaire' to the Surrealist poet in search of an image envisaged as 'création pure de l'esprit'.[35] Michel Carrouges (1950), one of the critics who examined the relationship between Surrealism and the scientific and philosophical discourse of the time, brought out the tendency of the movement to elevate experimental activities to a 'science of the imagination', which, one might add, seemed to make possible the objective validation of psychological phenomena as well as of the 'merveilleux' or the 'hasard objectif'. Carrouges even advances the idea of a conjunction between the 'merveilleux poétique' and the 'merveilleux scientifique'.[36] Fondane indicated that the Surrealists' apparent elevation of artistic creation to the level of theoretical knowledge, the definition of the 'merveilleux' in terms of a 'document mental', the effort to validate and justify the essentially unverifiable (non-scientific) value of poetic 'evidences' through methods of research supposed to match those of speculative thought and science, only managed to expose the precarious situation of a 'pure art' that had lost its existential, vital support:

> Cédant à l'Esprit du Temps, à la dialectique historique, à l'éthique qui nous est revenue plus virulente que jamais par le détour de la pensée révolutionnaire, la poésie de nos jours rompit avec son non-savoir existentiel, ambitionna le titre de: connaissance, prétendit au 'document' mental, se donna des airs scientifiques et pondit le plus bizarre des œufs que l'on puisse imaginer: le miracle *naturel,* le mystère *mécanique*, l'inspiration *automatique*.[37]

The existential critique of truth from the point of view of faith (relating notions of individual will, miracle and grace) departs from the Surrealist ideology, which in order to reconcile divergent tendencies within the movement opted for an aestheticization of madness and a dialectical synthesis of opposites, which held the promise of a unified, non-contradictory vision of human nature in relation to nature and society at large. The aestheticization of madness emerged in response to the new engagements of the 'reasoning period' and to the re-evaluation of the early Surrealist experiments in keeping with the new scientific drive in the field of cognitive-psychological and social theories. This effort of integration involved the aestheticization of mental alienation (as illustrated by Breton's concept of 'la beauté convulsive' in *Nadja*), which made possible a unifying project, culminating in Breton's theory of dream and his notion of 'mad love'. As Ferdinand Alquié remarked: 'Si, avec le surréalisme, nous voulons intégrer la nature totale à l'homme, nous ne pouvons le faire que par la voie du rêve: la valeur vérité est alors sacrifiée à la valeur beauté.'[38]

Like Chestov, Fondane insists on the truth of human suffering—the existential truth corresponding to Pascal's 'chercher en gémissant' as the only authentic 'method' of searching for truth:

> Chacun de nous aura raison
> car la raison de chaque vie
> est plus forte qu'aucune flamme
> [...]
> une vie est plus qu'une raison,
> le sang est plus qu'un théorème

que vaut-elle la vérité
la plus pure, la plus troublante,
auprès d'une goutte de sang?[39]

This redefinition of truth has major implications for the construal of consciousness within the existential line of thought. It leads to a non-unitary model of consciousness and to the notion of a paradoxical, sudden 'awakening to oneself'. The new understanding of consciousness, with reference to the notion of awakening, situates Fondane's existential thought in close relationship to Daumal and Gilbert-Lecomte's 'experimental metaphysics', as well as to Artaud's critique of rationality.

Awakening and Consciousness of Self

In existential thought, the notion of 'awakening' is related to the revival and further elaboration of traditional philosophical arguments that can be said to support the existential fight against self-evidence, insofar as they bring out the psychological origin and the relative value of non-temporal, 'eternal' truths of reason. One of the arguments frequently used by Chestov and Fondane concerns the role of 'hyperbolic doubt' in Descartes's *Meditations*. According to Chestov, the hypothesis of a Malign Creator who perverts all human cognitive efforts and makes mere delusions appear as self-evident truth to the human mind cannot be dismissed simply on account of God's perfection and the infallible evidence of man's existence.[40] If, as Chestov argues, God does deceive men, while nevertheless granting them the certainty of their existence, it might be that all other human truths are only relative (determined by the limited framework of human understanding):

Il se peut donc que d'autres êtres existent, anges ou dieux, que personne ne trompe et qui voient la vérité authentique. Du point de vue de ces êtres, la vérité humaine sera une vérité spécifique, utile et necessaire (peut-être, au contraire, nuisible, mauvaise) aux hommes, mais inapplicable dans les autres mondes.[41]

Chestov's re-examination of 'hyperbolic doubt' has at least two aims: (1) to question the foundation of Husserl's statement that 'truth is one and the same, whether men or non-men, angels or gods apprehend and judge it';[42] (2) to uncover the possible existence of another dimension of reality and being ('d'autres êtres', 'd'autres mondes'), which exceeds logical comprehension. The question that Chestov attempts to answer by advancing the notion of 'awakening' concerns the paradox that a rational being would be able to form the idea of something that exceeds rational comprehension. In Chestov's argumentation, the concept of 'hyperbolic doubt' thus reopens, with the question of the 'awakening' to another type of thinking, the debate over the criteria distinguishing sleep from waking consciousness, delusion from truth.

In order to illustrate the process of awakening from the reality governed by logical and rational a priori thinking, Chestov, like Fondane, takes the following example[43]: a man is asleep and dreams that he is the emperor of China and that he is about to inscribe monograms on the surface of a one-dimensional sphere. Not only is the sleeper unaware of contradictory aspects, which would seem inconceivable to his waking consciousness, but he does not even question the validity of such ideas as that of 'a one-dimensional sphere'. Chestov's argument is that, if the hypothetical sleeper no less than the waking man remains convinced of the self-evidence of the Cartesian *cogito* and the absolute certainty that Husserl attaches to the apprehended 'cogitationes', he cannot reject his ideas or the facts ('les données') supporting these ideas as absurd or as relative to this state of consciousness. Nevertheless, as Chestov and Fondane further argue, if the given self-evidence is no longer indifferent to the sleeper (like the indifferent possibility of a one-dimensional sphere), if the logic of his dream-world turns into a nightmare that threatens his own existence, the sleeper will want to wake up. Even at the risk of running counter to the principle of non-contradiction, he will denounce the self-evidence of his dream-reality as false evidence, and will no longer admit it as an absolute, eternal truth. The hypothetical sleeper, in Chestov, represents the epitome of the rational thinker who, unless forced to confront the question of his own existence and death, defines the possibilities of thought in terms of one-dimensional—a priori—conditions of truth.

More specifically, this argument provides a polemical reply to Husserl's emphatic postulation: 'We cannot agree to believe something to be psychologically possible if it is logically and geometrically absurd.'[44] The absurd psychological possibility of an 'awakening' to a type of thinking not governed by rational, eternal truths directly challenges the unity of consciousness, which constituted a fundamental tenet of Husserl's investigations. In *Ideen*, where Husserl proposes to take up Descartes's 'attempt to doubt everything' only 'as a device of method', he notes, 'We must describe the *unity of consciousness* which is demanded *by the intrinsic nature of the cogitationes*, and so necessarily demanded that they could not be without this unity'.[45] From this point of view, the otherwise common experience described in Chestov's example of the sleeper who wakes up only by doubting the unity of consciousness and the self-evidence of the so-called *cogitationes* and the principle of non-contradiction becomes logically and psychologically impossible. Not only the unity of consciousness but the unified field of experience, both of which are ensured through the theory of intentional constitution, prevent one from talking about the logical or psychological possibility of some other form of consciousness, some other form of truth and being beyond the limit of self-evidence. Husserl's 'plain correlation' between being and meaning supports the phenomenological conviction that one cannot relativize truth without relativizing being.[46]

> Quand en rêve l'homme écrasé, torturé par un monstre épouvantable se sent incapable non seulement de se défendre mais de bouger un de ses membres, le salut surgit avec la conscience contradictoire que le cauchemar n'est pas la réalité, qu'il n'est qu'une illusion passagère. Cette conscience est contradictoire, car elle suppose que le dormeur tient pour vrai que l'état de conscience de celui qui rêve n'est pas vrai; il s'agit par conséquent d'une vérité qui se détruit elle-même. Pour se débarrasser du cauchemar il faut chasser loin de soi le principe de contradiction sur lequel se fondent dans l'état de veille toutes les évidences.[47]

The 'self-destructive truth' of another type of thinking (of what Chestov and Fondane call 'the second dimension of thought') gives rise to a non-unitary, contradictory configuration of consciousness, a configuration that contains the possibility of a heightened state of awareness, of an 'awakening' that shatters the unity and the logical principles governing rational consciousness. In arguing that people spend their lives sleeping rather than thinking (that the activity which they call thinking is nothing else but slumber, paralysis of thought), Chestov and Fondane ultimately challenged the ontological implications of Husserl's theory of truth, which equates 'self-evident being' and 'true being', while ignoring the conditions of real, living individual human beings, irreducible to the non-temporal status of ideal entities of thought.

In reply to Husserl's objection that 'the psychological origin' of arithmetical concepts introduces a fallacious interchange between different genres (μετάβασις εἰς ἄλλο γένος), and that relativizing truth implies a relativization of being, Chestov remarked that the affirmation of the ideal character of truth relativizes, and even destroys the diminishing territory of reality and individual existence. It makes possible the μετάβασις between ideality and real existence:

> A l'encontre de ce que pense Husserl, je dirai: en affirmant l'existence absolue de l'idéal, on relativise, on détruit même toute réalité. Les efforts de Husserl pour concilier l'idéal et le réel, le rationnel avec l'individuel, en les faisant rentrer dans la même catégorie, celle de l'être où chacun dispose de droits égaux, ces efforts aboutissent non à la solution du problème mais à son obscurcissement, car on crée ainsi la possibilité d'une μετάβασις εἰς ἄλλο γένος légale pour ainsi dire, et où se réfugie ce même relativisme constamment traqué [...]. Ces deux espèces appartiennent au même genre, il est donc fort tentant et naturel de substituer l'idéal au réel, ou vice versa.[48]

The attempt to relativize truth, by pointing to the psychological origin of 'self-evidence' and the possible non-unitary configuration of consciousness, foregrounds the existence of the thinking subject as a temporally determined, living being, irreducible to ideal objects or entities of thought. Moreover, the fight against self-evidence is a fight against the necessary death of any temporal being, most clearly illustrated by the Kierkegaardian *Either/Or*, as formulated by Chestov: 'ou bien renversons le "deux fois deux quatre" ou bien admettons que la mort est le dernier mot de la vie, son tribunal suprême'.[49] Logico-mathematical truth and phenomenological self-evidence not only affirm their necessity independently of the thinking subject and his existence, but operate a rationalization of experience that amounts to the reduction of the 'hic et nunc' existence of the individual, for whom the impersonal, eternal '$2 \times 2 = 4$' becomes a principle of death. Chestov argued that subjective truth cannot be reconciled without violence with necessary, logical truth. Existential truth finds its source in the reality and the 'absurd' contingent experience bracketed by logico-mathematical knowledge. The existential non-unitary model of consciousness remains outside the framework and the aims of the mainstream Surrealist project.

The immanentist doctrine elaborated by Breton, starting from the exploration of dreams and the Freudian analysis of the interaction between consciousness and the unconscious, rejected the idea of a transcendent 'au-délà' as it rejected the ultimate implications of Hegel's idealism (which identifies Absolute Spirit with God). The significance of the Cartesian 'hyperbolic doubt' eluded the Surrealist quest for the 'true functioning of thought' and the Surrealist critique of rationality, which dismissed the hypothesis of a transcendent being, 'l'épouvantail de la mort, les cafés chantants de l'au-delà',[50] while maintaining the imperative of a dialectical synthesis of dream and reality, of conscious and unconscious processes of thought. There is a stark contrast between the Surrealist concern with unity and dialectical reconciliation of opposites on the one hand and the existential idea of contradictory, incompatible states of consciousness, distinguishing rational slumber from 'awakening', on the other. The notion of 'surréalité' has nothing in common with the existential notion of 'awakening', which implies the awareness of a second dimension of thought and of a transcendent reality relating to the existence of God.

Outside the confines of mainstream Surrealism, René Daumal elaborated a non-systematic line of thought, which can be said to share many distinctive aspects of the existential critique of the traditional concept of consciousness. In describing his project, Daumal referred to a 'perpetual race towards awakening' ('une course perpétuelle à l'éveil'), and spoke of the direct experience of 'l'INTOLÉRABLE'.[51] The notion of the 'unbearable' points to the existential non-unitary model of consciousness insofar as it involves (1) processes of thought exceeding the unifying framework of rational comprehension, and leading to what Daumal calls the 'Vision of the Absurd'; (2) an emotional dimension of the search for a 'lived truth', which Daumal explicitly qualifies as 'Suffering'. The existential emphasis on the Pascalian 'method' of inquiry ('chercher en gémissant') and the idea of 'awakening' find eloquent illustrations in Daumal's revolt against speculative thought, seen as deadly spiritual slumber: 'élève-toi par un éveil toujours nouveau, ou dors dans la mort spirituelle'.[52]

René Daumal and Roger Gilbert-Lecomte's project of an 'experimental metaphysics', focusing on the notions of 'awakening' and 'absurd evidence', emerged from a series of experiments with carbon tetrachloride[53] carried out in the years preceding the formation of the group *Le Grand Jeu*. Daumal provides two accounts of the so-called 'vision of the absurd' occurring in the carbon tetrachloride experiments,[54] and in both of them he struggles to overcome the problem of describing 'logically and geometrically impossible' images in conceptual terms. He insists however that the 'concepts' in this case overlapped with images (that is, his reasoning operated with images and *not* with linguistic entities of meaning) and that, despite the effort to analyse the vision using common categories of *space*, *time* and even mathematical *figures*, there was always an irreducible residuum—the 'absurd' evidence or certainty of entering another dimension of thought. In one of these accounts, Daumal points to the distinction between two simultaneously perceived 'realities':

> Je commencerai par les images, bien qu'images et concepts fussent simultanés. Elles sont visuelles et sonores. Les premières se présentaient comme un voile de phosphènes, plus réel que le 'monde' de l'état ordinaire, que je pouvais toujours percevoir au travers.[55]

The images constituting Daumal's vision present a special interest for the notion of 'awakening', illustrated by Chestov and Fondane with reference to the case of the sleeper who conceives the 'geometrically absurd' idea of a 'one-dimensional sphere':

> Un cercle semi-partie rouge et noir inscrit dans un triangle mi-partie de même, le demi-cercle rouge étant dans le demi-triangle noir et inversement; et l'espace entier était divisé indéfiniment ainsi en cercles et triangles inscrits les uns dans les autres, s'agençant et se mouvant, et devenant les uns les autres d'une manière géométriquement impossible, c'est-à-dire non représentable dans l'état ordinaire.[56]

Probably the most significant evidence brought to light or verified by the carbon tetrachloride experiment was that 'Quelque chose d'absurde peut être donné dans l'intuition.'[57] Both Daumal's and Gilbert-Lecomte's experiences showed that something logically and geometrically absurd can be given to the consciousness, and can therefore raise doubts about the common notions of certainty, possibility and impossibility. Their experimental activity represents in a sense the actual enactment of the hypothetical case presented by Chestov and Fondane in support of the idea of awakening to a different kind of evidence.

In a similar manner to Fondane, Daumal speaks of the 'awakening' to another kind of evidence, equally necessary but opposed to that given to common reasoning. The awakening emerges *suddenly* rather than through a process of logical elaboration, and it is rather a 'recognition' (*reconnaissance*) of a truth already known to the subject, though muted, as it were, in normal conditions:

> et, sous peine d'une perte irrémédiable, je devais, toujours sur ce rythme accéléré, répéter un mot imprononçable (approximativement: 'temgouef temgouef drrr...'); à un certain moment, le rythme devenait si rapide que je ne pouvais plus le suivre, et subitement je *reconnaissais* la vérité que j'avais connue depuis toujours, je m'éveillais à cette vérité. Avec une évidence, une clarté dont je ne puis donner la moindre idée, tellement ce caractère de certitude, de nécessité absolue, est ignoré de la pensée humaine normale, je comprenais le sens [...] de ce mouvement sonore et visuel: le dernier mot de tout, l'explication [...] de l'existence de mon esprit, tenait dans une sorte de raisonnement supra-logique terriblement simple, impossible à traduire.[58]

Daumal reaches the point of a radical, uncompromising critique of reason, corresponding to Fondane's 'fight against self-evidence'. The certainty and evidence that emerged from Daumal's initiation into another dimension of thought, 'un autre monde ou une autre sorte de connaissance', was nothing other than the revelation of his own 'asymptotic' annihilation at the limit of a logico-mathematical equation:

> et c'est là le centre de l'expérience — *c'est de moi qu'il s'agit*: je voyais mon néant face à face, ou plutôt mon anéantissement perpétuel dans chaque instant, anéantissement *total* mais non *absolu*: les mathématiciens me comprendront si je dis 'asymptotique'.[59]

In Daumal's experiment, the effort to ascertain existence through reasoning (in the manner of the Cartesian *cogito*) fails. The limit that Daumal confronts is none other than the limit of his reasoning, which cannot capture or stop the ineluctable temporal flow of his existence, and ultimately brings him face to face with his own 'anéantissement'. The certainty and evidence achieved in these conditions is no longer that of a unitary consciousness, but an 'absurd evidence', revealed as the 'déroulement illusoire de ma durée'.[60] The awakening to this truth of the temporary existence of the individual subject, as *the* most important thing rather than a meaningless variable in a logico-mathematical equation, occurs at the limit of near-death experiences like those in which Daumal and Gilbert-Lecomte engaged.[61]

Although the critics of *Le Grand Jeu* have often commented on the theme of awakening and the aspect of near-death experiences characterizing all the experiments of the group,[62] nobody so far has traced this theme back to Plotinus's philosophy, which is an explicit reference point not just for Chestov's and Fondane's writings, but also for Daumal's and Gilbert-Lecomte's 'vision of the absurd'. The example of the sleeper who dreams that he is the emperor of China about to inscribe monograms on a one-dimensional sphere was used by Chestov and Fondane precisely as an illustration of a process by which one can, in special circumstances, transcend common reason and follow Plotinus's awakening to what he called τὸ τιμιώτατον—'the most important'—the transient, temporally determined reality of individual existence. The awakening, Daumal specifies, is not a state but an immediate act—an act of revolt and absolute negation, which draws on Plotinus's 'negative theology'.[63] Daumal, like Chestov, remarked upon the 'scandal' and contradiction introduced into speculative, philosophical thought by the 'awakening to oneself' (ἐγειρόμενος εἰς ἐμαυτόν).[64] In rejecting common reason as mere delusion or sleep, man discovers the 'scandalous' or absurd nature of everything that exists without the necessary support of logical argumentation. Moreover, as Daumal comments, one does not ultimately need to resort to artificially-induced states of sensorial deprivation (like the experiments with carbon tetrachloride) in order to grasp the significance of this metaphysical question:

> Mais j'insiste sur ceci: pour que l'intuition de l'absurde acquière la pleine valeur d'une expérience métaphysique, il n'est pas nécessaire que tu fasses l'expérience particulière et assez exceptionnelle que j'ai racontée. Mais l'existence de chaque chose, de toutes les choses, du monde; la présence de quelque chose qui n'est pas toi-même, l'existence de personnes et de consciences distinctes de soi, ta propre existence, enfin, comme être individuel et fini, tout cela doit, si tu t'éveilles vraiment, t'apparaître comme intolérablement absurde. Tu dois commencer par penser comme absolument irrésoluble la double question: pourquoi quelque chose existe? pourquoi telle chose existe-t-elle? Tout ce qui t'est donné doit devenir avant tout une *matière de Scandale*.[65]

Self-subsistent, contingent existence is scandal to discursive thought and to conceptual definitions of being ('toute existence définie est scandale');[66] thinking in terms of the awakening to oneself, to one's particular, empirical existence, is scandalous to common reason: 'Toute réflexion est fille du scandale. Scandale dès que j'ouvre mes yeux.'[67] Like Fondane and Gilbert-Lecomte, Daumal identifies consciousness of self with this awakening and emergence of an absurd evidence contradicting the self-evidence of rational thinking. The individual subject knows himself and becomes conscious of himself through this perpetually renewed act of negation.[68] This is the sense of Daumal's 'perpetual race towards awakening', which exposes the self-evidence, the laws and necessity of speculative thought as 'spiritual death', or in Fondane's terms 'le commencement de la mort'.[69]

Artaud's understanding of the theatrical performance as an actual enactment of alternative possibilities of thought, exceeding common reasoning, supports and illustrates the existential opposition between dream and 'awakening', between the slumber of necessary, logical judgements and the wakefulness ('la veille') that reveals the subjective necessity and meaning of 'real life':

> Quand je vis je ne me sens pas vivre. mais quand je joue c'est là que je me sens exister. Qu'est-ce qui m'empêcherait de croire au rêve du théâtre quand je crois au rêve de la réalité? Quand je rêve je fais quelque chose et au théâtre je fais quelque chose. Les événements du rêve conduits par ma conscience profonde m'apprennent le sens des événements de la veille où la fatalité toute nue me conduit. Or le théâtre est comme une grande veille, où c'est moi qui conduit la fatalité.[70]

Just as Chestov gives the example of the man who, tortured by a monster in his dream, can only wake up by refusing to accept the 'self-evident' coherence of seemingly 'real' events, Artaud makes shouting ('le cri') the principle of a paradoxical fight against the slumber of rational thought: 'Je crie en rêve, mais je sais que je rêve, et sur les deux côtés du rêve je fais régner ma volonté. [...] Ce cri que je viens de lancer *est* un rêve. Mais un rêve qui mange le rêve.'[71] From Artaud's point of view, which converges with Chestov's and Fondane's understanding of awakening, shouting is less a method than a means of mobilizing the individual will in order to overcome the coherent, oppressive logic of the dream.

In fact, as Daumal argued, there can be no universal method or technique that used consistently would induce an alternative line of thought in a rational, analytical mind. All too often the use of a method paralyses thought and induces sleep rather than heightened lucidity. The investigations into the unconscious carried out by the Surrealists under the authority of psychoanalytical theory entertained the illusion of activity in an otherwise dormant reasoning, according to Daumal:

> En fait, la doctrine psychologique cherchée n'existe pas encore. Les techniques surréalistes peuvent constituer d'excellents moyens d'investigation dans certains domaines, si elles sont prises comme de simples techniques. Malheureusement, l'écriture automatique, l'onirisme, etc., deviennent trop vite pour les surréalistes des *moyens de penser*, des *mécanismes pensants*, autrement dit des procédés pour dormir, pour ne pas avoir à penser.[72]

Daumal's preoccupation in his 'experimental ontology' with the origin rather than the structures of consciousness and self-identity exposes the frailty of the rationalistic, reductive assumptions underlying psychological statements about self-consciousness:

Regarde, par exemple, le lamentable spectacle d'un psychologue à la recherche de la conscience. Il dit: 'ma conscience', comme si c'était une chose qu'il puisse posséder. Qui est cet 'il'? Qui est possédé? Et qui possède, sinon le conscient? La science de ces gens est vaine au point d'essouffler de rire. Ecoutez-les seulement parler de l'inconscient. Poussez-les à bout, et ils croiront exprimer une pensée, une pensée claire, même, et une vérité indiscutable en prononçant, toujours sans rire, cette phrase: 'dans le profond sommeil, je suis inconscient'. Demandez-leur maintenant ce que le mot 'je' signifie dans leur proposition. Les voilà bouche bée.[73]

The contradiction contained by the case of the sleeper in Chestov's argument (which is similar to the liar's paradox), is attributed here to the scientific discourse that postulates the truth of a sleeper's statement, 'I am unconscious'. Can one logically sustain the possibility of a subject, of a consciousness to which the evidence of being unconscious might be given? If a subject is unconscious, then the statement 'I am unconscious' or even 'I am' cannot be true; it is absurd. Like Chestov and Fondane, Daumal often uses paradox to question the rational postulate of the unitary framework of consciousness underlying the search for universal, absolute criteria of truth and certainty.

In addition to his experimental metaphysics, elaborated on the basis of the results provided by the experiments with carbon tetrachloride, Daumal proposed a kind of anti-science, 'la Pataphysique', articulated on the basis of the so-called 'logique formelle de la pataphysique'. This para-logical mode made use of 'sophismes pataphysiques', or reasonings in the form of 'vicious circles'. The vicious circle is the form taken by paradoxes, of which the best example used by Daumal is that of the liar.[74] Paradoxes provoke the subject to awaken from his slumber and start thinking. The object of pataphysics is 'l'irréductible'. Knowledge of this 'irréductible' comes by way of a negative progression, and an affirmation of the identity of opposites:

Connaître X = connaître (⁻X) seule façon de connaître l'irréductible. [...] Il n'y a de connaissance de l'irréductible que par l'identification de soi à tout — (car: irréductible à *quoi*? Posons: irréductible à X; il suffit de faire X = tout pour que ... etc.) D'où deux axiomes fondamentaux: 1) identité de contraires; 2) progrès de la conscience.[75]

Daumal's 'pataphysics' (which drew its inspiration from Alfred Jarry's *Gestes et opinions du Dr Faustroll pataphysicien*) relied on the force of the same negative principle invoked by Fondane: 'le rire'. The revelation of the 'absurd evidence' comes as the 'revelation of laughter': the first step is refusal, negation. Daumal specifies:

> Ce refus, partout où il se manifeste, c'est d'abord le grand *Rire*. C'est la plus grande approximation concrète que je puisse donner de cet acte précis, que j'invite chacun à accomplir. En usant toujours de mots tels que *négation*, plus exacts peut-être en leurs sens originels, je craindrais de laisser entendre cette opération comme un simulacre abstrait du discours, un vain schème vocal. Et, pour tâcher que tu ne retombes dans le sommeil de ton 'savoir' philosophique, je dirai donc plutôt, quand je parle bien du doute méthodique, *sarcasme* ou *dérision méthodique*; et je ne crains plus guère que tu prennes ce Rire pour de la joie.[76]

We are far from the Surrealist 'humour noir' here, despite the apparent resemblance to Vaché's conception of 'l'inutilité théâtrale et sans joie du tout'. Laughter, sarcasm and derision take on the aspect of a systematic disruption of 'sleep'—that is, of logical thought—in a constantly renewed attempt to subvert the foundations of all philosophical knowledge. Daumal's critique of rationality places a special emphasis on the opposition between 'sleep' and 'awakening', which plays a significant part in the existential 'fight against self-evidence' and finds no equivalent in the Surrealist doctrine.

Against the Surrealist immanentist interpretation of Rimbaud's 'raisonné dérèglement de tous les sens', the members of *Le Grand Jeu*, like Fondane,[77] considered Rimbaud as the messenger of the 'awakening' of an 'au-delà' of rational thought rather than the explorer into the reasoned enchantment of dream analysis and automatic writing. Roger Gilbert-Lecomte, for example, illustrated the position of his group with quotations from Rimbaud that clearly depart from the Surrealist interpretation while closely following Fondane's existential thought ('Nous ne sommes pas au monde'; 'Mais je m'aperçois que mon esprit dort, s'il était bien éveillé toujours à partir de ce moment, nous serions bientôt à la vérité qui peut-être nous entoure avec ses anges pleurant').[78] Fondane, like Daumal, pushes 'systematic doubt' to the limit, making destruction the principle of a nihilistic attitude which can ultimately provide the only 'kind of foundation, a theoretical basis'[79] for another dimension of thought. The revolt of the individual against himself, against the a priori conditions governing his thought, goes beyond the limited revolt against social or political conditions, engaging in the absurd yet decisive fight for life: 'Non, non à présent je me révolte contre la mort', Rimbaud wrote, leaving behind his quest for a visionary 'raisonné déréglement de tous les sens'.[80] The only way to overcome the idealistic and rationalistic fallacies involved what Fondane called 'Le Procès de la raison', which instead of considering the 'problem of knowledge' (the foundations of rational thought) will look at 'knowledge as a problem' ('le savoir en tant que problème').[81] A similar iconoclastic tone and the same 'absurd' questions emerge from both Fondane's and Daumal's writings:

> Et puisque la Raison convient qu'il n'est pas en son pouvoir de nous donner la liberté, que ne nous la sollicitons-nous à la Déraison?[82]

> (T)oute logique rejetée, pourquoi ne pas croire au déraisonnable? Puisque toutes les raisons de croire sont vaines, pourquoi ne pas croire à l'insensé?[83]

There is a striking resemblance between the defiant statements of the two authors, paying homage to nonsense and insanity ('la Déraison') as the irreducible other of Reason. Daumal's pataphysics underlies, in its profound sense, an ontology for which the Genesis, the dawn of existence is laughter, shattering the foundations of reason: 'A l'origine, le chaos fut illuminé d'un immense éclat de rire. [...] Ici nous sommes près du mystère de la séparation, de la négation, du Rire que j'ai dit contemporain de ce monde existant.'[84] Fondane similarly identifies the manifestation of the 'pure self' ('le moi pur') with the negative, destructive power of laughter: 'Tirer la langue aux évidences voilà une manifestation du "moi pur"'.[85]

Crying or shouting ('le cri') provides a second non-systematic means of disrupting the slumber of rational thought and uncovering the certainty of the 'awakening to oneself', in the sense of the emergence of a new consciousness of self: 'Le cœur même de cette certitude, le cri: "C'est moi cela! c'est de moi qu'il s'agit", ce cri doit effrayer les curieux qui voudraient, d'une façon ou d'une autre faire la même expérience.'[86] If laughter throws the individual outside the boundaries of an oppressive slumber in which being remains the attribute of logical self-evident truth, the sudden cry of awakening measures the abyss opened before those who have ventured into this second dimension of thought, where no solid ground and no rational light can guide their steps. In Artaud's writing, the cry is both the sign of awakening and a solitary call to revolt, the origin of human speech: 'un grand cri, une source de voix humaine, une seule et isolée voix humaine, comme un guerrier qui n'aura plus d'armée'.[87] To Chestov and Fondane, the inarticulate, spontaneous cry marked the moment when the individual breaks free from the logical, discursive thinking and re-establishes the lost communication with the transcendent and the divine. Crying out is thus no longer a sign of despair and helplessness but the beginning of a fight for life:

> *De profundis, ad te Domine clamavi*, criait Job, comme le psalmiste; et Nietzsche, Kierkegaard, Chestov, eussent compris que les 'cris de Job ne sont pas seulement des cris, autrement dit des clameurs absurdes, inutiles et fatigantes'; ils eussent compris qu'avec ses cris, Job abordait une 'nouvelle dimension de la pensée'; que le cri n'était pas là une façon d'abandonner la lutte, mais une *méthode de lutte*; [...] Le cri, en tant que méthode: voilà ce qu'oppose la pensée existentielle à l'*intelligere* de la pensée spéculative.[88]

In this paradoxical advance towards a certainty beyond rational knowledge, the individual encounters the discontinuity, arbitrariness and sudden changes of personal existence, which can no longer provide a unified, non-contradictory reflection at the level of consciousness. According to Fondane, the 'catastrophic moments' of revelation explode the 'automatism of the so-called objective consciousness'[89] and question the constitution of objective consciousness within both Hegelian idealism and Husserlian phenomenological description. The non-unitary, contradictory model of consciousness uncovered by the existential fight against self-evidence involves a radical critique of the theory of intentionality and of the interlocking of meaning and being in the rationalist philosophical discourse.

Intentionality vs. the Absurd Evidence

Chestov's and Fondane's critique of Husserlian phenomenology focused on the concept of self-evidence that underlies the intentional constitution of the pure ego and of true being as being-given-in-itself. The existential account of Husserl's project highlights the fact that the phenomenological search for certainty relied on the postulated primacy of autonomous reason and the necessary rather than actual correspondence between thinking and being. In Husserl, the *cogito* is no longer connected to the existence of the Cartesian subject but leads through the theory of intentional constitution to the self-evident identity of the transcendental Ego. The concept of constitution involves an act of endowing the object of intentional constitution with meaning. Being and meaning become interlocked, and as Leszek Kolakowski observes, 'the very concept of an absolute, self-supporting reality, not related to consciousness, [becomes] absurd and self-contradictory'.[90] This is the sense in which Fondane talked about a 'crisis of reality' and the need to go beyond the self-evidence of the intentionally constituted object, outside the unified, closed field of pure transcendental consciousness, in order to uncover the individual being and the paradoxical meaning or the absurd evidence of real, particular existence, bracketed out by phenomenological description. Within the Husserlian model of consciousness, the 'provisional' suspension of the problem of existence can no longer be reversed. The 'brackets' that exclude natural existence from the field of description are never taken off; they become an indestructible wall of evidence, protecting the 'perfect correlation' between meaning and being.

The emphasis on experience, consciousness and image (all of which are central to Husserl's *Philosophie als strenge Wissenschaft*) indicates the ground on which phenomenological and Surrealist investigations, phenomenological and Surrealist critiques of psychoanalysis might actually meet. In 'L'Ombre de l'inventeur', Aragon derives the notion of *surréalité* and the methodology defining Surrealism through comparison with a philosophical process of abstraction in two stages: the first (very similar to phenomenological reduction) results in the production of the 'unreal' (l'irréel—reminiscent of the Husserlian 'Nicht-Reell');[91] the second stage is a dialectical synthesis of opposites following the Hegelian model, by which reality (le réel) and the unreal are reconciled and overcome within the 'surréel'. This way the philosophical and Surrealist investigations seem to converge and make use of a similar method: 'la considération du réel, sa négation, sa conciliation et le médiateur absolu qui les englobe'.[92] Breton was never comfortable with the metaphysical implications of Hegelian idealism,[93] and, as some commentators remarked, his unyielding affiliation to the principle of dialectical synthesis indicated rather a critique of absolute idealism, a return to the values of experience and intuition.

Nevertheless, it is significant that in the same article, 'L'Ombre de l'Inventeur', Aragon speaks of Surrealist objects and games in terms of 'pure imagination' and 'pure invention' (related to their scientific and philosophical meaning) and ends by stating emphatically: 'Ce ne sont pas des jeux, mais des actes philosophiques de première grandeur.' The recurrence of the term 'pure', attached to notions such as invention, imagination, inspiration and meant to illustrate the rapprochement between philosophical and Surrealist investigations, seems to indicate more than an accidental instilling of phenomenological ideas into Freudian psychoanalytical theory, which dominated the development of Surrealist techniques in the early 1920s. Such a transition was not only apparent in philosophical and psychological research at the time,[94] but actually coincided with Breton's effort in the *Second Surrealist Manifesto* to recover the 'total comprehension' and the 'original purity of thought' through objectively validated methods of investigation. This process of renewal was situated in a 'place of the mind' ('lieu mental') rather than 'in the world'.[95] Aragon went even further onto phenomenological ground when positing that an image 'annihilates the entire universe' ('une image anéantit tout l'univers')[96] and adding the following remarks on reality and image:

> Un certain sentiment du réel. Pur sentiment. Car où prend-on que le concret soit le réel? N'est-il pas au contraire ce qui est hors du réel, le réel n'est-il pas le jugement abstrait, que le concret ne présuppose que dans la dialectique? [...] Sans doute l'image n'est-elle pas le concret, mais la conscience possible, la plus grande conscience possible du concret. [...] Mais l'image emprunte seulement la forme du fait, car l'esprit peut l'envisager en dehors de lui.[97]

The indubitable presence of a Hegelian turn added to this phenomenological account of the poetic image does not derive from an isolated, idiosyncratic misreading of Husserl's project within the Surrealist discourse. The same surprising annexation of Husserl's thought to Hegel's *Phenomenology of Spirit* characterized the entire French reception of phenomenology in the twenties, as H. Spiegelberg's informed study (1965) shows. It was not only the general interest in Marxism, shared by many French intellectuals of the period, that led back to Hegel and seemed to make the connection with the recently imported Husserlian phenomenology, but also the more specific misinterpretation (of Hegel's phenomenology as 'phenomenological description in the Husserlian sense of the term') circulated by a trained philosopher like Alexandre Kojève. A Russian Marxist, Kojève studied under Jaspers and then temporarily took over Alexandre Koyré's course on Hegel at the École des Hautes Études.[98] This also happened to coincide with a sudden impetus of Hegelian studies in France, beginning in the late 1920s. A reference point for this revival, as Spiegelberg remarks, was Jean Wahl's well-known study of 1929, *Le Malheur de la conscience dans la philosophie de Hegel*, examining the role of the 'unhappy consciousness' in Hegel's *Phenomenology of Spirit*. It is not difficult to see that the discussion of master–slave dialectics aroused a particular interest among young Marxists at that moment, judging for example by the references to Hegel contained in the Second Surrealist Manifesto and the subsequent new series of *Le Surréalisme au service de la révolution*.

Conversely, the common interest in the problem of consciousness that defined both Hegel's and Husserl's phenomenologies must have accounted for the tendency to 'Hegelianize Husserl', as Spiegelberg notes, something that can be observed not only in the Surrealist position on this matter but also in the more lucid interpretation of *Le Grand Jeu*. Daumal, however, who was a better informed reader of Hegel (and more perceptive of Hegel's absolute idealism than Breton might have allowed himself to be), never completed the mistaken identification of Hegelian and Husserlian phenomenologies and preferred to combine the former with a leaning towards mystical, Occult ideas or, in particular, Oriental philosophy.

Breton's reading of Hegel seems to have influenced the comments in the final part of *Les Vases communicants* about the disconnection of the 'poetic operation' from any notion of miracle—a 'violation of the Spirit' in Hegelian terms. Instead, Breton proposed that the poet of the future should himself produce the capital piece of evidence meant to put an end to the 'immemorial' indictment by rational knowledge against intuitive knowledge. More precisely, the poet will agree to carry out the poetic operation in 'plain daylight' ('au grand jour'):

> Eux-mêmes ils ne crieront plus au miracle chaque fois que par le mélange, plus ou moins involontairement dosé, de ces deux substances incolores que sont l'existence soumise à la connexion objective des êtres et l'existence échappant concrètement à cette connexion, ils auront réussi à obtenir un précipité d'une belle couleur durable.[99]

The 'more or less' unintentional chemical reaction of two equally neutral, indifferent modes of existence, more or less objectively determined, aspires to validate the truth of the poetic 'document mental' as the resulting substance of this pseudo-scientific experiment. The repeatability of this chemical operation makes it accessible to everyone, in a similar way to that in which the self-identical meaning of ideal objects in phenomenological description is given to consciousness in its unlimited iterability, free of any contingent determinations. 'C'est toute la dignification de l'objet qui est en jeu', Breton notes with reference to the similarly mechanical process by which the poetic image will be constituted, making present in a striking comparison two objects as distant from each other as possible. The emphasis, therefore, is not set on the perceiving subject or its consciousness but on the manner of manifestation of the object and its 'dignity'. Such displacement is not without consequences, as Fondane remarked in his *Faux Traité d'esthétique*.

The moment poetry agrees to amend or to reconcile its 'unthinkable' evidence according to a higher order of truth (that of 'objective connexions'), a certain 'conscience honteuse' has taken hold of the artist himself: he no longer believes in his unverifiable, absurd intuitions, he despises the 'charm' and the 'miracle', but he has yet to *prove* his 'knowledge', his mental document, his claims to truth. In short, he is trapped in a 'vicious circle', as Fondane observed:

C'est là la crise de la poésie, le signe de sa maladie: la conscience honteuse est en nous. Si tant est que la poésie est une 'connaissance', le poète ne se peut refuser à la règle du jeu: il doit *justifier* de sa nécessité. Cercle vicieux: car s'il réfuse de démontrer la beauté, elle n'est pas; et s'il veut la démontrer, elle s'évanouit. [...] M. Caillois a raison: la beauté est chose hétérogène et contradictoire; M. Breton a raison aussi: elle est un 'mélange plus ou moins dosé'; les deux ont vu juste: elle ne donne *aucune prise aux appareils de mesure de l'investigation scientifique.*[100]

In fact, as Fondane further argues, how could the poet prove in terms of reason the necessity and the value of objectivity of an intuition such as 'le vent, du ciel, jetait ses glaçons aux mares'? Not only does the poet preserve his liberty to modify this intuition *par caprice*, whenever he likes, but the truth of this intuition, if any, has nothing universal about it, cannot be thought or imparted as objective knowledge, least of all be imposed on all men by necessity. The original as much as the modified proposition 'le vent de Dieu jetait ses glaçons aux mares' will never achieve the certainty of '2 + 2 = 4'. It may belong to common-sense psychology or 'la psychologie des états', but it will never achieve the status of a phenomenon, no matter how much the Surrealist theory might insist on the 'unreal', 'irreal' and 'super-real' character of poetic image.

In Husserl's phenomenology, which introduced in contrast to psychology the distinction between the meaning of judgement and the act of judging, the possibility of objective knowledge ultimately corresponds to the ideal character of truth, which in turn resides in the apodictic certainty or evidence of the self-identical, atemporal meaning of judgements. From this point of view, 'le vent de Dieu jetait ses glaçons aux mares' is *nonsense*; not so much an error of judgement, something that can conceivably be corrected, but something *absurd*. And this is precisely its irreducible character. Fondane even introduces a crucial distinction between irrationality and the absurd, the former being reducible, more or less, to rational categories, while the latter expresses the irreducible residuum of any rational analysis. Surrealist poetry, Fondane argued, achieved this irreducibly different kind of certainty or evidence only insofar as it went against Surrealist theory, against the dialectical reconciliation of two orders of truth.

Fondane therefore insists on the incompatibility of poetic intuition and philosophical (especially phenomenological) intuition. He argues that the 'données' of poetic consciousness will always emerge from a process that remains radically 'other' than that of intentional constitution, and which can be described in terms of 'participation-inspiration':

> Il se trouve ainsi que la réalité livre à l'expérience poétique, par le moyen de la participation-inspiration, ce qu'elle refuse à l'intelligence, à la connaissance; elle livre à la poésie un *état*, alors qu'elle n'offre à l'intelligence que des rapports, épars dans le texte discontinu des catégories. Mais nous ne tenons pas à serrer de près l'acte poétique, de crainte que, défini, il ne s'évanouisse; il ne peut être un acte de *saisie du réel* que pour autant qu'il refuse d'être une 'connaissance'.[101]

Poetic experience, grounded in common-sense psychology rather than in conceptual thinking, is a 'saisie de réel' insofar as it opposes the rationalized notion of experience presupposed by any rigorous epistemological approach providing the foundation for philosophical and scientific knowledge. Fondane's idea of a different kind of intuition, that of 'participation-inspiration', found support in sociological and anthropological studies devoted to the totemic mentality of primitive societies, which in his view provided the most substantial critique of the 'theory of knowledge' and generally of the rationalistic propensity of modern philosophy. Fondane was well acquainted with Lévy-Bruhl's work, to which he refers in *Faux Traité d'esthétique*, and which he comments on at length in an article published in two consecutive issues of *La Revue philosophique de la France et de l'étranger*. The opposition between the primitive pre-logical mentality and rational thought provided a central argument to Fondane's existential interpretation of poetry as an alternative type of knowledge, establishing its own alternative order of evidence and truth.

Similar considerations defined the position of *Le Grand Jeu* in Gilbert-Lecomte's comprehensive presentation of the avant-garde groups (Dada, Surrealism, Philosophies/L'Esprit)[102] in 1929. The so-called 'lyrical state' represented a type of knowledge ('mode de connaissance') that, according to Gilbert-Lecomte, *Le Grand Jeu* opposed to logical thought. The reference to Lévy-Bruhl and James Frazer is used to illustrate the simultaneous presence in the primitive mind of two different modes of reasoning: the logical mode, common to Western society and primitive thought (in that it enables any man to work out that '2 + 2 = 4'), and 'the pre-logical, mystical mentality' related to the 'spirit of participation'. Gilbert-Lecomte explicitly mentioned here the irreducible character of the totem as a development of another type of thinking, namely participation. Like Fondane, he denounces the limitation of rational thought and argues for the alternative 'logic' of participation:

> Je crois que l'indéfini perfectionnement de la pensée logique correspond à la pensée occidentale, chez qui l'esprit de participation a presque complètement disparu, ou tend à disparaître, tandis qu'au contraire la pensée orientale, du moins en ses sommets, me paraît déterminée par une priorité donnée en dernière analyse à un esprit de participation épuré et devenu l'esprit mystique dominant et guidant une pensée logique également évoluée. [...] Cette pensée que j'ai définie tour à tour comme prélogique, mystique, orientale et qui existe, j'en suis persuadé, au fond de chacun de nous, succombe devant la pléthore, l'hypertrophie, le débordement de la pensée logique à travers le monde.[103]

There is no doubt that the primitive mentality exercized a similar fascination on Surrealist writers. However, in contrast to the conception developed by Fondane and *Le Grand Jeu*, this area of interest, alongside the preoccupation with the Occult, was carefully purged of any mystical or religious implications. Artaud encountered the alternative line of thought that characterized Fondane's position and the metaphysical standpoint of the members of *Le Grand Jeu*, insofar as he did not subscribe to Breton's rejection of the notion of miracle and his anticipation of the time when a 'précipité d'une belle couleur durable' would fuse together the objective and the subjective dimensions of human existence. Rather than attempting to reconcile and fix the subjective and objective worlds in a 'belle couleur durable', Artaud proposed to open them up to a transcendent dimension, focused around the magical energies captured by the totemic mentality. Artaud's experience of rituals and magical practices, the decisive influence of his encounter in Mexico with the Indian tribe of the Tarahumaras, left an indelible mark on his conception of theatrical representation, as presented in *Le Théâtre et son double*. The new physical language that he attempted to introduce opposed the Surrealist notion of 'jouissance', the Surrealist emphasis on the immanent 'merveilleux', from a perspective that revived the pre-logical mentality of primitive societies, centred around totemic participation in a transcendent order of signification:

> Le vieux totémisme des bêtes, des pierres, des objets chargés de foudre, des coutumes bestialement imprégnées, tout ce qui sert en un mot à capter, à diriger, et à dériver des forces, est pour nous une chose morte, dont nous ne savons plus tirer qu'un profit artistique et statique, un profit de jouisseur et non un profit d'acteur.// Or le totémisme est acteur car il bouge, et il est fait pour des acteurs; et toute vraie culture s'appuie sur les moyens barbares et primitifs du totémisme, dont je veux adorer la vie sauvage, c'est-à-dire entièrement spontanée.[104]

Within Artaud's conception of theatre, the return to primitive mentality and magical practices makes possible the reconstitution of a primitive, non-rational understanding of the divine. In this sense, Artaud denounces the speculative attitude of rational man, whose age-old intervention has ended up by 'corrupting' the divine:

> Si notre vie manque de soufre, c'est-à-dire d'une constante magie, c'est qu'il nous plaît de regarder nos actes et de nous perdre en considérations sur les formes rêvées de nos actes, au lieu d'être poussés par eux.// Et cette faculté est humaine exclusivement. Je dirai même que c'est une infection de l'humain qui nous gâte des idées qui auraient dû demeurer divines; car loin de croire le surnaturel, le divin inventé par l'homme je pense que c'est l'intervention millénaire de l'homme qui a fini par nous corrompre le divin.[105]

The infection or corruption of the divine by the human derives from the predominant inclination toward rational analysis and contemplation, which ends up by secularizing the miracle, the 'supernatural', or more accurately by reinventing the divine in man's likeness. Artaud's attempt to regain the lost 'double' of human thought and human language is a search for the divine, unlimited possibility of creation, a search for life that could only be carried out as direct, living experience rather than as a process of intellectual discovery. This is why Artaud invests the body with the power to manifest or materialize 'ideas' concretely in a language that appeals to the senses, that decentralizes the objective, constituted meaning of words. Theatre, he argues, goes back to 'le second temps de la Création, celui de la difficulté et du Double, celui de la matière et de l'épaississement de l'idée'.[106] It uncovers not just the moment of creation of the physical world, but that of language as well. The notion of 'l'épaississement de l'idée', or of the creative power of speech in the material world, comes up in the writings of *Le Grand Jeu*. The members of the group assert the identity between idea and speech ('Idée et Parole') in divine creation, and replace the opposition between spirit ('l'Esprit') and matter with the notion of 'Esprit-Matière', suggesting that the emergence of life corresponds to the embodiment of the creative, divine *Parole* into *Matière*.[107]

Fondane's critique of Husserlian phenomenology from the point of view of a theory of participation finds support in Artaud's conception of theatrical representation and his notion of 'souffle'. In 'Lettres sur le langage', and especially in 'Un athlétisme affectif', Artaud develops a conception of language and meaning that could hardly be more remote from phenomenological intentionality and generally from any speculative definition of objective meaning.[108] The insistence on singularity, the absence of repetition of what Artaud calls 'signs' in theatrical language, measures the irreducible distance that separates his conception from the theory of the intentional constitution of meaning and generally from any theory based on the repetitive character of the signifier in logical, discursive language:[109] 'le théâtre est le seul endroit au monde où un geste fait ne se recommence pas deux fois'.[110] Artaud reinvests poetic/theatrical language with its absurd resistance to conceptualization, by bringing its power to signify without repetition back to the most irreducible, ultimate outpost of living experience, the body: 'Je crie dans une armature d'os, dans les cavernes de ma cage thoracique qui aux yeux médusés de ma tête prend une importance démesurée.'[111] The violence of rational thought against the individual subject becomes in Artaud outright and 'obscene' violence of the concept against the body, against his body.

To make place ('faire place') for the body, the subject has to 'abolish the idea' ('supprimer l'idée'), to assert itself as 'irréflexion', as concrete, physical language, instituting an order of truth that cannot coexist with that of the mind, of articulated language. This emphasis on a communication originating in the physical, living manifestation of the body subverts the privilege of ideal, abstract signs, which characterizes the conceptual approach to reality.[112] Artaud's idea of an 'athlétisme affectif', based on the possibility of uncovering an 'affective' dimension of thought situated in the body, involves a radical questioning of man's rationally-derived notion of meaning and the search for a 'parole d'avant les mots'.

Chestov's and Fondane's exploration of a 'second dimension of thought' was governed by the same concern with the possibility of expressing ideas that exceed the limitations posed by the objective, universal character of principles at work inside language. Chestov, like Artaud, came to acknowledge that, in trying to go beyond the bounds of rational thought, one actually confronts the bounds of meaning, of what is to be considered 'meaningful' communication:

> Tout ce qu'on écrit est écrit pour autrui, est objectivé. Jusqu'ici, en tout cas, les hommes n'ont pas encore trouvé le moyen de s'exprimer adéquatement. L'écrivain, comme l'artiste, se trouve devant un dilemme: si tu dis ce que tu vois et entends, les autres n'entendront et ne verrons pas. Si tu veux qu'on voit et qu'on entende, adapte-toi aux circonstances extérieures, dis ce qui peut être compris par tous, toujours et partout.// Par conséquent il faut se taire? Par conséquent!... Il ne faut nullement se taire, il ne faut pas non plus se presser tellement de conclure! Il suffit de constater le fait; la conclusion viendra plus tard, un jour ou l'autre, en tout cas *pas tout de suite*; pas tout de suite, c'est cela l'essentiel.[113]

The difficulty of communicating the self-contradictory, self-destructive truth, which Chestov mentions in describing the process of awakening, seems to confine the anti-rationalist thinker to silence. Just as the existential eulogy of madness points to the only alternative, the absolute other of reason, silence might be taken to represent the only alternative left outside the boundaries of meaningful communication through language. However, Chestov's critique of Husserl's theory of self-evidence (relating to the self-evident, objective meaning of ideal objects) proves the contrary. Silence is not the only, and certainly not the most effective, weapon against the self-evident limitations of language. As Chestov's argument consistently shows, one can subvert if not completely suspend the principles of both rational analysis and rational communication by using given, universal means of expression in order to raise questions that expose the bounds of reason, questions whose answer exceeds the bounds of non-contradictory, logical discourse. From this point of view, it can be said that the existential investigation of 'the absurd' (which converges with Artaud's own examination of language) led to a re-evaluation of the interconnected issues of silence and madness, anticipating the more recent analysis devoted by Jacques Derrida to the Cartesian 'hyperbolic doubt' in 'Cogito et histoire de la folie'. If the ultimate moment of doubt verges on the absurd, and discloses 'le sans-fond du non-sens' as the actual origin of meaning, the search for an absolute grounding of truth does not dwell on the silence of madness, as Derrida argues, but is already opened to the reassuring clarity of rational speech:

> J'entends bien qu'il n'y a pas seulement, dans le mouvement qu'on apelle le *Cogito cartésien*, cette pointe hyperbolique qui devrait être, comme toute folie pure en général, silencieuse. Dès qu'il a atteint cette pointe, Descartes cherche à se rassurer, à identifier l'acte du Cogito avec l'acte d'une raison raisonnable. Et il le fait dès qu'il profère et *réfléchit* le Cogito. [...] Au fond, en passant sous silence le problème que pose le Cogito, Descartes semble sous-entendre que penser *et* dire le clair et le distinct, c'est la même chose.[114]

The problem 'passed over in silence' by Descartes is among those questions never raised by systematic philosophy, which Fondane mentions in defining the scope of the existential critique of rationality. The unavowed, ultimate implication of 'hyperbolic doubt',[115] along with the problem of madness as the origin of meaning and rational discourse, constitutes the fundamental problem of philosophy. In refusing to pass over such questions in silence (to resort to Descartes' reassuring identity of 'penser *et* dire le clair et le distinct'), the existential thinker uncovers the significance of a wilful acknowledgement of the role played by the absurd in the articulation of the rationalist discourse itself. The existential 'éloge de la folie' is not confined to silence; it is actually the opposite of silence: an avowal or acknowledgement of the obliterated questions of rationalist philosophy such as the possibility of defining meaning against Husserl's theory of intentional constitution, from the 'natural standpoint' excluded by phenomenological description. The psychological aspect associated with 'natural consciousness' enables Chestov and Fondane to question the absolute, universal validity of self-evident units of meaning (the self-evidence of ideal objects) and to define truth as related to rather than independent of the existence of the contingent, individual thinking subject.

Existential thought begins where rational thought and the consciousness of our powerlessness in the face of necessity end, Fondane argues.[116] It is the realm of the absurd, or the impossible. Similarly, Artaud declared: 'Car il ne peut y avoir théâtre qu'à partir du moment où commence réellement l'impossible et où la poésie qui se passe sur scène alimente et surchauffe des symboles réalisés.'[117] This paradoxical displacement of possibility and impossibility defines the existential fight against rational limitations; it opens a new dimension, both at the level of thought and at the level of language and meaning. Both Daumal and Artaud insist on the lucidity and sudden 'prise de conscience' that allow this relocation of the possible in the domain of the impossible and the absurd.[118] But is not our ability to think differently, our notion of 'possibility', limited by our ability to name things? Breton himself formulated this problem in *Point du jour*: 'La médiocrité de notre univers ne dépend-elle pas essentiellement de notre pouvoir d'énonciation?'[119] The whole question of redefining our conception of certainty, evidence and possibility vs. impossibility, highlighted by the existential line of thought, comes back to the limitations at work inside language. The possibility of thinking the unthinkable seems to depend on the possibility of expressing the inexpressible in some form or other.

In contrast to the Surrealist doctrine of automatic writing, the existential critique of rationalism traced the question of language and signification back to the biblical myth of Genesis. Is the same unlimited creative possibility as that of the divine Word given to our consciousness in our (rational, logically-articulated) language? Chestov argued that the act of free creation, the divine 'creatio ex nihilo', was replaced by human knowledge and reason, which introduced its own Law, its *Logos*, into the world, and 'created' universal, immutable principles[120] without, however, finding a way to maintain their postulated ideal being in existence for eternity otherwise than by *necessity*. Man was cut off from the sources of life after having named all the creatures. Why would this be so? The singular, non-repeatable character of everything around man was reduced along a utilitarian line to a kind of minimal extension or 'essence'.[121] And man could conceive or think of everything, including himself, only in terms of what went into this minimal description. The individual subject ceased to be a 'creature' and became an 'object' to himself, in search for the 'essence', the 'general', rather than the unique, the uncommon. Chestov recalls the biblical idea that man became mortal after having eaten of the fruit of the Tree of the Knowledge of Good and Evil. He argues that knowledge, as opposed to Life, brought about a need for certainty, a need to establish the way in which things *necessarily* are, and not that they simply are.[122] More accurately, knowledge introduced a rational dimension into language (and implicitly into experience), which underpins any theory of meaning, as ideal meaning or meaning-in-itself, constituted independently of the variable conditions of experience and of the thinking subject's existence.

In the second issue of *Le Grand Jeu*, the momentary lapse into irrationality provides the ground for regaining the divine power of creation through naming, outside the limiting frame of human reason. That is why Rimbaud's 'Je est un autre' can, in a sense, be translated as 'Je est Dieu en puissance.'[123] The necessary, binding character of the name, its deadly weight, came only with Knowledge, or the rational conception of consciousness, capturing and maintaining things in some form of ideal being through intentional constitution. In the case of Husserl's phenomenology, at which Chestov's critique of rationality is often aimed, the term 'intentional' also refers to linguistic expression and acts as a qualifier in the 'intentional experience' and the 'intentional object' (as opposed to the *reell* constituents of experience, including the data of sensation).[124]

According to Chestov and Fondane, human truth in contrast to divine truth is no longer a freely accepted or subjective truth but a universal truth supported by *necessary*, objective principles. And this is why human truth or human certainty confirms rather than questions the reign of death inaugurated by the Fall, insofar as it reduces the living individual to its eternal 'essence' or 'general being', and insofar as it places the notion of consciousness and its 'données' alongside the self-evident character of mathematical and logical propositions. As Chestov and Fondane argue, the implacable necessity, the self-identical meaning and objectivity of a judgement such as '$2 \times 2 = 4$' is a principle of death. In contrast, life and freedom correspond to the contingent, 'absurd' existence of the living individual and to the equally 'absurd' (logically unverifiable) existence of God. The mark of life, according to existential thought, is the struggle against the dissolving action of the universal, necessary character of logico-mathematical judgements, guiding the philosophical investigation into the origin of truth and being.

As I have previously argued, Fondane's critique of Surrealism from the point of view of existential thought brings out the similarities between artistic creation and the attempt to express the contradictory, self-destructive truth arrived at through the process of awakening. The 'truth-value' of a poetic affirmation such as 'Le vent de Dieu jetait ses glaçons aux mares' is unjustifiable in terms of the logical criteria of validation; but so is the truth of any philosophical judgement concerning the existence of God, or the contingent existence of the thinking subject itself. Fondane thus relates the existential fight against self-evidence to Artaud's, Daumal's and Gilbert-Lecomte's search for an alternative mode of knowledge, relating to the relative freedom from logical constraints displayed by primitive beliefs or by poetic, metaphorical language. The signs and the meaning of signs in Artaud's conception of the theatre subvert the notions of objectivity and intentionality supporting the system of logical communication. Words themselves are used in their acoustic dimension, as incantation, or even alongside crying or laughter as non-systematic methods of exploding the rational framework of language. All this finally leads to the re-conquest of the free creative powers that man supposedly had before the Fall. Artaud, like Fondane and Chestov,[125] refers to the 'dieu caché', in contrast to the manifest, 'visible' God identified with the Greek notion of *Logos*. Creation in the theatrical representation corresponds, in Artaud, to the 'tourbillon volontaire du bien', to the 'appétit de vie aveugle' manifest in the creation of the 'dieu caché.[126] This attempted reconstruction of a meaningful physical reality of creative communication beyond the limits of objective, logical discourse leads to a similar reconstruction of the notion of subjectivity.

Conclusions

Chestov's and Fondane's view of consciousness, analysed in this chapter with reference to Artaud, Daumal and Gilbert-Lecomte, attempted to subvert notions of objectivity, self-evidence and intentionality. The existential fight against self-evidence, as well as Daumal's and Gilbert-Lecomte's non-systematic methods of uncovering a second dimension of thought, opposed the Surrealist 'rational exploitation of the irrational', the scientific posturing of

Surrealist theories of language and poetic image. As I have tried to show with reference to Fondane's arguments, this tendency to realign the Surrealist doctrine with the main scientific theories of the time comes from the postulated convergence between the artistic domain and that of 'pure mental representation', insofar as this domain 'extends beyond real perception' and the representation occurs 'outside the physical presence of the object'.[127]

The existential fight against self-evidence was in particular designed to counteract arguments within Husserlian phenomenology and to subvert the complete rationalization of experience within the theory of intentionality. Chestov's and Fondane's approach disclosed a different understanding of consciousness and experience, starting from a paradoxical, anti-rational perspective, opposed to the process of intentional constitution and to the postulated unity of consciousness—which represented the necessary foundation for both Freudian psychoanalysis and Husserlian phenomenology. The process of awakening to a different order of truth, which was highlighted by the existential line of thought (and which finds relevant illustrations and support in Artaud's, Daumal's and Gilbert-Lecomte's writings), emphasized the non-unitary character of consciousness, the sudden nature of transition from logical to absurd evidence, and the emergence of a para-logical and paradoxical reasoning, which re-established the relationship between the human subject and the divine beyond the limitations imposed by rational analysis. Ultimately, the existential destruction of the logical principles and the necessity at work behind the postulated objectivity and iterability of the linguistic sign opened the way for a re-evaluation of the primitive, pre-logical mentality from the point of view of poetic and theatrical modes of expression, providing 'the only theoretical foundation' for an understanding of art as an alternative type of knowledge.

The existential critique of the interlocking of meaning and being, with reference to the ontological implications of the speculative discourse on consciousness, on ideal vs. real objects, also finds powerful expression in Artaud's revolt against the encroachment of rational thought and logic on the body, on the possibilities of verbal and physical communication outside the given criteria for intelligibility. The existential fight against self-evidence (as illustrated in Artaud, Fondane or *Le Grand Jeu*) is a fight for 'the impossible'. It aims at achieving the impossible return of the 'parole' to its divine creative source, avoiding the detour of logical reasoning. Even if human communication does contain 'un arrêt de mort', an apparently unsurpassable limitation, there is, however, an absurd possibility and a corresponding 'absurd evidence' that the individual will find a way to awaken the lost sources of life and to express the 'inexprimable'. The first step, which opens up this possibility, consists in exposing the limitations of rational discourse and acknowledging the questions obliterated by the history of systematic philosophy.

Notes to Chapter 1

1. It is interesting to note that, apart from Benjamin Fondane's remarks on the 'pure chemical state' in which current theoretical ideas of the 1920s and 1930s were represented by Surrealist theory (cf. *Faux Traité d'esthétique*, 22), later critics such as Sarane Alexandrian further illustrated this view by establishing a comparison between automatic writing and chemical reactions—specifically the process of 'precipitation' of chemical substances. Alexandrian (*Le Surréalisme et le rêve* (Paris: Gallimard, 1974), 94–5) also signals the influence of physics, not only in the title of the first Surrealist work, *Les Champs magnétiques*, but also in Breton's identification of various speeds (viz. v, v', v'', v''' and v'''') at which automatic writing can be performed.
2. Antonin Artaud, 'Le Pèse-nerfs', *Œuvres complètes*, i (Paris: NRF and Gallimard, 1976), 81.
3. Fondane, 'Un philosophe tragique', 142–50.
4. One of the first articles by Léon Chestov that came out in French was 'Dostoïevsky et la lutte contre les évidences', published with a presentation by Boris de Schloezer in *La Nouvelle Revue française* 101 (Feb. 1922), 134–58.
5. For the purpose of brevity, and in order to avoid repetitions, I do not intend to provide here an exposition of Husserlian phenomenology. Specific aspects relevant to the configuration of existential thought are discussed in various parts of this study. A good survey of the relationship between the concept of *Evidenz* and intentionality can be found in Quentin Lauer's 'Introduction' to Husserl's *La Philosophie comme science rigoureuse* (Paris: P.U.F., 1955), 36–49.
6. Similar reservations have been voiced by recent commentators like Jean-Luc Marion, who argues (*Réduction et donation: Recherches sur Husserl, Heidegger, et la phénoménologie* (Paris: P.U.F., 1989), 8) that: 'l'idéal de l'objectivité met en cause l'objectif même de la phénoménologie — le retour aux choses en question. Car il ne va pas de soi que les choses en question ne se donnent pas que sous la forme de leur objectivation constituée.'
7. Fondane, *La Conscience malheureuse*, pp. xxi, xxiv. For Chestov's critique of the 'probité intellectuelle', see Léon Chestov, 'La seconde dimension de la pensée', *La Nouvelle Revue française* 228 (1 Sept. 1932), 347–9 (aphorisms IV and V: 'L'honnêteté intellectuelle' and 'La vision intellectuelle'). See chap. 4 below for a detailed discussion of Chestov's and Fondane's interpretation of the 'unhappy consciousness'.
8. 'C'est parce que poser certains problèmes est une opération "tabou" pour la philosophie — "tabou" dont le viol nous couvre de honte — que nous avons été

obligés de partir en guerre contre la philosophie'; Fondane, *La Conscience malheureuse*, p. xx. Fondane previously quotes the extract from Kant's *Critique of Pure Reason* §A58 (Eng. trans. (London: Macmillan, 1993), 97) concerning 'absurd' questions that 'bring shame' on those who ask them.

9. See e.g. Léon Chestov, 'Kierkegaard et Dostoievsky: Les voix qui clament dans le désert', *Cahiers du Sud* 181 (Mar. 1936), 182.
10. See ibid.
11. André Breton, 'Introduction au discours sur le peu de réalité', *Œuvres complètes*, ii (Paris: Gallimard, 1992), 278.
12. Ibid.
13. Roger Caillois, *Le Procès intellectuel de l'art (exposé des motifs)* (Marseilles: *Les Cahiers du Sud*, 1935). On the relationship between Fondane and Caillois, see 'Lettre de Roger Caillois à Benjamin Fondane (13 juin 1936)', with a presentation by Michel Carassou, 'Caillois-Fondane, le dialogue malgré tout', Jean-Clarence Lambert (ed.), *Roger Caillois* (Paris: Éditions de la Différence, 1991), 205–9.
14. Fondane, *Faux Traité d'esthétique*, 34–5.
15. André Breton, *Manifeste du surréalisme*, *Œuvres complètes*, i (Paris: Gallimard, 1988), 346.
16. Fondane, *Faux Traité d'esthétique*, 15.
17. 'Die Frucht des Baumes der Erkenntniss des Guten und des Bösen, d. h. der aus sich schöpfenden Vernunft, das allgemeine Prinzip der Philosophie für alle Zeiten (The fruit of the knowledge of good and evil, that is to say of reason creating out of itself: the general principle of philosophy for all times)'; quoted from Hegel, *Werke*, xiv. 49, in Léon Chestov, *Athènes et Jérusalem: Un essai de philosophie religieuse* (Paris: Aubier, 1993), 115.
18. André Breton, 'Les Vases communicants', *Œuvres complètes*, ii. 208.
19. See the original quotation from Hegel, *Werke*, xiii. 124 in Chestov, *Athènes et Jérusalem*, 115. Cf. Hegel, *Lectures on the Philosophie of Religion*, iii (London: Routledge & Kegan Paul, 1968), 53–4.
20. André Breton, 'Qu'est-ce le surréalisme?', *Œuvres complètes*, ii. 233.
21. André Breton, 'Projet pour la bibliothèque de Jacques Doucet', *Œuvres complètes*, i. 631.
22. André Breton, 'Légitime défense', *Œuvres complètes*, ii. 292.
23. Antonin Artaud, 'Lettres aux écoles du Bouddha', *La Révolution surréaliste* 3 (15 Apr. 1925), 22.
24. Antonin Artaud, 'L'Activité du Bureau de Recherches Surréalistes', *La Révolution surréaliste* 3 (15 Apr. 1925), 31.
25. Jacques Derrida's interpretation of nonsense and madness as the 'origin of meaning', together with his comments on the will to express or avow this ultimate limit of rational inquiry, which characterizes the history of philosophy (see 'Cogito et histoire de la folie', *L'Ecriture et la différence* (Paris: Éditions du Seuil, 1967), 88–96), illuminate Artaud's remarks as well as the existential passionate advocacy of madness. Echoing Derrida's comments, Chestov writes in 'L'Eloge de la folie', *Les Commencements et les fins* (Lausanne: L'Âge d'Homme, 1987), 55: 'on peut appeler la Folie la Grande Raison et cela a, si on veut, un sens profond ou, plus exactement, une profonde virulence'.
26. Fondane, *La Conscience malheureuse*, 254.

27. Roger Gilbert-Lecomte, 'La force des renoncements', *Le Grand Jeu* 1 (Summer 1928), 15.
28. Ibid., 12.
29. Fondane, *La Conscience malheureuse*, 10–11.
30. André Breton, *L'Amour fou*, *Œuvres complètes*, ii. 689, 690.
31. Antonin Artaud, 'A la grande nuit, ou Le Bluff surréaliste', *Œuvres complètes*, i, rev. edn (Paris: Gallimard, 1970), 365.
32. Breton, *Situation du surréalisme*, 29.
33. Gilbert-Lecomte, 'La force des renoncements', 17.
34. Gilbert-Lecomte, 'Avant-Propos', *Le Grand Jeu* 1 (Summer 1928), 1.
35. Breton, *Manifeste du surréalisme*, 324, 346.
36. Michel Carrouges, *André Breton et les données fondamentales du surréalisme* (Paris: Gallimard, 1950), 364.
37. Fondane, *Faux traité d'esthétique*, 35.
38. Ferdinand Alquié, 'Humanisme surréaliste et humanisme existentialiste', *Cahiers du Collège philosophique*, special issue 'L'Homme, le monde, l'histoire' (1947), 160.
39. Benjamin Fondane, 'Philoctète (extrait)', *Le Mâche-Laurier*, Obsidiane 2 (June 1994), 34.
40. See Léon Chestov, 'Memento mori (A propos de la théorie de la connaissance d'Edmund Husserl)', *Revue philosophique de la France et de l'étranger* (Jan.–Feb. 1926), 35.
41. Chestov, 'Memento mori', 36.
42. Edmund Husserl, *Logical Investigations*, i (London: Routledge & Keegan Paul, 1970), 140.
43. This example was initially used by Chestov in his critique of Husserl's phenomenology; cf. 'Memento Mori', 5–62. Fondane here follows Chestov's argumentation as presented in *Le Pouvoir des clefs* (Paris: Vrin, 1936); see Fondane, 'Léon Chestov et la lutte contre les évidences', 35–6.
44. Quoted by both Chestov and Fondane from the German edition, *Logische Untersuchungen*, ii. 215: 'Wir werden uns nicht zu der Überzeugung entschliessen, es sei psychologish möglich was logisch und geometrisch widersinnig ist.' See Fondane, 'Léon Chestov et la lutte contre les évidences', 34. For the English translation, see Husserl, *Logical Investigations*, i. 425.
45. Edmund Husserl, *Ideas: General Introduction to Pure Phenomenology* (London: Collier Macmillan, 1962), 105.
46. This issue is discussed in more detail in my article, 'Evidence et conscience: Léon Chestov et la critique de la théorie de l'évidence chez Husserl', *Cahiers de l'émigration russe*, special issue 'Léon Chestov — Un Philosophe pas commes les autres' (Paris: Institut d'Études Slaves, 1996), 116–19.
47. Léon Chestov, 'A la mémoire d'un grand philosophe, Edmund Husserl', *Revue philosophique de la France et de l'étranger* 1–2 (Jan.–Feb. 1940), 29.
48. Chestov, *Le Pouvoir des clefs*, 279.
49. Chestov, 'Dostoïevsky et la lutte contre les évidences', 157.
50. André Breton, *Second manifeste du surréalisme*, *Œuvres complètes*, i. 781.
51. René Daumal, 'Les Provocations à l'Ascèse', *Tu t'es toujours trompé (1926–1928)* (Paris: Mercure de France, 1970), 33, 34.
52. Ibid., 34.

53. Carbon tetrachloride is a volatile liquid, similar to chloroform, but very toxic, which destroys the myelin of nerve-fibres and can be lethal.
54. The first account was written around 1930 for the fourth, unpublished issue of *Le Grand Jeu*. Later it was included in *L'Evidence absurde* (Paris: NRF and Gallimard, 1972), 51–6, with the title 'L'Asphyxie et l'évidence absurde', and in the reprint of the complete collection of *Le Grand Jeu* (Paris: Jean-Michel Place, 1977), 1–5, this time as 'L'inénarrable expérience'. The second account was written in 1943 at Jean Paulhan's request, who intended to publish a collections of 'souvenirs déterminants'. The project, however, did not materialize, and the article only appeared in *Les Cahiers de la Pléiade* 1 (1946), 168–73, bearing the title 'Une expérience fondamentale'. It was subsequently published in René Daumal, *Chaque fois que l'aube paraît* (Paris: Gallimard, 1953). It was also reprinted in Claudio Rugafiore's edition of *Les Pouvoirs de la parole*, ii (Paris: NRF and Gallimard, 1972), 112–20, as 'Le souvenir déterminant'. I shall refer to both accounts, because the actual experiments on which the articles were based date back to 1924–5, and because, despite the close resemblance of the two accounts, the second provides clarifications of aspects that are crucial for the understanding of the experience.
55. René Daumal, 'Le Souvenir déterminant', *Les Pouvoirs de la parole*, 115.
56. Ibid., 115.
57. René Daumal, 'L'Asphyxie et l'évidence absurde', in *L'Évidence absurde*, 51.
58. Ibid., 53.
59. Daumal, 'Le Souvenir déterminant', 117.
60. Ibid., 118.
61. This problem lies at the centre of Chestov's *Les Révélations de la mort*. Chestov developed his interpretation of death (and near-death experiences) as 'awakening' in a number of volumes that came out in the years when Daumal's and Gilbert-Lecomte's metaphysics emerged from the experiments with carbon tetrachloride. The publication of Chestov's books also coincided with the first, experimental stage of the Surrealist movement. See Léon Chestov, *Les Révélations de la mort: Dostoïevsky—Tolstoï* (Paris: Plon, 1923); *L'Idée de bien chez Tolstoi et Nietzsche: Philosophie et prédication* (Paris: Éditions du Siècle, 1925); *La Philosophie de la tragédie: Dostoïevsky et Nietzsche* (Paris: Éditions de la Pléiade and J. Schiffrin, 1926).
62. See Michel Random, 'La Métaphysique expérimentale', *Le Grand Jeu* (Paris: Denoël, 1970), 99–142; Jean Néaumet, 'René Daumal ou la volonté de connaissance', *René Daumal et le retour à soi* (Paris: l'Originel, 1981), 191–203; Virmaux, *Roger Gilbert-Lecomte et le Grand Jeu*, 189–206; Powrie, *René Daumal*, 33–53.
63. Daumal, *Tu t'es toujours trompé*, 65.
64. See Chestov's discussion of Plotinus' idea in relation to his critique of Husserl's phenomenology, 'Qu'est-ce que la vérité? (ontologie et éthique)', *La Revue philosophique de la France et de l'étranger* 1–2 (Jan.–Feb. 1927), 36–74. Fondane takes up Chestov's comments on Plotinus's τὸ τιμιώτατον in more than one article, e.g. 'Léon Chestov et la lutte contre les évidences', 41.
65. Daumal, 'L'Asphyxie et l'évidence absurde', 55–6.
66. René Daumal, 'La Pataphysique et la révélation du rire' (1929), *L'Évidence absurde*, 19.

67. René Daumal, 'La Vision de l'Absurde', *Tu t'es toujours trompé*, 43.
68. Ibid.
69. Cf. Fondane, 'Léon Chestov et la lutte contre les évidences', 21.
70. Antonin Artaud, 'Le Théâtre de Séraphin', *Le Théâtre et son double* (Paris: Gallimard, 1964), 229–30.
71. Ibid., 226–7.
72. René Daumal, 'Le Surréalisme et le Grand Jeu', *Le Grand Jeu* 4 (Autumn 1932), 11–12.
73. Daumal, 'Les provocations à l'ascèse', 42.
74. 'Est en ce sens pataphysique le fameux cercle vicieux: "Epiménide dit que les Crétois sont menteurs; or Epiménide est Crétois; donc il ment; donc les Crétois ne sont pas menteurs; donc Epiménide ne ment pas, et tous les Crétois sont menteurs."' Daumal also gives as an example the following Oriental story: a crocodile, wanting to know what truth is, told a woman who happened to pass by the river that he will not eat her if she tells him something true; the woman replied: the truth is that you are going to eat me. See René Daumal, 'Notes diverses sur la pataphysique', *Tu t'es toujours trompé*, 223–8.
75. Ibid., 223–4.
76. Daumal, 'La Vision de l'Absurde', 41.
77. In his controversial study, *Rimbaud le Voyou* (Paris: Denöel & Steele, 1933), Fondane approaches Rimbaud at the point when the promises of the rationally-based 'dérèglement' of the 'visionary' phase have turned into an incurable 'malaise': 'Maintenant, *je m'encrapule de plus en plus* [...] Je veux être poète et travaille à me rendre voyant.' Fondane's interpretation, inspired by Chestov's comments on Dostoevsky (specifically *Notes from the Underground*), is a polemical reply to the Surrealist appropriation of Rimbaud 'le voyant' and to the later objections levelled against Rimbaud in Breton's *Second Manifesto*; see *Rimbaud le Voyou*, 22–3.
78. The two quotations from Rimbaud appear in Roger Gilbert-Lecomte, 'L'Horrible révération, la seule...', *Le Grand Jeu* 3 (Autumn 1930), 15–16. Fondane's *Rimbaud le Voyou* came out in 1933. Interestingly enough, this book was in preparation three years before, when a fragment of it appeared in *Raison d'être* 7 (July 1930) 16–20, a publication closely associated in its spirit with *Le Grand Jeu*. The editor of *Raison d'être*, as of the earlier variant *Zarathoustra* (1928–9), was Jean Audard, brother of Pierre Audard, a member of *Le Grand Jeu*.
79. Cf. Benjamin Fondane, 'Le Procès de la raison: Léon Chestov, témoin à charge', *Cahiers de l'Étoile* 2 (1929), 360.
80. See Fondane, *Rimbaud le Voyou*, 39.
81. Cf. Fondane, 'Léon Chestov et la lutte contre les évidences', 21.
82. Fondane, 'Le Procès de la raison', 363.
83. René Daumal, 'La Révolte', *Tu t'es toujours trompé*, 59.
84. Daumal, 'La Vision de l'Absurde', 38, 41.
85. Fondane, 'Le Procès de la raison', 349.
86. Daumal, 'Le Souvenir déterminant', 118.
87. Artaud, 'Le Théâtre de Séraphin', 229.
88. Fondane, 'Léon Chestov et la lutte contre les évidences', 47–8.
89. Fondane, 'Le Procès de la raison', 349.

90. Leszek Kolakowski, *Husserl and the Search for Certitude* (New Haven: Yale University Press, 1975), 67.
91. The 'Nicht-Reell' is defined as the noematic aspect of the 'Irrealität' characterizing pure phenomenological consciousness. Cf. Edmund Husserl, *Ideas*, 235–40. See also the notes on Reality in the Analytical Index, ibid., 432.
92. Louis Aragon, 'L'Ombre de l'inventeur', *La Révolution surréaliste* 1 (1 Dec. 1924), 23.
93. See Ferdinand Alquié's comments on the relationship between Breton's ideas and Hegelian idealism in *Philosophie du surréalisme* (Paris: Flammarion, 1977), 41–7, 77; Elisabeth Roudinesco, 'André Breton entre Freud et Hegel', *La Bataille de cent ans: L'Histoire de la psychanalyse en France*, ii: *(1925–1985)* (Paris: Seuil, 1986), 37–49.
94. Bergsonian intuitionism and—most prominently—Jasper's explicit introduction to psychiatry of a descriptive phenomenological approach (and of a *verstehende Psychologie*) signalled the unavoidable confrontation and possible collusion of Freud's and Husserl's theories of intentionality and consciousness. By the end of the 1920s, the phenomenological critique of Freud (and the consequent redefinition of subjectivity) was no longer an understatement. A new generation of phenomenologists had come of age with the publication in 1929 and 1930 respectively of Heidegger's *Was ist Metaphysik* and Lévinas's *La théorie de l'intuition chez Husserl*. (On this subject, see Gerald N. Izenberg, *The Existential Critique of Freud: The Crisis of Autonomy* (Princeton: Princeton University Press, 1976), 14–18).
95. Cf. Breton, *Second Manifeste du surréalisme*, 782.
96. Louis Aragon, 'Discours de l'Imagination', *Le Paysan de Paris* (Paris: Gallimard, 1926; repr. 1976), 82.
97. Aragon, *Le Paysan de Paris*, 243–4.
98. See H. Spiegelberg, 'Phenomenology and Hegelianism', *The Phenomenological Movement: A Historical Introduction*, ii (The Hague: Martinus Nijhoff, 1965), 413–15.
99. Breton, *Les Vases communicants*, 209.
100. Fondane, *Faux Traité d'esthétique*, 36.
101. Ibid., 78.
102. The journal *Philosophies* came out shortly before *La Révolution surréaliste* in March 1924 and lasted for one year. Two issues in 1925 appeared under the title *L'Esprit*. The group formed around the journal was quite eclectic, including among others Pierre Morhange, Georges Politzer, Henri Lefebvre, Jean Grenier, Norbert Guterman, Max Jacob, Jean Cocteau and Pierre Drieu la Rochelle. For a short time, Daumal and Gilbert-Lecomte thought they shared the same ideals with Morhange, only to be later disappointed by his complete change of direction as editor of the orthodox *Revue marxiste*.
103. Roger Gilbert-Lecomte, 'Les Chapelles littéraires modernes', *Œuvres complètes* (Paris: NRF and Gallimard, 1974), i. 327–8.
104. Artaud, 'Le Théâtre et la culture', *Le Théâtre et son double*, 15–16.
105. Ibid., 13.
106. Artaud, *Le Théâtre et son double*, 77.
107. Cf. A. Rolland de Reneville, 'L'Élaboration d'une Méthode', *Le Grand Jeu* 2 (Spring 1929), 14–15.

108. See e.g. Artaud's considerations ('Lettres sur le langage', *Le Théâtre et son double*, 185–6) on 'les sources respiratoires, plastiques, actives du langage', which he associates with the purely sonic value of words.

109. On the precondition of the repetitive character of the linguistic sign in relation to Husserl's theory of intentionality, see Jacques Derrida, *La Voix et le phénomène* (Paris: P.U.F., 1967), 55: 'quand je me sers de mots, que je le fasse ou non à des fins communicatives, je dois d'entrée de jeu opérer [dans] une structure de répétition dont l'élément ne peut être que représentatif. Un signe n'est jamais un événement si événement veut dire unicité empirique irremplaçable et irréversible. Un signe qui n'aurait lieu qu'"une fois" ne serait pas un signe.'

110. Antonin Artaud, 'En finir avec les chefs-d'œuvres', *Le Théâtre et son double*, 117.

111. Ibid., 117. It is worth mentioning here that Gilbert-Lecomte also imagined 'des cryptogrames vasculaires', and spoke of 'concepts-limites' and extatic intuitions expressed through the 'rhytme frénétique de la rumeur du sang'. See Roger Gilbert-Lecomte, 'Epithalame', *Œuvres complètes*, ii. 116; 'Le cinéma, forme de l'esprit', ibid., 162.

112. It is significant, in this sense, to mention here Binswanger's critique of Freudian psychoanalysis as presented by Izenberg in *The Existential Critique of Freud*, 121: 'Rather one must realize that the 'somatic realm' [*das Körperliche*] or corporeality [*die Leiblichkeit*] is only a special form of human existence. One must realize and try to understand why is it that under certain circumstances it remains the only form of expression left to people, and that people henceforth use of its language, i.e., instead of scolding and raging, they sob, belch, screech and vomit.' Izenberg adds: 'Physical symptoms were thus not merely negative, *substitutions* for behaviour or language, but a different form of them that could be described in their own terms.' Taken out of their clinical, psychiatric context, these remarks might be said to describe the radically different dimension of language proposed by Artaud's theatre.

113. Léon Chestov, 'Conclusions', *Cahiers du Sud* 321 (Jan. 1954), 223.

114. Jacques Derrida, 'Cogito et histoire de la folie', *L'Ecriture et la différence*, 89–91.

115. On this issue, Chestov makes the following comments (*Athènes et Jérusalem*, 299): 'Le doute de Descartes était une feinte: le philosophe a fait mine de douter de sa propre existence puis de l'admettre en s'appuyant sur les preuves qu'il avait découvertes. Hume a parfaitement raison: si Descartes avait réussi à pousser jusqu'au bout son "doute radical", il ne serait jamais parvenu à s'en sortir. S'il avait douté de l'existence de Dieu, tout aurait été fini, et les "preuves" ne lui aurait été d'aucun secours. Avec une prudence qui nous fait songer plutôt à un somnambule qu'à un esprit philosophique, Descartes dirige ses doutes sur cette vérité que personne ne peut entamer. Et sur ce il crie victoire: les preuvent triomphent du doute le plus radical [...]. Mais il aurait dû raisonner autrement: je ne dispose pas des preuves de mon existence, mais je n'en ai pas besoin; par conséquent, certaines vérités, des vérités très importantes, se passent complètement de preuves.' The two important truths that existential thought proposes to defend, precisely insofar as they exceed the criteria of rational validation and logical argumentation, are the existence of God and the existence of the (particular, contingent) thinking subject.

116. 'La pensée existentielle commence, en effet, là où finit la pensée rationnelle en

général — cette pensée née, comme disait Épictète, de *la conscience de notre impuissance devant la nécessité*'; Fondane, 'Chestov et la lutte contre les évidences', 46.

117. Artaud, 'Le théâtre et la peste', 40.
118. Compare, for example, Daumal's remarks ('Les Provocations à l'ascèse', 45) on the emergence of a notion of possibility cut off from rational definitions of 'le domaine du *possible*', and Artaud's considerations ('Le Théâtre et la peste', 45–6) on the possibilities opened by theatrical representation, insofar as it mobilises the forces of 'life'.
119. Breton, *Œuvres complètes*, ii. 276.
120. On the controversy between the supporters of the 'vérités créées' and those of the 'vérités incréées' (which Chestov revived through the opposition between 'la vérité contraignante' and 'la vérité salutaire'), Fondane made the following remarks ('Chestov et la lutte contre les évidences', 23): 'Descartes soutient que si Dieu avait créé l'existence *ex nihilo*, il n'a pu manquer de créer également *ex nihilo* les vérités éternelles. [...] Certes, Descartes [...] était loin d'imaginer que, ayant créé ces vérités que nous connaissons, Dieu pût les changer en cours de route, arbitrairement; il pensait tout comme Sénèque que [...] les vérités avaient été créées au temps lointain où Dieu commandait et, le fait même que depuis, Dieu ne faisait qu'obéir, était la plus solide garantie de leur immutabilité.' Descartes's interpretation of divine truth eliminates the idea of freedom (inherent to any 'created' notion of truth), to the benefit of the supposed immutability of principles that, although created by God, could not be changed by Him. Man, like God, can only obey.
121. See on this issue Léon Chestov, 'La Balance de Job', *Cahiers du Sud* 244 (March 1942), 213.
122. Cf. Léon Chestov, 'Kierkegaard et Dostoievsky', *Cahiers du Sud* 181 (March 1936), 190–1.
123. The article containing this demonstration was published in the second issue of *Le Grand Jeu*, devoted to Rimbaud; see A. Rolland de Reneville, 'L'Élaboration d'une Méthode', *Le Grand Jeu* 2 (Spring 1929), 10–16. The title suggests a deliberate, coherent orientation inside the group, which is most clearly illustrated in the short preface to the essays on Rimbaud, where the members of the group subscribe to the statement that 'un homme peut, selon une certaine méthode dite mystique, atteindre à la perception immédiate d'un autre univers, incommensurable à ses sens et irréductible à son entendement'; cf. 'Essais', common tract, *Le Grand Jeu* 2 (Spring 1929), 9.
124. The most detailed analysis of the concept of intentionality in Husserl (as contrasted on the one hand to the Scholastic use of the tems 'intention' and 'intentional', on the other to Brentano's understanding of 'intentional') can be found in Herbert Spiegelberg, '"Intention" and "Intentionality" in the Scholastics, Brentano and Husserl', *The Context of the Phenomenological Movement* (The Hague: Martinus Nijhoff, 1981), 3–25.
125. In one of his articles ('Qu'est-ce que la vérité?', 37–49), Chestov starts his argument from the question 'Dans les Évangiles, il est vrai, Dieu est appelé Logos; mais peut-on identifier le Logos des Évangiles avec celui des philosophes?' His answer opposes the reconciliation between the two different orders of truth, i.e. that of the Scriptures, and that of the philosophical discourse on the Logos.

126. Artaud, 'Lettres sur la cruauté', *Le Théâtre et son double*, 159–60.
127. André Breton, 'Position politique de surréalisme', *Œuvres complètes*, ii. 490.

CHAPTER 2

❖

The Powerless Subject: Forms of Negative Reconstruction

Résigne-toi, mon cœur, dors ton sommeil de brute
BAUDELAIRE, 'Le goût du néant'

Il est douloureux d'accepter l'impuissance, mais combien plus douloureux encore de la repousser et d'accepter l'absurde!
FONDANE, 'Chestov et la lutte contre les évidences'

The existential critique of the rationalist unitary configuration of consciousness, as well as the re-examination of the problems raised by the Cartesian *cogito*, brought to the fore a concern with the substantialist view of the subject, which can be said to have played an equally important part in the elaboration of the Surrealist doctrine. Both existential thought and Surrealism explored in different ways the possibility of reviving and redefining the traditional understanding of the subject with reference to the real, particular existence of living individuals.

However, existential arguments pertaining to this issue are not elaborated from the immanentist perspective that characterized the Surrealist approach to the question of the subject. On the contrary, these arguments as presented by Chestov and Fondane were designed to support the metaphysical thesis of the immortality of the soul, while paradoxically relating this idea to the physical, bodily existence of the individual. Unlike the Cartesian postulation of the existence of God, which rationally confirms the thinking subject's existence through the *cogito*, existential thought emphasizes the paradox of the 'living God' ('Deus Homo', God who became Man), which in turn illuminates the paradox of an immortal, yet contingent, temporal subject. The existential notion of subject can be traced back to Kierkegaard's understanding of the 'particular individual' and of its one-to-one relationship with God. In Chestov's and Fondane's view, this relationship is defined in terms of the powerlessness of the subject, of its inability to transcend its condition through rational means.

Conversely, Surrealism tried to empower the subject by situating it within a theoretical context that could either establish its historicity along the lines of Hegelian idealism or underpin its social/political dimension from a Marxist perspective. The manner in which Surrealism appropriated and combined various philosophical and theoretical discourses (Hegelian idealism, Freudian psychoanalysis and Marxist historical materialism) accounts for the interpretation of the question of the subject as part of the debate surrounding the ideas of 'revolt' and 'revolution'. As I intend to show in the first part of this chapter, the mainstream Surrealist concern with the social and political empowerment of the individual gave rise to polemical replies from writers working on the fringes of the movement, who paradoxically associated 'revolt' with notions of powerlessness, renunciation or resignation rather than with a commitment to proletarian revolution.

This position signals a disengagement from Surrealist revolutionary practice, while opening up the possibility of a completely different engagement with issues discarded or glossed over by the mainstream doctrine of the movement. Daumal's and Gilbert-Lecomte's understanding of revolt as 'la révolte de l'individu contre soi-même', together with Artaud's emphasis on 'la métamorphose des conditions intérieures de l'âme' in his polemic with Breton, illustrated an attempt to redefine the question of the subject in relation to the individual revolt against inner rather than outer limitations and contradictions. The existential notion of the subject is connected to a similar interpretation of revolt (the fight against self-evidence), which exposes the limits of the rational definition of the subject and brings about a dissolution of the 'rational subject' (similar to the 'revolt of the individual against itself'). This dissolution is anticipated by the recurrent motifs of powerlessness and disengagement in *Discontinuité*, but its clearest formulation can be found in the writings of Gilbert-Lecomte and Artaud. The resulting idea of a 'powerless subject', defined in terms of its mortality and its struggle against both logical and natural necessity, functions within the existential critique of rationality as part of a process of negative reconstruction of the traditional notion of the subject from an eschatological perspective.

In contrast to the Hegelian and Freudian interpretations of subjectivity, which informed the Surrealist doctrine, the existential negative reconstruction of the subject involves a paradoxical type of argument, centred around the idea of 'creation out of nothing'. The second section of this chapter will examine Chestov's and Fondane's understanding of 'creatio ex nihilo', which can be described as the absurd movement of faith emerging from the confrontation with death, and uncovering the obliterated relationship between a living individual and God. This moment of creation is preceded by the reduction of the rational subject to nothingness, which finds illustration and support in the figuration of the void and in the various expressions employed by Artaud and Gilbert-Lecomte to describe the process of 'absorption' or 'résorption'.

Ultimately, the existential notion of 'creatio ex nihilo' will be shown to lead to a particular interpretation of tragedy and of the tragic experience as the encounter between the individual subject (the 'tragic' man) and the radically other (the living God). This singular development, which has no counterpart in Surrealist writing, emerges from Artaud's reconsideration of Greek tragedy in his 'theatre of cruelty' and from Chestov's and Fondane's understanding of 'the philosophy of tragedy'. The present chapter thus investigates three interrelated moments of the existential critique of the rationalist concept of the subject, leading to the negative reconstruction of a notion of subject defined in its relationship to the experience of tragedy and the encounter with God: (1) The dissolution of the rational subject; (2) Creatio ex nihilo; (3) The birth of the tragic subject.

The Dissolution of the Rational Subject

Artaud's remarks concerning the 'libération totale de l'esprit' shed light on the meaning of the existential fight against self-evidence, which involves a process by which reason comes to turn against itself and redeploy its violence against its own grounding principles. This negative, self-destructive movement opens up the possibility of 'awakening', of the 'awakening to oneself', by which a living individual becomes aware of its own existence and of its own mortality. The contradictory, non-unitary consciousness that apprehends in the process of 'awakening' both the rational, eternal truth of death and the 'absurd evidence' of something that transcends this rational limitation discloses the scandal introduced into speculative thought by the individual aspiration towards a truth relating to its own contingent, temporal existence. Roger Gilbert-Lecomte described the astonishment and anxiety that accompany the disclosure of this 'absurd evidence' in the following terms:

La stupeur fixe devant l'évidence absurde du scandale d'être, et d'être limité sans connaissance de soi-même. L'existence de la conscience est effrayante et insoluble. Devant cette angoisse essentielle à l'homme, dans son expression nue, toute autre pensée est vaine.[1]

Chestov and Fondane further relate the scandal of an interpretation of being that starts from the premiss of the contingent existence of a living individual to Kierkegaard's understanding of 'the scandal of faith', concerning the paradoxical nature of the 'living God'. As Kierkegaard argues:

Just as the concept 'faith' is a highly characteristic note of Christianity, so also is 'offence' a highly characteristic note of Christianity and stands in close relation to faith [...]. Offence has essentially to do with the composite term God and man, or with the God-Man. Speculation naturally had the notion that it 'comprehended' God-Man—this one can easily comprehend, for speculation in speculating about the God-Man leaves out temporal existence, contemporaneousness, and reality.[2]

Faith corresponds to the 'second dimension of thought',[3] uncovered through the process of 'awakening'. Unlike speculative discourse on 'l'Homme-Dieu' (for instance within Hegel's doctrine of Spirit), the second dimension of thought can accommodate not only the truth of the 'living God' but also the truth of the contingent existence of a living individual, as having both the attribute of temporality and that of timelessness. Chestov's and Fondane's redefinition of the notion of subject from an anti-rationalist perspective involves a paradoxical type of thinking that refers back to the 'absurd' argument preceding Tertullian's concluding remark on the resurrection of Christ: 'certum est quia impossibile'.[4] Daumal similarly mentions 'le fameux "Credo quia absurdum"'[5] in support of a non-systematic line of thinking, which dispenses with any method of rational analysis.

The same statement was also used by Roger Gilbert-Lecomte in his refutation of the rationalist conception of an eternal, immortal and 'homogeneous' or unique Spirit. Gilbert-Lecomte argued that it takes as much faith to believe in the truth of an immortal, abstract entity of thought (which contradicts all the evidence of our experience) as it takes to admit 'credo quia absurdum'.[6] Daumal's and Gilbert-

Lecomte's position converges with the existential critique of the rational conception of 'being' and the rational interpretation of the subject. The arguments that Chestov and Fondane elaborate in presenting the paradoxical existential idea of a subject that is both temporally determined and 'immortal' are explicitly related to Kierkegaard's critique of objectivity and in particular to the thesis that 'subjectivity, inwardness is the truth'.[7] In contrast to the Hegelian dialectical reconciliation of opposites, Fondane like Chestov adopts Kierkegaard's line of argumentation, which highlights the tension between the objective and subjective perspectives on truth, while proposing to attribute exclusive powers of validation to the latter:

'La superstition — écrit Kierkegaard — attribue à l'objectivité le pouvoir de la tête de Méduse, le pouvoir de pétrifier la subjectivité; et cette absence de liberté ne permet plus à l'homme de détruire l'enchantement'. Eh bien! maintenant c'est le contraire qui se produit: c'est la subjectivité qui acquiert le pouvoir de la tête de Méduse; en pétrifiant l'objectivité elle recouvre sa liberté [...] Ce n'est pas d'un autre Savoir qu'il s'agit, mais d'un *non-savoir*, d'une pensée qui ne veut pas 'comprendre' l'être, mais de parvenir à l'être.[8]

The existential attempt to challenge not only the traditional speculative notion of subject but also the rational understanding of being, by reasserting the obliterated relationship between individual, particular existence and the existence of the 'living God', remained outside the scope of the immanentist doctrine of the Surrealist movement. A significant change of emphasis in the Surrealist interpretation of the subject occurred during the mid-1920s, when its faint reverberations seemed at first lost amidst the clamour of more prominent political debates, of acrimonious rhetoric and public expulsions, which only confirmed a latent crisis eventually brought out into the open by the collective declaration 'Au Grand jour' (1927), signed by Breton, Aragon, Éluard, Péret and Unik. The ensuing polemic between Artaud and the signatories of this declaration uncovers the controversial issue of subjectivity obscured by the rhetoric of political recriminations.

In 'A la grande nuit, ou Le Bluff surréaliste', Artaud's individualistic interpretation of questions relating to the notion of subject comes into direct conflict with two of the recurring motifs of the Surrealist doctrine, revolution and action. From the Surrealist point of view, current political developments (the war in Morocco) had irreversibly changed the meaning of 'revolt', which no longer concerned what

Breton accusingly qualified and Artaud defiantly acknowledged as 'une métamorphose des conditions intérieures de l'âme'.[9] The imperative of action—of 'revolutionary' action—had become inextricably linked to the necessity of a clear, if problematical, political commitment. However, behind the declamatory statements of a desired political engagement, notwithstanding certain reservations, 'Au Grand jour' spoke most strongly in favour of the moral imperative, the 'moral attitude' overriding the poetic or political preoccupations of the moment: 'C'est encore de cela qu'il s'agit, et de cela seulement', writes Breton.[10]

The subject of the early nihilistic revolt, the subject of individual desire and non-conformist experimental activities, was called into question and made to confront the moral issue of a resolution of all antinomies through political revolutionary action. This constituted the essence of the message addressed to the 'non-Communist' Surrealists by the leaders of the movement: if Surrealism was to remain faithful to Hegelian dialectics, while also maintaining the idea of revolution as the only possibility of solving the antinomies of the real world, then the transition from Hegelian dialectics to Marxism and the affiliation of the movement to the Communist Party provided the only 'ideological safeguard' of Surrealist activity.[11] It is significant that, in trying to avoid the identification of the movement with 'une doctrine politique positive', Breton and the other signatories of the declaration consider that their specific contribution to the 'absolute necessity' of revolution could be defined as a certain proficiency in judging matters pertaining to 'the moral truth': 'nous sommes, pensons-nous, appelés à juger sans lacune et sans faiblesse de tout ce qui touche, de près ou de loin, la vérité morale que notre parti est seul à défendre au monde, et qu'il imposera'.[12]

To the rebarbative tone of this declaration, as inflexible in its condemnations as it is ambivalent in its commitment to party politics, Artaud responds with a defiant affirmation of disengagement, individualism and powerlessness ('impuissance'). The inability to recognize the limitations imposed on Surrealist activity by a direct involvement in political action made apparent, from Artaud's point of view, the 'impuissance native' of the members of the group, which he implicitly contrasts to 'mon irrémissible impuissance', insofar as the latter can neither be dispelled by the power associated with political commitment nor claim to effect any real transformation in the outside world.[13]

The paradoxical link established between the 'powerlessness' of political disengagement and freedom, or the possibility of deploying the energies of the subject in a 'revolution' carried out at a different level, runs through all the other writings of the period that illustrate the existential line of thought. The only issue of the magazine *Discontinuité* (June 1928), to which Benjamin Fondane contributed alongside Monny de Boully (a dissident member of the Surrealist group, subsequently affiliated to *Le Grand Jeu*), makes a point of rejecting the ethical imperative of political action of the moment: 'Nous ne sommes pas des Révolutionnaires dans le sens où nous *devrions* l'être' [my emphasis].[14] At the time when the question of 'devoir' dominates the need to clarify an ever-present concern for 'notre attitude morale' in 'Au Grand jour',[15] the Surrealist vocabulary of militant activism and political engagement finds its negative counterpart in the recurrent, emphatic presence of notions such as 'lâcheté', 'résignation', 'défaite', 'désespoir' in the programme of *Discontinuité*.

Concerning the ethical undertones of political debates, it is worth recalling here that the Surrealist rejection of the theological implications of Hegel's philosophy further led to the formulation of Breton's imperative 'devoir-vivre', which, starting from Hegel's 'devoir-être' (*sollen*), attempted to fuse Marx's hope to 'transformer le monde' and Rimbaud's desire to 'changer la vie'.[16] The correlation that Breton established in *Les Vases communicants* (1932) between the theory of convulsive beauty and the social and political determinations of the 'devoir-vivre' firmly situates the notion of subjectivity within a field of convergent ethical, political and aesthetic imperatives, carefully distinguished from the ideas of a transcendent being and of immortality, which guided the existential subject's revolt.

The polemical insistence on a radical negativism equally qualifies the position of *Le Grand Jeu*, whose programme appeared in the first issue of the journal with the same title, published at the same time as *Discontinuité* during the summer of 1928. A similar dissociation from the Surrealist rhetoric of active engagement is signalled in *Le Grand Jeu* by the paradoxical use of such characteristic terms as 'résignation', 'révolte invisible', 'renoncement'.[17] Three essays, gathered under the general topic 'La Nécessité de la révolte', define in more detail the position of the group, following an opening text ('Avant-propos') that ended with a statement that fuelled the Surrealists' controversy with *Le Grand Jeu* ('nous avalerons Dieu pour en devenir transparents jusqu'à disparaître'). The second essay, signed by Roger Gilbert-

Lecomte, explicitly states the paradoxical function assigned to powerlessness, resignation or renunciation, in close resemblance to the position adopted by Artaud, Fondane and the members of *Discontinuité*. An immediate indication of this paradoxical use of powerlessness and disengagement comes up in the title of Gilbert-Lecomte's article, 'La Force des renoncements', and is further reinforced by a series of statements that both reject the solution of direct political action as a false, inefficient answer to what Breton called 'the antinomies of the real world' and at the same time redefine revolt as 'the revolt of the individual against itself'.

What Gilbert-Lecomte has to say about the first alternative of political engagement and militant rhetoric is convincingly summarized in one sentence: 'ils luttent pour des fausses libertés, ils remplaceront les institutions qu'ils détruisent par d'autres analogues, ils font des petites crises ministérielles'.[18] To the plural employed to designate this collectivist ideal of a class insurgence, meant only to replace existing institutions by other forms of repression, the article opposes the singularity and the paradoxical power of the individual, whose radical revolt against the inner limitations posed by rationality and ethics starts with the refusal of any external imperatives, with absolute negation and 'resignation': 'A l'état de révolte doit succéder l'état de résignation; et *cette résignation postérieure sera, au contraire de l'abjection, la puissance même.*'[19] Gilbert-Lecomte refers to René Daumal's article, 'Liberté sans Espoir', the last of the three essays mentioned above, in support of this implicit declaration of rights of the individual pursuing its own revolution outside and against the social/ political engagements of the majority, as signalled in one of the polemic aphorisms running along the top of the pages of this first issue of *Le Grand Jeu*: 'Le droit commun n'est pas le nôtre'.[20] In Daumal's article, the notion of freedom is linked to individual choice and the 'acte gratuit', affirmed within a 'divorce avec le monde' and a perpetually renewed act of negation, which is 'créateur de la conscience et du présent'.[21] The subject affirms its paradoxical power of individual choice, free from any external constraints and rational imperatives, through absolute negation pushed far beyond the limitations of immediate action: 'Dans quelque forme que je me saisisse, je dois dire: *je ne suis pas cela*; [...] La conscience, c'est le suicide perpétuel.'[22]

In contrast to the social and political commitments promulgated by Breton and the other signatories of 'Au Grand jour', Daumal like

Artaud relocates the notion of revolt at the level of an individual struggle against inner limitations of thought and projects the aspiration towards freedom in a realm in which resignation, inactivity and disengagement prepare the paradoxically strong, propitious position of an encounter or confrontation between the subject and the radically other as God: 'C'est en cessant de chercher la liberté, que l'homme se libère; la véritable résignation est de celui qui, par un même acte, se donne à Dieu, corps et âme.'[23] The implications of this absolute form of revolt, in the confrontation of the individual with God, will be further elaborated in the last section of this chapter. For the moment, it is important to notice the recurrent, explicit rejection of the Surrealist doctrine of subjectivity (based on ethical commitment, activism and political engagement) in all the polemical statements that define the existential line of thought. Another example of this position can be found in the following statement from the programme of *Discontinuité*, which implicitly assigns individual power and freedom to the defiant avowal of defeat: 'Nous ne pouvons pas agir, marins les mains pleines de sable, alors que nous nous résignons, nous abandonnons toute vanité, nous avouons notre défaite.'[24]

Defeat, resignation and renunciation, which are related to despair and even suicide in the declarations of *Discontinuité* and *Le Grand Jeu*, signal a process of annihilation or self-destruction that further uncovers a figuration of the void, meant to indicate the destruction of rationality as part of the fight of the individual against itself and the regression to a state before rationality: 'nous n'isolons pas la cause de l'effet, nous n'aimons pas le vide mais ce qui le précède', write the members of *Discontinuité*.[25] Gilbert-Lecomte's considerations in 'La force des renoncements' similarly outline a process that evolves from 'revolt' to 'resignation' and ultimately to the 'purity of the void', described as the strength of a continued negation: 'Il faut qu'il arrive à faire naître peu à peu en lui un état d'innocence qui soit la pureté du vide. Sans jamais s'arrêter. Pas même au sein de la révolte.'[26] This is the alternative, 'invisible revolt', corresponding to the fight of the individual against his own rational and ethical limitations, which Artaud and Gilbert-Lecomte describe with reference to the notions of 'absorption' or 'résorption'.

Gilbert-Lecomte's understanding of power as 'le côté négatif des renoncements' points to a paradoxical advance, through a continued destruction of all rational barriers, towards a 'pre-natal' (pre-logical) state, which is reminiscent of Artaud's comments on 'le génital innée':

Je suis un génital inné [...]. Il y a des imbéciles qui se croient des êtres, êtres par innéité. Moi je suis celui qui pour être doit fouetter son innéité. [...] c'est-à-dire toujours fouetter cette espèce de négatif chenil, ô chiennes d'impossibilité.[27]

Artaud opposes the notion of 'un génital inné' to the concept of being derived according to the original, 'innate' right of rational thought ('la pensée [...] quand on la prend pour un fait inné') to judge and validate what really 'is' or exists. Because, as Artaud further argues, 'la pensée est une matrone qui n'a pas toujours existé'.[28] Nevertheless, the individual can only assert its being—its physical, contingent existence (captured by the attribute 'génital')—as the other, the negative of rational thought. The possibility of affirming what one is ('je suis un génital inné') thus results from a negative type of argumentation, which proceeds by suspending the 'innate' privilege of thought over being, and arrives at the paradox of something that is both 'innate' and non-rational: the truth of physical, individual existence, unsupported by reason.[29] The following lines from Artaud's 'Fragment d'un journal d'enfer' bear a striking resemblance to the statements defining the position of the subject in *Le Grand Jeu*, in which the notion of 'renoncement' is associated with the revolt of the individual against himself—against the rational structure of consciousness and of the self:

Je n'ai point d'appui, plus de base ... je me cherche je ne sais où. [...] Je finis par voir le jour à travers moi-même, à force des renonciations dans tous les sens de mon intelligence et de ma sensibilité.[30]

The negative progression towards a point of identification that paradoxically combines self-destruction (as the destruction of the rational self) and self-affirmation (as the power of transgression and access to a different configuration of the subject) corresponds in both Artaud and Gilbert-Lecomte to an obstinate return or reversal of the process of thought to an original void, signalled by the insistence of the two authors on the state of infancy, on birth or even on 'pre-natal' states. It might seem that this preoccupation with the early stages of an individual's evolution is no different from the Surrealist appreciation of the innocent, inherently poetic vision of children and of the primitive mentality. But the actual formulation of the question of regression, or rather of a destruction of reason through negative progression, in Artaud and Gilbert-Lecomte has no equivalent in the Surrealist writings. Throughout Gilbert-Lecomte's collected works and correspondence, the distinctive presence of highly idiosyncratic expressions such as 'la magie prénatale',[31] 'la divination extatique et intra-utérine',[32] 'chanter les Nénies prénatales'[33] points to an exploration of identity and self-consciousness that exceeds the Surrealist probing of unconscious processes, of the primitive and infantile mentalities.

The actual question posed by Artaud and Gilbert-Lecomte is not simply that of a return to childhood as a privileged state of innocence and 'non-savoir', but the question of an obliterated origin or birth that confronts the opposed movements of thought and of 'being' in the sense of individual, contingent existence. For the members of *Le Grand Jeu*, the process of 'resorption' involved the possibility of attaining a void in consciousness, 'un gouffre noir' according to Gilbert-Lecomte. Artaud understood this as the possibility of surpassing the deadly limitations of rational consciousness through a backward progression of thought ('penser en arrière'), so that thought ultimately becomes 'absorbed', ruptured by the sudden emergence of life:

> Il faut que l'on comprenne que toute intelligence n'est qu'une vaste éventualité, et que l'on peut la perdre, non pas comme l'aliéné qui est mort, mais comme un vivant qui est dans la vie et qui sent sur lui l'attraction et le souffle (de l'intelligence, pas de la vie).
>
> Cette possibilité de penser en arrière et d'invectiver tout à coup sa pensée.
>
> Ce dialogue dans la pensée.
>
> L'absorption, la rupture de tout.[34]

The revolt of the individual against itself and the emergence of the living subject are defined by this return to an original source of life, which precedes rational analysis and transcends the limitation of death.

In 'La Force des renoncements', Gilbert-Lecomte equates revolt and resorption within a negative progression, whose relevance for the positioning of the subject in relation to the other directly contradicts the Surrealist immanentist doctrine and its commitment to an active social and political integration of the subject: 'Toujours est-il que dans cette marche de l'esprit en révolte vers sa résorption en l'unité, rien ne peut jamais être considéré comme acquis.'[35] Unlike the meaning assigned to the dialectical progression towards unity in Surrealism, Gilbert-Lecomte's relentless regression to the void points to the transcendent existence of God. The paradoxical advance through resorption or regression situates the individual 'au-dessus de l'activité humaine'[36] at a transcendent level, at which resignation and dis-engagement or detachment make possible the transformation of the powerless subject into the individual that manifests itself as 'une force naturelle', 'un *Cataclysme Vivant*'.[37]

The return to a 'pre-natal' or pre-logical state is connected to a process of thought that both Daumal and Gilbert-Lecomte call 'paramnésie', which points to the encounter between a living individual and God. In the process of reminiscence, the subject accomplishes the transition from discursive knowledge to 'l'omniscience immédiate' and is suddenly projected 'au-dessus de l'activité humaine'.[38] The dissolution of the rational subject through the 'revolt of the individual against itself' and the negative advance toward the 'resorption/absorption' of rational thought opens up an alternative configuration of the subject relating to the idea of 'creatio ex nihilo', which is explicitly thematized by Chestov and Fondane and illustrated by the writings of Artaud, Daumal and Gilbert-Lecomte.

Creatio ex Nihilo

In existential thought, resignation does not primarily refer to a disengagement from social and political commitments insofar as they relate to outer rather than inner determinations of thought. Resignation more adequately designates what seems to be the only sensible attitude when man comes to confront the implacable truth of human mortality. In commenting on the meaning of Chekhov's 'A Dreary Story', Chestov highlights the sense of hopelessness and despair that overwhelms the main character as he is approaching death.[39] Chekhov's hero, once a respectable professor, discovers that the rational and ethical truths that he has been upholding throughout his life are of no help in preventing his own death. He cannot reassure himself, and he finds no consoling answer to his student's persistent question ('What should I do?'). The only thing he can say is simply, 'I do not know'. Chestov argues that the ambivalent meaning of this answer can be understood in view of Baudelaire's similar remark: 'Résigne-toi mon cœur, dors ton sommeil de brute.' What man discovers in the confrontation with death is not mere resignation (in the sense of a passive acknowledgement of 'eternal', rational truths), but resignation mixed with revolt:

> 'Résigne-toi mon cœur, dors ton sommeil de brute.' Voilà la seule chose que nous trouvons à dire devant le spectacle de la vie humaine telle que nous la montre Tchékhov. Soumission toute extérieure sous laquelle se dissimule une haine profonde, inextinguible pour cet ennemi insaisissable. Oubli,

sommeil tout apparent, car celui qui appelle son sommeil un 'sommeil de brute', n'oublie pas évidemment, ne dors pas.[40]

If in 'A Dreary Story' the dying professor finds nothing else to say than 'I do not know', it is because, as Chestov argues, 'l'hésitation est l'élément constitutif nécessaire des jugements de l'homme, que sa destinée a placé en face des derniers problèmes'. Hesitation already marks the beginning of a relentless fight against the reassuring logical and ethical reasoning that extols man's resignation and submission in the confrontation with death. Faced with the 'ultimate problems' of human existence, man suddenly understands that his stoical resignation is actually forgetfulness and sleep, 'un sommeil de brute'. Thus for the first time he comes closer to an 'awakening' to questions whose answer exceeds rational comprehension. In hesitating or refusing to dismiss such 'absurd' questions (concerning for example death, the existence of God, the immortality of the soul), man has to 'create' an alternative, second dimension of thought 'out of nothing', insofar as he relies no longer on rationally grounded judgements but on groundless, paradoxical statements such as Tertullian's 'certum est quia impossibile'.

However, as Chestov argues, man might be forced to undertake the 'inhuman task' of a 'creatio ex nihilo' even before the final confrontation with death. Most characters in Chekhov's short stories illustrate this unusual situation, according to Chestov. They are people who 'overstrained' themselves and suddenly, owing to an absurd, insignificant accident, lost the self-assurance, the 'mirth' and confidence in rational thought of their fellow human beings, of those whose lives seem meaningful, protected against misfortune by the power of noble ideas. Under normal circumstances, Chestov remarks, the man broken by despair, the man who can no longer take an active part in life owing to an incurable illness, an abnormality, has become 'un homme de trop' and should die. In a sense, this man is already dead. However, despite his abnormality, which horrifies any healthy, reasonable human being, he continues to live. He is, in actual fact, perpetually between life and death, a living-dead who undergoes the most extraordinary transformation: 'cet être brisé se trouve brusquement privé de tout sauf de la connaissance et du sentiment de la situation. [...] Il arrive souvent qu'un homme ordinaire, médiocre, se transforme jusqu'à en devenir méconnaissable.'[41] The acute lucidity that accompanies this experience of 'death-in-life' as described by Chestov and Fondane engenders an intolerance, an incredible resistance of the broken individual to the consolations of common, rational people. The promise of social change, the concerns of men who 'parviendront peut-être à s'organiser sur terre pour y vivre et mourir sans souffrance', cannot alleviate the suffering of a man trapped in a situation without escape, which Chestov concisely described in one sentence: 'le présent, c'est l'impuissance, l'invalidité; l'avenir inévitable, c'est la mort'.[42]

The only 'method', the only means left to the individual who has lost everything, who is condemned to death and can no longer bear the ethical consolations of his fellow men, is the absurd revolt, the cry that might bring down the wall of logical evidences: 'Aussi ne lui reste-t-il plus qu'un seul moyen, un moyen désespéré: il se met à crier à tue-tête, d'une voix atroce, d'une voix déchirante, protestant au nom d'on ne sait quels droits.'[43] In existential thought, this moment of revolt, when crying out in despair replaces logical argument, points to the biblical story of Job, whose significance provided a constant source of inspiration for Kierkegaard as much as for Chestov and Fondane. While rejecting the consolations and advice offered by his friends, Job enters into a direct confrontation with God. The 'inhuman', absurd power of Job's revolt paradoxically emerges from utter powerlessness and despair. Similarly, his 'inhuman', one-to-one communication with God is established not through speculative reasoning but through a revolt that destroys reason and re-discovers faith as the 'creation' of meaning and truth 'ex nihilo'.

Chestov contrasts the normal, rational individual, '[qui] ne détruit que pour reconstruire en utilisant les anciens matériaux [et qui] ne souffre jamais du manque de matériaux', with the 'abnormal' individual, who finds himself confronted with the necessity of creating from the void: on the one hand, misfortune has deprived him of all rational means of creation, while on the other he is forced to continue to live and 'create' or formulate answers to the questions of human existence.[44] The process of 'creatio ex nihilo' determines a negative reconstruction of the notion of subject, insofar as it both shatters the foundation of rational judgements concerning human existence and resituates the contingent, temporally-determined condition of the living individual in relation to the creative nature of the 'living God', which transcends the limitation of death.

The paradox of a creation out of the void occurs when the subject finds itself in a situation that is described as 'death-in-life' by Chestov and Fondane as much as by Artaud and Gilbert-Lecomte. In *La Vie l'Amour la Mort le Vide et le Vent* (1933), Gilbert-Lecomte explores his obsessive theme, 'la mort dans la vie', within the context of a dramatic dialogue in which God questions 'Son absence' about the meaning of life, death and love. The fact that all the answers are attributed to God's Absence in this imaginary dialogue signals an implicit, negative search for God, which mirrors the negative search for the meaning of life: 'Quel est le but de la vie? / C'est la mort'; 'Quel est le but de la mort? / C'est la vie.'[45] In his reply to the Surrealist 'Enquête' on suicide, Artaud similarly argued, 'Je souffre affreusement de la vie. [...] Et très certainement je suis mort depuis longtemps, je suis déjà suicidé. *On* m'a suicidé, c'est-à-dire.'[46] The question of suicide only makes sense to those who have the certainty of being alive, the certainty of their existence. But Artaud like Gilbert-Lecomte has lost this simple certainty: 'Avant de me suicider, je demande qu'on m'assure de l'être, je voudrais être sûr de la mort', he declares,[47] and Gilbert-Lecomte echoes the same thoughts: 'Un jour se réveiller tout noir / Et privé du seul don de la vie le délire / La souffrance'.[48] The paradoxical idea of 'death-in-life' also plays a important part in Daumal's 'Vision de l'Absurde': 'Vous voyez que je ne chante pas ce que cette foule de fantômes appelle "la vie", mais sa dissolution. Ah! vous n'avez pas encore fini de mourir de la vraie vie!'[49]

The position of the subject that has reached the limit of death-in-life brings out the imperative need to create from the void, or rather to redefine thought starting from the elements that are irreducible to rational analysis, as Gilbert-Lecomte argues: 'Il s'agirait aujourd'hui [...] de reprendre tous ces éléments irréductibles à la raison discursive, tout ce qui, dans les sciences anciennes, dans les superstitions, a été jusqu'ici écarté, laissé de côté comme un résidu inemployable.'[50] Beyond the rationally-grounded certainty of the Cartesian *cogito*, the only other way in which the thinking subject can affirm its existence involves a process of negative reconstruction, a creation from the void using the apparently 'useless', discarded residues of rational analysis. The dissolution of logical argument and of the notion of subject postulated on rational grounds uncovers the contingent, logically 'groundless' existence of the living individual in its relationship to the equally 'unfounded' hypothesis of the existence of the 'living God'.

The negative reconstruction of a notion of subject that is irreducible to the rational understanding of temporal existence as limited by death aims to overcome the objective determination of speculative self-consciousness. The subject that paradoxically perceives itself as both temporally determined and able to transcend the limitation of death shatters the premiss of the objective, unitary framework of consciousness and replaces it with the subjective experience of nothingness. The subjective confrontation with death engenders the sudden, 'absurd' revolt of the individual, which instead of accepting its own annihilation attempts to dissolve or reduce to nothingness the rational framework condemning any particular, contingent existence to destruction. In 'La force des renoncements', Gilbert-Lecomte speaks of revolt as the movement of a powerful whirlpool, a negative current with irresistible powers of suction, with an insatiable desire to engulf everything:

> A la place de ce qui fut lui-même, sa conscience, l'autonomie de sa personne humaine un gouffre noir tournoie. [...] Il y a dans la Révolte, telle que nous la concevons, c'est-à-dire un besoin de tout l'être, profond, tout puissant, pour ainsi dire organique (nous la verrons devenir une force de la nature) une puissance de succion qui cherchera toujours, poulpe de famine, quelque chose à avaler.[51]

The living individual, engaged in a vertiginous destruction (or 'absorption') of rational thought, becomes a natural force ('un Cataclysme vivant'), which draws its insatiable thirst of being back to an origin beyond all human limits: 'C'est en de tels instants que nous absorberons tout, que nous avalerons Dieu pour en devenir transparents jusqu'à disparaître'.[52] The 'gouffre noir' that Gilbert-Lecomte associates with the negative movement of revolt leading to a redefinition of the subject in its relationship to God can be contrasted with the 'conscience *pleine* du sujet', which characterizes the mainstream Surrealist doctrine according to the analysis devoted by Jacqueline Chénieux-Gendron to Breton's and Aragon's considerations on the notion of subject.[53]

As I have so far attempted to show, the mainstream Surrealist approach to the question of the subject rejected the negative, paradoxical line of argumentation elaborated in the works of dissident or non-affiliated writers such as Artaud, Daumal and Gilbert-Lecomte. This opposition is supported by Chénieux-Gendron's analysis, which distinguishes the mainstream 'conscience *pleine* du sujet' from the '*dissolution* du sujet', situated 'aux frontières du surréalisme, sur les frontières extérieures'.[54] Chénieux-Gendron further clarifies the former conception with reference to the tension between a so-called 'pure subjectivity' (defined by Breton's emphasis on ethical determinations) and the subject of action, of revolutionary practice. In using the term 'pure subjectivity' to define one aspect of the Surrealist understanding of the notion of subject, Chénieux-Gendron does not initially dwell on the implied rapprochement to phenomenological theory, which is only later considered when she talks about the presence of a 'phenomenology of perception' in Breton.[55] At first, this 'pure subjectivity' seems to designate the Surrealist introspective approach to consciousness along the lines of Freudian psychoanalysis, in contrast to a dynamic, action-based configuration of the subject, which Chénieux-Gendron traces back to Dada and to Nietzsche's Dionysiac exultation, rather than to the social/ political connotations of Surrealist 'activism' in the mid 1920s:

> *Entre* ces deux pôles antithétiques — l'immolation d'une conscience romantique dans l'*acte* (nietzschéen) ou le geste (dadaïste) et, d'autre part, le regard introspectif ou l'auto-analyse par tous les moyens —, se situe le champ du *sujet* surréaliste.[56]

According to Chénieux-Gendron, the 'dialectical tension' between these poles did not exclude the possible reconciliation of the opposites and the articulation inside the central Surrealist group (as contrasted with its 'external frontiers') of a unitary conception of the subject, with two complementary 'versions': Aragon's predominantly philosophical approach to 'la contingence du *moi*' and Breton's emphasis on the ethical determination of subjectivity. It is significant that, in the context of Breton's ethical conception of subjectivity, Chénieux-Gendron mentions a tendency that she calls 'la volonté d'indifférence'[57] as an illustration of the 'devenir pur' of the subject in the overcoming of the 'passion amoureuse'. Indeed, Breton writes in the 'Introduction au discours sur le peu de réalité': 'J'ai oublié systématiquement tout ce qui m'arrivait d'heureux, de malheureux, sinon d'indifférent. L'indifférent seul est admirable.'[58] This overcoming of passion through indifference seems to motivate Breton's strenuous attempts to reconcile dialectically an individualist position of the subject, which recast Dada nihilism in the mould of Freudian psychoanalysis, and the notion of a morally and socially engaged subject, aligned with the political imperatives of the Surrealist.

In the *Faux Traité d'esthétique* and in *La Conscience malheureuse*, Fondane relentlessly attacked the two sources of the Surrealist dialectical transition from the individual subject to 'pure subjectivity': Freudian psychoanalysis and Hegelian philosophy. As Fondane remarked, Breton adopts not only Hegel's aesthetic considerations on Romantic art, 'qui a pour conséquence l'absolue négation de tout ce qui est fini et particulier',[59] but also the implicit ethical overcoming of the individual subject in favour of the 'unité simple' and of the speculative notion of subjectivity:

Cette habile confusion des buts de la philosophie avec ceux de la poésie, [...], et cette fine trouvaille qui consiste à faire honneur à la 'subjectivité' de la longue et patiente destruction qui est l'œuvre de la raison, à la faveur d'un malentendu de terminologie qui use à bon escient du terme abhorré de 'subjectivité' alors que, pour Hegel, il sert à désigner ici l'esprit, ou la 'raison concrète', tout cela est d'une diabolique adresse.[60]

To the Surrealist 'volonté d'indifférence', which makes way for political engagement, for ethical and social determinations of the subject, existential thought opposes a defiantly affirmed interest in the individual, solitary struggle against reason and morality, which emphasises inaction (for instance 'la loi du *Non-Agir*' in Gilbert-Lecomte),[61] resignation, renunciation.

The notion of 'action' invoked by Chénieux-Gendron may perhaps resolve the 'tension entre une subjectivité "pure" et un acte "pur"' by which she defines the Surrealist subject, but it does not account for the social and political connotations of action, which pushed an opposite, existential understanding of the subject 'aux frontières extérieures du surréalisme'. From the perspective of this existential frontier of Surrealism, a far more effective interpretation of the internal tension of the movement would be achieved by considering the opposition between the subject of desire and the subject of action, rather than the dialectical pair of 'pure subjectivity' and 'pure action' proposed by Chénieux-Gendron. The effectiveness of the former interpretation can be appreciated in view of the fact that in existential thought the 'dissolution of the (rational) subject' emerges from an irreconcilable contradiction between two positions and not from their possible complementarity. The fight of the individual against itself manifests the irreducible conflict between the force of *desire* (in the sense of free will maintained by the negative 'force des renoncements') and the ethical, social or political imperatives of *action*. In contrast to the Surrealist use of dialectics, aiming to reconcile all contradictions, the existential negative progression involves the annihilation or 'resorption' of one term of a radical contradiction situated inside the subject itself. This existential situation of the subject is not concerned with the 'résultante d'*action practique*' that marked the evolution of Surrealism from Hegel to Marx and maintained the belief in man's liberation through proletarian revolution.[62] Moreover, what the existential critique of Surrealism particularly targets is the assurance with which Surrealists proclaim that 'le procès de la connaissance' no longer needs to be undertaken, since the solution to the problems of life, of death, of individual freedom can be expected to emerge from the investigation of dreams:

> Le procès de la connaissance n'étant plus à faire, l'intelligence n'entrant plus en ligne de compte, le rêve seul laisse à l'homme tous ses droits à la liberté. *Grâce au rêve, la mort n'a plus de sens obscur et le sens de la vie devient indifférent.*[63] [my emphasis]

The whole problematic of existential thought is thus either 'indifferent' or already solved, clarified thanks to the powers of dream. In fact, the question posed by the individual fight against self-evidence, by the process of 'awakening', exceeds the Surrealist solution of dream. Similarly, the existential 'desire', as irrational affirmation of the freedom of individual will to break the limitation of rational thought, exceeds the Freudian configuration of the 'pleasure principle' and refuses to accept the 'reality principle' and the necessary determinations of an action that is coextensive with the ethical and rational knowledge mediating this education of the will. Even when the notion of action (as opposed to desire) is taken out of the social and political context and relocated at the psychological level of 'pure subjectivity' (in the sense adopted by Chénieux-Gendron), the Surrealist 'position of the subject' does not coincide with the position of the existential subject. In agreement with the Freudian 'dialectic of roles', which (according to Paul Ricoeur's analysis) 'expresses the internalization of a relation of opposition, constitutive of human desire',[64] Surrealism always strove to reconcile the antithetical principles of desire and reality, even though more often than not it was a case of making reality conform to the principle of desire rather than the other way around. However, existential thought rejected this idealist solution and instead of trying to adapt or transform reality chose to destroy the foundation of the so-called 'reality principle'—its ethical and rational imperatives.

In contrast to the existential notion of 'creatio ex nihilo', the question of creation is posed by Surrealism starting from the premiss of the privileged role of language (in speech, in automatic writing, in the accounts of dreams, in hypnotic trances or in the simulation of mental afflictions), providing the means for the miraculous transformation of reality.[65] The unlimited confidence in the revolutionary potential of language oriented the Surrealist exploration of subjectivity and of the relationship between mental representations and their corresponding linguistic signs, as Breton later acknowledged:

> Il est aujourd'hui de notoriété courante que le surréalisme, en tant que mouvement organisé, a pris naissance dans une opération de grande envergure portant sur le langage. [...] On n'a pas assez insisté sur le sens et la portée de l'opération qui tenait à restituer le langage à sa vraie vie, soit bien mieux de remonter de la chose signifiée au signe qui lui survit, ce qui s'avérerait d'ailleurs impossible, de se reporter d'un bond à la naissance du signifiant.[66]

The restructuring of the world is thus operated by language and involves a creation with already existing materials (as is the case of automatic writing, automatic speech, simulated mental affliction, etc.), which resembles the Freudian archaeology of the subject, a resemblance brought to light by Paul Ricoeur's comparative analysis of Freud's and Hegel's conceptions, while remaining at all stages different to the existential creation *ex nihilo*. Ricoeur places 'the structure of the Hegelian self-consciousness at the very center of the Freudian desire', and relates Freud's concept of identification to 'the dialectic of the reduplication of consciousness'.[67] Ricoeur further connects the aesthetic and ethical components of sublimation to identification as part of an argument that proves to be directly pertinent to Breton's own understanding of subjectivity and creation in its allegiance to both Freudian psychoanalysis and Hegelian dialectics. What became an integral part of Breton's conception as a result of this double spiritual affiliation was the similar use of opposition in Freud and Hegel, observed by Ricoeur: '[the] style of opposition is intimately involved in the birth of meaning; the dichotomy is already dialectical'.[68] The process of sublimation, which Breton implicitly acknowledged in his theory of creation, uncovers not only the reduplication of consciousness pertaining to identification and the dialectical birth of meaning but also the profound relationship between desire and language, 'le pouvoir d'énonciation' by which the Surrealist subject asserts itself. 'If desire is the unnameable', Ricoeur argues in his philosophical interpretation of Freud, 'it is turned from the very outset toward language; it wishes to be expressed; it is in potency to speech.'[69] The transition from life to reflexive consciousness, the process of self-knowledge and identification guided by the original turning of desire towards speech, promises not only to reconcile the speculative notion of self with the absolute otherness of life[70] but actually to enrich life in the very process of knowledge, as Breton argued: 'Ce n'est qu'à ce prix qu'on pouvait espérer rendre au langage sa destination pleine, ce qui, pour quelques-uns dont j'étais, devait faire un grand pas à la connaissance, exalter d'autant la vie.'[71]

Instead of following Freud's therapeutic approach, Breton took up his idea of sublimation (implicitly referred to in the motto of *Les Vases communicants*, where he quotes from Jensen's *Gradiva*) and developed the Surrealist theory of convulsive beauty, in which the aestheticization of madness radically opposes the existential search for truth through a direct, lived experience of madness and suffering, the Pascalian 'chercher en gémissant'. In Surrealism the oneiric regression to a state before birth is a source of enjoyment. As Pascaline Mourier-Casile observes, the Surrealist imaginary topography of the unconscious celebrates, in contrast to the Freudian therapeutic approach, 'le paradis intra-utérin: la grotte et l'île océaniques'.[72] In Artaud and Gilbert-Lecomte, the negative progression to the pre-natal state through 'resorption' or 'absorption' is associated with suffering, with the painful search for truth frequently invoked by Chestov and Fondane.[73] Thus, on the boundary of Surrealism, the aquatic figuration of the unconscious signals a process of dissolution and death: it is the topos of the void and of the creation from the void.[74]

In order to elucidate the question of 'la subjectivité [qui] demeure en effet le point noir',[75] Breton alternately adopts the position of the psychoanalyst and of the philosopher, particularly preoccupied with avoiding 'toute erreur dans l'interprétation de l'homme', which might entail 'une erreur dans l'interprétation de l'univers' and consequently obstruct the transformation of outer reality whenever the exclusively subjective point of view prevails.[76] The only means of avoiding such errors, according to Breton, 'est de préparer à l'existence subjective une revanche éclatante sur le terrain de la connaissance, de la conscience sans faiblesse et sans honte'.[77] Fondane specifically referred to this passage from Breton's *Vases communicants* in his critique of the Surrealist effort to assimilate the more rigorous, systematic interpretation of the notion of subject provided by the Freudian and the Hegelian doctrines:

Ce ne sont là ni vérités physiciennes, ni vérités matérialistes; ce sont vérités du sur-moi éthique, idéaliste, cruellement armé pour la destruction du moi insensé, affectif, imaginatif, réel, qui tient que ses passions lui sont un principe autrement plus vital, plus vrai que la *rectitude d'interprétation*.[78]

Fondane's objections to the Surrealist dialectical and unifying configuration of the subject, which places ethical concerns above the anarchic, centripetal impulses of the 'moi insensé', can be better understood in view of the above-mentioned opposition between 'creatio ex nihilo' and Breton's doctrine of creation. As I have pointed out, the latter involved the assimilation of the Freudian concept of sublimation and led to the aestheticization of madness within the Surrealist theory of 'convulsive beauty'. This evolution has crucial implications for the Surrealist understanding of processes pertaining to the constitution of the subject. Unlike the existential emphasis on the non-unitary, divided nature of the 'moi insensé' (uncovered by the paradoxical processes of 'awakening to oneself' and 'creatio ex nihilo'), the Surrealist theory of 'convulsive beauty' highlights the Hegelian dialectical interpretation of the so-called 'material mechanism of individuality'. Breton's article 'La Beauté sera convulsive' explicitly mentions Hegel's notion ('le mécanisme matériel de l'individualité') and relates it to the special predilection for the crystal as figure of a unified self, engaged in a process of objectivization through dialectical reconciliation of opposites.[79] In the passage from Hegel's *Philosophie de la nature* to which Breton refers, the crystal or the 'determined figure' is no longer an 'interior figure' but a figure that exists in itself. As Hegel further argues, this figure corresponds to the material mechanism of individuality and is determined 'comme affranchie de toute condition et comme libre. [...] Par là la forme se manifeste spontanément.'[80] The Hegelian representational model adopted by Breton situates individuality at the level of this spontaneous formation of a crystalline structure, whose opposite is the plurality and the anarchic character of the coral.[81] When Breton outlines his understanding of creation with reference to the notion of 'beauté convulsive', he identifies creation with 'l'action spontanée' (pertaining to the Hegelian mechanism of individualization) insofar as the crystal constitutes the perfect expression of the couple creation–action: 'Je ne cesse pas, au contraire, d'être porté à l'apologie de la création, de l'action spontanée et cela dans la mesure même où le cristal, par définition non améliorable, en est l'expression parfaite.'[82]

Breton's apology of creation as spontaneous crystal formation and his theory of individuality from the vantage point of objective knowledge constitute the exact opposite of the absurd creation 'ex nihilo' that characterizes the emergence of the existential subject, whose 'knowledge' is the measure of individual suffering, of a lived rather than represented experience of madness and dissolution. In opposition to the Surrealist configuration of the subject and to its spontaneous crystallization in language, in the 'inépuisable murmure' of words that, as Abastado remarks, 'élucident l'opacité de la réalité subjective',[83] the existential experience of the absurd, through laughter, intense pain or the sudden crying out to God from the depth of despair, displays a certain powerlessness and limitation of language. At this point, the only alternative is creation *ex nihilo*, the emergence of a subject whose desire is not 'in potency to speech' but in the will to restore the (rationally impossible) communication between the human and the divine, starting from intense sensorial and emotional experiences (such as pain, despair, laughter, crying), whose nature remains irreducible to logical, speculative analysis.

This perspective governs Fondane's critique of the manner in which Surrealism appropriated Rimbaud's visionary 'dérèglement de tous les sens' as a privileged method of seeing, a rationally acquired power to envisage the irrational, which Rimbaud himself came to reject:

> Le désaveu de Rimbaud écarté, les affirmations du Voyant furent mises sous verre, munies des saints sacrements de l'objectivité scientifique, investies de pouvoirs surnaturels, et rendues à la fois universelles et obligatoires. L'expérience du Voyant devint, tout comme l'Immaculée Conception, l'objet d'un dogme infaillible et la source d'une infinité de décrets-lois tel celui-ci, d'André Breton: 'Je demande que l'on tienne pour un crétin celui qui se refuserait encore à voir un cheval galoper sur une tomate'.[84]

As Fondane suggests, the Surrealist questioning of the privilege of rational sight through poetic vision ended up with an alternative, equally dogmatic mode of seeing, which dispensed Rimbaud's devoted followers from experiencing his painful legacy and advancing beyond the letter of his 'mot d'ordre':

> Mais, [...], s'il nous était interdit de toucher au dogme, il nous resterait encore le droit d'examiner si, pour arriver aux conclusions mêmes de Rimbaud, ses disciples ont suivi loyalement la voie indiquée par le poète, s'ils ont vraiment 'vécu' toutes les formes d'amour, de souffrance et de folie afin que, le salon au fond d'un lac étant vrai, il s'ensuive nécessairement qu'un

cheval galopant sur une tomate, soit vraie aussi. La voyance étant obtenue au prix de 'toute la foi, de toute la force surhumaine', qui m'assure, Rimbaud l'ayant eue, qu'elle n'ait pas été refusée à Breton? Et que, ce que l'un a découvert au prix de sa propre folie, le second pourra l'acquérir froidement — je veux dire automatiquement?.[85]

From the existential perspective, the faithful advance along the visionary 'voie indiquée par le poète' implies the faith and 'superhuman' power needed to live through rather than reflect on a whole range of individual experiences, taking all the risks involved when one loses sight of any method, and does not seek to establish a method at the end of a perilous journey into the unknown.

The same emphasis on the indispensable lived quality of poetic vision as opposed to rational sight characterizes the second issue of *Le Grand Jeu*, entirely devoted to Rimbaud. The issue of verification, deeply embedded in the quest of truth and certitude through rational sight, is posed by Roger Gilbert-Lecomte in terms of living: seeing is living. From believing at the end of an intellectual exercise to actually living the truth manifested in the personal experience of seeing beyond rational evidence, there is an incommensurable distance, which separates the mode of being of the existential individual from the objectivity of the speculative concept of subject. Like Fondane, Gilbert-Lecomte sees in Rimbaud the 'rare témoin' who makes manifest rather than representing and conceptualizing the limiting, extreme experience of a particular individual:

Il montre la limite de tout individu parce qu'il vécu lui-même à la limite de l'individu: je veux dire que plusieurs points de son œuvre marquent le souvenir d'un être qui, ayant tendu toutes les facultés de son esprit à l'extrême des possibilités humaines, a suivi l'asymptote des impossibilités humaines. S'il a ou n'a pas *vu* au delà de ces limites (ce qu'on ne peut évidemment vérifier qu'à condition de revivre son expérience et à quel prix!) il a au moins vécu béant sur cet au-delà.[86]

Showing ('montrer') replaces the indirect, referential mode of speculative analysis and asymptotically approaches the 'impossible', absurd manifestation of another order of being, beyond human limitations and verifiable only through personal lived experience. To see is to experience the terrifying, direct confrontation with the 'au delà', the living God of mystical encounters, which the members of *Le Grand Jeu* do not hesitate to invoke in contrast to the professed atheism of Surrealist writers. André Rolland de Renéville, for example, distinguishes himself from Breton and the Surrealists when he poses the relationship between the individual subject and God (when he interprets Rimbaud's remark 'Je est un autre' as actually signifying 'Je est Dieu en puissance'). He also affirms the value of direct experience at all costs against the mere simulation of madness and suffering.[87]

There is an interesting tension in *Le Grand Jeu* between the informed adherence to Hegel's absolute idealism and the existential emphasis on the value of the subjective experience of 'lived truth' (especially through extreme, limiting situations such as suffering and madness), which supersedes the objective verification and validation of results. While Rolland de Renéville proposes the 'elaboration of a method' starting from Rimbaud's 'Lettre du Voyant', published in the same special issue of *Le Grand Jeu*, Roger Vailland denounces 'les tricheurs systématiques [... qui] ont systématisé la stupeur d'être'. Daumal's and Gilbert-Lecomte's deliberate choice of paradoxical formulations, their violent rejection of systematic philosophy and their reversal of logic through 'pataphysical' judgements, disprove the idea that the 'experimental metaphysics' was a mere offspring of Hegelian absolute idealism. It is true that both Daumal and Gilbert-Lecomte occasionally blend their destructive 'casse-dogme' statements with Hegelian exegesis, arriving at some point even to a definition of God that is perfectly compatible with Hegel's.[88] However, the originality of their thought can be said to reside in the affirmation of the value of individual existence, of subjective experience, and the emphasis on anti-Hegelian notions such as that of truth as 'vérité éprouvée', consciousness as 'réveil devant le Double, le Contradictoire, l'Absurde', revolt as 'la mort dans la vie'. It is also significant that *Le Grand Jeu* not only maintained God within, or rather at the limit of, human possible experience but also set the subject in a paradoxical relationship to the mystical 'Deus absconditus', which was also invoked in Fondane's and Artaud's writings.[89] The Surrealist position of the subject remained firmly opposed to any notion of a transcendent being or of God, as Breton stated in *Les Vases communicants*, quoting Lautréamont's words: 'Ma subjectivité et le Créateur, c'est trop pour un cerveau.'[90]

In existential thought, the possibility of pointing to or even of making manifest ('montrer') the presence of another order of being has to do with the revelatory nature of the tragic experience, which brings the individual in a direct, terrifying contact with the 'living

God'. This moment of the existential critique of speculative discourse corresponds to the reinsertion of the contingent being of the particular individual among the possibilities of thought, together with the simultaneous affirmation of the contradictory being of the temporal, living, yet timeless, immortal God.

The Birth of the Tragic Subject

The unacceptable, 'taboo' questions of philosophy that man dares to raise only when he reaches the predicament defined by Chestov as 'creatio ex nihilo' are not given to consciousness in the clear and distinct light of reason but in the darkness of despair and powerlessness. Such questions, Fondane argued, 'ne se posent pas dans la lumière de la sagesse, mais dans une nuit, soudain devenue si noire, que vous arrivez vous-même à vous croire aveugle'.[91] Only the temporary blindness of reason, which is in fact the awakening to another kind of consciousness, the paradoxical consciousness of the existential subject (both temporally determined and opened to immortality), can give the individual the power to doubt the apparently unshakeable laws of logic and ethics, the foundation of speculative thought, which makes death the necessary limitation of temporal existence.

Moreover, the awakening to the absurd evidence of self-subsistent existence (neither grounded in nor derived from speculative reasoning) involves the revolt against the apodictic character of the rational indictment of subjective valuations. The exasperated individual will supporting the affirmation of a subjective rather than objective valuation of contingent existence brings out the 'self-love' that Freud qualifies as man's most extreme resistance to truth, a narcissistic position condemned to suffer the blows inflicted by scientific research and ultimately to accept the principle of reality. As Ricoeur points out, the wounding of man's narcissistic desire has come in modern times from 'the cosmological blow inflicted by Copernicus', 'the biological humiliation from the work of Darwin', and finally from psychoanalysis itself.[92] The ancient imperative of self-knowledge (γνῶθι σεαυτόν), reaffirmed by the modern philosophies of Hegel and Husserl, is also present in the psychoanalytical project, which forms an integral part of the same history of self-consciousness, 'a self-consciousness taught by the reality principle, by Ananke, and open to a truth free of "illusion"'.[93]

To the existential thinker no less than to the systematic thinker, knowing oneself implies knowing one's limit, the limit that reason traces between the possible and the impossible, between truth and illusion. Ananke, logical and natural necessity, *is* this limit, which rules out 'tedious' or shameful questions of the sort posed by Chekhov in 'A Dreary Story' or by Tolstoy in *The Death of Ivan Ilitch*, which Chestov recalls before making the following remark:

Il y a dans l'univers on ne sait quelle force invincible, qui écrase, qui brise l'homme: c'est clair, c'est tangible même. [...] L'expérience quotidienne nous convainc à chaque heure, à chaque minute même, qu'en face des lois de la nature, l'homme faible et solitaire n'a qu'une chose à faire, c'est de s'adapter et de céder, de céder toujours.[94]

The only reasonable answer to suffering, despair, and death, to all the absurdities and the limitation of human existence is submission: 'Résigne-toi mon cœur, dors ton sommeil de brute'. Yet, Chestov argued, behind the apparent resignation of this line from Baudelaire's 'Le Goût du néant', which he repeatedly quotes in his essay 'La Création *ex nihilo*', an 'inextinguishable hate' against the necessary laws of nature and of reason always remains, the same resistance to truth that Freud expected to bring around to the principle of reality by means of a painful if redemptive humiliation. The 'primary narcissism', which Freud uncovers 'at the very heart of the Ego Cogito' according to Ricoeur, has actually been under attack, exposed to humiliation, ever since Greek philosophy adopted Epictetus's postulate, as Chestov argues: 'Ἀρχή φιλοσοφίας συναίσθησις τῆς αὐτοῦ ἀσθηνείας καὶ ἀδυναμίας περὶ τὰ ἀναγκαῖα' ['Le commencement de la philosophie est la conscience de sa propre impuissance et de l'impossibilité de lutter contre la nécessité'].[95] The beginning, the arché (ἀρχή) as original principle of philosophy, is already the acknowledgement of the limit of necessity, of the ananke (ἀνάγκη) that, as Aristotle said, 'cannot be persuaded to change'. Man, therefore, has to content himself with the things that lie in his power and find consolation in ethics and self-knowledge, which is itself 'man's greatest good'. Thus, Chestov argues, begins the replacement of ontology by ethics in philosophy and the education of man's desire to accept the principle of the greatest good, which is also that of the truth:

La vérité est que l'univers visible est soumis à la loi de la mort; le bien consiste à chercher non pas ce que l'homme désire, mais ce que la raison lui ordonne de reconnaître comme meilleur. Et le bien suprême, 'summum bonum', ce qui est le but de εὖ ζῆν [well-being], et non pas ἡδονή [pleasure]—car ἡδονή n'est pas soumis à la raison, de même que ce monde visible auquel appartient ἡδονή [pleasure]—mais la faculté de *juger* que ἡδονή[pleasure] est τὸ ἀγαθόν [the good].[96]

Ancient wisdom arrives in this way at an exaltation of the limit, of the rational power to judge what is pleasurable according to what is 'good', having established that the supreme good to which man can aspire consists precisely in knowing what he can reasonably expect. The visible world, Chestov says, the created world in which man came to recognize the absence rather than the presence of ancient gods, was replaced by the ideal world that reason itself engendered, as the only real creative power left to man, a power to create within given limits. As Chestov further argues, the principle of moderation in all things and the corresponding ethical condemnation of uncontrolled passions banished everything that lay beyond man's rational power (the immortality of the soul, the existence of God, absolute freedom) to the realm of illusion. The Greek notion of κάθαρσις (catharsis), 'the last word in ancient wisdom', accomplished the purification of excessive passions by re-establishing a limit, a boundary not only between the sphere of rational possibility and the sphere of illusive desires but also between man's determinate existence under the rule of Ananke and the terrifying, indeterminate existence of powers that exceed rational control.

Yet, as Chestov remarks, in ancient as well as modern times, not all thinking subjects reached the same conclusions in contemplating the truth that lies at the heart of the 'Ego cogito'. If Hegel, Husserl and Freud agree on what Ricoeur rightly calls 'the dispossession of immediate consciousness'[97] and the displacement of the ego from its central place as subject of the *cogito* to the position of an object of reflection or alternatively to the position of 'an object of desire', the existential subject refuses to accept both the premisses of this displacement and the resulting reduction of the individual being to the idea of being in general, to an objective concept. From the point of view of the living subject who has awakened to another kind of truth about his own existence, the necessary wounding and humiliation of self-love, as part of the long speculative history of self-consciousness, represents an unbearable offence against which he is prepared to fight at all costs. The existential subject no longer perceives the limit of the Ananke as an exuberant celebration of good measure, as the reassuring conquest of a long struggle for certainty and self-overcoming against the vicissitudes of passion and the lure of unfounded illusions. The limit and its wounding truth is an abyss ('le gouffre') placed by speculative thought at the very heart of the living individual being, a horrifying annihilation of the passion of both man's and God's existence. In this sense, Fondane recalls that in Kierkegaard's understanding: '*une limite* c'est, précisément, pour la passion *sa torture et son aiguillon*', while making the following comment on Hegel's and Heidegger's concept of nothingness: 'Le Néant, c'est-à-dire le Pouvoir Magique qui "néantit" l'existant, transforme le contingent en nécessaire, et ne nous laisse que le droit de le servir — ou de nous taire. Nous sommes enfermés dans le Discours; on ne peut en sortir.'[98]

Like Chestov, Fondane argued that the existential fight for the absurd possibility of man's and God's existence beyond the limit of the Ananke was not a defensive return to reassuring beliefs, or—one might add—the kind of pathological need for illusory consolations that Freud uncovered at the origin of religious phenomena, but a rejection of the certainty and reassurance that the rational thinker found in his glorification of the limit:

> C'est en un monde sans Dieu, en un monde où on *a tué* Dieu et où, selon la remarque de Nietzsche, *on ne s'est même pas aperçu*, que la philosophie existentielle est née. La philosophie de Kierkegaard et de Chestov qui aboutissent au *Dieu tué* peut nous faire croire (tout au moins au penseur pressé; et qui ne l'est pas?) qu'il ne s'agit que d'un *retour* à la foi perdue, par lassitude, besoin de sécurité, de repos, et non (ce qu'elle signifie en vérité) par horreur du repos, de la sécurité, de la certitude. On peut croire à des âmes lasses et non (ce qu'elle sont) des âmes *dangereuses*, qui veulent briser toute quiétude afin de ramener, avec la question, la possibilité de la réponse. On serait enclin de croire à une crise *religieuse*, et non à une crise *philosophique.*[99]

The mode of questioning that the existential thinker adopts brings about a philosophical rather than a religious crisis precisely because it departs from the assurance and, as Fondane would say, the haste with which Freud along with rational philosophers draws the ultimate conclusions from the 'death of God'. Whereas Surrealism uncritically subscribed to Freud's view of religion and refused to engage in any investigation pertaining to the existence of a transcendent realm of being, existential thought challenged both the premiss and the ultimate implications of the psychoanalytical account of faith.

In 'The Future of an Illusion', Freud declares that religion can be understood as 'the universal obsessional neurosis of humanity', which like infantile neurosis 'arose out of the Oedipus complex'.[100] Within the economy of the psychoanalytical project, the neurotic model, on which Freud bases his analysis of religion both in 'The Future of an Illusion' and in 'Moses and Monotheism', has the surprising function of an exorcism: not only does his refutation of religion 'mark the renouncement on the part of Sigmund Freud the Jew of the value that his narcissism could still rightfully claim', as Ricoeur points out,[101] but this refutation, based on the Oedipus complex as the history of human desire, which 'involves refusal and hurt' and the education of desire to reality,[102] manages to reinstate the reassuring omnipotence of reason over and above irrational impulses.

In his critique of systematic philosophy, Fondane unexpectedly reverses Freud's assessment of religion as 'obsessional neurosis' and applies the same analysis to the apparent self-assurance with which 'clear and distinct' reasoning protects itself against 'taboo' questions that exceed the limits of logical comprehension. In passing over such questions in silence, rationalist philosophy itself becomes an obsessional neurosis, exorcizing the otherness of nonsense and madness:

Il y avait là une grande clarté, si grande, que l'idée nous est venue sur le tard que, derrière cette clarté, se dissimulait une peur atroce, — la peur que ces évidences ne fussent ni vraies, ni premières, ni absolues — la peur que la philosophie ne fût autre chose qu'un acte manqué, une névrose obsessionnelle, un secret honteux qu'à tout prix il fallait taire — sous peine de sombrer, de toucher du pied l'angoisse, l'absurdité et la folie.[103]

Therefore, despite Freud's last confident words, 'No, our science is no illusion. But an illusion it would be to suppose that what science cannot give us we can get elsewhere',[104] the existential thinker remains unconvinced by this explicit 'plea for the renunciation of wishes and for the acquiescence in Fate',[105] and questions the ethical foundation of Freud's interpretation of Greek tragedy in relation to Oedipus.

The 'abnormal' or 'neurotic position', which psychoanalysis interprets with reference to the tragedy of Oedipus, belongs from the existential point of view to any living individual who has suddenly awakened to the terrible truth of his condition: 'Tout un chacun *peut* devenir une "exception"',[106] says Fondane. The man who has reached the limit posed by reason, found it incompatible with his desire, with his will, and failed to submit, has become an exception by virtue of his absurd refusal to understand and adapt to his condition. He no longer sees the world in the clear and distinct light of reason, and he has accomplished the most horrible crime, condemned by rational, thinking beings since ancient times: he is a 'μισολόγος', an adversary of reason. He is guilty of excess, of seeking things ' that are not in our power', of setting his stubborn blindness against the arguments of the Ananke. In Chestov's and Fondane's view, the tragic man uncovers 'une réalité nouvelle, inouïe, tenue cachée jusqu'ici';[107] he makes manifest the passion, suffering and despair dissimulated by ethical and rational ideals. This direct manifestation of something that remains hidden, invisible to rational sight, belongs to the sphere of monstrous, unheard-of ('inouï') phenomena. It infringes on the territory delimited by reason, it transgresses the boundary between the possible and the impossible. The tragic man, as an outcast of society, as an 'underground man', sees himself and is seen by others as a monster:

> Se jugeant lui-même un monstre, de qui pourrait-il espérer de l'indulgence, de la pitié, de la compréhension, somme toute: des circonstances atténuantes? Il craint d'être mis au rancart comme possédé, d'être enfermé comme fou, ou simplement d'être classé parmi les maniaques de la persécution, peu en faveur dans la cité.[108]

The experience of awakening, which suddenly illuminates the darkness and blindness of this solitary advance into another reality, transforms the tragic man into a 'beast' or monster. His paradoxical blind vision reaches beyond the frontier of the visible with an absurd clarity, as Daumal affirms:

> Si les hommes savaient voir! Et l'un pourtant sous une clarté absurde s'éveille au milieu de la nuit, changé en monstre; et tel autre, mort, se pense et pèse en lui mille arbres et milles bêtes possibles. Que chacun se voie selon son désir, et mange ses mains d'homme pour se transformer.[109]

The only place in which such a horrifying metamorphosis of man into beast and the unrestrained display of passion of the tragic man can be presented with relative impunity is in the theatre or the fictional space of the work of art. According to Chestov and Fondane, Greek tragedy has the meaning of a terrifying disclosure of the reality and truth of human existence, as an immoderate, passionate fight against rational limitations under the guise of an ultimately purifying, moral experience. The unabated determination to uncover this hidden existential truth supersedes the intended cathartic effect of the performance, as Fondane suggests with his question:

Sophocle (tout comme le Scribe de Job) n'aurait-il inventé de toutes pièces ces fictions, ces trames imaginaires, n'aurait-il amoncelé tant de maux sur la tête de ses héros, que pour rendre vraisemblable ce qu'il n'eût pas osé crier autrement à la face du monde, crier que lui, Sophocle (Job) se sentait accablé par l'injustice de Dieu (ou des Dieux), qu'à ses yeux seuls le destin réservé aux hommes semblait *inacceptable* et que c'est lui, lui seul, qui osait regimber contre la loi, provoquer les Dieux, exiger un arbitre pour trancher son différend avec eux?.[110]

Sophocles' tragedy *Oedipus rex* brings man and God together in the same violent, passionate confrontation recounted in the book of Job from the absurd perspective of faith, which rejects any ethical consolations (relating to the injustice of human destiny) as well as any rational appeals to moderation. According to Fondane's interpretation, Greek wisdom and the Jewish tradition of biblical thought clash as the tragic hero approaches the moment of the horrible revelation of his condition. Sophocles, no less than 'Job's scribe', conveys this revelation in its absurd clarity, writes Fondane: 'Il faudra supposer que, pour le héros tragique, la vie elle-même est un mal — un mal incurable — et cent fois plus grand que le mal imaginaire qu'il [Sophocle] invente de toutes ces pièces.'[111] The unbearable suffering and despair to which Oedipus and Job testify brings the tragic hero into a suddenly dangerous, unpredictable proximity to something that exceeds rational thought. This is the one-to-one encounter between the living subject and the 'living God' that the existential understanding of tragedy aims to uncover. God makes himself known in a situation of transgression and excess, when the rational boundary between the human and the inhuman has been abolished, when the two otherwise separated, mutually exclusive spheres of existence become indistinguishable, superimposed.

Chestov and Fondane argue that, throughout the history of rational thought, the limit posed by logical and natural necessity has made man and God equally powerless, has suspended any possible communication and any transition from one mode of being to the other. The 'god of the philosophers' (as opposed to the 'God of Abraham, God of Isaac, God of Jacob' invoked by Pascal) is bound by the same fundamental principles of rational thought that determine the limits of human understanding. René Daumal acknowledged this identical powerlessness of man and God (whose will cannot in principle alter the a priori, immutable postulates of reason) when he referred to 'le Néant de Dieu', and more significantly to 'l'Homme identique à Dieu dans son néant'.[112] The abolition of rational boundaries in the experience of the tragic transforms the equality based on powerlessness into an equality based on an unlimited creative power, by which man like God becomes 'un *Cataclysme vivant*', as Gilbert-Lecomte envisaged. This expression aptly captures the situation of terrifying indetermination that, according to existential thought, sets in motion the whole mechanism of Greek tragedy. The existential interpretation of tragedy and the birth of the existential tragic subject can be understood in the light of Hölderlin's remarks on *Oedipus rex*, included in the notes to his German translation of Sophocles' work:

> Die Darstellung des Tragischen beruht vorzüglich darauf, daß das Ungeheure, wie der Gott und Mensch sich paart, und grenzenlos die Naturmacht und des Menschen Innerstes im Zorn Eins wird, dadurch sich begreift, daß das grenzelose Eineswerden durch grenzenloses Scheiden sich reiniget.
> Τῆς φύσεως γραμματεὺς ἦν τὸν κάλαμον ἀποβρέχων εἰς νοῦν.[113]

> The display of the tragic depends especially on the fact that the Monstrous, in which God and man join together, and in which the power of nature and the innermost core of man become limitlessly one in anger, comprehends itself by the fact that the limitless unification purifies itself by limitless separation. 'He was the scribe of nature, dipping his pen in his mind.'

The suspension of the limit restores the indeterminate sphere of the monstrous or the manifest, in which man and God become one. The manifestation of God, as presented in Greek tragedy and in existential thought, is monstrous precisely because it shows, brings terrifyingly close—to the point of identification—the absolute alterity of a transcendent being. The monster, derived from the Latin *monstro* (to point out, to reveal), has a subtle etymological affinity with the act of manifestation—'manifest' derives from the Latin *manifestus* (palpable, evident). The monster reveals or makes evident what remains otherwise hidden, invisible, impossible to comprehend in the absence of a limit, of the distance posited by reason between 'the innermost core of man' and the outside world. When this inner boundary collapses, man himself is transformed, becomes a monster, points to another realm of being that exceeds rational comprehension. The regime of speculative demonstration is replaced by the act of 'monstrare', by plain revelation. The tragic man discloses through his experience the unlimited power of nature and unlimited human passion as one unheard-of reality. He displays, as Fondane said of Rimbaud, 'une monstrueuse sensibilité à autre chose',[114] which turns away from discursive thought and encounters a reality that can only be shown but not demonstrated. This disclosure does not need any demonstration because making manifest (in the sense of the Latin *manifestus*) means nothing other than making 'palpable', 'clear', 'plain'. The immediate character of manifestation is not only in no need of verification, but annihilates the concept of verification, which presupposes a mediated, reflexive approach to something given as a separate, objectified unit of meaning.

The manifestation and fusion of man and God cannot be separated from a direct experience whose violence or 'fury' [*Zorn*]—signalled by extreme pain, by crying, by a non-verbal, 'organic' expressivity—suspends the detachment necessary for the clear, distinct articulation of thought and of discursive language. This is precisely what Chestov says about the manifest nature and 'meaning' of the 'incomprehensible' in his essay 'La Balance de Job':

> Quant à l' 'incompréhensible' qui se manifeste à travers les cris, à travers les sons non-articulés ou d'autres signes extérieurs que le verbe est incapable de traduire, il ne concerne plus les hommes mais 'quelqu'un' qui est sans doute plus sensible au pleurs, aux gémissements, au silence même qu'au verbe: pour ce 'quelqu'un' (il doit certainement exister) ce qui ne peut être dit a plus de signification que les affirmations les plus claires, les plus nettes, les mieux fondées et démontrées.[115]

The transgression of the limit between two spheres of existence involves the correlative transgression of the bounds of sense as defined within rational discourse. In his unlimited display of passion, the tragic man like Job no longer addresses his fellow human beings but 'somebody' else. The tragic monologue, the 'language' of disarticulated cries and of silence that seems 'incomprehensible' to other people, actually responds to the manifestation of an 'unheard-of' reality ('la réalité inouïe') by establishing a different yet perfectly valid mode of communication with that 'somebody' else for whom the 'gémissements', the crying and the silence, have more meaning than the best-founded, demonstrable argument. According to Chestov's interpretation of the tragic experience, rational speech—in the sense of the Greek λόγος—institutes the limit that exorcizes the alterity of the 'living God' and purifies the human sphere by means of an unlimited separation and a de-monstration of the monstrous. The cathartic effect of the tragedy derives from the reinstatement of the limit of the Ananke through rational exposition, the verbal de-monstration of the identity between man and God, not in their monstrous fusion but in their separation and their equal submission to necessity:

La catharsis grecque, la purification, provient de cette conviction que les données immédiates de la conscience qui témoignent de la destruction inévitable de tout ce qui naît, nous découvrent la vérité antérieure au monde, éternelle, immuable, à jamais insurmontable.[116]

In purifying man's excessive, passionate appeal to a transcendent source of truth, the Greek 'catharsis' not only reinstates the unsurpassable temporal limitation of everything that is 'created' (or 'born') rather than rationally construed, but also demonstrates the inability of God as well as man to suspend or overcome the immutable death and destruction of any living being. The cathartic intervention of rationally grounded speech in tragedy (insofar as the Greek 'logos' stands for both reason itself and speech—the Latin 'oratio' and 'vox'—what is said or spoken), discloses the unsurpassable, ideal origin of the limit, while at the same time hiding the mystery of the living God's unlimited power to create over and above logical or natural necessity. The first-person subject behind a tragic discourse (the *logographos* or 'chronicler'), for example 'the scribe of Job', is not always or not entirely the same as the one whom Hölderlin referred to as 'the scribe of nature dipping his pen in his mind', although they inevitably share the same limited language. The tragic poet no less than the tragic hero attempts to transgress this limitation, to point to what lies 'beyond mind and thought' (ἐπέκεινα νοῦ καὶ νοήσεως) as Chestov said, quoting Plotinus.[117] The possibility of communicating or of manifesting both man's and God's paradoxical (temporal and timeless) existence, outside the categories of reason, involves a paradoxical use of language, a simultaneous fusion and separation between human speech and inhuman, unspeakable presence. Artaud's remarks on the language of theatrical representation adequately capture this interplay between meaningful communication and 'meaningless' or absurd manifestation, between hiding and disclosing something that exceeds rational comprehension: 'Tout vrai sentiment est en réalité intraduisible. L'exprimer c'est le trahir. Mais le traduire c'est le *dissimuler*. L'expression vraie cache ce qu'elle manifeste.'[118]

In Artaud's view of theatre, the body and the direct physical manifestation of emotion constantly subvert verbal, discursive representation: 'Toute émotion a des bases organiques. C'est en cultivant son émotion dans son corps que l'acteur en recharge la densité voltaïque.'[119] Artaud sought to restore the disarticulated crying, the notion of 'souffle', the intense terror, the cruelty and the sense of danger in the theatre, as means of communicating something that exceeds human comprehension. As in Greek tragedy, this unintelligible type of speech signals the intention to address an interlocutor to whom such an unrestrained display of passion and of cruelty has more significance than rational argument. Artaud did not attempt simply to change theatrical representation but actually to transcend the concept of representation altogether by suspending the mechanism of reference, of an indirect, mediated presentation, that characterizes rational speech. The identification of 'souffle' and 'vie' in Artaud's theatre tends to approach the moment of a monstrous, plain identification of theatrical performance and life, of man's and God's unlimited creative powers:

> Le dieu caché quand il crée obéit à la nécessité cruelle de la création qui lui est imposée à lui même, et il ne peut pas ne pas créer, donc ne pas admettre au centre du tourbillon volontaire du bien un noyau de mal de plus en plus réduit, de plus en plus mangé. Et le théâtre dans le sens de création continue, d'action magique entière obéit à cette nécessité.[120]

It would be a mistake to assume that 'necessity' designates here the limiting power of rational thought, of the Ananke. The 'cruel necessity', which Artaud relates to the hidden God's will to create, corresponds to the manner in which the tragic man as presented in Chestov's essay 'La création *ex nihilo*' comes to confront the absurd yet unavoidable possibility of a creation from the void. Having reached the boundary between death and life, having moreover transgressed this limit through the terrible experience of 'death-in-life', the tragic man has to continue to live and has to continue to create, although this no longer implies a rational de-monstration but a monstrous identification with the hidden God of creation in the 'tourbillon volontaire du bien'. Artaud emphasizes such a paradoxical new meaning of necessity, related to the process of creation, when he juxtaposes 'volonté' and 'cet appétit de vie aveugle'.[121] This blind affirmation of life is founded on the unlimited will—God's will as well as man's will—emerging from the experience of awakening, which Chestov and Fondane no less than Daumal and Gilbert-Lecomte defined in terms of a perpetual negation and transgression of rational thought. To the 'cruelty' of life as defined within the confines of rational philosophical discourse ('Du point de vue de l'esprit cruauté signifie rigueur, application et décision implacable, détermination irréversible, absolue')[122] Artaud opposes the cruelty and determination with which man decides to confront—to revolt against rather than submit to—his destiny:

Il semble encore et c'est bien d'une volonté semblable que le théâtre est sorti, qu'il ne doive faire intervenir l'homme et ces appétits que dans la mesure et sur l'angle sous lequel magnétiquement il se rencontre avec son destin. Non pour le subir, mais pour se mesurer avec lui.[123]

The tragic man regains the power to assert himself as 'the measure of all things', and this no longer implies the Greek apology of moderation but the passionate, immoderate identification with the living God's power to create all things. The powerlessness derived from the limit or measure set by reason to God, and the corresponding powerlessness of an appropriation of God in human terms, becomes the power of an unlimited communication/identification between man and God, whose measure is paradoxically defined as excess. Man measures himself up to God in the creation from the void:

C'est dans le ventre que le souffle descend et crée son vide d'où il le relance au sommet des poumons.

Cela veut dire: pour crier je n'ai pas besoin de la force, je n'ai besoin que de la faiblesse, et la volonté partira de la faiblesse, mais vivra, pour recharger la faiblesse de toute la force de la revendication.[124]

The possibility of communication and passionate identification between man and God corresponds to the existential reinstatement of the positive, full presence of the individual subject, together with the manifest presence of God, as the actual foundation of philosophical investigation. Existential thought exposes the speculative substitution of ethics for ontology[125] and proposes a Nietzschean transvaluation of all values, starting from a radical questioning of the value of rational, scientific truth, as Fondane argued:

L'existence de la 'valeur' entraîne l'existence de la non-valeur et celle de 'vérité', l'existence de l'erreur. [...] Toute recherche existentielle implique une lutte sans merci non seulement avec la logique et la morale, mais encore et surtout avec le 'concept' de vérité.[126]

Existential man becomes 'the measure of all things' because he is no longer constrained to adapt himself and to submit to necessary, eternal truths; he creates his own truth, he points to this manifest truth through his very presence. Like Chestov, Fondane considered that the tragic experience leading to the encounter between the living man and the living God forms the object of 'the philosophy of tragedy', which proposes to uncover the identity between truth and lived experience. This approach seems incompatible with the conventional definition of philosophical inquiry, insofar as the new philosophy of tragedy 'prétend que la vérité n'est pas au terme d'un savoir mais d'un pouvoir, pas d'une évidence a priori mais d'une présence effectuée, pas d'une chose que l'on sait mais d'une chose que l'on *vit*'.[127]

The critique of the concept of truth was also an integral part of Daumal's and Gilbert-Lecomte's project for an experimental metaphysics that questioned the annihilation of the living, individual subject by speculative discourse and began the paradoxical reconstruction or creation of this subject from the void. The classical theory of correspondence ('adaequatio rei et intellectus') is replaced with an understanding of truth in terms of a more profound identity between the subject and its effective, manifest presence in the world. The representational model of this theory of truth based on correspondence can be said to determine the rational limit of possible experience, according to the categories of understanding, the very limit that the existential investigation of the living subject suspends. The destruction of rational, scientific truth in turn makes possible the emergence of created truth, by which the individual subject affirms his existence. Gilbert-Lecomte establishes this correlation between existential, personal truth and being when he writes: 'Pas de vérité. Tout en moi est vérité. Quoique je dise je ne puis pas mentir. Tout ce que je rêve et je veux existe.'[128] The project of an experimental metaphysics aimed to subvert the privilege of rational analysis, to question the centrality of rational sight, the meaning of 'voir' embedded in the traditional conception of 'savoir' and 'pouvoir', as Gilbert-Lecomte states in his 'Psychologie des états: Métaphysique expérimentale': 'La naissance de la pensée concrète (métaphysique expérimentale) en sortant la vision de son expression artistique, transformera son savoir en pouvoir.'[129] Fondane similarly recalled in *La Conscience malheureuse* the mystical approach that 'supprime le savoir et institue une recherche du NON-VOIR'. Gilbert-Lecomte's affirmation supports Fondane's previously-mentioned belief that existential thought inaugurates a philosophical rather than a religious crisis. This means that the existential vision introduces a poetic and tragic dimension into the field of philosophical analysis, while at the same time refusing to limit the investigation to the apparent psychological or aesthetic implications of a concern with the contingent, individual subject by firmly situating this subject within an ontological critique of rationality. One of the strongest statements to this effect, which uncovers the full extent of the existential questioning of the concept of being and redefines the notion of subject as irreducible to conceptual analysis can be found in Artaud's later writings:

Le moi est ce qui veut conserver son être
non dans l'absolu mais dans le particulier,
énnemi-né de l'éternité,
que le particulier se renouvelle non à l'infini
mais dans l'indéfini indéfiniment multiplié
[...]
Parce que le moi conservateur ne conserve jamais
que son irréductibilité à l'idée de l'être,
je ne suis pas
mais ne me faites pas être ce que je ne suis pas
et que je ne suis pas,
vous mettriez tout le monde à la place de moi,
C'est toujours moi mais ce n'est pas ça.
Pas de philosophie de l'être, et pas d'être,
le refus du néant et de l'être,
la volonté de ne participer jamais aussi bien à être
ceci qu'à ne pas être cela,
ni à l'affirmation du ne pas être (ou être) ceci contre le ne pas être cela.[130]

The subject that paradoxically aspires to 'preserve' its being, not in the manner of speculative, timeless concepts but as a contingent, particular entity, illuminates the relationship between the living man and the contradictory, rationally-incomprehensible existence of the 'living God'. The existential critique of the concepts of being and of truth discloses a thinking subject that is no longer disconnected from the subject of empirical experience. Thought itself, in its interlocking with the concept of being, which runs through the whole history of philosophy from Parmenides to Hegel or Husserl, ceases to designate the rupture between contingent existence and 'une pensée autonome' and becomes, as Fondane says, 'une pensée solidaire de l'existence, qui 'participe' à l'existence'.[131] Truth acquires the existential dimension of a 'vérité éprouvée', directly involved in the process of awakening and of creation, which defines the living subject in Daumal's and Gilbert-Lecomte's understanding. The existential philosophy of tragedy ultimately points to an experience of excess and transgression that restores the unlimited identity between the living man and the living God and makes possible a further unlimited identification between thought and existence: 'une pensée en tant qu'existence, pensée de ce qui est, expérience interne, unique, secrète, incommunicable, solidaire de l'existence individuelle dont elle est comme la sécrétion en même temps que le principe du mûrissement intérieur'.[132] The monstrous birth of the tragic subject from the void and the darkness of unknowing thus heralds the manifestation or the terrifying proximity of an infinitely distant sphere of being, whose fusion with man's innermost core and whose disclosure of created truth can never be purified through rational demonstration or separated from the lived experience of this unlimited, monstrous beginning.

Conclusions

The Surrealist investigation of the subject abandoned the highly individualistic, purely negative stance of Dada in favour of a social and political integration of the individual, which placed a special emphasis on the ethical imperative involved in the dialectical resolution of all contradictions and the transformation of experimental activity into a revolutionary practice. Conversely, the existential rejection of ethical determinations and of social/political militancy led to a defiant valuation of powerlessness, defeat, resignation and disengagement, which uncovered a paradoxical notion of revolt, defined as negative progression towards the void. The figuration of the void in existential writing signals a radical dissolution of the rational subject as a fallacious site of identification within the process of awakening through which the living individual affirms its own existence against the conceptual derivation of being from self-evident, objective meaning. The existential critique of rationality opposed not only

Husserl's phenomenological reduction (to which my previous statement alludes, and which was discussed in the first chapter) but also the two influential sources of the Surrealist understanding of subjectivity: the Hegelian mechanism of individuation and the Freudian psychoanalytical approach.

Hegel's remarks on the spontaneous formation of crystalline structures inspired the Surrealist description of individuality in terms of the correlative pair 'cristal/corail'. The same process of crystallization informed the Surrealist notion of 'beauté convulsive', and made possible the insertion of ethical and social imperatives—dialectically contained in the idea of 'devoir-vivre'—at the very heart of the investigation of the subject. To the Surrealist topography of individuation, based on the pair crystal/coral, existential thought opposed the process of resorption or absorption, the return to a pre-natal state that dissolved the solid structures of the rational mechanism of individuation and confronted the subject with a situation described as 'death-in-life'. The negative progression to the void and the tragic experience of 'death-in-life' made possible the paradoxical creation *ex nihilo*, which resisted both the Hegelian and the Freudian dialectical overcoming of the particular, unreflective self.

In his investigation of the notion of subject, Breton assimilated the Freudian intuition of the original turning of desire towards speech in the process of self-knowledge and based Surrealist experimental activity on what he described as 'une opération de grande envergure portant sur le langage'. It is true that the aim of this vast exploration of language in relation to unconscious desire did not coincide with the Freudian envisaged education of desire to an acceptance of the principle of reality. Nevertheless, as I have tried to show, the Surrealist elucidation of the question of subjectivity through speech and writing remained within the confines of the traditional interlocking between the concepts of being and thought, insofar as it rejected the possibility of a transcendent, rationally incomprehensible form of existence and the idea of human communication with the divine through the tragic display of suffering and passion.

The existential critique of the foundational role of language within the Surrealist exploration of subjectivity developed in relation to a more profound critical re-examination of the concept of truth, which uncovered the paradoxical notion of 'vérité éprouvée'. The concern shared by the Surrealist and the existential thinkers with the privilege of sight in speculative discourse elicited quite different interpretations of vision, corresponding to conflicting notions of truth and subjectivity. Whereas the Surrealist negation of rational sight ended up establishing the privilege of visionary illumination, ultimately superseded by the pre-eminence of the original language-based approach to subjectivity, the existential emphasis on blindness and on forms of paradoxical vision pointed to the monstrous, non-visual sensibility of the subject in its confrontation with the radical alterity of God.

Notes to Chapter 2

1. Roger Gilbert-Lecomte, 'Retour à Tout', *Œuvres complètes*, i. 232.
2. Søren Kierkegaard, *Training in Christianity*, trans. Walter Lowrie (Princeton: Princeton University Press, 1944), 83. The French translation rendered the concept as 'scandale'.
3. In 'Chestov et la lutte contre les évidences', 50, Fondane concludes his presentation of Chestov's thought thus: 'C'est le domaine de la *seconde dimension de la pensée* — de la tragédie, ou encore de la foi.'
4. Fondane gives the full quotation from Tertullian's *De carne Christi* in 'Chestov et la lutte contre les évidences', 18: 'Crucifixus est Dei filius: non pudet quia pudendum est; et mortuus est Dei filius; prorsus credibile est quia ineptum est; et sepultus resurrexit; certum est quia impossibile'.
5. Daumal, 'La Vision de l'Absurde', 46.
6. 'Donc l'Esprit est en soi, homogène, éternel et ne peut mourir (toutes notions incompréhensibles pour notre raison, à base d'expérience, et qui ont d'autant plus de chances de symboliser la vérité de ce qui est pour nous également incompréhensible). Aussi bien ceci n'est que l'explication analytique du "*credo quia absurdum*" de Saint Paul, et l'on pourrait ainsi jusqu'à la démence reprendre point par point pour ce que tu poses en principe. [...] La raison est donc un mécanisme suranné de notre esprit, quelque chose d'inutile dont il nous faut nous débarasser'; Roger Gilbert-Lecomte, letter 'A Roger Vailland, Reims, 1925', *Correspondance* (Paris: NRF and Gallimard, 1971), 92–3.
7. *Kierkegaard's Concluding Unscientific Postscript*, trans. David F. Swenson (London: Oxford University Press, 1945), 183.
8. Fondane, 'Léon Chestov et la lutte contre les évidences', 46, 47.
9. See André Breton, 'Au Grand Jour', *Œuvres complètes*, i. 929; Antonin Artaud, 'A la grande nuit, ou Le Bluff surréaliste', *Œuvres complètes*, i (Paris: Gallimard, 1956), 284.
10. Breton, 'Au Grand Jour', 928.
11. Ibid., 933.
12. Ibid., 940.
13. Breton ('Au Grand Jour', 929) had used a rather crude 'argumentum ad hominem' in his incrimination of Artaud's activity: 'Il y a longtemps que nous voulions le confondre, persuadés qu'une véritable bestialité l'animait. Qu'il ne voulait voir dans la Révolution qu'une métamorphose des conditions intérieures de l'âme, ce qui est le propre des débiles mentaux, des impuissants et des lâches.'

Artaud polemically attributed a positive value to his 'impuissance', implicitly contrasting it to Breton's comments on 'les deux seules défections' (Soupault's and Artaud's) at the time when the limits of the Surrealist action ('qui, révolutionnairement parlant, ne sont pas imaginaires mais réelles'; ibid.) needed to be established. From Artaud's point of view, this limitation was itself an implicit acknowledgement of 'impuissance'.

14. 'L'Aube n'est pas une épée' (collective declaration signed 'Discontinuité'), *Discontinuité* 1 (June 1928), 3; repr. in *Lectures d'Adamov: Actes du colloque international Würzburg 1981*, ed. Robert Abirached, Ernstpeter Ruhe and Richard Schwaderer (Paris: Jean-Michel Place, 1983), 153–4.
15. Breton, 'Au Grand Jour', 928.
16. Breton introduces the expression 'devoir-vivre' in *Les Vases communicants*, *Œuvres complètes*, ii. 104; 'l'idée du "devoir être"' is equated with 'le fait historique' on p. 188. Concerning the fusion of Hegel's and Rimbaud's ideas in the notion of 'devoir-vivre', see Marguerite Bonnet's comments in Breton, *Œuvres complètes*, ii. 1376 n. 4. The envisaged synthesis between the 'interpretation' and the actual 'transformation' of the world (in keeping with Marxist doctrine) is repeatedly stated in *Les Vases communicants*, 108, 193.
17. Roger Gilbert-Lecomte, 'La force des renoncements', *Le Grand Jeu* 1 (Summer 1928), 12–18.
18. Ibid., 15.
19. Ibid. The second sentence (followed by an explicit reference to Daumal) also appears in René Daumal, 'Liberté sans espoir', *Le Grand Jeu* 1 (Summer 1928), 24.
20. Gilbert-Lecomte, 'La force des renoncements', 16–17.
21. Daumal, 'Liberté sans Espoir', 19, 20, 23.
22. Daumal, 'Liberté sans Espoir' Ibid., 23.
23. Ibid.
24. 'L'Aube n'est pas une épée', *Discontinuité* 1 (June 1928), 3.
25. Ibid.
26. Gilbert-Lecomte, 'La force des renoncements', 15.
27. Antonin Artaud, 'Préambule', *Œuvres complètes*, i. 9.
28. Ibid., 10, 11.
29. It would be interesting to consider Artaud's contentions in view of the debate over 'innate ideas' between the idealist and the empiricist philosophical traditions. One can argue that the paradox uncovered by Artaud refers to the fact that contingent, individual existence is neither an 'innate idea' (in the sense in which Descartes stated that all principles of science and knowledge are founded on truths that are 'innate' in the mind) nor completely dependent on experience. The notion of 'le génital inné' situates the subject's existence neither in relation to the 'clear and distinct' idea of the Cartesian *cogito* nor in relation to empirical knowledge, informed by sense experience. This paradox of the substantialist view of the subject (as neither wholly unconditioned, nor empirically given in experience) is tentatively dealt with in the Fourth Antinomy of Kant's *Critique of Pure Reason*.
30. Antonin Artaud, 'Fragments d'un journal d'enfer', *Œuvres complètes*, i. 107.
31. Roger Gilbert-Lecomte, 'Au fond de tout', *Œuvres complètes*, i. 175.
32. Roger Gilbert-Lecomte, 'Retour de flamme', *Œuvres complètes*, i. 176.

33. Roger Gilbert-Lecomte, letter 'A Pierre Minet' [1926], *Correspondance*, 147.
34. Artaud, 'Le Pèse-nerfs', 88.
35. Roger Gilbert-Lecomte, 'La force des renoncements', 14.
36. Ibid.
37. Ibid., 16.
38. Ibid. The notion of 'paramnésie' in *Le Grand Jeu* and the argument from reminiscence within existential thought are examined in relation to the interpretation of time in the last section of Chap. 3.
39. Léon Chestov, 'La création *ex nihilo*', *L'Homme pris au piège: Pouchkine, Tolstoï, Tchékhov* (Paris: Union Générale d'Editions, 1966), 79–119. The essay was originally published separately in Russian in 1905 (collected in 1908); the French translation appeared in *Pages choisies* (Paris: Gallimard, 1931), 53–105.
40. Chestov, 'La Création *ex nihilo*', 110.
41. Ibid., 84.
42. Ibid., 91.
43. Ibid., 89.
44. Ibid., 96–7.
45. Roger Gilbert-Lecomte, *La Vie, l'Amour, la Mort, le Vide et le Vent*, *Œuvres complètes* (Paris: Gallimard, 1977), ii. 6–7.
46. Antonin Artaud, 'Enquête: Le Suicide est-il une solution?', *La Révolution surréaliste* 2 (15 Jan. 1925), 12; repr. *Œuvres complètes*, i. 246.
47. Antonin Artaud, 'Sur le suicide', *Œuvres complètes*, i. 221.
48. Roger Gilbert-Lecomte, 'Suppositions mortelles', *Œuvres complètes*, ii. 50.
49. Daumal, 'La Vision de l'Absurde', 46. Powrie (*René Daumal: Étude d'une obsession*, 41) also mentions the correlation between death and revolt in Daumal.
50. Roger Gilbert-Lecomte, 'Retour à tout', *Œuvres complètes*, i. 239.
51. Gilbert-Lecomte, 'La force des renoncements', 12.
52. Roger Gilbert-Lecomte, 'Avant-propos' (signed 'en complet accord' by other members of *Le Grand Jeu*: Hendrik Cramer, René Daumal, Artür Harfaux, Maurice Henry, Pierre Minet, A. Rolland de Renéville, Josef Sima, Roger Vailland), *Le Grand Jeu* 1 (Summer 1928), 3.
53. Jacqueline Chénieux-Gendron, *Le Surréalisme* (Paris: P.U.F., 1984), 158. Chénieux-Gendron provides the most comprehensive analysis of the Surrealist interpretation of the notion of subject from a philosophical and psychoanalytical perspective. In what follows, I shall refer to relevant chapters from this volume as well as to ead., 'La Position du sujet chez Breton et Bataille', Jacqueline Chénieux-Gendron, Marie-Claire Dumas (eds.), *L'Objet au défi* (Paris: P.U.F., 1987), 59–76.
54. Chénieux-Gendron, *Le Surréalisme*, 158.
55. Ibid., 166.
56. Ibid., 157.
57. Ibid., 159.
58. Breton, 'Introduction au discours sur le peu de réalité', 271.
59. André Breton, *Misère de la poésie* (1932), repr. *Œuvres complètes*, ii. 18, quoting Hegel, *Cours d'esthétique*, i; see also the editor's notes, *Œuvres complètes*, ii. 1306. See Fondane, *Faux Traité d'esthétique*, 37–8.
60. Ibid.

61. Gilbert-Lecomte, 'Fondements du pouvoir social', *Œuvres complètes*, i. 244.
62. Cf. André Breton, *Qu'est-ce que le surréalisme?*, *Œuvres complètes*, ii. 233, 230.
63. J.-A. Boiffard, P. Eluard and R. Vitrac, 'Préface', *La Révolution surréaliste* 1 (1 Dec. 1924), 1.
64. Paul Ricoeur, *Freud and Philosophy: An Essay on Interpretation* (New Haven: Yale University Press, 1970), 387. Ricoeur's informed comparative analysis of Freudian psychoanalysis and Hegelian idealism illuminates the Surrealist appropriation of the two doctrines within a unifying interpretation of dream and reality, with reference to language and signification. I shall therefore use Ricoeur's analysis to elucidate philosophical issues relating to the Surrealist notion of subject, which sparked the polemic between existential thought and mainstream Surrealism.
65. See Claude Abastado, 'Les pouvoirs du langage', 'Théorie de la création', *Introduction au surréalisme* (Paris: Bordas, 1986), 60–5, 69–81. Chénieux-Gendron also signals (*Le Surréalisme*, 170–5) 'le privilège du langage, autour duquel la réalité elle-même se redéfinit', and relates ('La Position du sujet chez Breton et Bataille', *L'Objet au défi*, 69) Breton's 'conception "pleine" de l'individu' to 'une réflexion sur le langage et une pratique de l'écriture qui redonnent au langage sinon une priorité sur le sujet, du moins une importance *opératoire* décisive'.
66. André Breton, 'Du surréalisme en ses œuvres vives' (1953), repr. *Manifestes du surréalisme* (Paris: Gallimard, 1979), 170, 181–2.
67. Ricoeur, *Freud and Philosophy*, 481–2.
68. Ibid., 475.
69. Ibid., 457.
70. See ibid., 472.
71. André Breton, 'Les Mots sans rides', repr. *Les Pas perdus*, *Œuvres complètes*, i. 284.
72. Pascaline Mourier-Casile, *De la chimère à la merveille* (Lausanne: L'Âge d'Homme, 1986), 249, 251. An early mention of the prenatal state in Surrealist automatic texts can be found in Breton's and Eluard's *L'Immaculée Conception* (1930), which includes a chapter on 'La Vie intra-utérine', repr. Breton, *Œuvres complètes*, i. 842–3.
73. See e.g. Roger Gilbert-Lecomte, 'Acte de dépossession (tension)', *Œuvres complètes*, i. 232: 'La souffrance — rien que la souffrance — au fond de tout être vivant, témoigne de la vie (seul témoin irrécusable, universel, inséparable).' Artaud ('A la grande nuit, ou Le Bluff surréaliste', 286) explicitly disassociated himself from the Surrealists on this point: 'Ce qui me sépare des surréalistes c'est qu'ils aiment autant la vie que je la méprise. Jouir dans toutes les occasions et par tous les pores, voilà le centre de leur obsessions.'
74. In opposition to the Surrealist faith in the positive, enlightening quality of dreams, Antonin Artaud, 'Le Mauvais Rêveur', *Œuvres complètes*, i. 224, described himself as 'le mauvais rêveur': 'Mes rêves sont avant tout une liqueur, une sorte d'eau de nausée où je plonge et qui roule des sanglants micas. Ni dans la vie de mes rêves, ni dans la vie de ma vie je n'atteins à la hauteur de certaines images, je ne m'installe dans ma continuité. Tous mes rêves sont sans issue, sans château fort, sans plan de ville. Un vrai remugle de membres coupés.'
75. Breton, *Les Vases communicants*, 207. This affirmation seems directly drawn from Hegel's *Logic*, in which the 'I', as 'mere being-for-self' is characterized as 'the ultimate and unanalysable point of consciousness'; *Hegel's Logic: Being Part One of*

the Encyclopaedia of the Philosophical Sciences (1830), trans. William Wallace (Oxford: Clarendon Press, 1975), 38.

76. Breton, *Les Vases communicants*, 196.
77. Ibid.
78. Fondane, *Faux Traité d'esthétique*, 40.
79. See André Breton, 'La Beauté sera convulsive' [first published in *Minotaure* 5 (May 1934)], *Œuvres complètes*, ii. 681–2, quoting Hegel's *Philosophie de la nature*, i (Paris: Ladrange, 1863), §315 on the crystal (cf. the editorial note, Breton, *Œuvres complètes*, ii. 1709–10 n. 3).
80. Ibid., quoting Hegel's *Philosophie de la nature*, §§ 315, 310.
81. Cf. Breton, 'La Beauté sera convulsive', 681–2. See Chénieux-Gendron, 'La position du sujet chez Breton et Bataille', 65.
82. Breton, 'La beauté sera convulsive', 681. The first chapter of *L'Amour fou* (which incorporates 'La beauté sera convulsive') ends (*Œuvres complètes*, ii. 687): 'La beauté convulsive sera érotique-voilée, explosante-fixe, magique-circonstancielle ou ne sera pas.' The crystal, as spontaneous formation, can be considered as the prototype of the 'beauté explosante-fixe', as shown by Gérard Legrand, *André Breton en son temps* (Paris: Le Soleil noir, 1976), 119.
83. Abastado, *Introduction au surréalisme*, 62.
84. Fondane, *Rimbaud le Voyou*, 49.
85. Ibid., 49–50.
86. Roger Gilbert-Lecomte, 'Après Rimbaud la mort des Arts', *Le Grand Jeu* 2 (Spring 1929), 26.
87. See André Rolland de Renéville, 'L'Elaboration d'une Méthode (A propos de la *Lettre du Voyant*)', *Le Grand Jeu* 2 (Spring 1929), 10–16; id., letter to Breton, *La Nouvelle Revue française* (1 July 1932), 157.
88. 'Comme il nous est arrivé de désigner par le mot Dieu la réalité absolue et que nous ne voulons pas nous priver d'un mot sous prétexte qu'on en a fait les plus tristes usages, que ceci soit bien entendu: Dieu est cet état limite de toute conscience, qui est La Conscience se saisissant elle-même sans le secours d'une individualité, ou, si l'on veut, sans s'offrir aucun objet particulier'; René Daumal and Roger Gilbert-Lecomte, 'Mise au point ou casse-dogme', *Le Grand Jeu* 2 (Spring 1928), 2.
89. See Fondane, 'Chestov et la lutte contre les évidences', 33; Antonin Artaud, 'Lettres sur la cruauté', *Le Théâtre et son double*, 159. Daumal (*Tu t'es toujours trompé*, 65) speaks of the God of negative theology, referring to Plotinus.
90. Breton, *Les Vases communicants*, 207.
91. Fondane, *La Conscience malheureuse*, p. xxi.
92. Ricoeur (*Freud and Philosophy*, 425 ff.) refers to Freud's famous essay of 1917, 'A Difficulty in the Path of Psychoanalysis', in his philosophical interpretation of Freud's notion of 'primary narcissism' as compared to Hegel's and Husserl's conceptions of consciousness and subjectivity.
93. Ibid., 428.
94. Chestov, 'La création *ex nihilo*', 108; 110.
95. Chestov, 'Qu'est-ce que la vérité?', 48.
96. Ibid., 55–6. Chestov quotes (in Greek and French) Plotinus's *Enneads* I, 4, 2 in support of his argument: 'Le bonheur donc appartient non pas à l'être qui veut le plaisir mais à celui qui est capable de connaître que le plaisir est un bien; et la

cause du bonheur sera non pas le plaisir, mais le pouvoir de juger que le plaisir est un bien. Or ce qui juge est supérieur à l'affection: c'est la raison ou intelligence. Et jamais ce qui est irraisonnable ne saurait être mieux que la raison.'

97. Ricoeur, *Freud and Philosophy*, 423.
98. Benjamin Fondane, 'Le Lundi existentiel et le dimanche de l'histoire', Jean Grenier (ed.); *L'Existence* (Paris: Gallimard, 1945), 41.
99. Ibid., 49–50.
100. Sigmund Freud, 'The Future of an Illusion', *Civilization, Society and Religion* (London: Penguin, 1991), 226.
101. Ricoeur, *Freud and Philosophy*, 244. Ricoeur advances the idea that 'Moses and Monotheism' stands as an exorcism of Freud's own narcissism in relation to his Jewish origin.
102. Ibid., 387.
103. Fondane, *La Conscience malheureuse*, p. xviii. Similar considerations (relating to the tension and the interaction between madness and reason in philosophy) can be found in Derrida's 'Cogito et histoire de la folie'; see Chap. 1. In the concluding part of his essay, Derrida writes (p. 96): 'Je ne philosophe que dans la *terreur*, mais la terreur *avouée* d'être fou. L'aveu est à la fois, dans son présent, oubli et dévoilement, protection et exposition: économie. Mais cette crise en laquelle la raison est plus folle que la folie — car elle est non-sens et oubli — [...] cette crise a toujours et déjà commencé et elle est interminable.'
104. Freud, 'The Future of an Illusion', 241.
105. Ibid., 218. Fondane quotes this passage in his critical essay on Freud, *La Conscience malheureuse*, 140.
106. Fondane, 'Le lundi existentiel', 52.
107. Chestov, *La Philosophie de la tragédie*, 77.
108. Fondane, *Rimbaud le Voyou*, 37.
109. René Daumal, untitled text accompanying a photograph of André Masson's sculpture 'Métamorphose', *Le Grand Jeu* 2 (Spring 1928), 31–2.
110. Fondane, *Rimbaud le Voyou*, 35.
111. Ibid., 37.
112. René Daumal, 'Poème à Dieu et à l'Homme', *Tu t'es toujours trompé* (Paris: Mercure de France, 1970), 136, 129.
113. Friedrich Hölderlin, 'Anmerkungen zum Œdipus', *Sämtliche Werke* (Frankfurt am Main: Insel, 1965), 1188. I am grateful to Michael Inwood for the English translation of this fragment. I have rendered 'γραμματεὺς' by 'scribe' rather than 'interpreter of nature'; cf. H. T. Riley (ed.), *Dictionary of Latin Quotations [...] with a Selection of Greek Quotations* (London: H. G. Bohn, 1856), 551.
114. Fondane, *Rimbaud le Voyou*, 25.
115. Léon Chestov, 'La Balance de Job', *Cahiers du Sud* 244 (Mar. 1942), 214.
116. Léon Chestov, 'Kierkegaard et Dostoievsky', *Cahiers du Sud* 181 (Mar. 1936), 181. It is useful to recall here that Chestov refuses to identify the God of the Bible with the Greek notion of Logos ('Qu'est-ce que la vérité?', 37): 'Dans les Évangiles, il est vrai, Dieu est appelé Logos; mais peut-on identifier le Logos des Évangiles avec celui des philosophes?' 'Le verbe a été inventé pour la vie, pour cacher aux hommes le mystère de l'éternel et clouer leur attention à ce qui se déroule ici, sur terre'; Chestov, 'La Balance de Job', 213.

117. Chestov, 'Qu'est-ce que la vérité', 67. On p. 55 Chestov signals the equivalent function of the notions of 'λόγος' [logos] and 'νοῦς' [nous], designating 'reason' in Greek philosophy, with specific reference to Plotinus, *Enneads* I, 4, 2.
118. Antonin Artaud, 'Théâtre oriental et théâtre occidental', *Le Théâtre et son double*, 110.
119. Antonin Artaud, 'Un athlétisme affectif', *Le Théâtre et son double*, 210.
120. Antonin Artaud, 'Lettres sur la cruauté', 159–60.
121. Ibid., 160.
122. Ibid., 158.
123. Ibid., 169.
124. Artaud, 'Le Théâtre de Séraphin', 225.
125. Chestov, 'Qu'est-ce que la vérité?', 46, 49, 54, 57, 59, insistently mentions this original substitution of ethics for ontology as the foundation of rational philosophical thought.
126. Fondane, *La Conscience malheureuse*, 33, 37.
127. Ibid., p. xxiv.
128. Roger Gilbert-Lecomte, 'La Vision par l'épiphyse', *Œuvres complètes*, i. 183.
129. Roger Gilbert-Lecomte, 'Psychologie des états: Métaphysique expérimentale', *Œuvres complètes*, i. 197.
130. Antonin Artaud, 'Dossier d'Artaud le Mômo', *Œuvres complètes*, xii (Paris: Gallimard, 1974), 183–4.
131. Fondane, *La Conscience malheureuse*, p. xxii.
132. Ibid., 20.

CHAPTER 3

❖

Time and History: Forms of Temporal Existence

The time is out of joint: O cursed spite,
That ever I was born to set it right!

SHAKESPEARE, *Hamlet*

l'Histoire n'est qu'une absence totale de Dieu

FONDANE, *La Conscience malheureuse*

The interpretation of time brings out the full scope of the existential critique of consciousness and subjectivity as presented in the preceding chapters, with reference to both the philosophical sources and the psychoanalytical approach that informed the Surrealist position. From the existential perspective, the rational interlocking between being and thought is supported by a conception of time that obscures the condition of the particular, living individual. The epistemological and historical accounts of subjectivity in relation to time situate the concept of being outside the realm of contingent existence and within a direct correlation to thought. In this chapter I propose to compare the existential and Surrealist views of time and individual existence by focusing on three main aspects: consciousness of time, history and memory.

The first section of this chapter will consider the rational negative valuation of contingent, individual existence (as determined by the law of perpetual creation and destruction), together with the resulting speculative effort to objectify the consciousness of internal time. This effort of objectivization, which characterizes both the Hegelian and the Freudian approach to self-consciousness, involves the transition from a particular, temporally-determined subject to a pure, timeless subject of knowledge, so that the latter organizes and sanctions the experience of the former, its interaction with the external world. The most significant implication of the process of objectivization, which existential thought opposed and Surrealism tended to embrace despite certain reservations, is that it tends to homogenize the mode of existence of the thinking subject and the pure, timeless being of the ideal objects of thought. Existential thought emphasizes the irreducible character of lived time and of 'natural' experience; it attaches special significance to discontinuity, to arbitrary, sudden changes, which reveal the heterogeneity between thought and existence.

The second part of the chapter concentrates mainly on existential and Surrealist reactions to Hegel's understanding of history. The complete rationalization of time in Hegel's philosophy corresponds to a conception of 'history' as Logos of time, as 'chrono-logy'. The notion of 'chrono-logy' that I introduce in this chapter refers to the link between Hegel's doctrine of Spirit (as the conceptual rather than 'real' historical evolution of self-consciousness) and the tradition of onto-theo-logical thought that identifies God with the rational understanding of Logos or Absolute Spirit within the Hegelian phenomenology. History as 'chrono-logy' thus refers to the ontological implications of a complete rationalization and homogenization of the consciousness of time, which affects the interpretation of God as much as the interpretation of contingent, individual existence.[1]

Against the hierarchical rather than the linear temporal order of the three stages in the phenomenology of spirit (consciousness, self-consciousness and reason), existential thought constructs an argument that finds support in Kierkegaard's critique of Hegel as well as in the biblical interpretation of time. Whereas Surrealism rejects even the rational concept of God, which Hegel makes perfectly compatible with his understanding of History and Spirit, the existential writers object not only to this rational construal of God but, more significantly, to Hegel's fundamental premiss and the method leading to his identification of God and Absolute Spirit. The God of Abraham and Job, the God invoked by Kierkegaard and Pascal against rationalist theologians, is credited by Chestov and Fondane with the power to reverse time and 'to make what happened not have happened'. This position of faith involves a radical questioning of the concepts of causality and objectivity. The existential critique of the status of historical facts will be examined in relation to Chestov's and Fondane's considerations on the death of Socrates.

The last part of the chapter will be devoted to the relationship between time and memory, as illustrated by the existential interpretation of the notion of anamnesis. In existential thought, Plato's argument from reminiscence is related to an eschatological perspective of time and history. Chestov and Fondane combine Plato's enigmatic definition of philosophy as the 'practice of death' and his observations on the process of anamnesis in order to oppose the rational negative evaluation of individual life and open up its temporality to a different sphere of being and of truth. Surrealism explored the aesthetic potential of mental phenomena linked to memory along the lines of Freudian psychoanalysis, without adopting Freud's therapeutic approach but at the same time carefully avoiding the implication of an eschatological investigation—the existence of a transcendent, immortal soul. As I shall argue, the existential analysis of consciousness attempted to break the postulated unity of mental phenomena and to point to the heterogeneity of rational recollection and anamnesis: the two are mutually exclusive, and the latter should not be dismissed as an error of thought—an accidental distortion of the former. According to the existential interpretation, anamnesis is a perfectly legitimate return to rather than a fallacious recollection of another sphere of being and a different dimension of time. This peculiar understanding of 'reminiscence' in existential thought will be analysed with reference to Nietzsche's idea of the eternal return and to Kierkegaard's notion of 'repetition'.

Lived Time and the Question of Being

The analysis of time forms an intrinsic part of any configuration of consciousness and subjectivity. It is not only the relationship between internal processes of consciousness and the external world that rests upon an interpretation of time, but also the fundamental problem of the objectivity of external objects and the question of causality. Our claims to objective knowledge rely on the interpretation of time insofar as the relationship between internal processes of consciousness and the external world can or cannot justify such claims. The great historical divide and the contrary conclusions arrived at by the empiricist and rationalist philosophers concerning the possibility and limits of objective knowledge can be said to originate in the manner of answering questions that ultimately have to do with our understanding of time. The existential line of argument traces such questions as the objectivity or the universal and necessary character of cognition back to an original investigation of time. This genealogical approach constitutes an attack on Kantian and post-Kantian philosophies, which attempted to bridge the gap between the empiricist and rationalist traditions. It is in particular designed to counteract the scientific arguments leading to the implicit indictment and devaluation of contingent, individual existence.

From the scientific point of view, which seemed to hold the promise of the only firm foundation for modern philosophy, experience itself yields no necessity and provides no basis for universal, unquestionable criteria of knowledge. As Chestov repeatedly argued, the modern philosopher no less than the ancient Greek philosopher finds himself unable to derive any necessary, absolutely certain conclusions from experience and attempts to circumvent this obstacle by elevating himself above contingent conditions, above the realm of arbitrary, unpredictable changes. Any change that cannot be subsumed under an intelligible, universal rule potentially threatens to shatter the entire edifice of knowledge. In 'Le changement et le temps',[2] Chestov traces this negative perception of change, potentially destructive rather than beneficial, to the original interpretation of time emerging from experience and empirical observation: everything that exists 'in time' and is subject to change will have to die and disappear in the end. According to Chestov, the link between 'time' and 'death', forged in man's empirical consciousness since ancient times, led people to deify the unchangeable, the immutable, the eternal. The perishable character of anything contingent, including human existence (constantly menaced by unpredictable changes and death), conversely gave indisputable value and precedence to things that seemed to evade the law of perpetual creation and destruction and therefore promised to restore order and stability in a changing, arbitrary world. Having come to the conclusion that the only certain truth of contingent, temporal existence is death, ancient as well as modern philosophers placed their hopes in the immortal, unchangeable realm of ideas. The fundamental principles of formal logic and mathematics provided the only secure foundation for philosophical thought, the model on which any other laws and principles could be established through analogy, with equal certainty and necessity, precisely insofar as such fundamental principles seem exempt from change and destruction—they have no empirical origin, cannot be derived from experience, and are non-temporal. The existential critique of this scientific foundation of philosophical knowledge concentrates on two major objections, explicitly thematized in Chestov's and Fondane's work:

1. The analogy between the principles of formal logic and mathematics on the one hand and the principles of philosophical thought on the other is neither unquestionable nor inherently legitimate.
2. These principles themselves do have a traceable origin in time; they depend on rather than pre-determine human experience and are as such subject to possible change.

The existential argument is that, as long as philosophical investigation is governed by man's fear of arbitrary, temporal phenomena and by man's corresponding need for order, stability and necessity in all things, the search for truth will be defined by analogy with mathematical and formal logical principles—the only sources of certainty and necessity. Therefore, philosophers will seek to show that everything conforms to these principles, which no longer depend on or originate in man's own manner of posing the question of knowledge: they actually dictate the conditions of all knowledge for all time, independent of experience and ultimately even of human existence. This is how, over and above the condition of mortal human beings, eternal, autonomous principles come to enjoy what Chestov ironically calls 'the life of ideas':

Les idées vivent d'une vie absolument autonome, libre. Comme si les hommes n'existaient pas. [...] Et nous 'comprenons' cela; il nous semble que c'est très bien, que cela doit être ainsi, que cela est parfaitement conforme à nos conceptions dernières, empruntées à la science 'royale', les mathématiques. Les mathématiques ont l'idée de la droite, l'idée du point, celle de la surface. [...] Avec une nécessité qui fait notre joie, les idées donnent naissance à d'autres idées. Avec *nécessité* précisément, et une nécessité réjouissante, parce qu'elle nous enlève toute responsabilité pour leur agissements et nous est un exemple de régularité, d'immutabilité et d'obéissance à une loi suprême. Les médianes et les bissectrices ne peuvent échapper à leur destin: aujourd'hui comme hier, comme demain, maintenant comme dans l'infini du passé ou comme dans l'infini de l'avenir, à la face des hommes, des anges, des démons, elles se coupent toujours au même point. Elles ne craignent pas le temps destructeur.[3]

As Chestov argued in his polemic with Husserl, to which this extract implicitly refers, the analogy between philosophical and mathematical principles always operates to the detriment of human, individual existence. The truth that Husserl described as 'one and the same, whether men or non-men, angels or gods apprehend and judge it' tends to homogenize not only different spheres of cognition but also different spheres of being. Husserl's theory of truth reaffirmed the ancient correlation between thought and being and arrived (within the wider framework of his concepts of intentionality and of self-evidence) at what Quentin Lauer rightly calls 'une logique complète de l'être', 'une identification de ce qui est et ce qui est vrai: est ce qui est vrai et est vrai ce qui est posé par la raison'.[4]

Chestov argued against both the premiss of this investigation—the exclusion of empirical, contingent existence—and the implications of the coextensive concepts of truth and being resulting from a philosophical search for absolute certainty carried out in perfect agreement with the principles of formal logic and mathematics. The ideal 'timeless' being of these principles (such as the principle of contradiction or the fundamental principles of geometry) dictated much more than the conditions of objectivity, truth and absolute certainty: they determined the a priori conditions of being over and above human existence, which was excluded from consideration. The further implications of Husserl's theory can only be appreciated in view of his breathtaking positing of absolute truth and certainty as independent not only of the existence of the thinking subject itself but of the existence of the human species, of the existence of the world, of causal connections and of time.[5] Chestov argues that this complete autonomy of truth and of the correlative concept of being (as self-evident, true being) is reached by means of an illegitimate transition from logical and mathematical principles to philosophical first principles—a mistake described in logic as μετάβασις εἰς ἄλλο γένος (a transition into another field). Although the analysis carried out under these circumstances does seem to have an exhaustive and unquestionable character, there always remains an irreducible residuum of being, 'le résidu irrationnel de l'être', which as Chestov observes should be valued for what it is: a surplus, not a 'lack'[6]—something that scientific thought cannot account for, but that nevertheless exists.

The search for the criteria of necessity and strict universality of knowledge places a special emphasis on the values of homogeneity and of continuity above all. This means, on the one hand, that the unified concept of being (which homogenizes different spheres of existence) is defined in relation to the similarly homogeneous concept of truth that remains 'one and the same' for whoever apprehends and judges it; on the other hand, it means that the homogeneity of being requires and actually relies on the homogeneity and continuity of time. As Chestov argued in 'La vie des idées', the fundamental laws of geometry (such as that concerning the median and the bisector), on which philosophy models its principles, are valid today as they are yesterday, tomorrow, now and in the infinite of the past or in the infinite of the future. No other being, and least of all the mortal, empirical thinking subject itself, can hope to defy time in this way and acquire the timeless, absolute status of ideal objects.

As Chestov and Fondane often remarked, this interpretation of time and timelessness, as related to real vs. ideal objects, has to do with the rationalization of experience that Husserl, following the path opened by Kant's First Critique (and, in a different sense, even by Hegel), pushed to its last consequences. The unitary character of time, or rather the Kantian thesis of spatio-temporal unity, which affirms that there must be only one time and one space—one unified (spatio-temporal) framework of empirical reality by which all experience and its objects are circumscribed—is closely related to the necessary unity of consciousness as well as to the possibility of conceptualizing experience (which actually underpins the unity of consciousness). What all this means is that, although experiences occur in time and yield no necessary connections at the empirical level, they can nevertheless be constituted as experiences of a law-governed, objectively ordered world insofar as they belong to the one and only unified spatio-temporal framework, and insofar as the subject of such experiences can identify them as his own within the same unified framework, which also predetermines his receptivity. The thesis of the unity of consciousness, as well as the possibility of self-consciousness corresponding to this unity, thus remain inseparably linked to the homogeneity of time and the homogeneity of experience—the possibility of conceptualizing experience within a given, unified framework.

Yet, as Chestov pointed out to Husserl, despite ever-renewed efforts to provide a uniform, unified account of time and experience, and make even arbitrary changes or irrational residua seem homogeneous with the general explanatory framework, any deep probing into the origin of our first philosophical principles 'throws time out of joint'. According to Chestov's recollection of his discussions with the German philosopher, the two of them had independently of each other found themselves faced with Hamlet's dilemma over being and time ('To be or not to be [...]'; 'The time is out of joint [...]').[7] Their response to the dramatic, categorical formulation of the question of time, which as Chestov remarked required an equally categorical, 'either-or' choice of method (reminiscent of Kierkegaard's uncompromising *Either/Or*), reflected their opposed understandings of the aims and the 'utility' of philosophical investigation. Whereas Husserl decided to restore the 'joint in time' and provide an absolute, unshakeable foundation for truth at all costs (even if that meant completely disconnecting truth from human existence), Chestov attempted to situate human existence and the living individual at the centre of philosophical investigation, precisely insofar as the broken 'joint in time' makes this re-evaluation possible, by opening up a fissure in rational, homogeneous analysis that could not and should not be repaired at the expense of individual life.

The 'utility' and ultimate consequences of either of these positions cannot possibly be grasped from the exclusive perspective of their immediate impact on reality; as Chestov observed with reference to religion and metaphysics: 'tout le monde exige que la religion et la métaphysique soient visiblement, indubitablement utiles ici même, *sur les plages du temps*'[8] [my emphasis]. The full significance of the existential interpretation of time only comes out in relation to the reduction and devaluation of individual existence, which always implicitly underpins the process of objectification and homogenization carried out within the rational analysis of the concepts of being and time.

Fondane spells out in clear, uncompromising terms the devastating implications of the logico-mathematical analysis of time in relation to personal human existence by referring to Chestov's critique of transcendental and absolute idealism and to his distinctive notion of 'tragic man'. In his article on Husserl (1929), Fondane does not hesitate to equate the perfect homogeneity obtained by means of phenomenological reduction with an effective death of the individual subject:

> Husserl veut donc lui aussi réduire le monde qui apparaît à toute intuition humaine, absurde, étrange, fantastique, capricieux, injuste même et peut-être horrible, aux proportions d'une ruche lumineuse, où ne subsiste que le seul mécanisme de la Raison. Cela ressemble bien au fameux: 'le calme absolu règne à Varsovie', en surimpression sur un monceau de cadavres.[9]

The re-insertion of the existential, individual subject and of his tragic, irreducible plight back into philosophical reflection 'throws time out of joint'. Fondane like Chestov correctly intuits and criticizes the effects of the rational (logico-mathematical) analysis that can only grasp things 'sous la seule forme de l'homogène, réduisant la multiplicité à l'unité, le discontinu au continu, le concret à l'abstrait, le réel à l'idéal'. The question of individual existence has to do with an irreducible multiplicity, with discontinuity and heterogeneity—as opposed to the postulated unity of consciousness and to the ideal unity and continuity of time. Homogeneity and unity are the indispensable features of a description that aims to establish not only the principles of thought for all times but also the objects, the basic entities to which these principles can apply; and for this to be possible 'at all times', such objects (or ideal units of meaning, in the case of phenomenological analysis) need to be self-identical, immutable. Like any mathematical judgement, the objects of a rigorous scientific analysis must have a self-identical, self-evident meaning, which is valid not just 'once', under particular circumstances, but 'once and for all' and as such is infinitely repeatable, remaining always the same.

In his article 'Le Procès de la raison', Fondane rightly contrasts the status of real, individual objects and the repetitive, self-identical nature of ideal objects of thought. Discontinuity, arbitrary change, ephemerality, as linked to contingent existence, are thus opposed to repetition, immutability, timelessness. The rationalization of experience involves the replacement of the former characteristics by the latter; it brings the multiplicity of particular, dispersed instances under the generality of the concept. Thus, the concept of 'man' ('l'homme en général'), as Fondane remarks, reduces the unique and 'illogical' condition of *this* living man to the general and intelligible condition of *any* man: similarity prevails over dissimilarity, continuity over discontinuity. The existential approach places a special emphasis on 'les actes discontinus eux-mêmes, les pensées exceptionnelles et justement aux moments où elles se font jour, aux moments catastrophiques, où l'automatisme de la conscience dite "objective", éclate et saute, où la liberté se fait prendre un seul instantané au magnésium'.[10]

To the self-identical meaning and timeless status of mathematical judgements, Fondane opposes the exceptional, revelatory nature of what he calls 'jugements discontinus' or 'actes discontinus', mental acts that bring out the discontinuity and heterogeneity of lived, personal experience, outside the categories of rational thought.

Fondane's contention needs to be considered in relation to the distinction that Husserl introduced between the act of judging (e.g. my act of affirming that $2 \times 2 = 4$) as causally determined and the meaning of judgements (e.g. the self-evident truth that $2 \times 2 = 4$) as independent of causal and temporal determinations and independent of the thinking subject itself. Fondane, like Chestov, refuses to accept this crucial distinction, which ultimately justifies both the suspension of contingent existence and Husserl's claim to absolute, autonomous truth based on the self-evident meaning of judgements. It seems that, from the existential point of view, 'discontinuous judgements' are those that cannot be dissociated from the temporally determined mental act that affirms them and from discontinuous rather than continuous, unified notions of time and consciousness. Such judgements, as Fondane suggests, are paradoxical, contradictory; they concern the absolute freedom and the ontological status of individual, living man, as well as the freedom, omnipotence and ontological status of God. More accurately, such judgements attempt to capture the 'vivantes contradictions'[11] that belong to the irreducible residuum of being—individual man as much as the living God.

Situating individual man and the 'discontinuous judgements' related to his existence, his freedom, his relation to God at the centre of philosophical investigation explodes the postulated ideal unity of time as well as the corresponding unity of consciousness. Roger Gilbert-Lecomte provided one of the clearest formulations of the discontinuous, fissured and multiple rather than unitary configuration of consciousness from the perspective of individual existence:

> La personnalité humaine est le lieu géométrique de consciences multiples parallèles — une infinité d'espaces parallèles au nôtre — à cloisons étanches, hormis les rares stries de fissures pour l'intuition de drames simultanés, vécus sur une infinité de plans divers — leurs reflets, leur échos fragmentaires, fugitifs, séparés, étant la discontinuité même de la conscience.[12]

The collapse of the unitary spatio-temporal framework and of the correlative unity of consciousness reveals an infinity of different, parallel spaces and innumerable simultaneous events whose fleeting, fragmentary nature makes manifest the discontinuity of thought processes. In contrast to the unity and homogeneity that characterize the rational analysis of time and consciousness, existential thought brings out 'les antinomies tragiques', the heterogeneity of different yet coexistent dimensions of consciousness, the discontinuity, the ruptured, non-unitary temporality of the tragic, individual man, as Fondane argues: 'il n'est pas difficile de trouver l'arbitraire, le caprice, l'absurde dans ce qui vit, pas difficile de saisir que la grandeur de l'homme n'est pas dans sa fausse unité, mais dans le nombre d'antinomies tragiques qui se disputent son être'.[13] The existential interpretation of time from the point of view of the arbitrary, absurd character of life privileges the moment over duration, places a special emphasis on isolated instants, 'les moments catastrophiques' when the discontinuity and the tragic antinomies of reason are revealed, when the ideal unity of consciousness is broken and man stands alone, face to face with the inexplicable, the irrational, the irreducible heterogeneity of another dimension of being. The discontinuous character of lived time, the inner contradiction or rupture of consciousness also defined the position of *Le Grand Jeu*. In 'La nature de la conscience vivante', Gilbert-Lecomte noted: 'Ils croient que la vie est successive, quand elle est une rupture perpétuelle [...] la conscience humaine n'est aucunement successive, continue, complète, immédiate'.[14]

In contrast to rational thought, which presupposes continuity and logical progression between judgements, existential thought emerges from momentary 'discontinuous judgements' or, as Fondane says, 'procède par sauts, par mutations'.[15] Thus, the discontinuity in time, which is 'out of joint', corresponds to a discontinuity or rupture in logical reasoning, which from the existential point of view restores the actual right of the individual to place itself over and above ideal objects at the centre of philosophical reflection, by means of a reversal that Fondane refers back to Kierkegaard's thought: '[C]e qui ressort du drame kierkegaardien c'est *le droit absolu de l'individu de mettre "son drame" au centre du problème philosophique, dût-il faire éclater celui-ci en morceaux*'.[16]

This interpretation of time with reference to individual existence rather than to the objective and unified field of rational analysis also characterized the programme of *Discontinuité*. The atomized configuration of time as an arbitrary succession of disconnected moments corresponded, as in Fondane's own previously mentioned remarks, to a discontinuity at the level of thought, a deliberate fracturing of the logical, continuous chain of judgements:

Les actes, les gestes, les paroles, les événements de notre triste existence dont nous sommes à la fois le théâtre et les acteurs, il ne saurait être question pour nous de les réduire encore une fois à l'échelle pitoyable des valeurs et des hierarchies. [...] Ce n'est un concept ni une chaîne de jugements qui saurait trancher le problème du suicide et de son abandon. Dans n'importe quelle circonstance, toujours et à tout moment, la peur et le désir du néant forme la moelle de l'esprit.[17]

The hierarchical order of conceptual thinking no less than its homogeneity and continuity precludes any attempt to re-evaluate individual, empirical experience, as well as the wide range of affects that accompanies this experience but never seems to contribute anything to the process of thought or to the validity of judgements, insofar as the objectivity of judgements presupposes the exclusion of individual psychological variables. Husserl's distinction between the act of judging and the meaning of judgment was aimed precisely at the relativism attached to psychological interpretations. In contrast, existential thought used a genealogical account in order to bring out the inextricable link between the meaning or truth of judgements and the origin of these judgements in the human mind. This is also what Fondane's so-called 'discontinuous judgements' show: that eternal, immutable truths paradoxically originate in the temporally bound human mind, and that truth should not be disconnected from human existence and affectivity. The emphasis on extreme, irrational emotions—anxiety, 'le désir du néant'—that one finds in *Discontinuité* as well as in Fondane and Chestov (especially with reference to Kierkegaard, or sometimes to Dostoevsky) is closely related to the existential interpretation of time, in particular to the privileged significance of isolated moments, situated outside continuity and duration. In contrast to the homogeneity and neutrality of the objective account of time, the subjective, existential interpretation focuses on unique, privileged instants, on 'catastrophic moments' whose exceptional character is signaled by an excessive emotional charge. Because of this emotional intensity, such moments seem to be 'outside time', abstracted from the neutral, homogeneous flow, standing out as sudden, instantaneous flashes of inspiration. The notion of 'Événement', explicitly thematized in *Discontinuité*, suggests that these isolated moments in time have a similar meaning to 'revelation'—in the sense of Fondane's 'discontinuous judgements', which are valid not in virtue of a syllogistic demonstration but simply because of the emotional evidence (or, as Daumal would say, the 'absurd evidence') that is thus suddenly given to the individual:

Nous sommes prêts à tout abandonner pour un Événement que nous ne préparons guère ni n'espérons plus.

C'est en vain que nous escaladons les degrés de la connaissance. Lointain ou proche, nécessaire ou non, nous attendons toujours un Événement, nous cherchons une idée fixe.[18]

The last article of *Discontinuité* makes clearer the interpretation of time related to the notion of 'Événement'. The title of the article, 'Cette flèche blanche nous a frôlés dans le jour. C'est le dernier avertissement de l'archer imaginaire', is itself an extended metaphor of time, and the author seems concerned with the 'tragic antinomies' of time-perception, as he contrasts, in similar manner to Fondane, individual existence under the sign of perpetual change and the 'immobility' of eternal truths:

Je voudrais supprimer le Temps et parfois l'allonger, mais je change sans cesse tandis qu'autour de moi règne l'immobilité la plus obsédante. Vérités anciennes que j'admire, guérison du Temps ou fièvre de l'Amour, je disparais encore un immense gant à la main. Gant disproportionné à la taille de monde...[19]

Most probably 'the imaginary archer's warning' of the title refers to death itself, or the anticipated disappearance whose signal is the outsize glove, a metaphor equally used by Surrealists. In the First Manifesto, Breton associates the symbolic letter 'M'—for *Mémoire* (and one could add for *Mort*)—with the gloves 'shrouding' the hands of participants in a fictitious rite of passage, by which Surrealism promised to introduce its adepts to the secret society *par excellence*—Death: 'Le surréalisme vous introduira dans la mort qui est une société secrète. Il gantera votre main, y ensevelissant l'M profond par quoi commence le mot Mémoire.'[20] This is not the only example of the intense preoccupation with time and death in early Surrealism. Before the famous inquiry on suicide and even before the official inauguration of the movement in 1924, *Littérature* launched an inquiry on writing, which Breton recalls in *Les Pas perdus* with reference to the subtle connection between time-perception and writing:

Pourquoi écrivez-vous? s'est un jour avisée de demander *Littérature* à quelques-unes des prétendues notabilités du monde littéraire. Et la réponse la plus satisfaisante, *Littérature* l'extrayait à quelque temps de là du carnet du lieutenant Glahn, dans *Pan*: 'J'écris, disait Glahn, pour abréger le temps'. C'est la seule à laquelle je puisse encore souscrire, avec cette réserve que je crois aussi écrire pour allonger le temps.[21]

The editor of *Discontinuité* similarly reflected on the possibility of 'allonger' and 'supprimer le Temps' as a remedy against an immutable, objective order of things. Breton himself deliberately misquoted Pascal in order to support the subjective interpretation of time proposed in *Les Pas perdus*: 'je me moque de ceux qui disent que le temps me dure à moi et que j'en juge par ma montre: ils ne savent pas que j'en juge par fantaisie'.[22] Early Surrealism seems to adhere to the same atomized, discontinuous perception of time that characterizes existential thought. In *Discontinuité*, this similarity is further reinforced when the notion of 'Événement' becomes associated with the revelatory power of love. Under the magnifying glass of intense emotion (whether 'l'Amour, guérison du Temps' or anxiety, 'élan vers le "non être"'), time looks fragmented, its moments unusually 'enlarged' and its continuity suspended. Fondane, who contributed one poem entitled 'Le Regard de l'absent' to *Discontinuité*, captures this vision of time when he writes 'l'heure est pleine de trous'. The void and discontinuity revealed at the heart of subjective time-perception elicit different interpretations in Surrealist and existential writings, despite their shared preoccupation with distortions and suspension of objective time.

When Surrealism extols the freedom of dreams, of induced sleep, reverie and other related states in relation to time, one can look for the significance of this liberating discovery in what Freud called the 'timelessness' of the unconscious. Surrealism revelled in this timelessness, which in a sense also presided over the birth of the poetic image as the encounter of distant, unrelated aspects of reality. Such an understanding of poetry in its privileged relationship to time inspired Breton's famous remark in 'Le Discours sur le peu de réalité' (which later became his unintended epitaph): 'Je cherche l'or du temps.' The Surrealist exploration of the unconscious dispensed with psychoanalytical therapeutic finality and the attempted reinsertion of 'timeless' traumatic events into the linear chronology of consciousness. Freudian psychoanalysis argues that there is no reference to time and no negation in the unconscious, whereas consciousness presupposes temporal organization, along with negation, control of action, motor inhibition, which are involved not only in every thought process but also in the reality principle itself.[23] However, far from trying to find a way out of the labyrinth of his own desires and imagination, guided by the thread of the reality principle, the Surrealist explorer preferred to remain forever 'trapped' in this labyrinth like an enchanted Theseus; such is the gold-seeker's 'grande aventure':

[...] je cherche l'or du temps. Qu'évoquent-ils donc ces mots que j'avais choisis? À peine le sable des côtes, quelques faucheux entrelacés au creux d'un saule — d'un saule ou du ciel, car c'est sans doute simplement l'antenne à grande surface, puis des îles, rien que des îles... la Crète, où je dois être Thésée, mais Thésée enfermé pour toujours dans son labyrinthe de cristal.[24]

The labyrinth is thus the topography of the timeless unconscious that Breton aspired to preserve and reconcile with reality itself. The possibility of reconciliation presupposed a homogeneity between the two systems, although the Surrealist understanding of this homogeneity no longer tipped the balance in favour of consciousness as the regulating, ratifying power.[25] The systematic erosion of the control exercised by consciousness over the unconscious involved the implicit disruption of the temporal organization that characterizes consciousness. The privileged use of the present tense as an indeterminate temporal reference in automatic writing and in accounts of dreams aims to create a disorientation, a 'suspension' of time that interrupts the logical chain of thoughts and breaks the causal links between successive events. Everything can then follow or appear to follow from everything. The timelessness of the unconscious thus throws into doubt the fundamental principles of rational thought—for instance causality or the principle of contradiction. Breton intuited that one of the implications of the timeless, purely affirmative character of the unconscious was that within the framework of the dream itself nothing could in principle disprove the certainty and apparent authenticity of the events presented to the sleeper's consciousness: 'pourquoi n'accorderais-je pas au rêve ce que je refuse parfois à la réalité, soit cette valeur de certitude en elle-même, qui, dans son temps, n'est point exposée à mon désaveu'.[26] The Surrealist effacement of the boundary between dream and reality seems strikingly similar to the existential argument against the absolute validity of reality-testing criteria, which ultimately prove to be indistinguishable from the self-evidence of dreams or the certainty attached to a given mode of temporal perception ('cette valeur de certitude [...] dans son temps'). The same questions of certainty and objectivity as essentially related to temporal organization are involved in the existential 'fight against self-evidence' and the existential positing of the paradoxical awakening to oneself (with reference to the paradox of the sleeper, analysed in Chapter 1).

Breton correctly identified the dialectic at work in the Freudian analysis and used the analogy with Hegel in order to introduce the notion of 'surréalité' as the result of the dialectic synthesis between dreams and reality: 'Je crois à la résolution future de ces deux états, en apparence si contradictoires, que sont le rêve et la réalité, en une sorte de réalité absolue, de *surréalité*.'[27] More than once, starting with the sentence that comes after this statement in the First Manifesto ('C'est à sa conquête que je vais, [...] trop insoucieux de ma mort pour ne pas supputer un peu les joies d'une telle possession'), Breton associates the promise of an 'absolute reality' with joyful indifference towards death, as if to signal the overcoming of the corrupting, destructive action of time. From the existential point of view, the Surrealist solution to the 'tragic antinomies' of life, along the line of Hegelian dialectic, does nothing to challenge the rational indictment of individual, temporal existence but actually lends support to the idealistic attempt to homogenize all forms of existence and bring them under one, unified, timeless concept of being. It is not sufficient, as Breton might have thought, to shift the emphasis from the conscious to the unconscious system in order to recapture the meaning and value of the otherwise ephemeral human existence, limited by the law of creation and destruction. The unconscious corresponds to a topography whose rules have universal validity rather than arbitrary, individual application. Being free from any reference to time, the unconscious circumvents rather than actually solving the temporal antinomies of individual life.

In contrast to the Surrealist aspiration to an 'absolute reality', the existential critique of rationality aims to maintain the contradiction, the 'tragic antinomy' pertaining to the individual consciousness of time, and to restore the topography of thought proposed by Kierkegaard: 'Voici la première topographie à relever: "Oser à fond être soi-même, oser réaliser un individu, non tel ou tel, mais *celui-ci*, isolé devant Dieu."'[28] Fondane's comments on Kierkegaard thus point to a topography of the mind that is not concerned with the immanent, dialectically reconciled opposition between consciousness and the unconscious but with the radically other dimension of being, with the transcendent singularity of God and at the same time with the obliterated, irreducible existence of the living individual. This particular, unique, living individual in its one-to-one encounter with the 'living God' describes the condition of the 'tragic man', which underlies the new topography of the mind. The implicit existential equivalence between Kierkegaard's affirmation of personal existence as an act of courage ('oser être soi-même') and the emergence of the 'tragic man' is suggested by the similar aphorism from Nietzsche's *Birth of Tragedy*, which Fondane quotes in support of his critique of rational knowledge: 'Oser maintenant être des hommes tragiques: car vous devez être délivrés.'[29]

The interpretation of tragedy in relation to the condition of the living individual is actually bound up with the existential interpretation of time, and it most clearly brings into view the opposition to psychoanalysis on the one hand and to Surrealism on the other. Psychoanalysis approaches religious phenomena and tragedy itself (as exemplified by the archetypal story of Oedipus) with reference to the neurotic model and to the process by which unconscious narcissistic self-love has to be humiliated and taught the reality principle, or rather brought to consciousness, under rational control and within the temporal organization of the dominant system. Before Freud, Schopenhauer was one of the first to argue that madness was rooted in an affliction of memory and that 'soundness of mind' differed from insanity in respect of the mind's temporal organization—the ability to have 'perfect recollection' of events. Freud's interpretation of Oedipus from the perspective of pathological behaviour highlights the need not only for a reconciliation of opposites similar to the Hegelian account of the 'unhappy consciousness' but for an attempt to 'restore the joint in time' and provide an immanent, dialectical solution to the 'tragic antinomies' of human existence.

From a different perspective, which has nothing to do with 'correcting' the temporal distortion of the tragic consciousness in conformity with the reality principle but rather with an aesthetic overcoming of antinomies, Surrealism nevertheless arrives at a homogeneous account of time that tends to restore the 'broken joint' in time and re-establish one unified framework by suspending the lived, temporal flow and blurring the boundaries between desire and reality. This unflinching aspiration towards dialectical unity and homogeneity made Fondane, who was otherwise perfectly aware of the partial convergence between the existential and Surrealist critiques of rational thought, declare that Surrealism managed ultimately to obscure rather than solve the problem of individual existence: 'En effet, c'est du gros, bien que parfois du merveilleux, truquage. C'est le plus habile piège que l'on a inventé pour embrouiller le problème de notre existence et le rendre à jamais insoluble.'[30]

The existential topography of thought, focusing on the condition of the solitary individual, of the tragic man, exposed the fallacious overcoming of death and temporality through the homogenizing rational analysis of being from the perspective of eternal, timeless categories. Fondane's denunciation of the 'truquage' involved in the Surrealist interpretation of time within the dialectical, unifying framework of psychoanalysis and Hegelian philosophy implicitly referred to the conceptual reduction of personal existence and to the emergence of 'l'existence anonyme, ou l'"On"', 'la vie de l'On', by which 'la mort est escamotée'. He fully elaborates this argument in his article on Heidegger's early work, 'Martin Heidegger sur les routes de Kierkegaard et de Dostoiewski', in which, despite serious reservations, he nevertheless acknowledges the preoccupation with time and existence common to both Husserl's estranged disciple and existential thought:

L'être de l'existence et, pour nous rapprocher, l'être de l'existence humaine, se caractérise par le fait que son essence est inséparable de son existence: son 'essence est d'exister' et non, comme pour Husserl, d'être une conscience de l'existence. Dès que l'Être nous est donné, il est donné *dans* le monde; le temps est son sens fondamental, le temps en tant que 'succession qui passe'. 'L'être dans le monde' a deux modes de comportement; l'un, l'existence quotidienne, banale [...] il s'agit de l'existence anonyme, ou l'On, création de l'omnitude [...]. Mais il y a également le moi dépouillé de l'On, l'être authentique, 'l'existence qui s'est retrouvée elle-même', la voix de l'existence 's'angoissant dans sa situation délaissée'. [31]

The existential critique of rationality focuses exclusively on this unique, individual self—*le moi*—which it restores outside the conceptual, reductive framework of being in general, and which it relates, unlike Surrealism, to the 'authenticity' of despair, tragedy and anxiety. However, what distinguishes existential thought from the Heideggerian understanding of contingent existence with reference to time and anxiety is the link that the former establishes between the arbitrary, discontinuous configuration of time and the irreducible residuum of a transcendent form of being.[32] Neither the Surrealist notion of 'merveilleux' (which Breton carefully dissociated from the miraculous) nor the Heideggerian concept of Being allowed for the relationship of individual existence to something radically other than itself (i.e. God) or for a contradictory interpretation of time that opened up contingent existence to permanence, as Fondane argued: 'Si l'"essence de l'être est d'exister", comme le prétend Heidegger, il nous importe au plus haut point de conserver malgré et contre tout cette essence — et de lui donner enfin le *prédicat de l'éternité*.'[33] The simultaneous affirmation of temporality and eternity in relation to human existence maintains the 'tragic antinomy' of individual consciousness of time and situates this paradoxical notion of being at the centre of philosophical investigation. The existential emphasis on discontinuity, on 'catastrophic moments', on the rupture between rational thought and being leads to a critique of history and chronology within the Hegelian phenomenology of Spirit.

The Historical Dimension: Chrono-logy as the Absence of God

Existential thought uncovers the 'living contradictions' of the individual consciousness of time as simultaneously related to contingent experience and to conceptual analysis. The homogeneity between being and thought, which Hegel's phenomenology reaffirms, following a long philosophical tradition that goes as far back as the Eleatic school and the Stoics, relies on the possibility of conceptualizing experience and providing a homogeneous account of time. The concept of history in Hegel, which does not simply correspond to a real historical development but, most significantly, to the stages in 'the formation of a consciousness of the spirit',[34] accomplishes a complete rationalization of time in so far as the phenomenology of Spirit can also be said to be the chrono-logy of Spirit, the Logos of its manifestation in time.

The homogeneity between different types of consciousness as well as the homogeneity between different spheres of being, which emerges from the chrono-logy of Spirit—from the historical dialectical movement by which consciousness rises to knowledge—constitutes a solution radically opposed to what Fondane hoped to achieve when he proposed to preserve individual existence as the essence of being and to attribute to it the predicate of eternity. It is true that through the overcoming of the self-contradiction that defines the Unhappy Consciousness the particular individual and the universal, the essential and the inessential, the ever-changing and the Unchangeable, interpenetrate each other and form an objective unity within Hegelian dialectics, but this moment of so-called *oneness* presupposes the renunciation of anything related to the particular individuality—its will, its actuality, its immediate self-consciousness. The content of the action that mediates consciousness, Hegel says, 'is the extinction of its particular individuality which consciousness is undertaking'.[35] This process of mediation as described in the *Phenomenology of Spirit* involves 'self-renunciation', '*actual* sacrifice' (§229), 'surrender of one's own will' (§230) as a necessary stage in overcoming the 'wretchedness' of self-division, precisely by renouncing anything particular, 'the protean Changeable', in favour of the 'consciousness which becomes aware of individuality in general in the Unchangeable' (§210).

Existential thought most strongly resisted the conceptual transition from the particular individual, from the 'individual man' (Fondane argued) to 'man in general', even when, as in Hegel's phenomenology, the resulting universal, unchangeable essence is supposed dialectically to incorporate what has been superseded. Fondane no less than Chestov often remarked that the movement of 'elevation' or self-abnegation—the ethically justified flight from the subject of willing, desiring and feeling—betrays a fundamental disparagement of individual, contingent existence, which in turn reveals a deep-seated fear of the 'protean Changeable', the ephemeral and especially the unpredictable. The irrational residuum of any rational analysis, the ever-changing, vanishing individual life has to be renounced, 'sacrificed', if it cannot be reduced to the Unchangeable, the pure universality of thought. Such is the logic of the movement in time, the chrono-logy of Spirit, and the meaning of the history of Spirit: 'having learned from experience [...] that the *vanished individuality*, because it has vanished, is not the true individuality, consciousness will abandon its quest for the unchangeable individuality as an *actual* existence, or will stop trying to hold on to what has vanished' (*Phenomenology of Spirit*, §217).

In contrast, what Fondane affirmed when he demanded that eternity should be the predicate of existence was nothing other than the possibility of the 'unchangeable individuality' as an actual existence. From the perspective of existential thought, whose positive evaluation of Unhappy Consciousness stemmed from a passionate vindication of contingent existence, inward self-division signaled precisely the refusal to abandon the vanishing, changeable individuality. This was the paradoxical, 'salutary' wretchedness of the self, which existential thought wanted to preserve, to reinforce rather than supersede in the emancipatory journey of consciousness through its various stages.

Fondane argued that the Surrealist understanding of poetry in relation to time and reality weakened the essential link between artistic creation and the temporal, changing mode of existence and thus mirrored the Hegelian conception, which necessarily eliminates or 'extinguishes' particular individuality within the dialectical progression towards the unity of consciousness:

Quand le philosophe prononce: eau, arbre, feuille, il est persuadé d'avoir sauvé du naufrage des choses périssables et transitives, les essences de cette eau, de cet arbre, de cette feuille-ci, etc., qui peuvent désormais périr: 'Les voici qui s'échappent au temps!' Faut-il penser que le rôle du poète n'est que de seconder le philosophe dans ces travaux d'usinage où le réel vivant se transforme constamment en réel chimique, en concepts intelligibles?.[36]

According to Fondane, Breton's way of attributing the predicate of eternity to perishable, transitory existence was no different from the philosophical—that is, Hegelian—solution to the same problem. The intended homogeneity between real and ideal being, between temporal and non-temporal individuality, defines the idealistic project at all periods from Plato to Hegel, a project that succeeds insofar as it eliminates or reduces the accidental, the unpredictable, the arbitrary to the uniform and the intelligible:

M. Breton eut hautement et hautainement refusé les durs 'attendus' de Platon concernant la poésie; mais il se laisse séduire par un Hegel disant *les mêmes choses exactement*, éliminant dans sa définition de la poésie: imitation, réalité, accidentel, passionnel, erreurs d'imagination etc., toutes choses qui agaçaient déjà Platon et qu'il n'arriva guère à évincer.[37]

Fondane's argument finds strong confirmation in the conception that Breton expounds in 'Misère de la poésie' (1932) with reference to Hegel's comments on the evolution of art leading to the destruction of the individuality exalted by Romanticism:

l'absolue négation de tout ce qui est fini et particulier. C'est l'unité simple qui, concentrée en elle-même, détruit toute relation extérieure, se dérobe au mouvement qui entraîne toutes les êtres de la nature dans leurs phases successives de naissance, d'acroissement, de dépérissement et de renouvellement; en un mot repousse tout ce qui impose des limites à l'esprit.[38]

The ideal being, which in its simple unity escapes the law of perpetual creation (γένεσις) and destruction (φθορά) and overcomes the natural, perishable condition of finite or particular real being, is no longer fraught with contradiction but has achieved homogeneity through the negation of particular individuality and final synthesis. Breton posed the question of homogeneity in the context of the 'history of automatic writing' as part of the Surrealist activity: 'comment s'assurer de l'homogénéité ou remédier à l'hétérogénéité des parties constitutives de ce discours dans lequel il est si fréquent de croire retrouver les bribes de plusieurs discours; comment envisager les interférences, les lacunes'.[39] Writing was not expected to help shorten, lengthen or relativize time any more: it now concerned the possibility of smoothing over the gaps, of uncovering the homogeneity, the neutrality of an ideal unity, abstracted from the irreversible flux of time. Breton's affiliation to Hegelian thought comes out most clearly from the anticipated dialectical reconciliation of all antinomies of the real world in the Surrealist notion of a 'point suprême' where all contradiction will cease to exist.[40]

The progression leading to a final synthesis describes the manifestation of Spirit in time, the logic of the unifying movement that 'life' or nature itself lacks according to Hegel: 'organic life has no history', only spirit has a history insofar as 'history' is something different from mere repetition—the perpetual creation and destruction characterizing nature. In the sphere of nature and, more significantly, at the level of individual life, there cannot be any escape from time, any form of 'eternity' or absolute permanence. But this is exactly what Fondane stated: that the essence of man, of the particular individual, is none other than his actual existence, and that this existence should be granted the attribute of eternity, however paradoxical or contrary to logical laws this may seem. Gilbert-Lecomte expressed the same thought in a lapidary note: 'L'homme éternel, l'absent hagard de la nature',[41] which deplores without however endorsing the actual inexistence of 'eternal man'. Gilbert-Lecomte's note presents us with the haunting image of an obliterated presence rather than the acknowledgement of a logical impossibility. The ruptured, contradictory consciousness of this eternal yet individual, contingent mode of being—'l'homme éternel'—corresponds to the discontinuity, the temporal heterogeneity of life or in Hegelian terms 'organic life', 'nature'.

The other great Absent from the homogeneous account of time is the living God, a paradoxical notion that matches the no less paradoxical existence of 'eternal man'. Chestov not only remarked that individual man and the living God constantly remain outside the philosophers' field of interest—'tous les philosophes [...] sacrifient avec la même indifférence l'homme vivant et le Dieu vivant'[42]—but also emphasized the close relationship between the existence of eternal man and the 'living God', the God who adopted human form and temporal existence in order to support man's 'irrational enterprise':

Nous ne sommes nullement obligés de croire, pour satisfaire aux idées mal comprises des penseurs hellénistiques, que Dieu s'est fait homme afin que l'homme cesse d'être lui-même et devienne une parcelle idéale du monde intelligible. Cela pouvait être obtenu d'une façon toute 'naturelle', quoi qu'en disent les théologiens médiévaux. Si une intervention 'surnaturelle' fut nécessaire, c'est qu'il s'agissait de soutenir l'homme dans sa folle entreprise, dans l'affirmation absurde de son 'moi'. Dieu devint homme pour que l'homme, surmontant ses hésitations (qu'avait exprimés la philosophie hellénistique), maintînt sa décision première.[43]

Man did not commit a culpable impiety when he ventured outside the perfect unity of the One into particular, contingent existence. The philosophical indictment of individual life from the perspective of ideal, eternal being cannot be maintained in relation to the 'living God', whose essence is no other than man's own essence—existence. Unlike the rational concept of God, to which philosophy denies the attribute of 'life', the existence of the 'living God', of the God of Job and Abraham, supports the existence of individual man. Chestov's as well as Fondane's critique of Greek and modern philosophy is especially directed against the Hegelian speculative denomination of God as Absolute Spirit, which has at least two consequences: it renews the medieval logocentric doctrine that reconciles the living God of the Bible and God according to reason, and it reduces individual existence to an insignificant accident along the historical path of Spirit. As Chestov argued with reference to Hegel's conception of history: 'L'homme pour lui n'est qu'un moment de l'histoire de l'Esprit, et dans l'Esprit l'homme est déjà surmonté.'[44] But the supersession of particular individuality, which defines the moment of Stoic self-abnegation, makes possible according to Chestov the glorification of the idea over and above the rights of living beings: 'à la place de l'être vivant, réel, on érige l'idée, les hommes ayant perdu tout espoir de sauvegarder les droits de l'être vivant'.[45]

Similarly, God finds no place in the pantheon of eternal, non-temporal ideas insofar as He preserves the attribute of life, of actual existence in time. The Hegelian doctrine not only reconciles revelation and 'thinking spirit' (*denkender Geist*) within God as Absolute Spirit but also replaces the historical aspect of revelation and of any other temporally determined entity that takes place 'only once' with the immutable, timeless character of a judgement made 'once and forever'. In their critique of Hegel's philosophy of religion, Chestov and Fondane especially emphasized the implications of the speculative effacement of anything particular, of living beings and of real events whose essential feature is precisely a singular, instantaneous manifestation ('only once'), as contrasted to the permanent, always identical and repetitive nature of ideal beings: 'La naissance du Fils, l'incarnation, la mort du Christ étaient également çoncus non pas comme des faits particuliers qui s'étaient produits une fois, mais comme existant d'une façon permanente.'[46] The temporality of actual existence is thus replaced by the 'eternal' and necessary character of truth posited in relation to rational principles of thought. The obliterated singularity of religious experience, or the equally unique character of any particular empirical experience, which yields no necessity, no permanence, and therefore no firm criteria of truth, is directly related to the mode of being and the temporality of the living God, of living man as well, and cannot be reduced to the universal, necessary being of ideal objects, whose truth is a measure of their speculative abstraction from time. The homogeneity between the two interpretations of time and between the levels of empirical experience and of rational truth, which Hegel's justificatory project of an 'absolute religion' set out to achieve, amounts to a systematic extinction of any particular, contingent, living content of religious experience.

The Hegelian exegesis of Christianity and its central theme of reconciliation within the Trinitarian schema closely follows the doctrine of λόγος (logos), which as Chestov notes was used for the first time by the Jewish-Hellenistic thinker Philo in order to make biblical revelation compatible with the *lumen naturale* of rational analysis. From this perspective, Fondane passionately argued in *La Conscience malheureuse* that history as conceived within the Hegelian rationalization of time, or what I have here called history as 'chrono-logy', as the teleological progression of spirit toward self-consciousness in the Absolute Spirit, is nothing other than 'une absence totale de Dieu'. Hegel's philosophy of religion aims to smooth over and logically to reconcile the rupture between the finite and the infinite, the 'broken joint' in time, the self-division of the Unhappy Consciousness. In a poem entitled 'Le Temps est hors des gonds', Fondane insistently points to the link between logical discontinuity and catastrophic events or 'underground' alternative modes of thinking on the one hand and the actual production or 'generation' of lived time as contrasted to the homogeneous conceptual interpretation of time on the other: 'voici que le temps est venu des actions impossibles'; 'voici que le temps est venu de la nouvelle apocalypse'; 'voici que le temps est venu des actions souterraines'; 'voici venir le temps prodigieux des fous'.[47] It is highly significant for the existential critique to recall here that the essentially tragic view of history that Hegel proposes with reference to the perpetual conflict between man and his destiny or to the 'ruse of reason' in history nevertheless combines with an equally pervasive logic of historical development, or as Jean Hyppolite remarks: 'The pantragedism of history and the panlogism of logic are one and the same.'[48]

Against the panlogism that pervades the pantragedism of Hegel's conception, existential thought affirms the irreducible conflict between the living individual and the ineluctable movement of history, a conflict that is the source of inner self-division but also of a different interpretation of time, highlighting the moment (*l'Instant*) as opposed to the historical continuum. As Fondane argues in *La Conscience malheureuse*, 'le point de contact fatal entre l'éternité et le temps' corresponds to an instant, a moment in which the ruptured continuity of history uncovers the truth of a 'dieu de paradoxe et de scandale' rather than the homogeneity displayed by the speculative unity of man and God in Absolute Spirit.

Like Chestov, Fondane refers to Kierkegaard's critique of Hegel when contrasting 'la vérité révélée' to the speculative concept of truth. Revealed truth does not emerge from a mediated relation or a syllogism, as in Hegel's description of the movement of dual consciousness towards 'oneness', but from the personal 'témoignage' of the paradoxical encounter between the finite and the infinite in one discontinuous instant.

In this sense, Fondane comments on Kierkegaard's notion of faith: 'être chrétien c'est être, par conséquent, un témoin de la mort de Dieu, un témoin du scandale, un "témoin de la vérité"'.[49] Revealed truth is not immutable and 'eternal' like objective, rational truths but grounded in temporal, empirical experience, in particular facts that occur 'only once' and whose temporal discontinuity further uncovers a paradoxical discontinuity at the level of being itself. Chestov actually defines the mode of being of the living God in these terms, as opposed to the homogeneity and continuity of the concept: 'Dieu est absent. Dieu n'est pas toujours. Lui aussi apparaît et disparaît. On ne peut même pas dire de Dieu qu'il est souvent. Au contraire, d'ordinaire, le plus souvent, Il n'est pas'.[50] When individual man calls out from the depth of despair (*De profundis clamavi ad te, Domine*), the living God may or may not be present; in any case, there is a clear difference between this discontinuous mode of being and the later phenomenological concept of being as 'self-evident being', whose 'presence' is determined with reference to the self-identical and immutable meaning grasped by consciousness in the process of intentional constitution. In existential thought, both truth and being are open to the temporally grounded 'discontinuous judgement' of living man and of the living God rather than delimited by the definitive, immutable meaning of logico-mathematical propositions as in Husserl's phenomenology or the equally definitive 'verdict of history' within Hegel's teleological conception.

One of the most interesting illustrations of this point, which Chestov and Fondane repeatedly bring up in their critique of the Hegelian conception of history as well as of Husserlian phenomenology, refers to the status of historical facts and historical development in relation to human existence. The argument concerns Socrates's death by poisoning. Chestov points out that, although Socrates's poisoning as a historical fact has an empirical origin in time (399 BC) and should consequently have a logical end in time, any reasonable human being from Plato (Socrates' disciple) to present-day philosophers cannot escape the evidence, the immutable truth of the judgement 'Socrates was poisoned.' There seems to be no higher power in the universe that could reverse this 'verdict of history'. Chestov moreover observes that from the logical point of view one cannot even differentiate between judgements such as 'Fido the dog was poisoned' and 'Socrates was poisoned.' The argument actually probes into the foundations of historical truth (the classical correspondence theory, the law of causality) as well as the foundation of philosophical truth in general, established through analogy with the principles of logico-mathematical reasoning. On the one hand, any attempt 'to reverse' or annul the historical fact of Socrates' poisoning would come up against the Hegelian causal, irreversible configuration of time and the overall rational character of history. On the other, given two valid judgements, Husserlian phenomenological reduction equalizes descriptive and value judgements: 'red colour' is as good a phenomenon as 'love' or 'sacrifice', and in this sense the apparently provisional suspension of ontological questions (as Kolakowski remarks) 'promises to overcome not only epistemological but ethical relativism'.[51]

However, the existential argument elaborated by Chestov and Fondane questions much more than the homogeneity between descriptive and value judgements. It poses the question of the homogeneity between the 'truths of fact' and the 'truths of reason', or rather between 'temporal', contingent truths and a priori 'eternal truths':

tout ce qui a un commencement doit nécessairement avoir une fin; seules les vérités *a priori*—vérités indépendantes de l'expérience—ont le droit au prédicat de vérités éternelles. Par conséquent, une constatation de fait, une vérité d'expérience, celle par exemple qu'en l'an 399, Socrate fut empoisonné à Athènes, devrait mourir un jour, tout comme elle est née un jour. On ne peut tout de même admettre une vérité éternelle qui n'existait pas avant l'an 399, qui est née seulement en 399![52]

The transition from the truth of fact to the historical truth that despite its temporally determined origin acquires the value of an indisputable, 'eternal' truth discloses the same illegitimate process (the so-called μετάβασις εἰς ἄλλο γένος) that makes possible the homogeneity between real and ideal objects, between different modes of being. The apparent autonomy of the concepts of truth and of being in relation to the temporal law of γένεσις (creation) and φθορά (destruction), which seems to apply only to human, individual existence and 'real objects', actually obscures the origin in time of such concepts (even that of 'eternal', 'uncreated' truth), their genealogical source in experience, in the mind of the temporally bound thinking subject itself. As Chestov and Fondane argue, the concepts of truth and being should depend on and support temporal, individual existence rather than acquire absolute, 'eternal' validity independent of human existence. If, as Plotinus says, philosophical investigation is the most important thing (τὸ τιμιώτατον), our definitions of truth and being should enable us to grant the attribute of eternity to real, temporal individuals rather than to ideal objects and 'truths of reason'. Chestov suggests that this re-evaluation of the concept of truth heralds the existential attempt to situate the living, particular individual at the centre of philosophical reflection, as the one most important thing, over and above the truth of historical or logical judgements:

Plotin sentit soudain probablement, mais pour un instant, que τὸ τιμιώτατον c'est précisément Socrate, ce Socrate hic et nunc qui était le maître de Platon, que les Athéniens empoisonnèrent sur les accusations d'Anytos et de Mélithe. Il comprit que la philosophie ne pouvait pas se passer de Socrate vivant et qu'il valait mieux désobéir pour une fois à la raison que de refuser à Socrate une place dans le monde nouménal.[53]

The sudden refusal to accept the 'verdict of history', which existential thought illustrates with reference to the 'self-evidence' of the ignominious death of Socrates, also comes out from Surrealist writing, most prominently from Breton's passionate defense of Mayakovsky, who committed suicide on 14 April 1930. The first issue of the new official publication of the Surrealist movement, *Le Surréalisme au service de la révolution*, which was published the same year in July, includes an article devoted to the Russian poet's tragic death, in which for the first time Breton critically reflects on the possible clash between the revolutionary, collectivist cause and individual existence. The Hegelian need to supersede particular individuality and to reconcile it dialectically with universality no longer seems a straightforward imperative of revolutionary action, and Breton unashamedly talks of 'notre *nécessité individuelle*' in relation to the equally irresistible call of love. He emphasizes the revolutionary scope of love in Surrealism and his determination 'à vouloir déduire le devoir révolutionnaire du devoir humain le plus général', while noting with amazement the criticism Engels levelled against Feuerbach's return to metaphysics through an apology of sexual love: 'je crains qu'Engels, qui nous a habitués à plus de sévérité, ne fasse ici que de la critique de tempérament'.[54] Breton refuses to accept Engels's obtuse understanding of art, along the lines of socialist realism, as well as the objections brought by what he calls 'un révolutionnaire politique' against 'un poète révolutionnaire', and he reiterates in defense of Mayakovsky's exemplary destiny (which he compares with Rimbaud's) the two major themes of the First Manifesto: the invincible power of love and the individual need for absolute freedom. Especially on the latter question, that of freedom, Breton joins the existential fight for a fundamental re-evaluation of individual existence, of individual desire, above all other extraneous ethical or logical imperatives.

The insoluble contradiction that Breton observes between the 'common duty' or interest and individual impulses ('Cette apparente dérision: ne pouvoir faire passer, tout en étant révolutionnaire, l'intérêt commun le plus haut par dessus le désintérêt personnel') seems to leave his belief in revolution unscathed; nevertheless,

Mayakovsky's death occasions one of the most uncompromising statements on the unsurpassable character of individual existence in Breton's writing, which echoes the passionate existential revolt against Socrates' poisoning: 'Sur [les poètes] pèse toujours, il faut bien l'avouer, en 1930, la menace de dépeuplement du monde par la perte d'un seul être.'[55] The existential critique of Hegel's conception of history leads to a similar conclusion: that no idea of progress and ultimate perfection can justify the loss of even one individual life. In this sense, Chestov often referred to the 'unreasonable' demand made by the Russian writer Belinsky, who from the imagined high point of Hegelian historical development wanted to have a full account of each and every victim of Philip II's inquisition and of all the other victims of history, 'mes frères par le sang' as he said.[56] The individual revolt against the definitive 'verdict of history' attempted to expose the disparagement and actual destruction of personal existence that seemed to be an inevitable part of any idealistic advance towards ever higher stages in the development of 'humanity', of 'man in general'. Unlike later Existentialists such as Camus, Chestov took a much less optimistic view of the myth of Sisyphus as related to the idea of progress in history:

Il faut croire que les hommes, ces perpétuels Sisyphes, se remettront de nouveau, dans cinq ans, dans dix, dans vingt ans, à rouler patiemment l'immense rocher de l'histoire, et s'efforceront, tout comme naguère, de le hisser dans les tourments au sommet de la montagne jusqu'à la prochaine catastrophe, jusqu'à ce que se répètent encore tous les malheurs dont nous fûmes les témoins.[57]

The editors of *Discontinuité* made similar critical comments on evolutionist theories, especially in the wake of the unprecedented horrors of the First World War. One of their programmatic articles, 'Nos idées', rejects the idea of 'objective progress' and sets the catastrophic events of the contemporary historical scene next to the single, emblematic execution of Socrates more than two thousand years ago in a manner strongly reminiscent of Chestov's own comments on Socrates' death: 'Le progrès objectif n'existe pas. En quoi l'époque de Socrate est-elle inférieure à celle des gaz asphyxiants et des guerres mondiales?'[58] The existential critique of history as chrono-logy, as complete rationalization of time and experience from a teleological perspective, attempts to restore the meaning of individual life and death and to make the interpretation of time conform to this particular meaning. The contingent, particular event of one single death thus becomes a source of philosophical reflection no less significant than the disappearance of the entire universe. As Gilbert-Lecomte noted: 'La fin du monde — serait-elle individuelle au lieu d'universelle — n'en est pas moins proche.'[59]

The members of *Discontinuité* challenged the Hegelian view of history from the point of view of an understanding of time centred on the particular living individual and on the ironic, defiant affirmation of 'la culture du moi — l'egoïsme' as 'le but de la perfection' or 'le bonheur dans son sens le plus large'. These critical opinions highlight the unsurpassable character of life, 'Vie avec un grand V', and replace the conceptualized 'marche vers le progrès' of consciousness by the individual need for self-affirmation: 'faire le maximum possible pour la réalisation relative de son "moi"'.[60]

Insofar as Surrealism can be said to have maintained an integrationist position in relation to the most influential theoretical advances of its time (Freudian psychoanalysis, Hegelian phenomenology, Marxism), conversely existential thought can be said to have attempted to transcend its historical context. Roger Gilbert-Lecomte expressed the latter tendency in a long passage in his article 'La lézarde', in which his critique of Hegel's conception of history bears a strong resemblance to Chestov's comments on the same subject. One of the first articles Chestov published in France, 'Les Favoris et les déshérités de l'histoire: Descartes et Spinoza' (1923), argued that philosophy cannot be on the one hand 'the most wakeful consciousness', the opposite of 'somnambulism', as Hegel declared and on the other the unavoidably limited manifestation of a particular, temporally determined stage in the evolution of Spirit. Indeed, Chestov remarked, if philosophy and the particular individual ('son of his people, of his country') cannot escape the limitation of the spirit of their time, then truth itself, the result of historically determined philosophical reflection, remains 'une vérité accidentelle, limitée', which men must nevertheless accept as binding and definitive:

> Mais si ce qu'il a dit de l'esprit du temps est exact, la philosophie, ou ce que Hegel appelle de ce nom, est un pur somnambulisme, et la conscience philosophique est la conscience la plus assoupie.[61]

Gilbert-Lecomte points to the same terrible 'blindness' or numbing sleep that characterizes human existence inasmuch as the historical perspective of the evolution of spirit and the pre-determined relationship between philogenesis and ontogenesis guide our understanding. The meaning of individual life is forever obscured and continues to elude man's 'blind' interpretation of time as the ineluctable unfolding of a teleology of Spirit. Caught within the frame of the particular moment or stage in the evolution of Spirit, man can only fulfil, give expression to, the essence of that given stage, while remaining unaware of his own 'blindness' or of the 'somnambulism' that philosophical consciousness seems bound to perpetuate:

Quelle cécité, quel engourdissement, quel sommeil écrasent tous les hommes? [...] Où va l'esprit humain, l'esprit total de tous les hommes? Mais aujourd'hui, où va chaque homme, du jour de sa naissance à la nuit de sa mort? Il n'en sait rien, il dort. S'il ne dormait pas, il ne pourrait supporter de vivre le temps d'un clin d'œil clair.[62]

The unbearable lucidity or awakening that discloses the real nature of human existence, its discontinuity, its fleeting manifestation between the moment of birth and that of death, constantly succumbs to the 'drowsiness' of idealistic argument, which situates all possibility of meaning and of being at the level of the supra-individual, continuous, teleological progression of Spirit in time. This view of contingent individual existence as justified only in relation to the meaningful higher order of History was seriously undermined by the scale of destruction and loss of life during the First World War. The more general, fundamental objections to Hegel's conception seemed particularly relevant within the context of post-war questionings about the meaning of life and the role of creative personalities in the history of human thought: 'Nous vivons une heure très sombre. Jamais nuit plus noire à nulle heure de l'Histoire. Il s'agit de l'Histoire de la pensée humaine, réflétée dans l'esprit des créateurs.'[63] As Chestov similarly argued, philosophical consciousness remained soundly asleep through the darkest night of history, which extended further back than the disparagement and destruction of individual life in the First World War, to the symbolic moment in the history of thought when man killed God. The two issues—the death of the living, individual subject and the death of God—are actually interconnected within the existential critique of speculative thought: 'La philosophie n'est possible qu'à la condition que l'homme soit prêt à renoncer à soi-même et à se détruire. [...] Ils sacrifient avec la même indifférence l'homme vivant et le Dieu vivant.'[64] The revolt against this double sacrifice of human life and of the living God involves the process of awakening from what Chestov calls the 'one thousand and one nights' of the history of speculative philosophy. The critique of the Hegelian doctrine of history as 'chrono-logy' leads to an interpretation of time that focuses on synchronicity rather than causal sequentiality, on 'anamnesis' rather than historical objectivity.

Memento Mori: Time and Reminiscence

The traditional, rationalist analysis of the concept of time aims to solve the connected problems arising from the relativity of time-perception and the inescapable finitude of human existence. If time exists only in relation to a thinking and perceiving subject rather than having independent, objective existence, and if this subject is a temporal being itself, not exempt from change and eventual destruction, then any interpretation of time remains flawed by relativity and prone to insoluble contradictions. Newtonian physics and Kantian idealism carefully distinguish time from temporal things, the things to which time, movement and chronological order apply. But whereas Newton introduces the notion of 'absolute time' (time as something existing in its own right), which avoids the contradiction involved in saying that time has only an ideal, mind-dependent existence although it can nevertheless exist independently of temporal things (of which the subject's mind itself is one), Kant maintains the ideality of time, its dependence on the human mind and the human 'point of view', yet establishes it *a priori*, prior to any experience in time and independent of the temporal existence of the empirical perceiving subject. In Kantian transcendental idealism, time is the a priori form of intuition that makes experience possible. Long before Kantian apriorism and Hegel's critique of the 'unhappy consciousness', Zeno's paradoxes had shown that any coherent account of time in relation to a thinking and perceiving subject had to bridge the gap between 'natural' perception and the rational analysis of temporal processes. What Kant's conception of time provided was precisely the logical homogeneity between these two incompatible levels of interpretation: empirical experience and rational understanding. The thesis of temporal unity, which postulates that there must be only one time (as there must be only one unified spatial framework), played a crucial part in the process of conceptualizing experience.

The unified field of possible experience ensured the exhaustive character of the description of any temporal and spatial phenomena—

nothing was left out, as there could be nothing outside the one, unified spatio-temporal framework. The existential critique of the transcendental idealist interpretation of time focused on this conceptual claim to exhaustiveness, derived from the postulated unity of time and of space in its relationship to the unity of consciousness. While sharing the view that time had a relative and ideal (that is, mind-dependent) ontological status rather than an absolute and real existence, Chestov and Fondane called into question the Kantian axiom regarding the unity and homogeneity of the spatio-temporal framework, which defined the limits of the so-called 'human perspective' and predetermined any possible experience without exception. Although Kant admitted at least in principle that there might be another perspective beyond the apparently all-inclusive, exhaustive human viewpoint, he also categorically stated that we as humans can know nothing about such an alternative, heterogeneous mode of representing things, neither can we have any experience of it (within the unknowable realm of noumena). The existential thinker not only affirms the possibility of a different, heterogeneous perspective, which contradicts our conceptual assumptions about the unity of consciousness and the spatio-temporal framework underlying this unity, but also advances the paradoxical possibility of experiencing such an alternative perspective from within the human system of reference itself.

In their critique of the transcendental idealist interpretation of time, Chestov and Fondane often start from a consideration of Plato's doctrine of *anamnesis*. If all knowledge is but recollection, as Plato argues in the *Phaedo*, then the state preceding any process of learning does not correspond to complete ignorance but to a lapse of memory, to forgetfulness. Chestov mentions in this respect the passage in which Plato speaks of birth as the moment when oblivion replaces the memory of a previous existence, as an angel comes down and touches the baby's upper lip, which thereafter preserves the mark of this fleeting touch.[65] Yet, Chestov comments, there are moments in life, privileged intervals of lucidity (*lucida intervalla*) when the individual suddenly remembers, or rather, 'awakens' from the oblivion that characterizes all existence in time. According to Chestov, such moments bring out the discontinuity, the gaps in the logically derived continuity and homogeneity between two otherwise incompatible spheres of being and between two radically different interpretations of time. The existential line of thought thus combined Plato's argument from reminiscence and Plotinus's notion of 'awakening' in order to emphasize the contradiction resulting from the simultaneous affirmation of opposite modes of time perception and of different levels of description.

Whereas the Platonic doctrine led to the postulation of a realm of eternal, timeless Ideas, the existential re-evaluation of anamnesis highlighted the later surreptitious insertion of living individual beings into the noumenal realm, as attempted by Plotinus with reference to Socrates. Chestov closely follows the subtle dislocation that occurs in the structure of the argument from reminiscence, when the intended demonstration no longer concerns the immortality of the soul in general but the question of the immortality of *this* existing individual in particular:

> Plotin, de même, parle ouvertement non seulement de l'idée de l'homme, mais aussi de l'idée de Socrate, sans crainte des contradictions irréconciliables, ainsi qu'il appartient aux grands philosophes. Une fois il écrit que les idées se rapportent au général, non à Socrate mais à l'homme (V, 9, 12). Mais une autre fois il déclare sur le même ton catégorique (V, 7, 1, début): s'il y a un Socrate et si l'âme de Socrate existe, il y a aussi un Socrate en soi, pour autant que l'âme individuelle existe là-bas (dans l'univers nouménal).[66]

Plotinus's paralogism aims to restore the reality and being of the contingent, particular individual as opposed to the apodictic, timeless existence and absolute reality of Ideas. The fallacy of the demonstration, which deliberately adopts an appearance of logical consistency, undermines speculative reasoning from within by questioning the universal validity of the principle of contradiction.

Similarly, Fondane explores the antinomies that emerge on the boundaries of logical argumentation when he comments on Heidegger's affirmation that the essence of being is existence. If this is the case, Fondane remarks, then existence should not only be maintained (rather than overcome in the process of conceptualization) but should also be endowed with the predicate of eternity insofar as it is defined in terms of 'essence'—the consistency of the concept of essence itself depends on this subsequent attribution of timelessness and immutability to existence. Such a derivation can certainly be exposed as illegitimate, because the premiss already involved a logically fraudulent identification between contingent existence in time and 'essence', but Fondane's intention was simply to disclose the conceptual gap that separates Heidegger's initial postulation from his ultimate replacement of existence by the concept of Being, which smoothes out the logical incongruity of the premiss. Instead of maintaining the contradiction between temporality and timelessness within the mode of being of the particular individual, so that the contingency of this individual would be simultaneously posited along with attributes of absolute reality and eternity (in the manner in which Plotinus talked about 'the idea of Socrates'), Heidegger preferred to ensure the homogeneity of his interpretation of time through speculative mediation. The existential critique of Heideggerian ontology reopens an older debate concerning the priorities that govern philosophical discourse: are logical consistency and the mediation of opposites more important, indeed more necessary, than the possibility of inquiring freely about such admittedly contradictory yet fundamental matters as the immortality and timelessness of individual human beings?

The paradoxical argumentation that existential thought adopts in resetting the priorities of philosophical investigation subverts the conceptual framework justifying the legitimacy or illegitimacy of any question likely to unsettle the order of a priori rationalist discourse. Whereas the attribution of eternal being and absolute reality to transitory, contingent individuals would be met with the strongest resistance by the principle of contradiction and would be declared illegitimate (insofar as this question is bound to elicit a nonsensical answer), the same principle of contradiction would find nothing invalid or unacceptable in a statement such as 'Socrates was poisoned', which, despite the startling association of 'Socrates' and the predicate 'poisoned'[67] remains as immune to logical objections and the passing of time as $2 \times 2 = 4$. Chestov argued that Plato developed his doctrine of anamnesis in response to the logical and historical legitimacy bestowed on the inconceivable 'truth' of Socrates's poisoning. However, Chestov remarked, in the transition between Plato's immediate reaction to Socrates's death and the definitive, intelligible thought that the philosopher could impart to the masses, a crucial intuition was lost: the 'absurd' possibility of preserving and carrying through into eternity the contingent existence of a particular individual, despite the opposition of the principle of contradiction.[68] The existential interpretation of anamnesis focuses on the profound sense of revolt, on the sudden insubordination to the basic principles of thought, that must have inspired Plato's daring postulation of an invisible realm of being. It aims to uncover the ' prediscursive' level at which this intuition coincided with the particular rather than the universal conditions under which human mortality can be superseded.

The reminiscence of an eternal order of things with specific reference to one particular living individual as the determined subject of a process of thought that can modify the perception of time and open up a different ontological perspective is directed against the apodictic judgments and syllogistic argumentation used by transcendental idealists like Kant in their refutation of the doctrine of the immortality of the soul. In the *Critique of Pure Reason*, Kant illustrates 'the function of reason in its inferences'—the universality of knowledge—with reference to a syllogism concerning precisely the mortality of human, temporal beings:

All men are mortal
Caius is a man

Caius is mortal

Although, as Kant admits, the proposition 'Caius is mortal' could be derived from experience, the syllogism is designed to establish 'a concept (in this case, the concept "man") that contains the condition under which the predicate of this judgment is given'.[69] Existential thought contests on the one hand the a priori analytic character of the major premiss ('All men are mortal'), which means that the predicate 'are mortal' is already contained in the concept 'man', while the full extension of this predicate (of the type 'All S are P') is not derived from experience—can be established a priori. On the other hand, existential thought also objects to the manner in which the conclusion then claims to restrict the predicate to a specific object ('Caius' or 'Socrates'), precisely on the basis of the major premiss considered in its full extension—'All men are mortal'. The validity of this type of postulation has to do with the foundations of a priori knowledge, with the very legitimacy of Kantian apriorism over and above the legitimacy of alternative modes of thinking (such as the paradoxical argumentation employed by existential thought).

It is interesting to note here the striking resemblance between the existential critique of the syllogistic deduction of the inevitability of individual death and Breton's remark from 'La Conféssion dédaigneuse':

Pierre n'est pas nécessairement mortel. Sous l'apparente déduction qui permet d'établir le contraire se trahit une très médiocre supercherie. Il est bien évident que la première proposition: Tous les hommes sont mortels, appartient à l'ordre des sophismes.[70]

Plato's argument from reminiscence is occasionally mentioned by Breton with reference to the 'Surrealist' use of language, as in the following fragment from the First Manifesto, which suggests that the effect of estrangement ('dépaysement') resulting from the arbitrary employment of words taken out of their usual context actually corresponds to the subliminal recollection of their long-forgotten original meaning:

Il m'est arrivé d'employer surréellement des mots dont j'avais oublié le sens. J'ai pu vérifier après coup que l'usage que j'en avais fait répondait exactement à leur définition. Cela donnerait à croire qu'on n''apprend' pas, qu'on ne fait jamais que 'réapprendre'.[71]

The remark correctly grasps the relation between anamnesis and the Freudian notion of the unconscious as a 'storehouse' of obliterated memories. Psychoanalysis proceeds through 'successive retro-references' or 'associations'[72] to disclose the first foundation, the deepest layer of meaning, in an endeavour that, considering the Freudian configuration of the unconscious as timeless, can be said to rejoin Plato's uncovering of an eternal realm of Ideas through anamnesis. However, the crucial difference between existential thought and Surrealism lies in the opposite conclusions derived from the negation of the inevitability of individual death. Whereas Breton was not prepared to admit the idea of the 'immortality of the soul' and the existence of God, existential thought might be said to have adopted a more consistent position in relating the refutation of the necessary temporal limitation of individual life to the immortality of the soul and the existence of God. Although the previously quoted remark about Pierre who 'is not necessarily mortal' stands in blatant contradiction to both Kant's and Hegel's judgements about individual existence, Breton continued to seek the solution to the problem of Pierre's (or Jacques Vaché's) death in Freudian and Hegelian arguments likely to support the Surrealist immanentist, aesthetic and ethical answer to human mortality.

In existential argument, anamnesis exceeds the limits of mere recollection and becomes an active process of 'awakening', through which the subject simultaneously projects itself into the 'future' (in the sense in which it situates itself in the timelessness beyond the moment of death) and returns to itself in a present that coincides with and 'reconstructs' rather than passively recollecting the past, down to the timelessness before birth. Roger Gilbert-Lecomte explicitly mentions Plato's argument from recollection in support of the idea of an active process, 'la lutte contre l'amnésie',[73] which uncovers a different dimension of thought, another type of knowledge, 'la poésie, mode de connaissance'. The notion of 'paramnésie', by which Gilbert-Lecomte designates the fight against oblivion, against the 'amnesia' associated with rational, speculative thought, illuminates an alternative configuration of time based on simultaneity rather than causal linearity, as well as an alternative view of human existence and of reality. Like Fondane, Gilbert-Lecomte maintains the paradoxical affirmation of the eternal, timeless essence of temporal reality, which he relates to simultaneity and to a mode of perception which transcends the rational concepts of linear time and duration:

L'essence éternelle de la réalité
Simultanément
(car la simultanéité universelle opposée au concept de temps et de durée est le talisman nuptial qui permet de faire rentrer dans l'unité l'intelligence des prémonitions d'une part et de l'influence des rêves sur la malléabilité du monde extérieur d'autre part.[74]

According to Gilbert-Lecomte, 'prévoir c'est engendrer', and reality therefore is as much a result of our 'creative' power of dreaming or actively anticipating events as what we call 'learning' is the result of anamnesis. The two directions or dimensions of time-consciousness, anticipation and recollection, lose their extensional significance and become fused in an instant without duration, which defines the configuration of time in terms of 'universal simultaneity'. In contrast to the universality of syllogistic reasoning, Gilbert-Lecomte proposes '[une] généralité non conceptuelle mais sentie'. He relates simultaneity to the aesthetic potential of 'la lutte contre l'amnésie', to the aesthetic type of knowledge occasioned by 'la paramnésie' and 'l'émotion paramnésique', while ranging this active process of reminiscence among psychic phenomena ('un mécanisme psychique évidemment simultané') rather than attempting to give it syllogistic legitimacy.

Plotinus's paralogism concerning the possibility of 'awakening to oneself' and the attribution of the divine quality of immortality to a mortal human being also contains a simultaneous affirmation of God's existence and of absolute freedom, although the possible inference of immortality from the premiss of the relationship between God's existence and freedom has nothing necessary or a priori about it;[75] it is rather the result of 'daring', an act of defiance against reason (the Greek νοῦς) and against the syllogistic legitimacy of philosophical questioning, as Chestov points out:

Comment un mortel ose-t-il même songer à une telle destinée: se confondre avec Dieu et s'élever au-dessus de ce qui fut créé par le νοῦς? Et que signifie donc: 'se réveiller à soi-même?' Cela ne revient-il pas à accorder de la valeur à ce qui est soumis à la γένεσις et condamné à la φθορά? Cela n'équivaut-il à placer, contre toutes les traditions consacrées, cette chose destinée à périr, sous la protection d'une force 'essentiellement différente de la raison'? Enfin, le 'réveil', ἐγρήγορσις: sous ce mot se cache quelque chose de tout à fait inacceptable pour la raison: une contradiction interne. L'âme donc dort toujours et toute son activité rationnelle s'écoule pour ainsi dire en rêve; pour participer à la réalité, il faudrait, au préalable, se réveiller.[76]

The idea of awakening opens up an internal contradiction because it rejects the postulations concerning the unity of time and the unity of consciousness. If the thinking subject needs to 'awaken' in order to make any valid judgments about time and reality, then in fact, consciousness is not 'unified' but 'divided' between the usual state of sleep and the occasional 'waking' or lucid intervals. Internal division of the perceiving consciousness also discloses a division or rupture in time between the homogeneous, unified temporal framework corresponding to the 'sleeping' consciousness and the heterogeneous, contradictory temporality corresponding to the 'waking' consciousness. The latter replaces the conceptual, ideal homogeneity of the former with the contingent, real discontinuity of experience, which resists conceptualization. Whereas the former, homogeneous configuration of time presupposes a linear, 'one-dimensional' continuum underpinning the a priori, universal law of causality, the latter emphasizes discontinuity and simultaneity, illustrated by the paradoxical idea of a 'one-dimensional sphere'.[77]

In his article 'Memento mori (A propos de la théorie de la connaissance d'Edmond Husserl)', Chestov examines the hypothetical situation of a man who is asleep and dreams that he is the emperor of China, and that he is about to inscribe monograms on the surface of a one-dimensional sphere. Within the system of reference of the dream, the man's consciousness readily accepts the 'self-evident' character of his representations, and anything that might remind him of a different order of things (one in which he is not Chinese or, even more pertinently, in which a sphere by definition cannot be 'one-dimensional') is ruled out as contrary to the consistent logic of the dream. Similarly, Chestov suggests, the principle of contradiction and the limitations of logical reasoning maintain, within normal, 'waking' consciousness, the impossibility of even imagining a way out of what seems to be the only, all-encompassing spatio-temporal framework. Leszek Kolakowski remarked that Husserl's suspension of the natural standpoint provided a way of going 'beyond the island of consciousness' in order to attain a new, unprejudiced insight into things. But once the suspension has been accomplished, there is no possibility of ever reversing the process, of removing the brackets or posing again the question 'How can I leave the island?'[78] The exhaustiveness and absolute certainty to which phenomenological description aspires means precisely that there is no 'outside', nothing 'beyond', and nothing left out of the unified and unifying field of consciousness as ultimate system of reference.

Awakening occurs as a sudden reminiscence, 'un brusque *memento*', Chestov notes, as the accidental eruption of a different temporal configuration into an apparently uninterrupted, linear and homogeneous flux. Consciousness is ruptured by the emergence of this memento, which contradicts all four logical postulates governing possible experience: (1) nothing happens through blind chance (*in mundo non datur casus*); (2) no necessity in nature is blind, but always intelligible necessity (*in mundo non datur fatum*); (3) the principle of continuity forbids any leap in the series of appearances (*in mundo non datur saltus*); (4) the principle of continuity forbids any gaps or cleft between two appearances (*in mundo non datur hiatus*).[79] What is remembered in awakening relates precisely to blind chance, to unintelligible determinations, to leaps and gaps that punctuate the apparent continuity and exhaustiveness of the chrono-logical account of time. The interval in which the thinking subject 'remembers' its own death and looks back on its own temporal existence from a point situated beyond the logically unsurpassable limit posed by human mortality can be said to exist outside the linear continuum and causal sequentiality of rational argumentation.

Plato's doctrine of anamnesis opens up not only a different interpretation of time, but also a different understanding of philosophy itself as the practice of death—μελέτη θανάτου. Existential thought no longer situates death at the end of a linear progression from birth or creation (γένεσις) to destruction (φθορά); death becomes a starting point, an interval that recalls and restores the timeless value, the meaningfulness of individual life. In this sense,

Fondane writes in one of his articles: 'Il faut traverser la mort, le désespoir, pour en ressortir vivant.'[80] Artaud similarly emphasizes the positive, affirmative nature of the 'investigation of death' and relates it to the revelation of the divine: 'C'est pourtant dans l'investigation de la mort que nous rencontrerions le Secret de l'emprise divine et de la configuration spirituelle du monde.'[81] He further associates the disclosure of a second temporal and ontological dimension in death with the experience of hypnosis or of dreaming: 'Et j'imagine qu'il doit y avoir dans la mort cette inquiétude de l'homme qui dort et se demande avec angoisse si c'est vraiment un rêve.'[82] The 'awakening' to the paradoxical truth of the immortality of a temporal being emerges from the sudden confrontation with death, or rather from the sudden superimposition of temporality and timelessness in anamnesis.

Kierkegaard's notion of 'repetition' and Nietzsche's 'eternal return' both illuminate from different angles the existential interpretation of anamnesis as 'awakening to oneself (Plotinus' ἐγειρόμενος εἰς ἐμαυτον).[83] In contrasting the thought of the eternal return and the ancient Greek doctrines (especially those attributed to the Pythagorean school), Chestov brings out the opposition between powerful self-affirmation and idealistic self-abnegation, between Nietzsche's passionate commitment to life and the speculative, ascetic indictment of individual existence:

> Que pouvait lui donner la conviction que son existence, telle qu'il l'a vécue, avec toutes ses horreurs, s'était déjà déroulée un nombre infini de fois et se répèterait encore sans la moindre modification jusqu'à l'infini? Si Nietzsche n'avait vu dans l''éternel retour' que ce qu'y voyaient les pythagoriciens, il n'aurait pu y découvrir nulle raison d'espérer. Mais puisque cette pensée lui infusa de nouvelles forces, c'est qu'elle lui promettait autre chose que la simple répétition à l'infini de cette réalité qu'il connaissait.[84]

The correlation of 'eternal return' and 'amor fati' in Nietzsche's writing might suggest a position of fatalistic self-denial and Stoic resignation. However, Chestov focuses on the equally pertinent correlation of 'eternal return' and the 'will to power', in order to highlight the unprecedented affirmation of all aspects of contingent existence, including the ugly, painful, evil aspects, which idealistic doctrines seek to overcome through moral elevation, and which 'amor fati' polemically embraces: '*Amor fati*: let that be my love henceforth! I do not want to wage war against what is ugly. [...] And all in all and on the whole: some day I wish to be only a Yes-sayer', writes Nietzsche in *The Gay Science* (§276). Chestov attributes a crucial argumentative significance to this refusal to 'wage war' against the 'horrors of life'. The willed 'yes-saying' and the 'eternal return' subvert the foundations of modern epistemology, Chestov argues, by aiming to invest contingent, temporal being with the attribute of eternity: 'il cherchait à obtenir l'éternité pour ces choses, qui selon notre conception de la vérité, sont condamnés à l'anéantissement'.[85] The interpretation of time that corresponds to Nietzsche's thought of eternal return directly challenges the postulates of Kantian transcendental idealism, which as Chestov points out had already come under attack in Schopenhauer's doctrine of the world as will and representation:

Si le temps est une forme de notre connaissance, si, par conséquent, nous percevons comme passé, présent et futur ce qui en réalité se produit hors du temps, c'est-à-dire en même temps (c'est la même chose), par conséquent nous ne savons pas voir le passé et l'avenir non pas parce qu'une telle perception est en général impossible, mais à cause de l'organisation de nos facultés de connaissance. Mais ces facultés, de même que toute notre organisation, ne sont pas immuables. On peut admettre la possibilité d'exceptions parmi les milliards d'hommes normaux; on peut admettre l'apparition des cerveaux qui ne percevrons plus les phénomènes dans le temps, et pour lesquels le passé et l'avenir se confondront dans le présent; ils pourront donc prévoir des événements non encore accomplis et distinguer ceux que l'histoire a déjà engloutis.[86]

Unlike Schopenhauer, Nietzsche places the greatest argumentative weight on individual will in his critique of asceticism and speculative discourse. However, as Chestov seems to suggest, existential thought shares Schopenhauer's and Nietzsche's understanding of timelessness in terms of simultaneity ('hors du temps, c'est-à-dire en même temps [c'est la même chose]'). Simultaneity also implies, according to Chestov, 'la possibilité d'exceptions', the emergence of an alternative, 'non-temporal' and non-homogeneous configuration of consciousness. Nietzsche's thought of 'eternal return' lends support to the existential interpretation of notions of 'chance', 'exception', discontinuity and heterogeneity with reference to the consciousness of time.

In opposition to Schopenhauer's doctrine of the objectification of the will leading to a 'pure, will-less, painless, timeless subject of knowledge', Nietzsche's Zarathustra epitomizes 'the redeemer of chance', the powerful 'yes-sayer' who 'creates' past and future by making them conform to his will: 'I taught them to create the future, and to redeem by creating—all that *was past*. To redeem the past of mankind and to transform every "It was" until the will says: "But I willed it thus! So shall I will it—" this did I call redemption, this alone did I teach them to call redemption.'[87] The thought of eternal return encounters the emphatic *amor fati* precisely in so far as redemption, according to Nietzsche, actually needs to 'create' rather than simply restore or recollect the past. Creativity, as manifestation of individual will, redeems through positive affirmation the irreversible, causal, linear configuration of time that inhabits the exhaustive discourse of rational knowledge. Chestov insists on the crucial distinction between recollection and the willful redemption of the past, between the historical, chrono-logical dimension of memory and the existential, illogical affirmation of 'eternal return', which directly contradicts a basic postulate of all rational thought since Descartes, *quod factum est infectum esse nequit* (what has been done cannot not have been done). Individual will, powerful self-affirmation prevails over syllogistic mediation, over the doctrine of 'sacrifice' and 'self-renunciation' underpinning not only Schopenhauer's dismissal of temporal existence as 'non-being' but also Hegel's historical unfolding of the movement of Spirit in time. The will redeems by breaking down the irreversible and immutable temporal order that constitutes the very fabric of memory and rational thought:

Et la mémoire cède: ce qui fut n'a jamais été. Dans *Zarathoustra*, Nietzsche reprend ce thème: racheter le passé et transformer tout 'cela fut' en 'je voulais que cela fût ainsi'. Et il y revient encore une fois dans la troisième partie du chapitre 'Des anciennes et des nouvelles Tables'. [...] Lui qui attaquait si violemment la Bible, il ose parler de 'rédemption'. Rachat du passé de l'esclavage sous la loi et des lois grâce auxquelles uniquement ce passé demeure inébranlable.[88]

The implacable order of things that the historical, chrono-logical discourse projects onto the deepest recesses of individual memory can only be overcome through the willful affirmation of the possibility of 'redeeming the past of mankind', the absolute past to which the Fall belongs, the past in which Knowledge itself is rooted.[89] The sudden awakening of the will divests the law of causality and the law of contradiction of their 'eternal', unshakeable power over temporal, contingent existence and transfers this power to living individual beings, who are no longer bound to recollect the past but can 'redeem' it, can attribute or withdraw the value of truth to historical as much as syllogistic judgments:

Or c'était quelque chose d'infiniment plus important que l'éternel retour. Nietzsche découvrit qu'en dépit de la loi *quod factum est infectum esse nequit*, non pas la mémoire qui reproduit exactement le passé mais une certaine volonté [...] avait de sa propre autorité rendu le passé inexistant; et il découvrit que c'était cette volonté qui lui apportait la vérité. [...] Sous l'éternel retour de Nietzsche se cache, semble-t-il, une force d'une puissance infinie et qui est prête à écraser le monstre répugnant qui règne sur la vie humaine, sur l'être tout entier: *Creator omnipotens ex nihilo faciens omnia* de Luther.[90]

From Chestov's perspective, the thought of eternal return points not only to the redemption of the past through willful self-affirmation but, most significantly, to the possibility of suspending time and the irreversible succession of events that governs human memory by appealing to the 'immemorial' being of the 'all-powerful creator [who] makes all things out of nothing'. The existential interpretation of time corresponding to 'eternal return' uncovers the link between the living man and the living God, whose will can create an alternative sequence of events *ex nihilo*, just as it can make 'what happened not have happened'. This view challenges the rational understanding of eternity as the realm of ideal and conceptual rather than real and living being and advances the notion of simultaneity precisely insofar as it provides an alternative configuration of time, within which temporality and timelessness are not mutually exclusive but can both be attributed to the irreducible residuum of rational analysis—to the living man as well as to the living God.

Existential thought situates the relationship between man and God not only beyond good and evil, but also beyond truth and error—'par-delà la vérité et l'erreur', as Chestov and Fondane argue. The paradoxical possibility of making 'what happened not have happened' triggers off the actual annihilation of the principle of contradiction and ultimately suspends the dichotomy between truth and error, good and evil. More significantly, it allows for the possibility of refusing to bestow the quality of real being on error or evil. According to Chestov, in the presence of God evil and error cease to exist, turn into nothingness, 'non seulement dans le présent, mais aussi dans le passé: ils ne sont plus et n'ont jamais été, en dépit de tous les témoignages de *la mémoire humaine*'.[91] History and human memory, which underpins the logical, causal, sequential unfolding of historical events, strongly oppose the idea of an erratic, willful intervention in the chrono-logy of things and exclude the possibility of changing the past. As Chestov points out in an article devoted to the existential fight against self-evidence: 'L'objet principal de la science de l'histoire, telle qu'on la comprend toujours, est de rétablir le passé sous l'aspect d'une série d'événements reliés entre eux par la causalité.'[92] The unlimited power of God, supporting the equally powerful will of the living individual, consists precisely in the freedom to escape the implacable chrono-logy of the past, so that the consciousness of time is no longer necessarily bound to re-establish the self-evidence and eternal character of personal or historical facts, irrespective of how horrible and unbearable some of these 'truths of fact' might be. As Chestov argues, the mode of being of God, insofar as it corresponds to a simultaneous manifestation of all moments in time, instantaneously suspends or 'abolishes' the rational configuration of time, the chrono-logical unfolding of causally determined events or the 'horrors' of the 'history of humanity':

L'histoire de l'humanité, ou plus exactement toutes les horreurs de l'histoire de l'humanité se trouvent 'abolies' par la parole du Tout-Puissant, cessent d'exister, se transforment en fantômes, en mirages: Pierre n'a pas renié, David a tranché la tête de Goliath mais il n'a pas été adultère, le larron n'a pas tué, Adam n'a pas goûté au fruit défendu, personne n'a jamais empoisonné Socrate. Le 'fait', le 'donné', le 'réel' ne nous dominent pas, ne déterminent pas notre destin, ni dans le présent, ni dans l'avenir, ni dans le passé.[93]

Chestov's interpretation of time discloses the full scope of the thought of eternal return in its profound correlation with the idea that the individual will, supported by the will of God, can 'redeem the past of mankind'. It is not only the horrors and the implacable facts inscribed in the personal past that need to be redeemed, but the immemorial past in which the Fall inscribed the memory of an unsurpassable Knowledge, the chrono-logical and Manichean type of thinking that thereafter limits man's understanding to the opposition between good and evil, truth and error, temporal and timeless existence.

Gilbert-Lecomte's remarks on the genuine meaning of Plato's doctrine of anamnesis, or rather on the implications of the possibility of reminiscence beyond the logic and irreversibility of temporal existence, are especially pertinent in this context:

son appel à la palingénésie peut engendrer immédiatement le sens de l'éternel, par négation de la vie individuelle et d'une existence non réversible du temps. Autrement dit: 'Je me souviens', devient: j'ai la mémoire immémoriale du temps où j'étais intemporel.

The paradoxical idea of 'immemorial recollection', of individual memory as capable of recapturing a moment before the beginning of time, suggests that timelessness surpasses the confines of logical consistency, and simultaneously defines the immemorial being of God and the present being of an existing individual projecting itself beyond the historical, chronological judgment of individual life.

In stating that the judgment 'Socrates was poisoned' might not have any legitimate claim to truthfulness or immortality (alongside eternal 'truths of reason' such as $2 \times 2 = 4$), Chestov is attacking not only the thesis of temporal irreversibility but the foundation of logical thought, the principle of contradiction that dictates that what has happened cannot not have happened—*quod factum est infectum esse nequit*. The self-evidence of temporal irreversibility persists insofar as it has already become bound up with chrono-logical memory and with the apodictic principle of contradiction. The existential fight against the irreversible order of the historical continuum thus involves the fight against the inner record—the individual memory—of this chronology of self-consciousness and ultimately attempts to disclose the instantaneous contact between temporality and timelessness, between individual man and God, within the limitless display of passion that characterizes the transgressional movement of tragedy.

The 'philosophy of tragedy' that Chestov and Fondane developed in relation to their critique of Nietzsche actually displaced the notion of 'the tragic' from the aesthetic sphere into the religious, thus taking over and modifying both Nietzsche's interpretation of tragedy and Kierkegaard's understanding of 'the three stages of life'. According to Kierkegaard, the tragic hero is situated within the moral sphere, above the first, aesthetic sphere or stage of existence but below the third and final religious stage: he has overcome his particular condition in order to reach the level of generality, but lives under the moral law and as such is unable to go beyond the dichotomy of good and evil. Kierkegaard's argument signals the profound affinity between the Greek doctrine of catharsis, which determines the evolution of the tragic hero in the moral sphere, and the Hegelian critique of the 'unhappy consciousness' from the perspective of the history of Spirit or its 'chrono-logy' as the complete rationalization of time-consciousness. Dialectical movement and ethical laws intrinsically belong to and govern both the Greek doctrine and the Hegelian perspective. Only in view of this constant critical reference to Hegel can one fully grasp the meaning of Kierkegaard's observation that the tragic hero needs the historical dimension and that he remains in every respect different from 'le chevalier de la foi', the representative of the third and final stage of existence, inasmuch as each stage corresponds to a different interpretation of time.

'Repetition' describes the paradoxical movement by which a momentary contact between eternity and temporal existence is established. This contact does not emerge from rational reflection and the dialectical mediation of opposites. Kierkegaard explicitly associates the notion of 'repetition' with the sudden turning away from Hegel and the decision to join the obscure 'penseur privé' of the Bible, Job, crying out to God from the depth of despair. In contrast to Hegel's conception of history, the personal story of Job holds the promise of an interpretation of time no longer dependent on causality and irreversibility. This legendary 'exception', as Kierkegaard calls it, manifests God's power to make 'what happened not have happened', to wipe away misfortune and restore an original state of affairs, over and against rational principles, even the most fundamental, firmly established principle of contradiction. In opposing Job to Hegel, Kierkegaard thus places the notion of 'repetition' within the sphere of the absurd, the level at which religious faith defies logical reasoning, more precisely the level at which individual, exceptional, unique occurrences disrupt the 'chono-logical' discourse, the homogeneous flux of historical continuity. 'Repetition' belongs to a different dimension of thought and a different interpretation of time from Plato's anamnesis, as Fondane argues with reference to Kierkegaard:

> Il oppose l'interne à l'externe, l'individuel au général, le possible au réel, la vie qui *va en avant* à la compréhension qui *retourne en arrière*, le destin individuel à l'Histoire de la Chine, le discontinu au continu et, *à l'image de lui-même*, nous propose une pensée caractérisée par le saut, l'humeur, le soudain, la passion et la fièvre. Son dilemme: 'Entweder Oder', ne comprend que deux termes: le ressouvenir et la répétition, l'esprit et l'absurdité, le secret et le général, la foi et l'indifférence.[94]

Kierkegaard articulates his thought 'in his own image', as lived, personal experience, defined by discontinuity, by sudden leaps, by gaps in the series of appearances. It might be said that, in contrast to rationalist philosophers such as Kant or Hegel, the existential thinker 'creates' his own spatio-temporal framework, similar to the way in which God created the world ('in His own image'). The possibility of 'repetition' involves the suspension of causality and the full *restoration* rather than the mere recollection of time past. 'Repetition' brings about a *restoratio in integrum*, which Job's story eloquently illustrates, and which Fondane contrasts to the purely speculative effectiveness of reminiscence:

Car Job s'oppose à Socrate; frappé dans son corps et dans ses biens, il ne se résigne pas à demander au ressouvenir platonicien la joie de contempler ce qui fut [...] mais exige, en frappant du pied, la répétition de *ce qui a été*.[95]

In refusing to accept the irredeemable loss of the past, in maintaining his stubborn conviction that his misfortune can be wiped out of existence, whereas the reality of a logically 'irretrievable' yet desirable past must once more be made present, Job re-establishes the obliterated link between the human and the divine will, between man's and God's power to 'recall', to bring into being, a moment in time rather than submit to an 'inevitable' temporal unfolding. Fondane is particularly sensitive to the shift in emphasis that this view of time and personal existence inaugurates. According to him, Kierkegaard's notion of 'repetition' replaces the speculative quest for eternal, timeless ideas with the existential search for a living body, 'la recherche du corps',[96] as manifest illustration of an alternative interpretation of being. Instead of the syllogistic demonstrations that conventionally legitimize any attribution of being, existential thought discloses the argumentative power of the immediate, non-referential movement of a living body in time:

[D]e même qu'il parle au début de sa 'Répétition' de Diogène démontrant aux Éléates que le mouvement existait, en marchant — c'est en vivant que Kierkegaard démontrera l'être. Il est une 'réfutation vivante' de la plupart des idées de son siècle — de tous les siècles — et, s'il s'opposa à Hegel, ce n'est pas de système à système, mais de vie à vie, d'être à être.[97]

Against the Hegelian indictment of particular existence, Kierkegaard mobilizes mostly non-discursive, pre-reflexive means of argumentation. As Fondane comments, the critique of the Hegelian system from the point of view of existential thought tends to become a 'living refutation' of the chrono-logical, historical movement of

Spirit in time. Kierkegaard's re-evaluation of the living, particular individual uncovered a mode of thinking that ceased to represent 'une *réflexion* sur l'existence' and started to manifest 'le mouvement même de cette existence vers le vivre'.[98] This movement corresponds to a configuration of eternity that does not involve the speculative overcoming of individual existence. Like Job, Kierkegaard rejects the consolations of an abstract, eternal realm of ideas and demands the full restoration of his temporal, particular existence and his temporal self, that is, his body. Repetition connects eternity and integrity: the 'movement of existence towards the living' restores those very aspects of the self that rationality declares irretrievably lost, not worth hanging on to. 'It is a great thing to seize eternity, but to keep hold of temporality after having given it up is greater still', Kierkegaard writes. Having lost everything in the range of temporal possessions, including his own health and integrity, Job decides to rebel against the moral law and abandon his obedience to God; he ceases to praise Him and even ceases to comprehend the logic of temporal irreversibility. A humble mortal categorically demands the annihilation of the past and the reinstatement of the reality that was forcefully taken away from him. This unprecedented confrontation between man and God, beyond good and evil, inspired Kierkegaard's comments on the possibility of repetition as part of the different configuration of time emerging at the final, religious stage of existence.

The existential interpretation of time, as presented in Chestov's and Fondane's writing, ultimately uncovers the close interweaving of teleological, chrono-logical conceptions and ethics. The suspension of temporality involves the 'suspension of the ethical', which makes the transition from the ethical to the religious stage of existence in Kierkegaard's thought. The possibility of making 'what happened not have happened' exceeds both the rational and the ethical framework of understanding, which underpins the configuration of time as an irreversible, causally determined sequence of events. Socrates's acquiescent attitude, more than his death sentence, has to be reversed, transcended, as the inner rational limit that prevents the 'redemption of the past', the reversibility of temporal events. According to Chestov and Fondane, the moral exaltation of the limit, of what is logically possible and within 'our power', has to give way to the affirmation of individual free will, to Plato's sudden τῆς ἐμῆς βουλήσεως (by my own will),[99] which replaces logical discourse, the teleology and the chrono-logy of rational argument, and restores the realm of unlimited freedom, where temporality and death do not acquire the attributes of truth and reality.

Conclusions

The existential interpretation of time uncovers the rupture between contingent experience and conceptual analysis, between the discontinuous character of empirical time-consciousness and the search for the criteria of necessity and strict universality of knowledge, which places a special emphasis on the values of homogeneity and continuity. The necessary correlation between the homogeneous concepts of truth and being relies on the speculative, homogeneous interpretation of time, which eludes or dialectically supersedes the rupture between real, temporal and ideal, timeless beings in order to ensure the unified, universal understanding of truth, independent of any contingent, time-bound determinations. The existential critique of the Husserlian conception of truth and being on the one hand and of the Hegelian conception of history on the other aims to show that the reinsertion of the existential, living subject into philosophical reflection 'throws time out of joint'—brings out the discontinuity and heterogeneity of time-consciousness, insofar as the investigation of time is connected to the status of living rather than abstract, timeless beings. The positing of an 'irreducible residuum of being', which encompasses the existence of the living individual as well as the existence of God, emerges from an alternative type of thinking based on 'jugements discontinus' or 'actes discontinus'. Such judgements and acts of affirmation are designed to counteract and subvert the homogeneous, immutable and timeless character of necessary judgements about truth and being, construed in analogy with the principles of mathematics and logic. In disclosing the 'lived antinomies' of thought, the existential interpretation of time opens up individual, temporal being to timelessness, by recalling the obliterated link between the two aspects of the irreducible residuum of any speculative analysis—the existence of the living individual and the existence of the living God.

Although similar to the existential 'jugements discontinus', the Surrealist considerations on the relativity of time-perceptions and the questionable ground of syllogistic inferences that establish the unsurpassable character of death lead to different conclusions. In contrast to existential thought, Surrealism continued to seek the answer to the 'lived' or 'tragic antinomies' of philosophical reflection in shared commitment to the dialectical reconciliation of opposites displayed by Freudian psychoanalysis and Hegelian phenomenology. The quest for an ultimate synthesis of dream and reality, life and death, past and present reiterated rather than subverted the speculative mechanism that ensured the homogeneity of an interpretation of time designed to supersede rather than maintain the irreducible alterity of God's existence as well as that of the existence of the particular individual.

The existential effort to overcome causality, linear sequentiality and the teleology of historical development ultimately comes up against a moral imperative that underpins the very foundation of rational thought. The next chapter will examine the relationship between Fondane's notion of 'the end of finitude' ('la fin du fini') and Kierkegaard's understanding of 'the suspension of the ethical'. Nietzsche's genealogical account of morality is equally relevant to the existential investigation of freedom, with reference to the idea of a 'teleological suspension' of morality, which brings temporal irreversibility and death as 'finitude' to an end.

Notes to Chapter 3

1. The way in which the notion of 'chrono-logy' functions in the economy of the present argument will become clearer in the course of the second and third sections of this chapter. Fondane's idea that history is a complete absence of God can be traced back to Chestov's critique of the philosophical and theological tradition that identifies God with the concept of Logos as opposed to the 'living God' of the Bible. More significantly, the notion of 'chrono-logy' refers to the speculative, homogeneous interpretation of time that culminates with Hegel's teleological interpretation of 'history' as the manifestation and the evolution of Spirit in time. Insofar as Hegel's philosophy 'is not a philosophy of history but the recollection of world history in an individual consciousness that is rising to knowledge' (Jean Hyppolite, *Genesis and Structure of Hegel's Phenomenology of Spirit* (Evanston: Northwestern University Press, 1974), 46), the existential critique of Hegelian phenomenology attempts to dislocate the traditional intertwining between processes of memory and the rationalization of time consciousness by advancing an alternative interpretation of time with reference to the notion of 'anamnesis' and to Kierkegaard's notion of 'repetition'. This aspect of 'chrono-logy', related to memory and processes of internal time-consciousness, will be investigated in the last part of this chapter.
2. Léon Chestov, 'Le changement et le temps', *Athènes et Jérusalem,* 315–17.

3. Léon Chestov, 'La vie des idées', *Sur la balance de Job: Pérégrinations à travers les âmes*, trans. Boris de Schloezer (Paris: Flammarion, 1971; 1st French edn Paris: YMCA-Press, 1929), 188. See *In Job's Balances: On the Sources of the Eternal Truths*, trans. Camilla Coventry and C. A. Macartney (London: J. M. Dent & Sons, 1932).
4. Quentin Lauer, Introduction to Husserl, *La Philosophie comme science rigoureuse*, 38. The previous quotation about truth, to which Chestov often refers in his polemic with Husserl, can be found in Husserl, *Logical Investigations*, i. 140.
5. It is interesting to mention here one of the more recent critiques of the Husserlian project. Leszek Kolakowski, *Husserl and the Search for Certitude*, 25–6, questions the validity of a notion of truth and self-evident meaning that bypasses human existence. He argues that if the ideal units of meaning do not originate in human thought, if they are independent of human psychology, biology and history, it is difficult to see what reasons we should have to believe in this realm of being. He also questions the unfathomable 'modus essendi' of these entities 'which are neither Plato's ideas nor psychological acts' and asks: 'What other reasons could we offer on their behalf except that otherwise we cannot legitimate the claims of science to "truth" in the traditional sense?'
6. See Chestov, 'Le résidu irrationnel de l'être', *Sur la balance de Job*, 219–23.
7. On the polemical yet mutually respectful relationship between Chestov and Husserl (who met for the first time at a philosophical congress in Amsterdam in 1928), see Chestov, 'A la mémoire d'un grand philosophe, Edmund Husserl', 5–32; Fondane, *Rencontres avec Léon Chestov*, 44–5, 67, 93–4, 114; Baranoff-Chestov, *La Vie de Léon Chestov*, ii. 10–16, 20, 24–6, 31–4, 38–40, 54–5, 62–3. Three letters from Husserl to Chestov were published in Valevicius, *Lev Shestov and His Times*, 139–42.
8. Léon Chestov, 'De l'utilité de la philosophie', *Athènes et Jérusalem*, 317–18. Benjamin Fondane, 'Edmund Husserl et l'œuf de Colomb du réel (de la philosophie phénoménologique allemande)', *Europe* 20 (1929), 342, also indirectly referred to this question of the relationship between a particular philosophical system and reality in his critique of Husserl: 'En un mot: pendant que Husserl s'abstient de la position du réel, le réel à son tour s'abstient-il de la position de Husserl?' When he comes back much later to this question, Fondane adds the following striking comment (*La Conscience malheureuse*, 295 n.): 'J'écrivis cela et le publiai dans "Europe", en 1929. Je ne croyais pas si bien dire. Pendant que Husserl, maître incontesté de la pensée allemande, s'abstenait du réel, le réel, lui, agissait. Il transformait la société allemande, instaurait la dictature, le nazisme, la défaite de la raison, le massacre légal des juifs. Il arrachait Husserl à son socle du plus grand philosophe allemand actuel et en faisait un simple non-aryen que l'on destituait purement et simplement, non pour gagner une place à distribuer, car il avait déjà pris sa retraite, mais pour lui infliger ce que Heidegger appelle la "brutalité de l'interdiction" et "l'humiliation du refus". Si je faisais état des "on dit" — mais je m'y refuse — c'est Heidegger qui, en qualité de doyen de la Faculté de Friburg, aurait revêtu de sa signature l'acte de destitution.' From this retrospective point of view, Chestov's contention that logico-mathematical analysis only manages to patch up or dissimulate the fissure between speculative discourse and reality, the broken 'joint in time', seems all the more pertinent in

the context of the tragic devaluation of individual existence during the Second World War.

9. Fondane, 'Edmond Husserl et l'œuf de Colomb du réel', 342.
10. Fondane, 'Le Procès de la raison: Léon Chestov, témoin à charge', 349.
11. Fondane, 'Un philosophe tragique: Léon Chestov', 147.
12. Roger Gilbert-Lecomte, 'La nature de la conscience vivante', *Œuvres complètes*, i. 201.
13. Fondane, 'Un philosophe tragique: Léon Chestov', 146.
14. Gilbert-Lecomte, 'La nature de la conscience vivante', 200, 201.
15. Fondane, 'Le Procès de la raison: Léon Chestov témoin à charge', 357.
16. Fondane, 'Sœren Kierkegaard et la catégorie du secret', *La Conscience malheureuse*, 225.
17. Programmatic text on the inner cover of *Discontinuité* 1 (June 1928). The page contains the title of the publication, the names of the editors (Ar[thur] Adamov, Monny de Boully, Claude Sernet), a photograph and the above-mentioned, unsigned, untitled text.
18. *Discontinuité* 1 (June 1928), 1. The second sentence opens the article 'L'Aube n'est pas une épée' (signed 'Discontinuité').
19. Ar[thur] Adamov, 'Cette flèche blanche nous a frôlés dans le jour. C'est le dernier avertissement de l'archer imaginaire', *Discontinuité* 1 (June 1928), 12.
20. André Breton, *Manifeste du Surrealisme, Œuvres complètes*, i. 334.
21. Breton, *Les Pas Perdus*, 196.
22. Breton, *Les Pas Perdus*, 197; cf. the editorial note, 1225–6 n. 1.
23. Cf. Ricoeur, *Freud and Philosophy*, 76, 315.
24. Breton, 'Introduction au discours sur le peu de réalité', 265; cf. the editorial note, 1445–6 n. 2.
25. It is significant to recall here Ricoeur's remark (*Freud and Philosophy*, 430): 'the unconscious is homogeneous with consciousness; it is its relative other, and not the absolute other'.
26. Breton, *Manifeste du surréalisme*, 318.
27. Ibid., 319.
28. Fondane, 'Sœren Kierkegaard et la catégorie du secret', 204.
29. Fondane, 'La Conscience malheureuse', *La Conscience malheureuse*, 45.
30. 'Lettre de Benjamin Fondane à David Gascoyne' [July 1937], London, British Library, Add. MS 56060 (typed copy of the original letter), p. 26. Fondane makes a similar remark about Bergson's thought (*La Conscience malheureuse*, 124): 'il a préféré embrouiller les questions, les rendre insolubles, donner 'deux' sources à la morale et "deux" à la religion, une morale et une religion qui font pendant à l'intelligence, et une morale et une religion qui font pendant à l'intuition'. It is interesting to note that in his letter to David Gascoyne Fondane mentions enclosing a copy of *La Conscience malheureuse*, which had just been published.
31. Benjamin Fondane, 'Martin Heidegger sur les routes de Kierkegaard et de Dostoiewski', *La Conscience malheureuse*, 187, 188.
32. Fondane's critique of Heidegger will be further investigated in the following chapter. For more information, see ibid., 169–98.
33. Fondane, 'Léon Chestov, Sœren Kierkegaard et le Serpent', *La Conscience malheureuse*, 257.

34. Jean Hyppolite, *Genesis and Structure of Hegel's Phenomenology of Spirit* (Evanston: Northwestern University Press, 1974), 38.
35. G. W. F. Hegel, *Phenomenology of Spirit*, trans. A. V. Miller (Oxford: Clarendon Press, 1977), §227, p. 136.
36. Fondane, *Faux Traité d'esthétique*, 15.
37. Ibid., 37.
38. André Breton, 'Misère de la poésie: "L'Affaire Aragon" devant l'opinion publique', *Œuvres Complètes*, ii. 18, quoting G. W. F. Hegel, *Cours d'esthétique* (Paris: Joubert, 1851).
39. Breton, 'Le Message automatique', *Point du jour*, repr. *Œuvres complètes* ii. 380–1.
40. It is useful to recall here the equivalence between Breton's notion of a 'point suprême', already advanced in *Nadja*, and the notion of 'le Point sublime', both derived in keeping with the same Hegelian model of dialectical reconciliation of opposites. On Breton's aesthetic doctrine in its relation to Hegel's aesthetics, see Gerard Legrand, *André Breton dans son temps* (Paris: Le Soleil Noir, 1976), 57: 'Cette *présence d'esprit* passe du subjectif à l'objectif en s'assignant un *lieu*, ainsi baptisé par le nom d'un site des gorges du Verdon (le "Point sublime") où cesseraient d'être perçues contradictoirement les catégories de l'entendement.'
41. Roger Gilbert-Lecomte, 'Terreur sur la terre ou la vision par l'épiphyse', *Œuvres complètes*, i. 172.
42. Léon Chestov, *Le Pouvoir des clefs/Potestas clavium* (Paris: Flammarion, 1967; 1st French edn Paris: La Pléiade, 1928), 49.
43. Chestov, 'Cur Deus homo?', *Sur la balance de Job*, 180.
44. Chestov, *Le Pouvoir des clefs*, 48.
45. Ibid.
46. Ibid., 42.
47. Benjamin Fondane, 'Le Temps est hors des gonds', *Cahiers de l'Étoile* 16 (July-Aug. 1930), reprinted in *Sens* 6 (1981), special issue 'Benjamin Fondane', 144.
48. Hyppolite, *Genesis and Structure of Hegel's Phenomenology of Spirit*, 31.
49. Fondane, 'Sœren Kierkegaard et la catégorie du secret', 215. Concerning the existential theme of the confrontation between Athens and Jerusalem (or Greek thought and Biblical thought), it is interesting to recall that, in his early writings, Hegel considered unhappy consciousness as 'intermingled at its origin with Judaism' (cf. Hyppolite, *Genesis and Structure of Hegel's Phenomenology of Spirit*, 36).
50. Chestov, *Le Pouvoirs des clefs*, 40.
51. Kolakowski, *Husserl and the Search for Certitude*, 40–1. This issue will be further investigated in the next chapter.
52. Benjamin Fondane, 'Léon Chestov et la lutte contre les évidences', 31. Socrates' death provides one of the most prominent, recurrent themes of reflection in Chestov's work; see 'Regarder en arrière et lutter', *Forum philosophicum* 1 (1930), 98–9; *Sur la balance de Job*, 210; *Athènes et Jérusalem*, 343–4, etc.
53. Chestov, 'Memento mori', 43.
54. André Breton, 'La barque de l'amour s'est brisée contre la vie courante', *Œuvres complètes*, ii. 312, 315.
55. Ibid., 316.

56. Chestov mentions Belinsky's letter on the victims of history in many of his writings; see e.g. *L'Idée de bien chez Tolstoi et Nietzsche*, 33.
57. Chestov, *Le Pouvoir des clefs*, 53.
58. Victor Aranovitch and Arthur Adamoff, 'Nos idées', *L'En dehors* 84 (July 1926), 4; repr. *Lectures d'Adamov*, 140.
59. Roger Gilbert-Lecomte, 'Terreur sur terre ou la vision par l'épiphyse', *Œuvres complètes*, i. 185.
60. Aranovitch and Adamoff, 'Nos idées', 141.
61. Léon Chestov, 'Les Favoris et les déshérités de l'histoire: Descartes et Spinoza', *Mercure de France* (15 June 1923), 644.
62. Roger Gilbert-Lecomte, 'La lézarde', *Œuvres complètes*, i. 187.
63. Ibid.
64. Léon Chestov, 'Mille et une nuits', *Potestas clavium*, 48, 49.
65. See Chestov, *Sur la balance de Job*, 213, aphorism XXXVII, 'L'anamnèse'.
66. Chestov, 'Memento mori', 42–3.
67. See Chestov, 'Regarder en arrière et lutter', 98, aphorism XVI, 'Le possible et l'impossible': 'Un carré rond ou du fer en bois est une absurdité et, par conséquent, une impossibilité, car la liaison de ces concepts a été faite à l'encontre du principe de contradiction. Mais "Socrate empoisonné" n'est pas une absurdité, c'est donc une possibilité: le principe de contradiction autorise le rapprochement de ces concepts.'
68. Chestov, 'Memento mori', 43–4: 'Bref, la théorie des idées, telle que le jeune Platon la découvrit en une minute d'inspiration particulièrement heureuse, signifiait que l'idée est la quintessence de la réalité, l'être κατ'ἐξοχήν [*par excellence*] dont les images de la réalité quotidienne ne nous présentent qu'une copie affaiblie. Ce n'est que plus tard, lorsque sous la pression d'une nécessité extérieure il fallut transformer les idées en un bien commun à tous, permanent et immuable, lorsqu'on fut obligé de les défendre devant l'opinion de la foule et démontrer à tout venant ce qui par son essence même était indémontrable, lorsque, en un mot, il fallut faire de la philosophie "une science", c'est alors que Platon se vit dans l'obligation de sacrifier la réalité et de faire passer au premier plan ce qui pouvait être "évident" pour tous. Et l'étape dernière fut la théorie des idées-nombres, car on ne peut rien imaginer de plus évident que les mathématiques.'
69. Immanuel Kant, *Critique of Pure Reason* (London: Macmillan, 1993), §A322, p. 315.
70. André Breton, 'La Confession dédaigneuse', *Œuvres complètes*, i. 195. The quoted passage has a special significance in a text devoted chiefly to the memory of Jacques Vaché. One can say that the suicide of Vaché troubled Breton as much as the death of Socrates did Plato or Chestov.
71. Breton, *Manifeste du surréalisme*, 335.
72. See Paul Ricoeur's analysis of the retroreferential progression in the Freudian exegesis of the unconscious, *Freud and Philosophy*, 380–2.
73. Roger Gilbert-Lecomte, 'Notes sur les rapports de l'esthétique et de la paramnésie', *Œuvres complètes*, i. 203.
74. Roger Gilbert-Lecomte, 'Méditations', *Œuvres complètes*, i. 178–9.
75. In the *Critique of Pure Reason*, §B395, p. 325, Kant states: 'Metaphysics has as the proper object of its enquiries three ideas only: *God, freedom* and *immortality*—so

related that the second concept, when combined with the first, should lead to the third as a necessary conclusion.' The possibility of a priori synthetic knowledge, which the First Critique undertakes to establish, ultimately fails to establish the legitimacy and the necessity of immortality as derived from the relationship between the ideas of God and of freedom.

76. Chestov, 'Qu'est-ce que la vérité?', 62.
77. See Chap. 1 for a discussion of the context in which Chestov and Fondane introduce the paradoxical notion of a 'one-dimensional sphere'. The question of awakening, which is closely related to the existential interpretation of time, plays an important part in the critique of the unity of consciousness (with reference to Kantian and Husserlian a priorism). Chestov and Fondane bring together Plotinus's notion of 'awakening to oneself' and Descartes' hyperbolic doubt concerning the possibility that a 'diabolical demiurge' might deceive man and induce him to form a 'clear and distinct' idea of something that, in truth, is nothing else than a consistent dream.
78. See Kolakowski, *Husserl and the Search for Certitude*, 73
79. See Kant, *Critique of Pure Reason*, §A228–9, pp. 248–9.
80. Fondane, 'Chestov et la lutte contre les évidences', 38.
81. Antonin Artaud, 'Excursion psychique', *Œuvres complètes*, i. 168.
82. Ibid., 169.
83. In their turn, Nietzschean and Kierkegaardian ideas of time emerge from the radical critique of transcendental idealism, of a priori synthetic judgements on time and human existence. Whereas in empirical, a posteriori synthetic judgements like the example given above concerning the mortality of a particular man named Caius, the middle term (in this case the concept 'man') can be derived from the complete experience of the object ('Caius' or 'Socrates'), which is thought through the concept, in a priori synthetic judgements this help is entirely lacking. It is as if we actually had to deal with an immediate inference of the type 'That is a man' → 'That is mortal', more precisely, as if the predicate 'is mortal', although quite different from the concept 'man', belonged, and indeed necessarily belonged to the subject. Existential thought rejects this immediate inference and the necessary, a priori character of synthetic judgements such as 'Caius (or Socrates) is mortal', which not only invalidate the idea of the immortality of the soul, but also indirectly contribute to the disparagement of temporal, contingent existence, in so far as syllogistic argument—and reason itself, Kant argues—aspire to a priori, necessary, timeless principles, operating outside the realm of transient, empirical beings.
84. Chestov, *Athènes et Jérusalem*, 157.
85. Ibid.
86. Chestov, *La Philosophie de la tragédie: Dostoïewsky et Nietzsche*, 185–6.
87. Friedrich Nietzsche, *Thus Spoke Zarathustra* (London: Penguin, 1969), 'Of Old and New Law-Tables', §3, p. 216.
88. Chestov, *Athènes et Jérusalem*, 156, 157.
89. It is interesting to note that Nietzsche also connects 'awakening' to the 'abysmal thought' of eternal return. This confirms Chestov's idea that Nietzsche arrived at his interpretation of temporality and timelessness by pursuing a radical critique of speculative knowledge and philosophy. In 'The Convalescent', §2, *Thus Spoke Zarathustra*, 235, Zarathustra makes desperate efforts to 'awaken' his 'abysmal

thought', and turn his 'ultimate depth into light', but is soon overcome by disgust and loses consciousness in the confrontation with the eternal return. Later, he evokes the symbolic struggle with a snake, which had crept into his throat and choked him. The same terrifying situation is revealed in 'The Vision and the Riddle' (with reference to 'a shepherd'), and in both cases man's salvation depends on the courage to bite off and spit away the head of the monster. From the existential point of view, this recurrent parable uncovers the profound relationship between eternal return and redemption, between Zarathustra's awakening of his 'abysmal thought' and man's struggle to break free from the choking grip of knowledge, the Knowledge of Good and Evil after the Fall. 'The great disgust at man—*it* choked me and had crept into my throat: and what the prophet prophesied: "It is all one, nothing is worth while, knowledge chokes."'

90. Chestov, *Athènes et Jérusalem*, 156–7.
91. Ibid., 157.
92. Chestov, 'Dostoïevsky et la lutte contre les évidences', 145.
93. Chestov, *Athènes et Jérusalem*, 37.
94. Fondane, 'Sœren Kierkegaard et la catégorie du secret', 209.
95. Ibid., 207.
96. The problem of the living body will be further investigated in the next chapter, with reference to ethics and freedom.
97. Fondane, 'Sœren Kierkegaard et la catégorie du secret', 208.
98. Ibid., 203: 'Voici un homme vivant, dont la pensée n'est pas une *réflexion* sur l'existence, mais le mouvement même de cette existence vers le *vivre*.'
99. See Chestov's references to Plato in *Athènes et Jérusalem*, 56–9; also the rest of chap. 1, 'Parménide enchaîné', 60–106.

CHAPTER 4

❖

Individual Choice and Freedom: Between the Categorical Imperative and the Suspension of the Ethical

> Si je ne crois ni au Mal ni au Bien [...] le principe même en est dans ma chair. Je détruis parce que chez moi tout ce qui vient de la raison ne tient pas.
>
> ANTONIN ARTAUD, *Manifeste en langage clair*

> Sin is opposed not to virtue, but to faith.
>
> SØREN KIERKEGAARD, *The Sickness unto Death*

The existential critique of the concepts of consciousness and subjectivity, in its relationship to the rationalist interpretation of time, ultimately aims to expose the twofold—ethical[1] and logical—foundation of systematic thought in order to arrive at a new understanding of freedom. In its attempt to transgress the ethical and logical valuations underpinning the dichotomous conception of temporal vs. timeless existence, Chestov's and Fondane's critique of rationality (with reference to Kierkegaard, Nietzsche and Dostoevsky) seeks to establish a configuration of freedom that would make possible a radical redefinition of being. The freedom leading to such a redefinition (one that simultaneously attributes temporality and timelessness to real existence) poses the relationship between man's and God's existence insofar as this relationship transcends the dichotomy between good and evil, as well as the correlative, logical dichotomy between truth and error. More adequately, freedom, from the existential viewpoint, exceeds the twofold (logical/ethical) limitation imposed by the rational configuration of time, inasmuch as logical and ethical postulates themselves rest on and reinforce an underlying interpretation of time. This final chapter will therefore consider the profound ethical implications of the interpretation of time-consciousness in relation to the epistemological foundation of truth, to the idea of the good and to the possibility of freedom.

The Surrealist approach to questions of freedom and choice, to political and ethical commitments, along the lines of the Hegelian conception of history and of Marxist ideology will be contrasted to the existential attempt to uncover the close interweaving of teleological, chrono-logical arguments and ethics as the underlying assumption of transcendental idealism and of dialectic historical materialism alike. Existential thought situates the question of choice in the context of the critique of the rational concept of truth previously undertaken by Nietzsche and Kierkegaard. The argument advanced by Chestov and Fondane traces back the genealogy of ethical as well as logical judgements justifying the disparagement of temporal, individual existence to an original interlocking of ethical and epistemological imperatives, which underpins the search for objective truth and self-knowledge as self-overcoming. The possibility of setting the conditions of truth in relation to temporal beings rather than timeless, ideal ones depends on the freedom of choice that transgresses the ethical dichotomy between good and evil in order to disclose the deeper antinomy between ontology and ethics. The first section of this chapter will focus on the existential critique of the Husserlian conception of truth in relation to ethics and will provide a comparative analysis of different views of truth and of different interpretations of the question of choice developed within or outside the boundaries of the Surrealist movement.

The second section will consider the Surrealist and existential interpretations of the idea of the good with reference to Hegel's analysis of the unhappy consciousness and to Kant's categorical imperative. The existential refutation of the ethical arguments underpinning Hegel's dialectical reconciliation of opposites revives and complements the critique of Hegelian phenomenology previously elaborated by Kierkegaard from the standpoint of the relationship between the particular individual and God. In its approach to ethical and socio-political questions, mainstream Surrealism supported rather than undermined Hegel's assessment of the unhappy consciousness by consistently trying to reconcile the position of the particular individual and the imperatives of historical development. Whereas the

Surrealist conception of freedom does not involve the complete dismantling of either Hegel's postulated identity between the principle of Reason and the idea of the Good or Kant's categorical imperative, existential thought dislocates the fundamental intertwining of rationality and ethics in both philosophical systems before proceeding to examine the possibility of freedom. The existential emphasis on Hamlet's line 'the time is out of joint', which points to a temporal as well as a cognitive dislocation, further qualifies this attempt to situate freedom within a new interpretative context starting from the critique of the rational and ethical foundations of knowledge.

The last part of the chapter will be devoted to the understanding of freedom that existential thought aims to uncover by dislocating the ethical and logical grounds of the traditional homogeneous interpretation of time in relation to the possibility of knowledge. The existential approach to the problem of freedom questions the a priori validity of Kant's categorical imperative and explores the implications of Kierkegaard's 'suspension of the ethical' together with those of Nietzsche's genealogical account of morality. The result of the existential re-evaluation of non-systematic arguments against the Kantian conception of freedom or against the later Hegelian view of freedom within the dialectical movement of self-knowledge as self-overcoming has no perfect equivalent in Surrealism, but it provides a significant reference point for 'dissident' projects pursued outside or on the boundaries of the movement itself. Chestov's and Fondane's affirmation of freedom 'beyond good and evil' as the paradoxical end of temporality (*la fin du fini*), which heralds the end of the dichotomous ethical thinking underpinning the disparagement of temporal existence, finds eloquent illustrations in Artaud's, Daumal's and Gilbert-Lecomte's writings and invites a reconsideration of the Surrealist conflicting concerns with ethical and political commitments on the one hand and with the possibility of individual freedom on the other.

Individual Choice and the Question of Truth

In recognizing the unprecedented character of Husserl's breakthrough, Chestov pointed out that the critical examination of the origin of scientific principles that presided over the elaboration of the phenomenological method uncovered a categorical, 'either/or' choice: either accept the relative, transient value of scientific knowledge and the impossibility of acquiring absolute certainty, or establish firm, unshakable criteria of truth and objectivity, even at the cost of disconnecting these criteria from human existence. Phenomenology and existential thought shared this essential, acute awareness of the uncompromising nature of truth and certainty. They provided utterly opposed solutions to the problem of knowledge, but started from an equally radical choice.

In the previous chapter, I have discussed the implications of the phenomenological and the existential approaches to the question of truth with reference to their different interpretations of time. However, the line from *Hamlet* ('The time is out of joint'), which haunted both Chestov and Husserl and prompted their common recognition of a crucial, 'either/or' choice, signals a profound ethical dilemma, a rupture at the level of moral consciousness, contained within the interrogation of a perceived break in temporal continuity. It is not only a choice between temporal, real beings and timeless, ideal ones, which Husserl like Chestov faced in setting the criteria for truth—either according to the aim of achieving absolute, scientific objectivity or according to the subjective aspirations of particular individuals. The choice, the 'either/or' of the philosophical quest for truth is also that between an engagement with and a disengagement from ethics. As Kierkegaard remarked in *Either/Or*: 'My either/or does not in the first instance denote the choice between good and evil; it denotes the choice whereby one chooses good *and* evil/or excludes them.'[2]

Similarly, Chestov's and Fondane's critique of the scientific conception of truth focused on the original interlocking of rationality and ethics, of the idea of truth and the idea of the good. Any attempt to redefine truth against the all-pervading analogy with the principles of mathematics and logic (running through the history of philosophy from Aristotle and Spinoza to Kant and Husserl), would need to dislocate both the correlation between philosophical and scientific first principles and the further interdependence of philosophical and ethical oppositional pairs (true : false :: good : evil). Kierkegaard's *Either/Or* advances the paradoxical possibility of moving beyond the dichotomous ethical framework through a choice that seemingly replicates the binary opposition (either/or) that it seeks to overcome. However, in choosing not to choose, or more accurately in choosing to exclude the pre-determined choice between good and evil, the philosopher opts out of the ethical framework and poses an alternative that undercuts the binary opposition of an ethical either/or, opening up the possibility of a complete disengagement from ethics. This movement of disconnection extricates the problem of truth from its interlocking with the speculative choice between good and evil and brings it into immediate contact with the existence of a particular individual. What Kierkegaard chooses in demobilizing a mode of thinking that links ethics to the search for truth and certainty is himself and/or the freedom brought out by the affirmation of the timeless, eternal value of his own temporal existence:

> But what is it I choose? Is it this thing or that? No, for I choose absolutely, and the absoluteness of my choice is expressed precisely by the fact that I have not chosen to choose this or that. I choose the absolute. And what is the absolute? It is myself in my eternal validity. [...] But what, then, is this self of mine? [...] It is the most abstract of all things, and yet at the same time it is the most concrete—it is freedom.[3]

In his article on Husserl's phenomenology, 'Qu'est-ce que la vérité? Ontologie et Éthique', Chestov argues that the rational consideration of the question of truth in the perspective of eternity or necessity (*sub specie aeternitatis vel necessitatis*) maintains the link between 'speculation' and 'wisdom', between what is philosophically true and what is ethically good or 'the best' (*optimum*). With reference to Spinoza and indirectly to Husserl, Chestov questions the grounds of the established correlation between *philosophia vera* and *philosophia optima*, between the idea of truth and the idea of the good:

> Quel rapport y a-t-il entre *verum* and *optimum*? *Verum* doit-il se conformer docilement à *optimum* ou bien, au contraire, est-ce *optimum* qui est asservi à *verum*? Et il y a là même une série de questions. Qu'est-ce que *verum*? Qu'est-ce que *optimum*? Qui a le pouvoir de déterminer le caractère du rapport entre le 'vrai' et le 'meilleur'?[4]

Chestov further comments that the nature of the relationship between *verum* and *optimum* depends on and reinforces an underlying perspective or interpretation of time: 'Le véritable objet de cette formule *sub specie aeternitatis* est d'établir un pont entre *vera philosophia* et *philosophia optima*.'[5] According to 'the perspective of eternity', the value of 'truth' as well as that of 'the good' can only be attributed to what is timeless, therefore immutable and necessary. The power that determines the indissociable link between *verum* and *optimum* relies on the speculative movement that first abstracts the idea of truth from any temporal, subjective variables (including the existence of the thinking subject itself) and then identifies this ideal, eternal concept with the 'good'. The movement of idealization, which accomplishes the transition from a temporal to a timeless perspective, confers a privileged ontological status on ideal, immutable entities of thought and places the existence of real, particular individuals outside Husserl's realm of true being (inasmuch as being and truth become intertwined), while subsuming it under the necessary correlation between truth and 'the good'. If a real, living individual cannot acquire immortality or aspire to the eternal status of conceptual entities, it can nevertheless achieve the 'highest good' (*summum bonum*) by renouncing everything that is transient and perishable and elevating itself to the understanding that the immutable truth, although disconnected from human existence, coincides with the good:

La raison [...] seule est juge de la vérité et du bien. La vérité est que l'univers visible est soumis à la loi de la mort; le bien consiste à chercher non pas ce que l'homme désire, mais ce que la raison lui ordonne de reconnaître comme meilleur. Et le bien suprême, 'summum bonum', ce qui est le but de εὖ ζῆν [well-being], est non pas ἡδονή [pleasure]—car ἡδονή n'est pas soumis à la raison, de même que ce monde visible auquel appartient ἡδονή—mais la faculté de *juger* que ἡδονή est τὸ ἀγαθόν [the good].[6]

The identification of *philosophia vera* and *philosophia optima* operates on the assumption that reason and ethics have congruent aims or, as Chestov argues, that reason alone determines the grounds and the validatory criteria for both the idea of truth and the idea of the good. Kantian transcendental idealism (to which this commentary on Plotinus's doctrine alludes) does not break with the ancient and the medieval line of argument, according to which *summum bonum* should not be sought in what the transient, mortal individual considers to be pleasurable or desirable, or in ἡδονή (pleasure) and affectivity as such, but in the superior faculty of judgement, which gives the measure of 'the good', of what is to be considered as 'pleasurable', in the perspective of eternity and necessity.

As Chestov's analysis indicates, the rational interpretation of time governs not only the movement of idealization or conceptualization, operating throughout the history of systematic philosophy, but also the less apparent replacement of ontology with ethics. Chestov calls this speculative process 'replacement' insofar as he considers that the philosopher is faced with the choice formulated by Kierkegaard—that of either engaging with or disengaging from ethics in considering the problem of individual existence. Actually, the movement of idealization already pre-empts the possibility of such a choice: the interlocking of *verum* and *optimum* only attaches itself to and strengthens the validity of the more fundamental interlocking of truth and being (νοεῖν and εἶναι) reiterated by philosophers from Parmenides to Hegel.

In affirming the 'plain correlation' between meaning and being, Husserl also advances a conception of truth that from the outset re-establishes the connection between (onto-)logical and ethical reasoning.[7] One of the most important consequences of this is that phenomenological reduction equalizes descriptive judgements and value-judgements. A striking confirmation, which Chestov fails to mention in support of his argument, can be found in the 'Prolegomena' to the first volume of Husserl's *Logical Investigations*. The general remarks on 'a certain unity of validatory interconnection' (§10) required by science barely hint at ethical imperatives through metaphors of elevation, ascent etc. However, the 'normative' character that Husserl assigns to logic only acquires more definite ethical undertones when he probes into the 'original sense' of 'shall'- or 'should'-predicates:

> If we say 'A soldier should be brave', this does not mean that we or anyone else are wishing or willing, commanding or requiring this. [...] 'A soldier should be brave' rather means that only a brave soldier is a 'good' soldier, which implies (since the predicates 'good' and 'bad' divide up the extension of the concept 'soldier') that a soldier who is not brave is a 'bad' soldier. *Since* this value-judgement holds, everyone is entitled to demand of a soldier that he should be brave, the same ground ensures that it is desirable, praiseworthy etc., that he should be brave.[8]

In a similar manner to Kant's syllogistic approach to the problem of individual existence (which I discussed in the previous chapter with reference to the proposition 'Caius is mortal'), Husserl proceeds to establish a concept ('soldier') that contains the condition under which the predicate is given. The apodictic foundation of the two predicates, 'good' and 'bad', which are supposed to 'divide up the extension of the concept', is ultimately determined according to the rules governing logical relationships between judgements taken in their full extension: 'We may in general, take as identical or at least as equivalent the forms "An *A* should be *B*" and "An *A* that is not *B* is a bad *A*", or "Only an *A* which is a *B* is a good *A*."'[9] Husserl leaves no doubt over the criteria that dictate the attribution or the denial of positive or negative value-predicates: they are the same criteria that have to be met in establishing the truth (in the sense of logical validity) of a given proposition. What decides whether something is to be considered 'good' or 'bad' comes down to the 'necessary and sufficient conditions' to be met when stating that something is 'true'. The aims of logic as a 'normative discipline' become intrinsically bound up with the aims of ethics, insofar as Husserl's 'concept of the normative judgement' promises to ensure the sought-after 'unity of validatory interconnection' by providing the 'basic norm', whose role, Husserl specifies, 'is, e.g., played by the categorical imperative in the group of normative propositions which make up Kant's Ethics, as by the principle of the "greatest possible happiness of the greatest possible number" in the Ethics of the Utilitarians'.[10]

The alternative envisaged by Kierkegaard and Chestov emerges from the sudden realisation of an absence of choice: 'Il n'y a pas de place en philosophie pour le choix et l'arbitraire', Chestov notes in 'Qu'est-ce que la vérité?'. There is no 'either/or' as long as the foundation of logical and ethical normative judgements remains unquestioned, as long as the choice between good and bad, truth and error is predetermined *sub specie aeternitatis* by the necessary and sufficient conditions set in analogy with the principles of logic and mathematics, independent of the wishing or willing, the desire of the living individual. The existential alternative does not involve a choice that could be equated with a simple logical negation—choosing not to choose. Instead of merely negating, the 'either/or' suspends the framework of logical and moral normative reasoning. This suspension reverses the apodictic speculative movement that excludes temporal individuals from the realm of true being, starting from the premiss that mortality constitutes the ultimate truth of human existence. Fondane comments on the consequences of such a reversal with reference to Heidegger's early position (from *What is metaphysics?*):

> Si Heidegger dit vrai — si le néant précède la négation, il se pourrait par conséquent, que l'Etre précédât l'affirmation, et le Réel l'Idée; il se pourrait [...] que l'absurdité précédât l'évidence, le caprice le principe de la contradiction et que la liberté fût née avant la nécessité.[11]

However, this mode of thinking, which links freedom to a notion of being preceding its logical affirmation, insofar as it uncovers a random, subjective 'choice' or an alternative that undercuts the ground of logical validatory arguments, bears little resemblance to Heidegger's own conception as he developed it in *Being and Time.*

Fondane did not fail to notice that the apparent revival of Kierkegaardian themes in Heidegger's ontology remained tributary to an interpretation of time that pre-empted the existential possibility of opting out of the necessary attribution of finitude and mortality to individual being as opposed to the timeless, universal concept of Being. Fondane's remarks anticipate the more recent criticism formulated by philosophers like Jean-Luc Nancy, who situate Heidegger within rather than outside the history of 'une pensée de la finitude de l'être' while pertinently recalling the grounding and the implications of an ontological project which starts from the premiss that 'le *Dasein* est être-à-la-mort'.[12]

When Fondane quotes Heidegger's statement, 'Plus primordial que l'homme lui-même est sa finitude', at first his objections seem exclusively aimed against the logic of a redefinition of being that comes back to the more fundamental interdependence between temporal existence and death: 'L'Être n'est plus qu'un accessoire de "ce qui meurt" — que dis-je? de sa propre mort'.[13] However, it soon becomes clear that Fondane's refutation of the philosophy of 'the finitude of being' has different if not further-reaching goals than the current critical re-evaluation of the onto-theo-logical tradition undertaken by Jean-Luc Nancy among other contemporary thinkers. In contrast to recent debates on phenomenology and ontology, Fondane and Chestov attempted to expose and destroy the ethical grounding of the speculative concept of truth and to trace the interlocking of rational truth and being back to the significance of the biblical fable of the Fall of Man. According to Chestov's and Fondane's understanding, the Fall is the inaugural event of rational knowledge, the Knowledge of Good and Evil that pre-empts the possibility of an alternative affirmation of Life, preceding the dissociation and the choice between good and evil as well as the dissociation between truth and error based on logical validatory arguments. The Fall symbolically designates an 'event' that otherwise has no corresponding reference in time or in history, insofar as rational thought has no definite origin or beginning and no end; it only subtends an ontological horizon *sub specie aeternitatis vel necessitatis*.

In Chestov's and Fondane's interpretation, the movement to idealization, the transition from particular entities to general and universal concepts, is but one with the ethical movement of self-overcoming; more adequately, the dawn of logical reasoning coincides with the trans-historical advent of the dichotomy between good and evil. The genealogical account that Chestov and Fondane elaborate in relation to the question of the timelessness and the lack of origin of rational thought recaptures the meaning of Nietzsche's gnomic statement: 'The drive towards knowledge has a *moral* origin.'[14] In trying to suspend or even annihilate the foundation of the logical, dichotomous investigation of truth, existential thought aims to overturn the moral grounding of the drive towards knowledge.

It can be said that, up to a certain point, Surrealism pursued the same destruction of rational, scientific truth by affirming the value of imagination, of dreams and individual affectivity, as non-systematic means of knowledge. Breton did not hesitate to relativize truth and set it in relation to personal, variable faculties, or to a more general but unquantifiable creative ability to seize valuable insights: 'La vérité particulière à chacun de nous est un jeu de patience dont il lui faut, entre tous les autres, et sans les avoir jamais vus, saisir les éléments au vol.'[15] More significantly, Breton's reflections on truth indicate his constant preoccupation not only with individual existence but also with the question of mortality, of temporal finitude, which delimits any investigation of the concept of truth. In 'La Confession dédaigneuse', Breton illustrates his approach by quoting Tolstoy's words: 'Si seulement un homme a appris à penser, peu importe à quoi il pense, il pense toujours au fond à sa propre mort. Tous les philosophes ont été ainsi. Et quelle vérité peut-il y avoir, s'il y a la mort?'[16]

The Surrealist examination of the problem of truth emerged from an exploration of language, of the relationship between thought-processes and linguistic communication. Breton's famous observation from the 'Introduction au discours sur le peu de réalité' accurately pinpoints the fundamental question raised by Surrealism: 'La médiocrité de notre univers ne dépend-elle pas essentiellement de notre pouvoir d'énonciation?'[17] The revolutionary potential of a new theory of the poetic image, developed in conjunction with experimental techniques meant to change rather than simply reinterpret reality, soon acquired ethical undertones. The exploration of language becomes closely interwoven with a deep concern for ethical exigencies imposed by the revolutionary practice that Surrealism inaugurated. Having to defend and reconcile conflicting tendencies within the movement, Breton abandons a provisional individualistic and nihilistic stance in favour of Hegelian dialectics and finally embraces the ethics underlying Hegel's conception of history. In 'Légitime Défense', Breton comes to affirm that 'La réalisation de la nécessité seule est d'ordre révolutionnaire', and, as if to substantiate this point, he then situates the Surrealist investigation of language within the framework of the Hegelian doctrine of the Spirit of the Time:

Encore une fois, tout ce que nous savons est que nous sommes doués à un certain degré de la parole et que, par elle, quelque chose de grand et d'obscur tend à s'exprimer à travers nous, que chacun de nous a été choisi et désigné à lui-même entre mille pour formuler ce qui, de notre vivant, doit être formulé.[18]

Despite a sudden interruption, which sounds like an exclamation of revolt against the Hegelian thesis ('Mais c'est comme si nous y avions été condamnés de toute éternité'), Breton carries on undisturbed: 'Écrire, je veux dire écrire si difficilement, et non pour séduire, et non, au sens où l'on entend d'ordinaire, pour vivre, mais, semble-t-il, tout au plus pour se suffire moralement.'[19]

The 'vital tension' between the two terms of a poetic image constitutes, as Claude Abastado interestingly remarks, the necessary but not sufficient condition, to which Breton insistently added 'une autre exigence, qui, en dernière analyse, pourrait bien être d'ordre éthique'.[20] From the perspective of Fondane's existential critique of Surrealism, it is precisely this ethical exigency that brings back an alternative, poetic search for truth under the authority of speculative reasoning subject to logical validatory arguments. The willingness to establish the ethical justification and the logical validity of one's position on truth reinstitutes the double (ethical and logical) foundation of systematic thought. In deciding or in willing to comply with the requirements of this double imperative, one makes a choice that is still determined by the dichotomy of truth and error, good and evil, as Kierkegaard observed:

That the man who chooses good and evil chooses the good is indeed true, but this becomes evident only afterwards; for the aesthetical is not the evil but neutrality, and that is the reason why I affirmed that it is the ethical which constitutes the choice. It is, therefore, not so much a question of choosing between willing the good *or* the evil, as of choosing to will, but by this in turn the good and the evil are posited.[21]

Daumal's and Gilbert-Lecomte's critique of morality leads to a similar interpretation of choice and freedom. The position of *Le Grand Jeu* was from the outset polemically detached from the emerging ethics of revolt developed within the Surrealist movement in response to current social and political debates. The articles published in the first issue of the magazine might seem to indicate that the members of *Le Grand Jeu* reversed the sequence of the three stages of life described by Kierkegaard (the aesthetic, the ethical and the religious) and proceeded to dismantle ethical reasoning from a position of complete indifference or of a suspension of choice, which Kierkegaard would qualify as 'aesthetic':

> Après la révolte qui cherche la liberté dans le choix possible entre plusieurs actions, l'homme doit renoncer à vouloir réaliser quelque chose au monde. La liberté n'est pas libre arbitre, mais libération; elle est la négation de l'autonomie individuelle. L'âme refuse de se modeler à l'image du corps, des désirs, des raisonnements; les actions deviennent des phénomènes naturels, et l'homme agit comme la foudre tombe.[22]

'Tout m'est égal, j'égale tout', reads one of the striking mottos running on the top of the pages of the first issue of *Le Grand Jeu*. However, the notion of 'renunciation' on which Daumal and Gilbert-Lecomte based their paradoxical understanding of freedom successively negates the aesthetic and the ethical stages of life in order to arrive at an existential revaluation of religion compatible with Kierkegaard's own interpretation. As Daumal suggests, the aesthetic suspension of choice and the affirmation of free will already contain the marks of the next, ethical position. Thus, the first negation uncovers a choice or a pure affirmation of the will, which as in Kierkegaard operates within the boundaries of ethical thinking. Concerning the individual who adopts the first, aesthetic stage of revolt, Daumal writes: 'Il veut choisir librement et de lui-même. [...] Il veut vouloir pour vouloir, agir par pur décrets. L' "acte gratuit" est, dit-il, le seul acte libre.'[23] Aesthetic 'indifference' involves not only a negation of choice but also an act of detachment from the world and of self-abnegation, which already makes the transition to 'irony', to the Stoic attitude of the ethical thinker, according both to Kierkegaard and to Daumal:

> Ce divorce d'avec le monde, qui fait le monde indifférent à l'esprit, est souvent proche du désespoir; mais c'est un désespoir qui rit du monde. Si l'esprit se sépare des choses, le corps en même temps, se sépare des autres corps; son raidissement l'isole, et couvre le visage du masque musculaire de l'ironie. [...] L'esprit prend l'habitude de dire à tout ce que subit ou fait le corps: 'Ce n'est pas important'. Et l'homme croit avoir trouvé le salut. L'existence et les biens de ce monde perdent leur prix, rien n'est à craindre, et l'âme continue sa recherche de la pureté dans ce raidissement d'orgueil, celui du stoïcien.[24]

Daumal's considerations on the grounds and development of the Stoic attitude parallel the critical remarks made by Chestov in his article 'Qu'est-ce que la vérité?', in which the ancient Greek story of the Bull of Phalaris[25] functions as a reminder of the question posed by extreme physical suffering to the ideal of moral endurance and self-abnegation, presiding over the edification of any ethical discourse. The negation and the disparagement of temporal, bodily existence, which enables the plain identification between *verum* and *optimum*, all too often avoids confronting the consequences of the idealistic demand that the virtuous man can and should find *summum bonum* even inside the Bull of Phalaris. The notion of *renoncement*, defined by Daumal and Gilbert-Lecomte, moves beyond ethical self-abnegation, insofar as it annihilates or reduces to nothingness the ground of ethical choice—the pure act of willing, the will to will, which still poses the choice in terms of good and evil. In emphasizing the possibility of recapturing 'the innocence of the void', while affirming the positive value or power of perpetual negation and renunciation (*la force des renoncements*), Daumal and Gilbert-Lecomte advance a new, paradoxical understanding of 'abnegation': '*L'essence* du renoncement est d'accepter tout en niant tout',[26] by which the individual overcomes the limitation of ethical reasoning and encounters God as the 'alternative', or absolute alterity. This position confirms Fondane's comments on the possibility that 'nothingness' might precede logical negation and that real, individual existence might precede the logical affirmation of Being at the point at which the 'renunciation' no longer refers to temporal, physical being but to the speculative judgement on temporal being according to the logic of good and evil. The 'either/or' configuration of individual existence in relation to the existence of God thus involves a 'choice' that exceeds both the logical and the ethical construal of being in its plain correlation to the rational understanding of truth.

The Unhappy Consciousness: The Idea of Good as the Categorical Imperative

Fondane, like Daumal and Gilbert-Lecomte, considered that the act of annihilation or 'renunciation', leading to an alternative interpretation of freedom, involves a struggle, a confrontation that is played out within the living individual itself, within its consciousness. As Fondane implicitly argues, every individual carries within itself the principle of reason, which it seeks to overcome:

Et si, d'après Pascal, chacun de nous porte en lui un Montaigne, il est vrai d'autant et même plus que chaque homme porte en lui son Husserl. Si Husserl n'avait pas été, dit Chestov, pour pousser jusqu'à ses conséquences ultimes les droits de la Raison, il m'aurait fallu le faire moi-même d'abord, pour pouvoir me réfuter ensuite; il m'aurait fallu être Husserl, pour arriver à être Chestov.[27]

Even when the refuted principle seems to become completely objectified and external, so that the conflict appears to refer to something outside the subject itself (in this case, Fondane's witty paraphrase of Pascal makes Husserl the 'embodiment' of Reason), the individual in its fight against rational self-evidence confronts an inner 'adversary' and the question of its own, ruptured consciousness.

The source and mechanism of this confrontation are amply described in the section of *Phenomenology of Spirit* that Hegel devotes to self-consciousness and freedom. The 'life-and-death' struggle between competing 'shapes of consciousness' that seek to eliminate each other is played out within self-consciousness, like the further-developed relationship between Master and Slave—between 'pure self-consciousness' and '*immediate* consciousness, or consciousness in the form of *thinghood*'.[28] Among the three phases of the life-and-death struggle in the rational progression of self-consciousness to freedom, 'the unhappy consciousness' provides the most accurate account of the inner conflict opened up by the existential 'fight against self-evidence'.

While noting the pertinence of the Hegelian description, Fondane like Chestov exposes the underlying ethical argument that presides over the dialectical reconciliation of the opposite terms of the 'inwardly disrupted consciousness'. The overcoming of the 'wretchedness' of divided self-consciousness is achieved through the 'elevation' from 'the protean Changeable' to 'the pure formless Unchangeable' (*Phenomenology of Spirit*, §§209–13), through an ethical as much as a cognitive movement of idealization, which leads from the temporal, 'vanished individuality' to the 'unchangeable Being'. The ethical valuation of the two opposed sides of self-consciousness comes more prominently into view in the last part of the *Phenomenology of Spirit*, that on the revealed religion, when Hegel defines one side of the antithesis, 'the side of evil', as that 'for which natural existence and individual self-consciousness count as essence' (§781). He further adds that the self, in having to withdraw from natural existence and retreat into itself, has to become evil (§782), but that the 'inwardizing', which involves 'the *knowledge of evil* as something that is *implicit* in existence' already constitutes 'the first moment of reconciliation' (§783).

Fondane argues that this negative valuation of empirical existence, which posits that the knowledge of evil is 'implicit in existence', constitutes one of the fundamental tenets of speculative thought of all times. Since such apodictic statements do not rely on particular judgements derived from experience, one can wonder whether the truth regarding the 'evil' that rational analysis identifies in empirical existence was not 'surreptitiously' introduced from the outset into existence by speculative thought. The formulation of this idea in Fondane's article 'Chestov et la lutte contre les évidences' bears a striking resemblance to a remark in Nietzsche's essay 'On Truth and Lies in a Nonmoral Sense':

> When someone hides something behind a bush and looks for it again in the same place and finds it there as well, there is not much to praise in such seeking and finding. Yet this is how matters stand regarding seeking and finding 'truth' within the realm of reason.[29]

Like Nietzsche, Fondane denounces the moral imperative that underpins this manner of seeking and finding truth. As Nietzsche remarks in the above-mentioned essay, 'to be truthful means to employ the usual metaphors. Thus, to express it morally, this is the duty to lie according to a fixed convention, to lie with the herd and in a manner binding upon everyone.'[30] Similarly, Fondane attacks both the moral foundation of the rational drive for truth, and the universally 'binding', necessary status of 'eternal' or immutable truths, especially those predicating the inherent evil of temporal, empirical existence:

> Il ne s'agit pas là d'une querelle de mots: la pensée ne porte que sur des essences; eh bien, nous nions qu'il existe une *essence du mal*; la pensée porte sur des nécessités intrinsèques; nous nions qu'il y ait une nécessité intrinsèque du mal; la pensée juge que le mal est nécessaire et qu'il ne peut *être* que si, émergeant du contingent, du transitif et du provisoire, il est immuable et éternel; nous nions, nous, que jamais mal sur terre eût semblable figure.[31]

According to Fondane, the postulation of an ineradicable evil attached to transient, contingent existence actually reflects the cognitive as much as the ethical aspiration towards a realm of timeless, immutable truth, which comes to be identified with the 'highest good' in opposition to the unavoidable, therefore 'necessary', misfortune of living under the incidence of perpetual change and final destruction. Fondane's interpretation of natural existence contrasts the ethical imperative of self-overcoming, which underpins the Hegelian movement of conceptualization based on dialectical reconciliation, and Kierkegaard's attempt to dislocate the interdependence of the concept of truth and the idea of the good by emphasizing the moment of 'separation', the rupture within consciousness.

Fondane acknowledges that Hegel's analysis of consciousness uncovers an aspect of crucial importance for existential thought: 'l'existence historique d'un *hiatus irrationalis* qui, en termes de conscience, est malheur, division, tragédie ou, comme [Hegel] le dit expressément en parlant du judaïsme: "horreur"'.[32] What existential thought objects to is the speculative overcoming of this moment, within a historical development whose teleology predetermines the aims and the final conclusion of the analysis:

En effet, la conscience est engagée dans une sorte de devenir historique; sa division absolue apparaît pour la première fois dans l'horreur de la catégorie du maître et de l'esclave, au sein du judaïsme; cette catégorie s'atténue et s'adoucit grâce au christianisme qui en prend la suite; l'universel devient concret, Dieu devient homme, Dieu est mort.[33]

As Fondane further argues, the consequence of the speculative, historical movement of 'inwardization' of the other, of 'the master' as exteriority or alterity ('l'intériorisation du maître'), is the gradual, complete rationalization of God as absolute otherness. Hegel's analysis leads not only to the reconciliation or the equivalence between the human and the divine but to the further conclusion that 'the dead divine Man or human God is *in himself* the universal self-consciousness' (*Phenomenology of Spirit*, §781). This complete humanization of the divine, safeguarding the aims of the speculative drive towards the universal 'in the sense of the universality of Reason' (§249), is paralleled by a similar rationalization of external reality. The Stoic attitude, Fondane comments, suspends 'non pas seulement l'extérieur comme Dieu, mais aussi l'extérieur comme réalité',[34] while replicating the dichotomy 'dans l'intérieur du terme qui restait' and completing the process of internalization. However, Stoicism constitutes a false return to unity insofar as 'l'esclave devient le "maître du maître"'. Fondane's perceptive interpretation of the historical evolution of self-consciousness, which leads to the recognition of the '*non-essentialité de l'autre* par rapport à *l'infinité de la pensée*', attempts to expose and dislodge the grounding of the rational construal of the notion of God within Hegel's speculative interpretation of 'revealed religion'. In dialectically overcoming the *horror religiosus* of the inwardly disrupted consciousness, and in reconciling the confrontation between the individual and the absolutely other with the aims of a rational elevation towards the united and unifying Absolute Spirit, Hegelian phenomenology puts an end to the religious *hiatus irrationalis* only to replace it with what Fondane calls 'the religion of reason':

Le Dieu vivant, ni le Dieu mort n'existent plus; ils ont été *dépassés*; à leur place s'est installé l'universel conciliateur, l'*Esprit*: la religion est devenue raison et la raison est devenue religion. Cette religion de la raison — à laquelle un Husserl essaiera de donner, plus tard, des fondements absolus — commence par 'la rationalisation d'un fond que la raison n'atteint pas'.[35]

Fondane interestingly points out that the conceptualization of the irreducible residuum of rational analysis (of 'natural existence' as well as the existence of God) enslaves rather than frees consciousness insofar as it generates a new unsurpassable instance of authority. Reason and rational necessity become the new master, in relation to which the individual thinking subject is a perpetual slave. As Fondane comments:

nous n'avons fait que de changer de 'maître': nous sommes à présent *les esclaves de la Nécessité*. *Amor fati*, tel est aujourd'hui le signe de notre malheur. Il nous faut aimer le malheur, il nous faut aimer la guerre, il nous faut aimer la mort et, ce qui pis est, *il nous faut les introduire en nous-mêmes, les rendre nous-mêmes*.[36]

While indirectly recalling Nietzsche's remark on the decision to sacrifice God 'and out of cruelty against oneself worship stone, stupidity, gravity, fate, nothingness' (*Beyond Good and Evil*, §55), Fondane emphasizes the double—logical and ethical—imperative that the living individual confronts as an inner, unsurpassable limit. The exaltation or the 'idolatry' of the limit posed by rational necessity, which has ensured the continuity of a 'philosophy of the finitude of being' from ancient to modern times, relies on the conceptual identification between truth and being as well as on the further correlation between the drive towards knowledge and the ethical striving towards 'the highest good'. The complete rationalization of being, which both Hegel's and Husserl's phenomenologies carried out in different manners, seems to relegate the existential 'fight against self-evidence', the confrontation between the existential and the conceptual interpretation of being, to the level of the living individual itself and of its temporally determined consciousness:

Ce conflit est d'autant plus angoissant que l'adversaire est logé dans notre propre moi et que c'est en elle-même, au sein d'un individu déterminé, que l'existence rencontre les résistances de la raison, et la raison l'opposition désespérée de l'existence. L'adversaire le plus terrible de Husserl, c'est sa propre existence, et l'adversaire le plus embêtant de Chestov, c'est sa propre raison.[37]

This situation of conflict within an individually and temporally determined framework is crucial for the existential 'alternative' definition of being and truth. It is not so much dictated by the previous Hegelian or Husserlian configurations of self-consciousness as it is found adequate to meet the existential aim of dislocating an interpretation of time, which underpins the interlocking of the concepts of being and truth. In refusing to solve this conflict either in terms of the Hegelian historical evolution of self-consciousness or in terms of the Husserlian phenomenological reduction, which isolates the pure transcendental consciousness, existential thought undercuts the fundamental premiss of any speculative, systematic search for truth: the idea that truth is the result of a necessary movement of conceptualization that either dialectically supersedes or phenomenologically 'brackets' the level of 'natural existence' and of 'natural consciousness'. Moreover, in situating the tension between the existential investigation of truth and the rational, transcendental investigation of truth at the level of the temporal, lived experience of a particular individual, Fondane's and Chestov's approach challenges the interpretation of time that underlines the definition of truth with reference to timeless, immutable principles. It is also important to note at this point that the existential critique of the rational interpretation of time aims to destroy not only the foundation of the concept of truth, but also the foundation of the concept of freedom; for the understanding of freedom itself is determined by the same assumptions concerning the opposition between temporal, empirical existence and timeless, necessary being.

Within Kantian as well as Hegelian transcendental idealism, the possibility of freedom becomes intrinsically bound up with the possibility of knowledge, with the movement of conceptualization that seeks to overcome the empirical conditions of temporal existence, 'the protean Changeable', in order to attain the realm of timeless, immutable and necessary being. Fondane and Chestov argue that what the transcendental idealistic analysis of freedom actually establishes in relation to the interpretation of time is the freedom or, more adequately, the autonomy of reason itself (as absolutely free from temporal, empirical determinations). On this ground, autonomous reason proceeds to establish the conditions under which the particular, living individual can aspire to and achieve a degree of freedom.

Fondane, like Chestov, points to the double (logical and ethical) commandment underpinning the rational configuration of freedom, quoting Seneca's words: 'si vis tibi omnia subjicere te subjice rationi (if you wish to subject all things to yourself, subject yourself to reason)'. What the existential critique of rationality attempts to expose and annihilate is a fundamental, unquestioned subjection or bondage of the particular individual in relation to reason, insofar as this relationship determines the ground and the possibility of freedom. The disclosure of this new master–slave relationship exceeds the Hegelian reconciliatory project. The existential manner of posing the problem of the 'unhappy consciousness' uncovers a more profound contradiction that is irreducible to the dialectical reconciliation within the unifying framework of rationality itself. Existential thought advances a notion of being that precedes and undercuts the bondage or subjection to rational necessity, to rational validatory arguments:

> Ce n'est pas d'un autre Savoir qu'il s'agit, mais d'un *non-savoir*, d'une pensée qui ne veut pas 'comprendre' l'être, mais parvenir à l'être, et ne veut pas se soumettre à l'impossible, mais se le soumettre et lui commander.[38]

In moving beyond the boundary of logical intelligibility and validatory argument, Fondane and Chestov aim to recapture a notion of freedom grounded in the simultaneous existence of an empirical and transcendent residuum of rational analysis that precedes the dichotomy between truth and error or the correlative dichotomy between good and evil. The transcendent existence of God makes manifest the possibility of dislocating the intertwining of rational truth and being, insofar as His existence as well as the creation of Man precedes rational knowledge, the Knowledge of Good and Evil. The empirical existence of a particular individual, Fondane argues, similarly precedes the rational affirmation or negation of being and dislocates the rational interlocking of the search for truth and the aspiration towards the 'highest good'—the ethical imperative of self-overcoming, which underlies the movement of conceptualization. However, in stating that existence 'precedes' rational argument, Fondane does not refer to a relationship defined in terms of chronological anteriority. Existence 'precedes' rational analysis only in the sense that it uncovers a more fundamental question, that of an irreducible residuum of being, something that exceeds the framework of the rational interpretation of time.

René Daumal criticizes scientific knowledge for its failure to address questions that resist rational elucidation. As Daumal argues, the scientific endeavour to identify the unchangeable principles of what is perpetually changing comes up against 'des choses qu'il est impossible d'identifier, [...] des "irréductibles"'.[39] The critique of scientific methods of investigation develops into an opposition between Kantian and Hegelian transcendental idealism insofar as the former constitutes a philosophy of the *status quo*, which sets not only the a priori conditions but also the limits of human understanding, while the latter has the advantage of affirming the possibility of a limitless progress of consciousness as well as of our understanding. One might conclude that the exhaustiveness of the Hegelian interpretation is actually the model on which Daumal based his search for an alternative mode of thinking, in opposition to what he calls 'la science discursive'. However, the last sentence of his article provides a different answer to the limitations of scientific analysis: pataphysics, in the sense of 'un humour redoutable', replaces the previous reference to Hegelian dialectic. The difference is significant because Daumal's notion of 'l'évidence absurde', related to the paradoxes of pataphysical thinking, is hardly if at all compatible with Hegel's exhaustive rationalization of reality and consciousness. In order to appreciate the contrast between the pataphysical and the Hegelian solutions to the irreducible residuum of scientific investigation, one need only consider the following explicit description of the type of 'demonstration' that Daumal associated with pataphysical thinking:

> [C]e genre de démonstration pose avec force le caractère irréductible de l'existence individuelle et, par *la réduction à l'absurde*, procédé proprement pataphysique, dessine le cercle vicieux de la science tout en lui échappant. En résumé: l'irréductible est absurde; réduisons donc à l'absurde pour prouver l'évidence.[40]

Pataphysical reasoning not only confounds and playfully ridicules the working of the logical mind but also subtly circumvents the exhaustiveness of Hegel's dictum, 'everything real is rational', and turns the conclusive judgement derived from this premiss into its exact opposite: 'l'irréductible est absurde' (unlike everything that is real, the irreducible character of individual existence is absurd). The method proposed for proving the truth (*l'évidence*) of this affirmation—*reductio ad absurdum*—is not surprisingly in stark contrast to the Hegelian dialectical progression to ever higher levels of rational elucidation. The parodic, subversive appropriation of speculative argumentation by pataphysics has the same function and aim as the existential 'fight against self-evidence': both critical strategies seek to bring out the contradictory, irreducible nature of individual existence. Striking similarities emerge when one compares Fondane's or Chestov's configuration of a 'second dimension of thought', focused on the 'irrational residuum of being' and Daumal's definition of an alternative mode of knowledge. Pataphysics, Daumal argues, is 'la connaissance du particulier et de l'irréductible. Or l'existence de l'irréductible est un autre aspect de mon existence en tant qu'être particulier, existence contradictoire, puisqu'en même temps je me sais partie de l'Un.'[41]

According to Gilbert-Lecomte, *Le Grand Jeu* made manifest a tendency that was also shared by the writers gathered around another ephemeral publication of the period, the magazine *L'Esprit*. Their philosophical investigations, Gilbert-Lecomte argues, did not provide a solution to the 'irreconcilable contradiction' of 'the unhappy consciousness', to the opposition between 'pouvoir et savoir', between 'savoir et vivre'.[42] There is good reason to believe that the same might apply to the understanding of freedom that *Le Grand Jeu* developed around the notions of 'résignation' and 'renoncement'. Instead of situating these notions within the framework of the Hegelian movement of self-overcoming and the dialectical reconciliation of opposites, *Le Grand Jeu* emphasized the moment of negation as part of a continuous process of destruction, an advance towards the void. 'Résignation' no longer designates 'self-abnegation' in the sense of a conceptual movement of elevation. Gilbert-Lecomte understands renunciation ias the 'regression' to the void (to the pre-conceptual level). This tendency, he argues, 'résiste à toute analyse rationnelle'. Like the existential fight against self-evidence, the negative movement of resignation or renunciation might be part of an attempt to dislocate not only the cognitive but also the ethical foundation of rational thought.

Judging by Gilbert-Lecomte's remarks, this movement of renunciation aims to destroy '[les] idoles Vrai-Bien-Beau' by creating a kind of whirlpool of perpetual negations that empties the consciousness and provokes a process of 'resorption'. Gilbert-Lecomte's description of 'resorption' suggests that the progression towards the void has its own momentum and its own power of suction, which threatens to engulf the ground of logical dichotomous thinking. Renunciation thus signals a continuous disengagement with logical argumentation. It creates a moment of discontinuity, which like the existential 'either/or' makes possible a new interpretation of freedom: 'Quiconque a le désir profond de se libérer doit volontairement nier tout pour se vider l'esprit, et renoncer toujours à tout pour se vider le cœur. Il faut qu'il arrive à faire naître peu à peu en lui un état d'innocence qui soit la pureté du vide.'[43] Like Fondane (who describes the existential approach as 'non-savoir'), Gilbert-Lecomte defines the negative, inverted evolution towards a preconceptual level in terms of a suspension of rational knowledge: the meaning of 'le renoncement' is 'le désapprendre'.[44]

Gilbert-Lecomte's negative advance towards a prespeculative affirmation of Life in opposition to Knowledge involves the replacement of the universality of scientific reason with '[une] généralité non-conceptuelle mais sentie' based on 'la catégorie affective, ni aristotélicienne ni kantienne'.[45] In this respect, one can argue that Gilbert-Lecomte shared Fondane's understanding of the relationship between an alternative, existential mode of knowledge and poetic experience. Their critique of the rational, scientific approach to truth and being assigns a central role to poetic emotion, to 'vision' and 'revelation', to notions of mystical or prelogical 'participation', which point to rather than conceptually validate the 'irreducible residuum' of speculative analysis.

However, in *Le Grand Jeu* and in Fondane's writing, 'poetic' or existential knowledge is situated beyond the level of aesthetic experience. Fondane, like Chestov, considered that the search for a new understanding of being exceeded not only the aesthetic but also the ethical framework (the first two stages of life, according to Kierkegaard). The movement of 'renunciation' described by Gilbert-Lecomte leads beyond an aesthetic rejection of rational categories, while nevertheless failing to suspend moral determination altogether. A new morality of perpetual negation emerges after the 'death of art' heralded by Rimbaud.[46] Interestingly, Gilbert-Lecomte redefines the idea of 'beauty' with reference to this morality of revolt in a manner that is certainly compatible with the Surrealist notion of 'convulsive beauty': 'la beauté [...] ne sera que le reflet de l'idée morale de révolte, c'est-à-dire que pour tous cette beauté sera à jamais révoltante'.[47] The negative advance towards the void ('renoncement') does produce a disengagement with ethics, which comes from Gilbert-Lecomte's explicit rejection of the Kantian categorical imperative as well as from the systematic, normative foundation of what he calls 'la morale abstraite'. However, he contrasts the speculative elaboration of ethical doctrines, corresponding to the development of Western philosophical thought, to the 'dynamic morality' of Oriental cultures. He defines the latter, non-systematic variety as 'une force de la nature, un progrès vraiment qualitatif, [...] une évolution spirituelle vers le mieux-être'.[48]

Insofar as Gilbert-Lecomte argues that the foundation of this 'dynamic morality' could be thought of in terms of the possible application of the dialectical method to an 'enlarged' understanding of psychoanalysis (one that would replace the restrictive notion of 'libido' with the Jungian-derived idea of an all-encompassing 'psychic energy'), it is doubtful whether the affirmation of religious belief in *Le Grand Jeu*, as the 'antithesis' of an affirmation of reason, ever escaped the Hegelian reconciliatory project. Daumal's and Gilbert-Lecomte's ambivalent attitude to Hegel's philosophy, as well as their interest in the relationship between Hegelian phenomenology and Freudian psychoanalysis, brings their investigation of ethical questions much closer to the Surrealist dialectic morality of revolt than to the existential 'suspension of the ethical', which situates individual existence and the existence of God 'beyond good and evil' (beyond the logical and ethical foundation of normative value-judgements).

The self-contradictory, ambiguous position of *Le Grand Jeu* makes the Surrealist and existential projects seem more consistent in comparison. On the one hand, Daumal and Gilbert-Lecomte propose to uncover an irreducible residuum of being through a negative advance towards the void, a revolt of the individual against itself, which apparently resists rational analysis. On the other, their understanding of God does not ultimately challenge the theological and philosophical interconnection between truth and the idea of the 'good', between the human aspiration towards the divine and the rational drive towards the 'highest good'. Indeed, in *Le Grand Jeu*, God still is the embodiment of the Moral Law. The affirmation of God's existence does not suspend the opposition between temporal and timeless being or the negative logical and ethical valuation of empirical, transitory existence.

Conversely, Surrealism rejects any notion of God or of transcendent being, and elaborates a morality of revolt/revolution in keeping with

Marxist historical materialism and with the Freudian and Marxist critique of religion. Hegel's identification of the 'divine Man' with the 'human God' foreshadowed the concept of the death of God. From the point of view of Hegelian phenomenology, the absolute alterity of a realm of being that is irreducible to human understanding (a role played by the 'thing-in-itself' in Kantian apriorism) no longer poses a limit to rational knowledge. It becomes a stimulant to knowledge insofar as it constitutes the term of an opposition that is now situated and constantly overcome within self-consciousness itself. The 'unknowable' ceases to be an unattainable 'outside' or an absolute otherness, as the dialectical movement ensures the infinite progression towards the knowledge of what may seem unfathomable but can be and actually is continuously refashioned, remoulded in the process of rational elucidation. This approach enables the construal of 'unknowable' otherness as the 'not yet known', an 'outside' that is still 'inside'—within the greater framework of human rationality and the teleological advance of self-consciousness towards the Absolute Spirit. The 'death of God' occurs against the background of the gradual speculative reduction of the distance between self and absolute otherness, between the inside and the outside of an ever-expanding field of rational comprehension.

Chestov's and Fondane's critique of the logical and ethical arguments that underlie the speculative appropriation and the humanization of the divine anticipates more recent attempts to re-examine Marxist theory in the wake of the historical, onto-theological identification of God with the universality of human reason. Jean-Luc Marion traces back this identification to the constitution of a 'phenomenology of the *eidolon*', which has its source in ancient and medieval metaphysical doctrines and culminates in Hegel's 'idolatrous' construal of God with reference to absolute Knowledge. *L'Idole et la distance* (1976) indirectly supports and resituates the existential critique within a contemporary philosophical context. Marion's ample analysis, uncovering the historical evolution of a discourse that works to reduce the distance between the human and the divine while subjecting God to the human conditions of the experience of the divine, brings to the fore at least two major conclusions directly relevant to existential thought:

1. The idol of the 'Christian God' that Nietzsche declares dead is constructed in relation to the notion of truth and to the will for truth

as the figure of the will to power. The idol that dies is therefore the idol that the moral law (as expression of the will to power) has produced.[49]

2. The idolatrous identification of 'God' with absolute Knowledge in Hegel provided the basis on which Feuerbach's and Marx's theories of alienation could empty one concept of its meaning to the benefit of another within a metaphysical system of communicating 'vessels'. This allowed for the development of an understanding of religion in terms of a 'commerce' between the human and the divine, by which the more man invests in God the less he possesses.[50]

Chestov's and Fondane's attempt to uncover an 'irreducible residuum of being' that resists rational analysis involved a similar critique of the onto-theo-logical construal of God with reference to the epistemological and ethical imperatives guiding the search for rational truth. In proposing to dislocate the correlation between truth and being, existential thought aimed to pre-empt the speculative humanization of the divine, which makes possible the interpretation of the relationship between human existence and divine existence in terms of 'commerce', of an economy of loss and dispossession. From Chestov's and Fondane's perspective, this relationship exceeds rational calculation, and it can only be seen as a 'loss' insofar as it is an unaccountable residuum of a speculative economics of being that aspires to exhaustiveness. The irreducible character of both man's and God's existence makes possible a simultaneous, paradoxical affirmation of being in which the two terms 'comprehend' (as much as they include) each other beyond logical and ethical calculations of truth and error, good and evil.

Surrealism subscribed to Feuerbach's and Marx's destruction of the concept of God provided by the Hegelian phenomenology of Spirit. The revolutionary practice promoted by Surrealism configured the relationship between man and God in terms of 'alienation' and 'exploitation', pertaining to the ideology of the proletarian struggle for social and political liberation. In *Signe ascendant*, Breton remarks: 'Il faut, non seulement que cesse l'exploitation de l'homme par l'homme mais que cesse l'exploitation de l'homme par le prétendu "Dieu" d'absurde et provocante mémoire.'[51] Both Marxist and Freudian analyses of man's iredeemable investment in God (as part of an economy of expenditure and return) indicate that the refutation of a concept whose speculative history is also that of the transcendence of the moral law does not actually lead to a corresponding refutation of dichotomous ethical valuations. Rather, both the historical-materialist and the psychoanalytical assessments of the human condition promise to fulfill the rational aspiration towards the 'highest good' through a dialectical reconciliation of opposites and a movement of self-overcoming that reinforce the ethical foundation of the drive for knowledge.

From the existential point of view, Surrealism failed to notice that the Marxist as well as the Freudian refutation of religious belief left intact what Fondane called the 'religion of reason'. Following the speculative humanization of the divine, the death of God as the idol that the moral law had produced enabled a transfer of attributes from the dead concept of 'divine being' to the new concept of 'man'. However, man himself, like the former rational notión of God, remained bound to unsurpassable first principles of thought that determined the possibility of freedom in relation to the ethical, imperative drive to knowledge. The humanist conception that was developed within the Surrealist movement supported this fundamental moral exigency and anticipated, in this sense, the declared humanist orientation of Sartrian Existentialism. As Ferdinand Alquié observes, the two projects converge in their aspiration to found a 'coherent humanism' that makes any aspect of reality and any value relative to man.[52] It is true that Chestov and Fondane often quoted Protagoras's famous saying, 'Man is the measure of all things.' However, to them, this statement also contained the less apparent Nietzschean call for a 'transvaluation of all values', which questions the very production of cognitive and ethical value judgements. If man is the measure of all things, then his existence can be disentangled from the production of truths or 'usual metaphors'. Chestov also argued that, insofar as reason itself rather than 'man' sets the measure that determines the philosophers' quest for truth, there are issues that exceed speculative 'measurement', that remain incommensurable with the established limits of human understanding.[53]

In contrast to the Surrealist and the Existentialist position, Fondane declares, 'Nous contestons que l'homme soit la seule réponse à l'homme.'[54] The problem of human existence, the contradiction of the 'unhappy, inwardly disrupted consciousness', may not find a definitive answer within humanistic conceptions that continue rather than subvert the traditional 'philosophy of the finitude of being'. The idea of values and truths that man 'creates', in the Surrealist and

Existentialist sense, does not suspend the ethical exigency that presides over this creation and governs the social practice attached to it. Fondane argues that social revolutions, political commitments and new ethical imperatives will not alter the rationalist manner of posing the question of human mortality. Insofar as the logical and ethical foundations of rationalist philosophy remain unchallenged, the examination of the three most important problems confronting an existing individual (the immortality of the soul, the existence of God and the possibility of freedom) will be determined by the underlying postulate of the finitude of temporal being. The existential quest for freedom, which probes the foundation of the rational interpretation of time, proceeds from the critique of the concepts of truth and 'the good' to a Kierkegaardian 'suspension of the ethical'.

Freedom Beyond Good and Evil: *La Fin du fini*

Like Nietzsche's critique of the concept of truth, the existential approach points to the gap between our cognitive capacities and our cognitive interests and desires.[55] This means that what one desires to know, especially those things one considers of utmost importance, may not be within the reach of one's cognitive capacity or even within the limits of rational elucidation. The question that arises from this remark, and the question that the existential analysis of truth brings out, is: Who decides what can and should be the object of cognition, what are the aims and the limits of human understanding? If the immortality of the soul, the existence of God and freedom constitute the three issues of utmost importance to any human being, who or even 'what' determines whether our cognitive interests should reside within the boundaries of our rational capacity of understanding? And if any or all of these issues prove to exceed our cognitive capacity and the limits of rational demonstrability, who or what decides that such issues are also beyond our cognitive interests?

In this respect, Chestov and Fondane often recall Aristotle's imperative warning, ἀνάγκη στῆναι (one must stop), or Kant's similar caution about those 'absurd' questions that 'not only [bring] shame on the propounder of the question, but may betray an incautious listener into absurd answers'.[56] The appeals to 'shame', as well as Aristotle's imperative interdiction of trespassing over a limit beyond which the greatest misfortune (to become μισολόγος, an adversary of reason) befalls the incautious propounder or listener of 'absurd' questions, signal the presence of an ethical commandment underlying the call for moderation. We need to moderate our cognitive interests and desires if we are to avoid the shame and misfortune of asking and trying to answer questions that exceed our own cognitive capacities. As Fondane observes, the rationalist philosopher 'a fait de ses opérations logiques des principes de *moralité;* la vertu-science de Socrate a été fondée; désormais, toute infraction à la vérité logique est devenue un crime de lèse-morale'.[57]

Thus, any attempt to formulate questions that can have no 'reasonable' answer, in the sense in which the legitimacy of the question and the validity of the answer cannot be logically established, comes up against an ethical as much as a cognitive injunction stipulating that 'one must stop'. The risk of ignoring this injunction is to disgrace oneself, through a deliberate disregard of one's *probité intellectuelle* or *probité scientifique*, as Chestov and Fondane remark. Consequently, the μισολόγος not only risks excommunication from the community of self-respecting philosophers who understand, like Kant, that 'to know what questions may reasonably be asked is already a great and necessary proof of sagacity and insight' (*Critique of Pure Reason*, §A58); the 'adversary of reason' also risks excluding the problems he intends to raise from the field of respectable, scientific investigation altogether. However, Chestov consistently argues against the idea that this should 'consequently' be the case:

Par conséquent? Par conséquent, direz-vous, il faut oublier la Bible et suivre Spinoza et Kant [...]. Mais si l'on essayait pour une fois de conclure autrement, si l'on disait: 'par conséquent', il faut envoyer au diable l'honnêteté intellectuelle pour se débarasser des postulats de Kant et apprendre à parler à Dieu comme lui parlaient nos ancêtres! L'honnêteté intellectuelle consiste à se soumettre à la raison, non par crainte, extérieurement, mais de tout cœur. Elle est une vertu si le pouvoir de la raison est légitime. Et si la raison s'était emparé du pouvoir illégalement? Notre soumission à ses décrets ne serait-elle pas alors un esclavage honteux?[58]

What is at stake is not simply the 'revealed truth' of the Bible against the scientific validity of rationally established truth; it is the freedom of posing the question of freedom itself, as related to the other 'ultimate' questions concerning the immortality of the soul and the existence of God, in other terms than those determined by the limits of our 'cognitive capacities', of our ability to demonstrate and validate potential answers. The issue that is at stake here might in fact be expressed in the following way: Is Kierkegaard's 'either/or' possible? Does one have the possibility of disengaging with the ethical and cognitive imperatives governing our search for truth in order to redefine our understanding of 'freedom'?

From the perspective of the Aristotelian and Kantian cautionary postulates about the aims and the necessary limits posed to our cognitive desires, this 'either/or' is not a reasonable possibility; it is not a possibility at all. In fact, as Chestov and Fondane point out, the ethical and logical call for moderation, reiterated throughout the history of systematic thought, actually determines the conditions of what is to be considered 'possible' and sets the limit between the 'possible' and the 'impossible', between what is within and what is beyond our cognitive capacities, our power of understanding. Since ancient times, the ability to grasp and submit to the distinction between τὰ ἐφ᾽ ἡμῖν (what is in our power) and τὰ οὐκ ἐφ᾽ ἡμῖν (what is beyond our power) has not only been 'a great and necessary proof of sagacity and insight', but the beginning, the first postulate of any rational philosophical investigation. As Chestov recalls, quoting Epictetus, 'Le commencement de la philosophie est la conscience de sa propre impuissance et de l'impossibilité de lutter contre la nécessité.'[59] This acknowledgement finds its ethical rather than purely logical justification, in that man actually 'does not aspire to the impossible' as Aristotle argues: προαίρεσις μὲν γὰρ οὐκ ἔστιν τῶν ἀδυνάτων, καὶ εἴ τις φαίη προαιρεῖσθαι δοκοίη ἄν ἠλίθιος εἶναι ('l'homme n'aspire pas à l'impossible, et s'il y aspire, tout le monde le considérera comme un faible d'esprit').[60]

The bottom line of this reasoning is the ethical appeal to one's *honnêteté intellectuelle*. By confronting the one who disregards the limits (or 'powerlessness') of rational investigation with yet another attribution of powerlessness (*faiblesse d'esprit*), while acquiescence seems to entail a certain 'power'—the attribution of 'sagacity' and 'insight'—the rationalist philosopher appeals to the virtue of man's intellectual 'honesty'. More accurately, as Chestov comments, this argument relies on man's submission to the postulates of reason, which determine the limits of our cognitive interests and the point at which one 'should stop'. It is a question of universal consent, of general agreement, which supports the fundamental postulation about what is reasonably 'possible', and 'within our power', as opposed to what is 'impossible', 'beyond our power' of understanding, therefore 'not to be pursued'. But, as Chestov further argues, man often forgets that in the realm of rational possibility and impossibility, the imperative call for moderation and 'free' submission to existing limitations ('non par crainte, extérieurement, mais de tout cœur') relies on general consent or, more adequately, on agreed conventions.

Nietzsche's comments on truth bring into view the 'forgetfulness' that ensures that the conventionally agreed boundaries of both our cognitive capacities and our cognitive interests appear to be universally binding, necessary, therefore unquestionable:

> What is then truth? A movable host of metaphors, metonymies and anthropomorphisms: in short, a sum of human relations which have been poetically and rhetorically intensified, transferred and embellished, and which, after long usage, seem to a people to be fixed, canonical and binding. Truths are illusions which we have forgotten are illusions.[61]

In arguing that '*by means of this unconsciousness* and forgetfulness [man] arrives at his sense of truth',[62] a Nietzsche points to the same consensus or acquiescence in existing conventions that Chestov identifies as man's 'free' submission to the postulates of reason. The sudden 'recollection' or recognition of the consensual character of what is to be considered as rationally 'possible' within the set limits of our cognitive capacities constitutes the first step of the existential fight for a redefinition of freedom. Kierkegaard's 'either/or' uncovers the forgotten possibility of disengaging with the general consensual framework of rational investigation and of undertaking a solitary search for truth that defies the ethical appeals to 'shame' or the threat of 'weakness' and 'greatest misfortune' attributed to μισόλογοι (adversaries of reason). If man himself is the one who establishes the consensus about what is 'possible' and 'impossible', then he also has the freedom to redefine existing conventions and pursue cognitive interests that exceed the set boundaries of human cognitive capacities. Although this description of the existential view of freedom might seem to involve very specific, if not relatively modest, objectives, one need only consider the actual implications of the Kierkegaardian 'either/or' in order to grasp the full scope of the existential project. The possibility of disengaging with the consensual framework of rational investigation implies that:

1. the boundaries of our understanding and of our cognitive interests are conventionally established—relative and open to alteration;
2. we have only a relative measure of truth within set boundaries of human understanding;

3. the rational interlocking of 'truth' and 'being' is only valid by consent, within agreed boundaries of what is rationally 'possible' (what we can know and logically validate) and what 'is' (what we can rationally affirm as 'being');
4. we can legitimately aspire to a notion of 'truth' and a notion of 'being' that are incommensurable with or exceed conventional boundaries of rational understanding and logical validation;
5. the rational interlocking of 'truth' and the idea of the 'good', of epistemological and ethical cognitive interest is also valid only by consent.

This last statement actually targets the underlying, 'forgotten' postulate in relation to which any other statements concerning the boundaries of human understanding, the concepts of truth and being, the aims and limits of legitimate cognitive aspirations appear binding (necessary), universal and timeless (independent of the empirical, temporal conditions of human existence). Nietzsche's and Kierkegaard's critique of systematic philosophy uncovered the moral origin of the drive for knowledge. Recalling this origin as well as the relative (consensual and temporal rather than timeless) value of the ethical imperatives that underpin the 'necessary' character of rational postulates forms an integral part of the existential strategy for arriving at a new understanding of freedom.

References to the notions of 'anamnesis', *paramnésie*, 'forgetfulness' vs. 'recollection' and so on play an important role not only in Chestov's and Fondane's writing but also in *Le Grand Jeu*. Despite obvious similarities with processes that belong to the Freudian interpretative framework, the existential use of 'anamnesis' or *paramnésie* as part of a genealogical critique of rationality has quite different aims from psychoanalysis. Instead of trying to reconcile desire with reality and to 'educate' or bring the 'pleasure-ego' under the injunction of the 'reality principle',[63] existential thought attempts to maintain and legitimate 'desire'—in the sense of cognitive interests or desires that contradict and exceed existing limits of rational 'possibility' and of human cognitive capacities. At the same time, this attempt to legitimate such cognitive aspirations undermines the foundation and the necessary, universal character of the 'reality principle' itself. What the existential 'anamnesis' aims to recapture is man's option to engage with, or disengage from, the logical and ethical conventions that underpin the 'reality principle'.

Insofar as the Freudian and the Hegelian interpretations of consciousness, with reference to time, converge in recognizing the tension between conflicting desires and in seeking to resolve this tension through a process that involves the internalization of oppositional relations and the dialectical reconciliation of opposites, existential 'anamnesis' attempts to undermine the foundation of both psychoanalytic and phenomenological cognitive frameworks.[64] In existential thought, the process of recollection does not simply target the 'forgetfulness' associated with the hidden topography of the unconscious in opposition to consciousness; it further signals the oblivion that Nietzsche associated with the speculative search for truth as well as the oblivion of the origin and status of the ethical and logical postulates underlying this search for truth. The same ethical imperative of self-knowledge as self-overcoming operates in the Hegelian historical movement of self-consciousness and in the Freudian interpretation of human desire in terms of a history that 'involves refusal and hurt' and through which 'desire becomes educated to reality through the specific unpleasure inflicted upon it by an opposing desire'.[65] The existential process of 'anamnesis' thus aims to reverse this historical evolution and to uncover the obliterated point at which the principle of Life was overcome and replaced by the principle of Knowledge, that is, the Knowledge of Good and Evil:

Le fait même que notre Savoir se donne comme un 'progrès infini', progrès que l'Histoire nous permet aisément de mesurer, ne nous autorise-t-il pas à *refaire la trajectoire en sens inverse* jusqu'à la découverte d'*un point* où, *pour la première fois*, l'existence a été accablée de sa propre connaissance et où le sujet a été affligé, pour la première fois de l'objet?

Qu'il nous faille considérer l'entreprise philosophique [en son *essence*, bien entendu, et avant même qu'elle ne fut devenu 'philosophie' — je veux dire dès son point de départ, qui est rupture avec le concret, division de l'homme avec le réel, par l'entremise d'un bien et d'un mal dont on vient de *prendre conscience* (Cf. la *Genèse: 'Et ils connurent qu'ils étaient nus'*...)], comme une simple activité historique, voilà une opinion qu'il faudra ranger un jour parmis les *naïvetés* de cet âge.[66]

The regressive movement of 'anamnesis' in Fondane's and Chestov's writing parallels the negative advance towards the void, the movement of 'resorption' described in *Le Grand Jeu*. The existential 'fight against self-evidence', which makes possible the 'awakening' to a different understanding of truth or to the 'absurd evidence' (posited by Daumal and Gilbert-Lecomte), is a fight against 'forgetfulness'. In trying to recapture a moment that precedes or rather undercuts the historical evolution of systematic philosophy from its 'origin' to the present, the existential 'anamnesis' involves a retrospective destruction of the continuous chain of 'self-evident' truths leading back to the 'first', original intertwining of morality and the drive for knowledge. Chestov's and Fondane's argument thus brings together Nietzsche's genealogical account of morality, his remark on the moral origin of the drive for knowledge, and his critique of the forgetfulness through which man arrives at the conventional understanding of 'truth'. But the most significant implication of the existential interpretation of 'anamnesis' is that it undermines the rational interpretation of time that supports the conventional concepts of truth and being, their plain correlation and their dependence on the ethical dichotomous opposition between good and evil. Insofar as the recalled 'origin' of speculative thought escapes historical determinations (it is not situated 'in time'), the process of existential anamnesis aims to recapture a perspective that subverts the foundation of the linear, chronological and teleological interpretation of time.

The obliterated moral 'origin' of the drive for knowledge contains not only the emerging dichotomy between good and evil but also that between temporal, mortal being and timeless, eternal being or the further dichotomy between the empirical, heterogeneous experience of time and the abstract, homogeneous configuration of time. In trying to recall this origin, and the initial rupture or inner division within the consciousness of the knowing subject, existential thought actually seeks to go beyond the apparently unsurpassable limit of an original, fundamental choice between good and evil, between the 'highest good' associated with the drive for knowledge and the 'evil' inscribed in natural, temporal existence. The point of the recollection process is to retrieve the meaning of the biblical story of the Fall of Man and to uncover the obliterated link between death and the fruit of the Tree of the Knowledge of Good and Evil. From this perspective, death is not the first and ultimate truth of natural existence, contrary to what Hegel argued, reiterating the main postulate of systematic philosophical thought from ancient to modern times. Death is inscribed in the Knowledge of Good and Evil and initiates a drive for knowledge that remains at all times opposed to the principle of Life. The 'philosophy of the finitude of being' emerges from and finds its justification in the unsurpassable truth of human mortality.

The ethical imperative of self-knowledge as self-overcoming reinforces the premiss of the speculative, negative valuation of temporal existence while obliterating the link between death and the advent of the 'Moral Law'. Chestov explicitly recalls this forgotten link by tracing back the origin of 'death' to the 'knowledge of good and evil' with reference to the Fall of Man in the Book of Genesis:

[L]e premier homme ne distinguait pas le bien du mal, ignorait la loi, et quand il a cueilli et goûté le fruit de l'arbre de la connaissance du bien et du mal, c'est-à-dire quand il a commencé à distinguer le bien du mal, quand il a reçu 'la loi', il a, avec la loi, reçu la mort.[67]

From the existential point of view, the interdependence between ethics and rational knowledge is grounded in the fundamental postulate of the unsurpassable character of death, which poses a limitation to man's quest for truth and freedom. In contrast to the philosophy of the finitude of being, which places man under the imperative of the Law and defines his existence in relation to death, Chestov and Fondane advance the project of a philosophy of Life, which is also a philosophy of unlimited freedom. Existential thought uncovers the obliterated link between Life and unlimited freedom by means of a radical disengagement with rational knowledge, which Fondane expresses in uncompromising terms when he writes, 'N'est-il plus exact de dire que là où il y a connaissance il n'y a pas de liberté, et que là où il y a liberté il n'y a pas de connaissance? que la liberté cesse précisément là où commence la connaissance?'[68] The possibility of an alternative manner of posing the question of freedom, as related to life rather than to the unsurpassable limit of death, arises from the recollection of the fundamental question of rational knowledge, which Fondane argues was 'conjured away', eluded from the very beginning:

Etait-ce bien possible que la connaissance — cette pure sagesse, cet antique savoir — trichât, afin que l'on oubliât qu'elle avait escamoté sa première question, *la première question entre toutes*: 'Pourquoi, au fond, la connaissance? pourquoi des évidences premières et absolues? pourquoi des évidences qui doivent et peuvent soutenir l'édifice du savoir? Et que fera-t-on des évidences qui *doivent, mais ne peuvent* soutenir cet édifice? à quoi bon ce savoir *fondé sur le sacrifice*? La vie en avait-elle besoin pour vivre? ce savoir était-il nécessaire, indispensable à la vie? ou bien, tout au contraire, s'agissait-il d'*un refus à la vie*, d'un suicide, d'un essai d'évasion, de quelque chose dont la vie *ne voulait pas*?'[69]

Depending on the recognition or the denial of the legitimacy of this series of questions, the philosopher makes a choice between two irreconcilable lines of argument. From the existential perspective, the obliteration of these questions, dismissed as improper or illegitimate (insofar as they elicit absurd answers), characterizes the history of speculative thought, which attributes a fundamental role to ethical problems while relegating ontology to a secondary position. In this case, as Chestov observes: 'l'être se trouvera limité par la pensée'.[70] The other line of argument brings out the Kierkegaardian alternative: the affirmation of life is made possible by the simultaneous disengagement with rational thought and with ethics. The existential philosopher thus defines himself with reference to 'le désir de passer "par delà le bien et le mal"', and 'le souvenir (anamnésis) de ce que voyait le premier homme'.[71]

Whereas the rational line of argument determines the possibility of freedom in relation to the epistemological and ethical aims of the search for truth (according to necessary and universal conditions, to concepts of 'the highest good' and of 'duty'), the existential redefinition of freedom involves the dislocation of the interlocking of freedom and ethics, of freedom and necessity. Chestov's critique of the Kantian ethical theory brings out the implications of an investigation of freedom that proceeds from the double (ethical and logical) grounding of rational necessity. Although philosophers have always expatiated on the question of freedom, what they sought was actually necessity[72]—necessary laws, independent of empirical and temporal determinations. As Chestov also argues, the 'ultimate truths' reached within this type of investigation are truths that 'chain' rather than 'liberate' man. The existential desire to look for freedom 'beyond good and evil' proves to be incommensurable with Kant's statement that 'the "ought" pronounced by reason confronts such willing with a limit and an end—nay more, forbids or authorizes it'.[73]

Insofar as the freedom of the will is defined in relation to the existing limits of human understanding and to the ethical pronouncements of reason, man's cognitive desires and personal inclinations have to comply with the boundaries set by rational necessity. According to Kant's conception, an action is to be considered 'free' only inasmuch as it is performed 'out of duty', independent of personal inclinations and of any empirical grounds of the will. Conversely, Chestov and Fondane argue that to disconnect the idea of 'freedom' from the empirical conditions of individual existence, from the personal inclinations and desires of a particular individual, amounts to denying the real possibility of individual freedom in the sense in which it preempts the possibility of a 'free choice' based on empirical grounds. Although possible in principle, such choice would not be considered 'free' from the perspective of Kant's ethical theory.

In the *Critique of Practical Reason*, Kant affirms that no empirical determining grounds of the will should be incorporated with the moral law as a 'condition', 'for this would destroy all moral worth just as surely as any admixture of anything empirical in geometrical axioms would destroy all mathematical certainty'.[74] Chestov's and Fondane's argument is directed against Kant's understanding of freedom with reference to the moral law and the concept of 'duty', insofar as the analogy with geometrical axioms and mathematical certainty guides the investigation of the determining grounds of the will and of the possibility of freedom.

Chestov traces back the analogy between the necessity of the moral law and mathematical certainty to Spinoza's *Ethics*, in which the author proposes to examine the existence of the soul, the existence of God and the motives of human actions in the same way in which one would examine geometrical concepts. This manner of posing the problems of the existence of the soul and of the existence of God within an ethical framework that endeavours to attain the certainty of geometrical argumentation fails to take into account the difference between real and ideal beings. As Chestov argues, the homogenization of moral and mathematical judgements prompts the following question:

> [S]i nous formons nos jugements sur Dieu, sur l'âme, sur les passions humaines de la même manière que sur les lignes, les plans et les corps, alors qu'est-ce qui nous donne le droit d'exiger ou même de conseiller à l'homme d'aimer Dieu et non un plan, une pierre ou un billot? Et pourquoi la demande d'aimer Dieu est-elle adressée à l'homme et non à une ligne ou à un singe?[75]

The ontological status of the real, living individual, as much as that of the 'living God', is incommensurable with the ideal status of objects of thought such as lines, surfaces and geometrical bodies. For ethical judgements to be formulated by analogy with the principles of mathematics presuppose the homogenization of two different modes of being. In order to uncover this presupposition and its implications for individual existence, Chestov raises two questions: (1) To whom are ethical and rational postulates addressed? (alternatively, What is the ontological status of the subject required by such necessary judgements?); (2) What is the ontological status of the object of human will? Spinoza's affirmation that God should be the object of human aspirations, of human 'love', is not incompatible with apodictic judgements concerning lines, surfaces or geometrical bodies insofar as the 'living God' has already been replaced by an ideal, timeless concept that man can and should aspire to, should 'love', 'même lorsque Dieu n'existe pas, ou lorsque à la place de Dieu est mise la nécessité objective, mathématique et rationnelle, ou l'idée du bien humain qui ne se distingue en rien de la nécessité rationnelle'.[76]

This speculative homogenization between the mode of being of the 'living God' and the ideal, conceptual status of the moral law makes possible the postulation of a necessary ethical commandment, according to which the actual object of the human will is 'the good'. In the *Critique of Pure Reason*, Kant dispenses with his previously established argument and states outright that the object of the will, 'thought of as practically necessary through the categorical imperative directly determining the will', is 'the highest good'.[77] The subject to which ethical demands are addressed, the subject whose willing is confronted by the 'ought' pronounced by reason, undergoes a similar process of speculative homogenization. If the imperative demand to 'love God' or, more adequately, to aspire towards 'the highest good' is addressed to man rather than to a geometrical line or to a monkey (as Chestov hypothetically submits), it is insofar as the rational living individual can be thought of in terms of the intelligible, universal concept of 'subject'. Only an 'acting subject' that 'in its intelligible character' does not 'stand under any conditions of time'[78] can support the idea of freedom derived in accordance with the postulate of the 'highest good' as the necessary object of the will, rather than in relation to personal desires and inclinations or even in relation to the existence of the 'living God'. The homogeneity between real, temporal beings and ideal, timeless conceptual entities thus ensures the inexorable, unsurpassable character of the moral law, which predetermines the investigation of freedom.

The existential 'suspension of the ethical' uncovers the irreducible nature of individual, particular existence and the possibility of a different understanding of freedom, beyond necessity—the necessity of the moral law as well as the necessity of the 'eternal', timeless truths of reason. Chestov and Fondane argue that the freedom that emerges 'beyond good and evil' is neither necessarily nor universally given. In amending Bergson's affirmation about 'the self', which is infallible in its immediate observations, feels free and declares it, Chestov argues that at the level of immediate, empirical experience one should rather speak about 'my self' and avoid making universal inferences from particular, contingent premisses. It might happen that some individuals would arrive at the contrary conclusion starting from the same premiss. To illustrate his point, Chestov recalls Spinoza's intriguing remark about the relativity of freedom. If a stone were endowed with consciousness, Spinoza writes (*Correspondence*, letter 58 (62), Schüller 1674), it would be convinced that it falls freely to the ground, although to us it would be obvious that the stone cannot but fall. Chestov elaborates on this possibility and draws a striking parallel between the speculative mode of thinking that derives freedom from necessity and the fallacious reasoning of the conscious stones:

> Mais Spinoza se trompait. Si la pierre avait une conscience, elle serait convaincue qu'elle tombe à terre en vertu de la nécessité de la nature pierreuse de l'être. 'Il s'en suit' que l'idée de nécessité n'a pu naître et se développer que dans des pierres douées de conscience. Et comme l'idée de nécessité est si profondement enracinée dans l'âme humaine qu'elle apparaît à tous comme primordiale, comme le fondement même de l'être (ni l'être ni la pensée ne sont possibles sans elle), il s'en suit encore que l'immense, l'écrasante majorité des hommes ne sont pas des hommes quoi qu'il semble, mais des pierres douées de conscience.[79]

The idea of necessity functions as a speculative proviso that invalidates any attempts at relativizing freedom. From the point of view of rational argument, it is absurd to say that some people, like Spinoza's conscious stones, might think that 'they fall freely to the ground', while others clearly perceive that the necessary law of gravitation makes any other course of action simply impossible. Chestov suggests that the structure of 'consciousness' itself is so defined in relation to the categories of understanding or the more general distinction between human rationality and organic life or nature that any being endowed with consciousness cannot think otherwise than in conformity with the fundamental principles of rational comprehension. The necessity of natural laws, the necessity of mathematical and logical principles is not a matter of choice. Man cannot 'choose' to think otherwise than the constitution of his consciousness, and the categories of human understanding determine him to think.

If this is the case, Chestov argues, then man's freedom resembles very much the freedom of Spinoza's 'stones endowed with consciousness'. To affirm that man is nevertheless 'free', despite or even precisely insofar as he thinks and acts according to the predetermined limits of his understanding and the inexorable, necessary laws of logical and ethical argumentation, amounts to little more than the certainty that stones might achieve in the hypothetical case that they were conscious beings, aware of the law of gravitation yet convinced that they 'fall freely to the ground'. The only difference is that, contrary to the implications of Spinoza's example, such certainty becomes universal and 'absolute' (as opposed to relative) within the framework of rational understanding. The speculative homogeneity of the concept of 'consciousness' excludes the possibility of relative, disjunctive points of view pertaining to those 'beings' (men, stones, etc.) to whom 'consciousness' can be attributed. Thus, as Chestov remarks, the 'idea of necessity' in the sense of the necessary laws of rational understanding seems to belong to the inherent nature of 'being', to its fundamental structures.

This argument, following on the critique of Spinoza's and Kant's ethical theories and conceptions of freedom, in fact relates to the debate between existential thought and Husserlian phenomenology over the questions of truth and being. In disconnecting the concept of truth from any psychological or historical determinations, and in further positing the certainty of 'self-evident' truth as independent of human existence, Husserl attempted to put an end to all sources of 'relativism' including the moderate Kantian claim about the limited 'human perspective' within which we can know anything with scientific, a priori certainty. It was Husserl rather than Kant who made consciousness 'the measure of all things' and affirmed that 'truth is one and the same, whether men or non-men, angels or gods apprehend and judge it'.[80]

The complete homogeneity and rationalization of the field of possible experience, coupled with the complete homogenization of consciousness, allowed for the complete homogenization and correlation of being and truth. Within the Husserlian project, self-evident being and truth constitute the absolute rather than the relative 'measure of all things'. If, according to Chestov, Spinoza's rationalization of being led to the conclusion that 'le vrai nom de Dieu est nécessité',[81] and if Hegel fulfilled the complete humanization and rationalization of the divine by identifying God with the Absolute Spirit, no other philosopher before Husserl went so far as to state that absolute truth and certainty must be independent not only of the existence of God but of the existence of the human species, of the existence of the world, of causal connections and of time. It was thus

Husserl more than any of his rationalist predecessors who gave added legitimacy to Chestov's objection that man's freedom resembles that of 'stones endowed with consciousness', insofar as there can be no other, alternative perspective (human or non-human), no alternative mode of thinking and no residual form of being whose consciousness and understanding might escape the postulates of reason and open up a different interpretation of freedom.

Chestov's and Fondane's critique of the rationalist view of freedom specifically targets two arguments within Husserlian phenomenology: (1) that something that is 'geometrically' impossible is also psychologically impossible; (2) that the relativization of truth implies the relativization of being. The first argument has to do with the speculative homogeneity or the 'unity' of consciousness, which makes meaningless, 'absurd'—if not totally impossible—the attempt to adopt an 'alternative' perspective that exceeds the established framework of 'consciousness'. The second argument is directly related to the first, because any attempt to relativize truth by adopting a different (e.g. a psychological) perspective on the origin and the validity of logical judgements threatens to dissolve the conceptual unity of 'being' as correlative to the conceptual unity of 'truth'. In stating that this conceptual unity relies on consensus, that it represents nothing else than a convention or an 'illusion' that men have forgotten is an 'illusion', the existential critique of truth aims to bring out an irreducible residuum of being, which resists rational analysis and can, therefore, be disentangled from the necessary correlation with the 'eternal' truths of logical, as much as ethical, argumentation. As Fondane affirms: 'le rôle de l'être est de relativiser constamment ces vérités, les suspendre, les abolir, afin de pouvoir ... se réveiller'.[82]

The process of awakening, which is equally invoked in Daumal's, Gilbert-Lecomte's and Artaud's writings, enables the particular individual to relativize rational truth in order to affirm the truth of its own, temporal existence. This truth of a physical, bodily presence in time proves incompatible and incommensurable with the pure, timeless existence of geometrical bodies, which provide the model on which ethics and logical reasoning establish their postulates through analogy. Artaud expresses in uncompromising terms the existential redefinition of truth in relation to the physical, temporal being of a particular individual:

Si je ne crois ni au Mal ni au Bien, si je me sens de telles dispositions à détruire, s'il n'est rien dans l'ordre des principes à quoi je puisse raisonnablement accéder, le principe même est dans ma chair. Je détruis parce que chez moi tout ce qui vient de la raison ne tient pas. [...] Je me sens maintenant capable de départager l'évidence. Il y a pour moi une évidence dans le domaine de la chair pure, et qui n'a rien à voir avec l'évidence de la raison.[83]

In destroying the double (ethical and logical) foundation of rational thought, the living individual encounters an 'evidence' of a totally different kind, unlike any of the 'self-evident' truths of mathematical and philosophical argumentation. If Daumal talked about a paradoxical 'absurd evidence', the attribution of 'absurdity' need not be taken literally. Far from being 'absurd', such evidence has meaning, a meaning that, Artaud himself argues, remains irreducible to rational analysis ('[il est] irréductible par la raison'). The 'fight against self-evidence' recalls and recaptures the meaning and the full value of truth of individual, particular existence. The relativization of truth, which recalls the conventional, 'illusory' character of necessary, 'eternal' truths through anamnesis and recaptures man's fundamental role in the production of 'truth' through the process of 'awakening', exposes the fallacious attribution of true, real being to timeless, ideal concepts in opposition to living, temporal individuals.

The freedom that man reclaims by undertaking the 'fight against self-evidence' is the freedom to pose the problem of his own life, the problem of the desires, suffering and aspirations of his own physical, bodily existence, over and above ethical and rational imperatives. In his essay on Kierkegaard, Fondane echoes Artaud's remarks about the 'evidence' of the flesh and examines the possibility of an affirmation of life that includes rather than ignores the presence of the body, 'un corps d'homme vivant [...], un corps qui désire, qui aime, qui se veut immortel, et qui, loin de se résigner à la nécessité, exige les pleins pouvoirs'.[84] If there is an irreducible 'evidence' of the body, then the question that both Artaud and Fondane insistently ask is whether this body has the right to pronounce its own 'truth' or, more adequately, 'si le corps *a le droit* de penser tout haut'.[85]

Within the existential critique of rational truth, the problem of the body of a living individual, which 'far from resigning itself to necessity, demands full powers', refers to the possibility of reclaiming man's right to decide whether his cognitive interests, his personal inclinations, desires and suffering, should play any part in the investigation of the three questions of utmost importance to human life—the existence of God, the immortality of the soul and freedom.

Like Job, whose story is often quoted by Kierkegaard, Chestov and Fondane alike, the existential thinker revolts against the necessary limitations of logical and ethical argument, refuses the ethical consolations of his fellow men, in order to present his plight, his physical suffering and unappeasable yearning for immortality and freedom to God, the one who 'transcends intellect, transcends knowing'.[86] In disengaging with ethics and rational knowledge, existential thought rejects the speculative notion of 'God' (whose 'true name is necessity', as Chestov observed), aiming to re-establish the obliterated communication between the 'living man' and the 'living God'. This communication exceeds rational comprehension. According to Chestov, God always demands 'the impossible', and man only turns to God when he himself needs to ask for the impossible, while in asking for things that are possible within the limits of rational comprehension, he addresses his fellow men.

Unlike Aristotle's inexorable Ananke, which 'cannot be persuaded to change' (Ἡ ἀνάγνκη ἀμετάπειστόν τι εἶναι), the 'living God', 'God of Abraham, God of Isaac, God of Jacob, not of philosophers and scholars' (as Pascal states in his *Mémorial*, fr. 913), can be persuaded, can respond to man's desperate outcry: *De profundis clamavi ad te, Domine*. But in order to be able to cry out from the depth of despair like the Psalmist of the Bible, man has to break up 'the enchantment' of rational self-evident truths, he has to free himself from the all-pervasive power of ethical and logical imperatives. This is the meaning of Kierkegaard's affirmation that 'the opposite of sin is not virtue, but faith'. Faith opens up an alternative mode of understanding, the existential 'second dimension of thought', which is situated beyond good and evil, beyond virtue or 'merit', beyond logical arguments based on the dichotomy between truth and error. Man's salvation, his freedom and immortality, lie in faith alone (*Sola Fide*, as Chestov insisted, reiterating Luther's watchword).

The existential paradoxical type of argument subverts the foundation of logical and ethical postulates from within the established framework of rational understanding. While refusing to submit the 'truths of faith' to the mechanisms of logical validation, the existential philosopher also refuses to be bound by the principle of non-contradiction and the 'obligation' either to use logical arguments in conformity with this principle or to refrain from using logical arguments. Fondane emphasizes the freedom of the thinking subject both to employ and to dispense with logical validating arguments:

La preuve étant une arme rationnelle, comment la pensée de l'existence pourrait-elle, à son tour, *prouver*? là où il y a preuve, il y a contrainte; et la pensée de l'existence est liberté. Mais pourquoi renoncerons-nous à la preuve rationnelle? pour être *logiques*? si nous sommes libres de la rejeter, nous sommes également libres de l'employer.[87]

The existential use of rational 'proofs' functions as a predominantly negative, subversive device, meant to disrupt the unfolding of speculative demonstrations by exploring latent or obliterated antinomies of thought. If Kant argues that '"ought" in nature has no meaning', and Hegel similarly states that 'organic nature has no history' (in the sense of the historical evolution of Spirit, displayed in the raising of self-consciousness to absolute knowledge), then existential thought adopts their arguments, and proceeds to investigate the 'irreducible residuum of being', the natural, organic, bodily presence of a living individual, precisely insofar as the ethical and rational pronouncements, the 'ought' and the 'should' judgements, have no hold on this 'organic life'. This applies not only to Fondane's and Artaud's contention about the alternative 'evidence' of the body. While making use of the Hegelian trinitarian schema and of Hegelian dialectics, Daumal and Gilbert-Lecomte insist on the analogy between processes of consciousness and biological phenomena of 'sudden variation'. An individual who has found the 'right attitude' suddenly goes beyond the realm of 'human activity' and accomplishes the transition between 'discursive knowledge' and 'the tendency towards immediate omniscience' through 'un phénomène de variation brusque' similar to the transformation of a reptile into a bird.[88]

As Fondane and Chestov repeatedly state, the truths of faith are neither 'necessary' nor 'universal', and the existential type of argumentation proposes to uncover such truths, not to 'prove' them according to the conventional rules of logical validation. In contrast to the binding, inexorable character of self-evident truths given within the rational framework of consciousness, 'ces vérités [de la foi] sont données librement, elles sont librement acceptées'.[89] The mode of thinking based on the 'absurd evidence' of freely given and freely accepted truths corresponds to the re-establishment of the unlimited communication between the 'living man' and the 'living God'. The possibility of a negative reconstruction of this communication (negative insofar as it proceeds by destroying the speculative concept of 'God' and the unified and unifying framework of human consciousness) involves the suspension of the ethical. However, as

Fondane observes, the suspension of the ethical leads to the further suspension of temporal finitude, to an affirmation of life that opens individual existence to immortality while simultaneously maintaining and supporting the reality of man's physical, bodily presence in the world. In defining man's being in time in relation to life rather than death, in relation to the 'living God' rather than the Law, existential thought uncovers a realm of freedom that is incommensurable with the rational interpretation of time.

The God of Abraham, the God of Isaac and of Job can 'make what happened not have happened'. He can not only reverse but altogether suspend the implacable, linear chronology of events. He can restore the meaning and the certain, 'truthful' reality of temporal, living beings, in contrast to ideal, timeless entities of thought, thus abrogating the negative ethical valuation of transient, human existence. In stating that individual, human existence is irreducible to rational analysis and exceeds ethical judgements based on the idea of the finitude of temporal being, Chestov points to a realm of freedom that involves an alternative, paradoxical configuration of time.

The relationship between Kierkegaard's notion of 'repetition' and 'the suspension of the ethical' forms an integral part of the existential redefinition of freedom. However, Fondane considered that the suspension of the moral law and of the linear temporality associated with dichotomous reasoning was only a temporary strategy in Kierkegaard's thought, and that it remained unable to effect the desired 'redemption of the past', the transition from contingent temporality to timeless existence:

> Kierkegaard n'envisage l'action de suspendre le moral que comme un acte exceptionnel, momentané, cet acte de négation par lequel Orphée s'évade du fini jusque dans l'Enfer, mais, ayant ravi Euridyce (Isaac, Régine, les filles et les troupeaux de Job), s'en revient dans le fini et *réaffirme la temporalité d'abord niée*.[90]

In contrast to the notion of 'repetition' as return to temporality, Fondane argues, the suspension of morality in Chestov's thought coincides with an actual and definitive suspension of morality, of individual life as limited, finite experience in time: 'l'action de suspendre le moral comporte *la fin du fini*'. The end of finitude, the end of the linear temporality that leads inevitably to death, comes about in a paradoxical manner: the transgression of the limit posed by morality and dichotomous thought brings linear temporality, death and nothingness to an end. From this perspective, real being can legitimately be ascribed to individual, particular existence, in so far as it now opens on to eternity and absolute freedom. With *la fin du fini*, time no longer limits human existence but uncovers the relationship between the 'living man' and the 'living God'.

The recurrent theme of the death of Socrates in Chestov's work implicitly contrasts the situation of the man of faith, Job, and the situation of the man of reason, the Fallen Man *par excellence*, whose redemption involves much more than 'repetition'. Fondane's concluding remarks concerning the meaning of this major theme of reflection in Chestov's writing focus on the difference between 'repetition' followed by reaffirmation of temporality (as illustrated by the mythical journey of Orpheus) and the integral restoration of a state before or rather beyond the temporal framework to which the Fall and the dichotomy of good and evil belong. The suspension of the 'past of mankind' implies the suspension of the moral law, of the Knowledge of Good and Evil, which remains intertwined with the Fall. Death, the death of Socrates, the death of Man, as the final triumph of the rational configuration of temporality over faith, has to be superseded, and individual freedom has to replace the general economy of the historical continuum:

> Là où il y a liberté il n'y a aucune place pour le général. Aussi ne demande-t-il (i.e. Chestov) pas que l'on rendît à Socrate, empoisonné, le 'tout au double'; cette 'récompense' n'est encore qu'un terme de morale, un *hommage* à la morale; il en appelle au règne de la liberté *où la temporalité ne saurait en aucun cas recevoir le prédicat de la vérité et de la réalité*, où il apparaîtra que le procès de Socrate *n'a pas eu lieu* et que le plus sage des hommes *n'a pas été* empoisonné. Si ce qui a été *est* une fois pour toutes, qu'importe que l'on reçoive le tout au double! Le premier effet de la suspension téléologique du moral, c'est de faire que ce qui a été, sous le régime de la nécessité, du général et de la morale, *n'ait jamais été*![91]

In order to attain the 'reign of freedom' in which the understanding of time is no longer bound up with the law of temporal irreversibility, as well as with the necessary character of the double (logical and ethical) foundation of rational thought, man has to suspend Knowledge—the original Knowledge of Good and Evil, which establishes the inevitability of death after the Fall. This act of suspension makes paradoxical use of the concepts that it brings to an end. It is a 'teleological' suspension of the moral law in the sense in which it targets and returns to an obliterated origin—the reign of absolute freedom before the Fall—which then abolishes by its very nature any teleology. The possibility of making 'what happened not have happened' exceeds the framework of rational thought, the configuration of time as an irreversible, causally-determined sequence of events. It also exceeds the speculative understanding of 'freedom' as determined by the logical and ethical imperatives that govern man's 'drive for knowledge' and limit his expectations to what is 'rationally possible' in conformity with established conventions for the investigation and validation of truth.

Conclusions

The question of individual choice played a crucial role in the existential as well as the Surrealist investigations of freedom. The Surrealist movement evolved from an initial aesthetic view of choice, characterized by the revolt against established conventions and radical negation, to a moral determination of choice with reference to the social and political implications of acting upon a certain chosen course. The belief in the possibility of effecting real changes in the outside world by unlocking man's potential of artistic creation marked the transition from a nihilistic attitude of aesthetic 'indifference' or detachment (which Kierkegaard associated with the 'first stage of life') to an ideology of moral engagement, reconciling the individual with the social aspiration to freedom. In trying to contain and reconcile its inner contradictory tendencies, the Surrealist movement remained firmly committed to the Hegelian dialectical framework and the Hegelian solution to the problem of the 'unhappy consciousness'. Conversely, the existential critique of the concept of truth aimed to expose and destroy the double—logical and ethical—foundation of rational thought, which supported not only Hegel's doctrine of dialectical reconciliation of opposites but also the necessary character of the movement of conceptualization pervading the whole history of systematic philosophy.

Insofar as the moral origin of the 'drive for knowledge' dictates the conditions of an investigation of freedom that presupposes the superseding of temporal, individual beings and the privileged status of timeless, autonomous, conceptual beings, existential thought uncovers the irreconcilable contradiction between man's temporally-determined cognitive interests (including his personal desires, his physical presence in the world, his unquenchable thirst for immortality) and the 'eternal' ethical and logical imperative to limit such interests or desires to cognitive capacities, ultimately defined in conformity with the aim of rational knowledge itself. In suspending this ethical and logical imperative, which predetermines the 'possibility' or the legitimacy of man's claims to freedom (for instance his freedom to establish the conditions of 'truth' and 'being' in relation to rather than independently of his real, temporal, physical presence in the world), existential thought dislocates the apodictic interlocking of rational truth and the idea of the 'good'. If man's cognitive aspirations do not necessarily coincide with the aims and limits of the rational search for truth, posited as the 'highest good' attainable by a living individual, then man himself may choose to look for the answers to his questions 'beyond good and evil', beyond the ethical valuations underpinning the disparagement of temporal, contingent aspirations to 'truth' and 'being'. He may choose to do so precisely insofar as he recalls the conventional, consensual character of the ethical and rational understanding of truth, insofar as he fights against the 'forgetfulness' that makes such understanding the ultimate, unsurpassable and 'desirable' limit of human cognitive aspirations.

The disengagement with ethics and logical validatory arguments uncovers an alternative type of knowledge, a 'second dimension of thought', within which truth no longer depends on necessary, universal judgements or on the principles of rational demonstrability. When truth emerges from a cognitive approach that defines itself as related to rather than independent of the existence of the 'living man' and of the 'living God', it ceases to be universally binding or necessary. Unlike the 'eternal' truths of rational investigation, 'truths of faith' are freely given and freely accepted. They are 'manifest' instead of being pure, ideal representations that rely on validatory arguments. They manifest the irreducible, physical presence in the world of a living individual (a presence not mediated by rational analysis) and the relationship of the living individual with the 'living God'. Thus, the dislocation of the interlocking between existence and rational analysis makes possible the re-establishment of the obliterated link between individual life and the existence of God. The relationship between man and God in faith is 'unlimited' in the sense that it uncovers an alternative understanding of 'freedom'—unlimited by ethics, rational necessity and validatory arguments. It is unlimited insofar as neither of the terms involved in this relationship needs the support of logical argument and necessary principles of thought. Existence, the existence of God and the existence of a living individual, 'has no need of a support, as if it cannot support itself' (οὐ δεῖται ἱδρύσεωσ ὥσπερ αὑτὸ φέρειν οὐ δυνάμενον).[92] If existence exceeds rational understanding, as Chestov insisted in quoting Plotinus's *Enneads*, then it needs no rational ground or support. Its 'groundlessness' is its irreducible freedom.

Notes to Chapter 4

1. The term 'ethics' is here used in the sense of R. M. Hare's definition, as designating 'the logic of moral language'. Similarly, the term 'ethical' refers to Hare's understanding of 'ethical theory' as providing 'the conceptual framework within which moral reasoning takes place', a framework that actually 'dictates the form of the reasoning'. See R. M. Hare, *Freedom and Reason* (Oxford: Clarendon Press, 1965), 97, 89. It is in view of such general, theoretical definitions of these terms that I discuss the existential critique of the foundations of rational knowledge with reference to the underlying, logical framework of both epistemological and ethical arguments throughout the history of philosophy from Aristotle to Spinoza, Kant, Hegel and Husserl. As my analysis shows, the more specific problem that the existential critique of rational knowledge aims to uncover is the interlocking between the idea of truth and the idea of the good.
2. Søren Kierkegaard, *Either/Or*, ii, trans. Walter Lowrie (Princeton: Princeton University Press, 1959), 173.
3. Ibid., 218.
4. Léon Chestov, 'Qu'est-ce que la vérité?', 41.
5. Ibid., 45.
6. Ibid., 55–6.
7. In relation to the interdependence of the concepts of being and truth in Husserl, one would need to consider the implications of Husserl's doctrine of being (the constitution of true being through the intentional consciousness): true being is being-given-in-itself, or self-evident being. See Quentin Lauer, Introduction to Edmund Husserl, *La Philosophie comme science rigoureuse*, 42. I deal with this question in more detail in my article, 'Evidence et conscience: Léon Chestov et la critique existentielle de la théorie de l'évidence chez Husserl', *Cahiers de l'émigration russe* 3 (1996), 111–25.
8. Edmund Husserl, *Logical Investigations*, i. 82.
9. Ibid.
10. Ibid., i. 85.
11. Benjamin Fondane, 'Sur la route de Dostoyewski: Martin Heidegger', *Cahiers du Sud* 8 (1932), 383.
12. Jean-Luc Nancy, *Des lieux divins* (Mauvezin: Trans-Europ-Repress, 1987), 14.
13. Fondane, 'Sur la route de Dostoyewski', 387.
14. Friedrich Nietzsche, *Philosophy and Truth: Selections from Nietzsche's Notebooks of the Early 1870's*, ed. and trans. Daniel Breazeale (Atlantic Highlands, NJ: Humanities Press, 1993), 35.

15. André Breton, *Point du jour* (Paris: Gallimard, 1970), 62; in *Œuvres complètes*, ii. 304.
16. Breton, *Les Pas Perdus*, 193. The quotation is taken from Maxim Gorky, 'Souvenirs sur Tolstoi', *La Nouvelle Revue française* 87 (1 Dec. 1920), 862–922.
17. Breton, *Œuvres complètes*, ii. 276.
18. André Breton, 'Légitime défense', *Œuvres complètes*, ii. 291.
19. Ibid.
20. André Breton, *Signe ascendant* (Paris: Gallimard, 1947), 11, quoted in Claude Abastado, *Introduction au surréalisme* (Paris: Bordas, 1986), 90.
21. Kierkegaard, *Either/Or*, 173. This statement needs to be considered in view of Kierkegaard's doctrine of the three stages of life: i.e. the aesthetic, the ethical and the religious. In *Either/Or*, Kierkegaard mainly deals with the first two stages. In *Stages on Life's Way*, he fully elaborates this conception, and emphasizes the importance of the religious stage. Each 'stage' represents a different 'sphere of existence', which supersedes the previous one; the transition between the ethical and the religious sphere is not dialectical but can only be accomplished through 'a leap of faith'.
22. René Daumal, 'Liberté sans espoir', *Le Grand Jeu* 1 (Summer 1928), 23.
23. Ibid., 19.
24. Ibid., 20.
25. Phalaris was a tyrant of Akragas (Agrigentum) in Sicily *c.*570–554 BC; he was notorious for roasting his victims alive in a brazen bull. Chestov's critique of the Stoic attitude in face of adversity often takes its cue from a lapidary note on ancient cruelty in Aristotle's *Ethics*; see 'Dans le taureau de Phalaris', *Athènes et Jérusalem*, 109–98.
26. Daumal, 'Liberté sans espoir', 20.
27. Fondane, 'Edmond Husserl et l'œuf de Colomb du réel', 343.
28. Hegel, *Phenomenology of Spirit*, §§188–90, pp. 114–15.
29. Nietzsche, 'On Truth and Lies in a Nonmoral Sense', *Philosophy and Truth*, 85. Similarly, Fondane ('Léon Chestov et la lutte contre les évidences', 26–7) comments on the apodictic truth of the 'evil' inscribed in empirical existence: 'qui nous assure, ses "*intérêts*" exigeant que le mal soit inscrit dans les structures de l'être, que la pensée spéculative n'a pas, d'elle-même, inscrit dans l'être, subrepticement ou de bonne foi, les vérités mêmes qu'elle prétend y découvrir'.
30. Nietzsche, 'On Truth and Lies in a Nonmoral Sense', 84.
31. Fondane, 'Léon Chestov et la lutte contre les évidences', 27.
32. Fondane, 'La Conscience malheureuse', 48.
33. Ibid., 49.
34. Ibid.
35. Ibid., 50.
36. Ibid., 51–2.
37. Ibid., 26.
38. Fondane, 'Léon Chestov et la lutte contre les évidences', 47.
39. René Daumal, 'Pseudo-matérialisme et Emile Meyerson contre la dialectique hegelienne', *Le Grand Jeu* 4 (Autumn 1932), 27.
40. René Daumal, 'La Vision de l'Absurde', *Tu t'es toujours trompé*, 55.
41. Ibid., 52.

42. Roger Gilbert-Lecomte, 'Les chapelles littéraires modernes', *Œuvres complètes*, i. 324.
43. Roger Gilbert-Lecomte, 'La force des renoncements', *Le Grand Jeu* 1 (Summer 1928), 15.
44. Roger Gilbert-Lecomte, *L'Horrible Révélation, la seule...* (Paris: Fata Morgana, 1973), 69.
45. Gilbert-Lecomte, *Œuvres complètes*, i. 202.
46. Roger Gilbert-Lecomte, 'Après Rimbaud la mort des Arts', *Le Grand Jeu* 2 (Spring 1929), 31: 'Car l'œuvre de celui qui a voulu se faire voyant est soumise, jusqu'à sa condamnation finale, et au delà, à la seule morale que nous acceptions, à la morale terrible de ceux qui ont décidé une fois pour toutes de refuser tout ce qui n'est pas *cela* en sachant pertinemment à l'avance que, quoiqu'ils atteignent, ce ne sera jamais *cela*.'
47. Ibid.
48. Gilbert-Lecomte, *Œuvres complètes*, i. 329.
49. See Jean-Luc Marion, 'L'Effondrement des idoles et l'affrontement du divin: Nietzsche', *L'Idole et la distance* (Paris: Grasset, 1977), 49–60.
50. Ibid., 103: 'Feuerbach, Stirner, Marx s'appuient sur l'identification suprêmement idolâtrique du "Dieu" au Savoir absolu que leur a construite Hegel pour vider un concept de son contenu au profit de l'autre, en un système métaphysique de vases communicants.' Ibid., 111: 'L'équivalence et l'autosubsistance des attributs/prédicats permettent seuls, chez Feuerbach, leur transfert de "Dieu" à l'homme. L'absence radicale de théologie négative devient ainsi l'explicite condition d'une destruction strictement idolâtrique.'
51. André Breton, *Signe ascendant* (Paris: Gallimard, 1968), 158.
52. See Ferdinand Alquié, 'Humanisme surréaliste et humanisme existentialiste', *Cahiers du Collège Philosophique* (Grenoble and Paris: B. Arthaud, 1948), 139–63.
53. This argument, which permeates Chestov's entire work, finds an elliptic formulation in 'Regarder en arrière et lutter', 97–8, aphorism XIV, 'Protagoras et Platon': 'Protagoras affirmait que l'homme est la mesure des choses. Platon, lui, disait que c'est Dieu. [...] Cependant, Platon lui-même dit autre part que les dieux ne philosophent pas, ne recherchent pas la sagesse, étant sages eux-mêmes. Et qu'est-ce que donc que philosopher et rechercher la vérité? N'est-ce pas "mesurer" les choses? Une telle occupation ne convient-elle pas davantage aux faibles et ignorants mortels qu'aux dieux puissants et omniscients?'
54. Fondane, *La Conscience malheureuse*, 31.
55. For a detailed analysis of Nietzsche's early critique of the concept of truth as 'illusion', as contrasted with Cartesian and Kantian theories, see Maudemarie Clark, *Nietzsche on Truth and Philosophy* (Cambridge: Cambridge University Press, 1990), 40–93.
56. Kant, *Critique of Pure Reason,* §A58, p. 97.
57. Fondane, *La Conscience malheureuse*, 35.
58. Chestov, 'L'Honnêteté intellectuelle', *Athènes et Jérusalem*, 291. See also id., 'Sine effusione sanguinis: De la probité philosophique', *Hermes* 1 (Jan. 1938), 5–36.
59. Ἀρχὴ φιλοσοφίας συναίσθησις τῆς αὐτοῦ ἀσθηνείας καὶ ἀδυναμίας περὶ τὰ ἀναγκαια; quoted in Greek and French in Chestov, 'Qu'est-ce que la vérité?', 48.

60. Aristotle, *Ethics* 1111^{b}20, quoted by Chestov, *Athènes et Jérusalem*, 245.
61. Nietzsche, 'On Truth and Lies in a Nonmoral Sense', 84.
62. Ibid.
63. Freud initially elaborates his concept of reality in the context of the theory of neuroses and dreams. At this stage, as Paul Ricoeur comments (*Freud and Philosophy*, 261–2), reality in general 'is the correlate of the function of consciousness'. The opposition between the two regulative concepts dividing 'mental functioning', 'the pleasure principle' and 'the reality principle', is later dramatized by Freud as part of the 'remythicizing' of the instinct theory. Ricoeur points out: 'The real is no longer simply the contrary of hallucination; it is harsh necessity, and at times even Ananke. [...] In short, what at first was merely a principle of "mental regulation" now becomes the cypher of possible wisdom.' My argument refers to the later, 'stronger' interpretation of the reality principle as Ananke, which makes clearer the similarities between the Freudian and the Hegelian views of divided consciousness.
64. Insofar as this argument continues the previous examination of the existential view of the 'unhappy consciousness', it is interesting to mention here that the psychoanalytic relationship between the 'reality-ego' and the 'pleasure-ego' mirrors the master–slave relationship of Hegelian phenomenology. In both cases, the internalization of the conflict and the dialectical reconciliation of opposites follows the postulation of a logical and ethical necessity of overcoming self-division and of reaching a unifying, intelligible frame of reference, which contains and supercedes particular variations. For a detailed comparative analysis, which I consider relevant to the present argument about common assumptions and methodological similarities in Freud's and Hegel's interpretations of consciousness, see Ricoeur, 'A Philosophical Interpretation of Freud', *Freud and Philosophy*, 375–88, 461–82.
65. Cf. ibid., 387. The question of the relationship between ethics and the analysis of consciousness in Freud deserves further investigation and cannot be elucidated in the course of the present argument. I would only mention here the interconnection between the history of morality and the history of consciousness in Freud's work. This refers to the role assigned to the notion of 'taboo' (whose psychopathology extends into the Kantian imperative in *Totem and Taboo*). Freud considers that the explanation of taboo throws light on 'the origin of consciousness' ('taboo consciousness is probably the earliest form in which the phenomenon of consciousness is met with'); on the other hand, 'taboo' is a 'social institution' associated with the reality principle. For a further, detailed commentary on these aspects, see ibid., 204–5, 449. The original, constitutive function that Freud assigns to the moral imperative in relation to consciousness also characterizes Hegel's view of self-consciousness (as distinct from 'natural consciousness'): 'ethical substance is the essence of self-consciousness'. The transition from natural consciousness to self-consciousness in Hegel is thus governed by the same ethical principle that presides over the 'origin of consciousness' in the sense assigned to this notion by Freud (i.e. in opposition to the system of the unconscious). See also Hyppolite, *Genesis and Structure of Hegel's Phenomenology of Spirit*, 460–1.
66. Fondane, *La Conscience Malheureuse*, 33, 18 n. 1.

67. Léon Chestov, 'Les Favoris et les déshérités de l'histoire', 667–8.
68. Fondane, *La Conscience malheureuse*, 46.
69. Ibid., p. xix.
70. Chestov, 'Regarder en arrière et lutter', aphorism XXI, 'Le choix', 101.
71. Ibid.
72. Cf. ibid., 106.
73. Kant, *Critique of Pure Reason*, §A548, p. 473.
74. Immanuel Kant, *Critique of Practical Reason*, trans. Lewis White Beck (New York: Macmillan, 1993), 97. For an interpretation of this passage, see Henry E. Allison, *Kant's Theory of Freedom* (Cambridge: Cambridge University Press, 1995), 117–20.
75. Chestov, 'Descartes et Spinoza', 670.
76. Ibid., 671.
77. Kant, *Critique of Practical Reason*, 141. It is interesting to note that at this point the ontological problematics concerning the existence of God and the immortality of the souls has already moved into a position of secondary importance in relation to ethics. The concepts of God and of immortality, along with the concept of freedom, need to be 'presupposed' and are described 'as actually having objects' only 'because practical reason inexorably requires the existence of these objects for the possibility of its practically and absolutely necessary object, the highest good'. This only confirms the conclusion reached in the First Critique, which demonstrated the impossibility of the task attributed to metaphysics: to combine the concept of freedom to the concept of God in such a way so that the relationship between these concepts should lead to the concept of immortality as a necessary conclusion. The reformulation of this task in the Second Critique consists in assuming the three concepts whose objective reality failed to be established by speculative reason, in order to arrive at the conclusion of the inexorable and necessary character of 'the highest good' as the object of the will. Thus it is only in relation to 'the highest good' that freedom acquires 'reality'—practical reason 'exhibits' its reality 'in the moral law'—and God acquires 'significance'—becomes 'a condition of the possibility of the object of a will determined by [the moral] law'.
78. Kant, *Critique of Pure Reason*, §§A539–40, p. 468.
79. Chestov, 'Regarder en arrière et lutter', aphorism XXII, 'Les pierres douées de conscience', 102. See also id., 'Descartes et Spinoza', 664.
80. Husserl, *Logical Investigations*, i. 140.
81. Chestov, 'Descartes et Spinoza', 666.
82. Fondane, 'Léon Chestov et la lutte contre les évidences', 36.
83. Artaud, 'Manifeste en langage clair', *Œuvres complètes*, i. 238.
84. Fondane, 'Sœren Kierkegaard et la catégorie du secret', 206.
85. Ibid., 207.
86. Chestov (*Athènes et Jérusalem*, 218) quotes Plotinus, *Enneads* V, 3, 12 in support of the existential interpretation of God: '[The One] as it transcends intellect, transcends knowing; as it needs nothing, it does not even need knowledge, which pertains exclusively to the second order of nature'.
87. Fondane, 'Léon Chestov et la lutte contre les évidences', 34.
88. Gilbert-Lecomte, 'La Force des renoncements', 16.

89. Chestov, 'Regarder en arrière et lutter', 91.
90. Fondane, 'Chestov, Kierkegaard et le Serpent', 252.
91. Ibid., 253.
92. Cf. Chestov, *Athènes et Jérusalem*, 218.

CONCLUSIONS

The 'case' of Surrealism and of its dissident fringes serves as a poignant example of the conflict between divergent types of philosophical investigation, which Chestov's and Fondane's critique uncovers throughout the history of philosophy from ancient to modern times. This conflict can be traced back, as it is explicitly by both Chestov and Fondane, to the oppositions between Descartes and Pascal, between Montaigne and Pascal, between Kant and Nietzsche, between Hegel and Kierkegaard. Moreover, this conflict belongs to, informs and pervades the evolution of French thought and the debates in which Chestov, Fondane and the Surrealist writers were themselves involved. Chestov's and Fondane's specific contribution during the 1920s and 1930s consists in bringing to light those latent and overt tensions of a philosophical tradition that led on the one hand to the emergence of Husserlian phenomenology in Germany or to the resurgence of Hegelian phenomenology in France, and on the other to the revival of Kierkegaardian and Nietzschean themes of reflection in both Germany and France.

In response to the rise of scientific rationalism, mainly prompted by the French reception of Husserlian and Hegelian phenomenologies, an increasing preoccupation with theories and aesthetic practices relating to the absurd emerged at the beginning of the twentieth century. Surrealism was among the earliest avant-garde movements to undertake an exploration of the creative potential of irrationality through a wide range of techniques meant to subvert logical thought and conventional forms of expression. However, political and ideological pressures within Surrealism (which dictated the assimilation of some of the main rationalist conceptions of the period, especially as regards Hegelian and Freudian accounts of history, human nature and so on) pushed more radical subversive tendencies to the external frontiers of the group. Dissident and expelled members found themselves sharing the same uncharted territory as maverick philosophers who had started investigating the notion of the absurd and its various manifestations in an attempt at overcoming traditional argumentative logic. In both cases, the polemic vindication of a transgressive discourse focusing on the absurd corresponds to a radicalized understanding of revolt.

The tension between the notions of revolt and revolution within the Surrealist movement itself can be said to mirror the wider confrontation between a highly individualistic, anti-rationalist trend (which defined revolt in terms of the absurd, unqualified rejection of conventional thought) and a moderate questioning of reason, ultimately committed to social and political reform. Thus, the literary and philosophical conceptions of the absurd more often than not brandish an intransigent, deliberate isolationism. Their nihilistic protests against the established order of things subtend either metaphysical or transhistorical concerns (such as the human condition, personal experience, God, death, the meaning of existence), which allow for a polemically declared independence of any integrationist projects, of current social and political engagements.[1]

The existential critique of Husserl, developed in Chestov's and Fondane's works during the 1920s and 1930s, had a significant impact on philosophical and literary debates that questioned the predominant rationalist discourse, and it fostered a sweeping reassessment of the values of lived experience, sensibility and imagination. This shift of emphasis from scientific objectivity to an approach that endeavoured to recapture the vast area of human existence and personal experience (excluded by the Husserlian methodology) accurately defines the context of the French reception of German phenomenology, especially inasmuch as its decisive preference for ontological (over epistemological) issues is concerned. French Existentialism would not have been the same without Lévinas's, Sartre's and indeed Camus's critical reaction to Husserl, which found added support in Heidegger's own strand of existential phenomenology.

As one of the first commentators of Husserl's phenomenology in France, Leon Chestov[2] had a major although rarely acknowledged role in shaping the conceptions of a generation of writers and philosophers who reclaimed the heritage of irrationalist thinkers such as Kierkegaard, Nietzsche and Dostoevsky. Among the prominent personalities of the time, Camus remains Chestov's privileged interlocutor, the one whose work displays perhaps the most conspicuous examples of the ongoing dialogue between existential thought and

French Existentialism. The two most probably never met, although Roger Quilliot argues that Camus started to read Chestov (along with Kierkegaard, Nietzsche, Husserl and Heidegger) as early as 1936–7, a period when the project of the *Mythe de Sisyphe* was beginning to take shape.[3] Chestov died in 1938, and Camus's famous essay came out in 1942, the same year as *L'Étranger.* As it often happened, the task of engaging in direct exchanges with the young generation of French intellectuals was left to Fondane, who actually met Camus in 1943[4] and shortly afterwards replied to Camus's critique of existential thought in a long article that came out in the collective volume *L'Existence*, edited by Grenier.[5] If Camus had accused Chestov of fleeing the 'commandments of the absurd' by attempting to overcome reason only to reinforce the authority of an irrational, incomprehensible God, Fondane raised serious doubts about the aims of a revolt whose absurd hero is ultimately happy with his lot:

> '*Il faut imaginer Sisyphe heureux*', écrit-il à la dernière ligne de son ouvrage. Mais c'est de cette difficulté même qu'est née la pensée existentielle. Que Sisyphe *s'imagine* heureux, c'est tout ce que demande la pensée platonicienne, stoïcienne, hégélienne; qu'il consente à 's'imaginer' heureux c'est tout ce que lui demande le νοῦς, l'Esprit, la raison universelle, que sais-je? il fait preuve par là qu'il n'est pas un misologos, un contempteur de la raison, il renonce à l'absurde. [...] Car ce que craint la raison c'est justement un Sisyphe qui refuserait de *s'imaginer* heureux, qui désespèrerait du 'sérieux', qui en appellerait à l'Absurde — justement! Toute acceptation, toute résignation chasse l'absurde du réel, ou l'imprègne d'intelligibilité.[6]

As Fondane argued, Camus's attempt at situating the Absurd within the confines of a moral (or, even hedonistic) account of human existence runs the risk of taking resignation or mere contentment for revolt. In turn, Camus brilliantly summarized the differences between his own conception of the absurd and that of existential thought when he argued, 'Pour Chestov, la raison est vaine, mais il y a quelque chose au-delà de la raison. Pour un esprit absurde la raison est vaine et il n'y a rien au-delà de la raison.'[7] During the post-war period, possibly in the wake of Fondane's polemic with Camus, literary critics of Existentialism such as Albérès commented on the Stoic undertones of Camus's idea of revolt and highlighted the paradoxical blend of Epicurean and ascetic values that characterized works of the same period as *Le Mythe de Sisyphe* (*L'Étranger, Caligula*):

> Quoique issu surtout de Chestov, le *Mythe de Sisyphe* renvoie donc à des

formules qui ne sont pas très éloignées de celles de Nietzsche, et le stoïcisme primitif de Camus se transforme en un épicurisme ardent. L'homme absurde n'est pas très différent au fond de cet aristocrate, méprisant et jouisseur dont Montherlant a voulu créer avec lui-même le type. [...] Mais l'aristocratisme du *Mythe du Sisyphe* d'ailleurs habilement déguisé dans la personne du petit employé qu'est Mersault, tout comme *Caligula* et *Le Malentendu*, ne semblent avoir dans l'œuvre de Camus qu'une valeur d'ascèse.[8]

However, one cannot help noticing that both the ascetic and the hedonistic stances in Camus's view of the human condition derive from his understanding of the absurd as an existential critique of reason, qualified by the crucial proviso that there is nothing beyond reason. And this very limitation of the absurd to a purely immanentist framework prompted Fondane's objection concerning the possibility of revolt within rather than beyond the bounds of reason: 'Il est impossible de poser l'Absurde avec l'*assentiment* de la raison universelle; [...] et c'est pourquoi, pour Chestov comme pour Kierkegaard, l'Absurde n'est pas *en deçà*, mais au delà de la Raison.'[9] The argument is interestingly reminiscent of Fondane's remarks concerning the Surrealist 'rational exploitation of the irrational' with reference to Breton's theory of poetic vision, based on the Rimbaldian 'raisonné déréglement de tous les sens'.[10]

Undoubtedly, the influence that existential thought had on French literary and philosophical debates during the first half of the century can be attributed to Chestov's salient critique of Husserlian scientific rationalism, as well as to his groundbreaking comparative studies of Nietzsche and Dostoevsky, Nietzsche and Tolstoy. Nevertheless, it must be said that Fondane played an invaluable role in disseminating and interpreting Chestov's ideas and, most significantly, in applying the existential method of analysis to a wide range of artistic and theoretical pursuits well beyond the scope of traditional philosophical discourse. Fondane's polemic with the Surrealists (which produced a series of articles and at least two major works, *Rimbaud le Voyou*, 1933, and *Faux Traité d'esthétique*, 1938) helped situate existential thought in relation to competing avant-garde conceptions of the absurd.[11]

In fact, Fondane's first published volume in French was a collection of 'cinépoèmes',[12] an avant-garde genre at the boundary between automatic writing and 'découpage', which figured under different guises among the early Surrealist experiments (for instance Desnos's and Soupault's scenarios). The preface to this volume surprisingly reads as a manifesto of existential thought, starting with the title, '2 × 2', which takes up Chestov's critique of logical reasoning (based on Dostoevsky's famous exhortation against the rule of '2 × 2 = 4' in *Notes from the Underground*). According to Fondane, cinema provided the ideal medium for a radical break with rational, discursive thought owing to its inherent discontinuity and its ability to replace logical succession with the free play of simultaneous signifiers.[13] The passing reference to Artaud's theatrical project of 1927 in the preface to the 'cinépoèmes' can be taken as a declaration of spiritual allegiance (over and above Fondane's polemical remark on the classical repertoire of the Alfred Jarry Theatre). As a matter of fact, Fondane later expressed his admiration and support for Artaud's conception in a letter that passionately defended the Alfred Jarry Theatre against mainstream Surrealism with reference to a set of values strongly reminiscent of the preface to the 'cinépoèmes' ('un lyrisme particulier de l'éclairage', 'l'arbitraire du geste, du mouvement, la conception nette du tragique d'aujourd'hui', etc.).[14]

Fondane's similar affinity with members of *Le Grand Jeu* and *Discontinuité* together with his involvement in avant-garde projects for the theatre and cinema and his poetry bear witness to a sustained attempt at translating the existential critique of reason across a wide range of artistic activities. The analyses that Fondane devoted to the interaction between personal experience and transgressive conceptions of art in the works of Rimbaud and Baudelaire (along the lines of Chestov's previous studies of Nietzsche, Tolstoy and Dostoevsky) further substantiate his efforts to give positive expression to existential thought through new aesthetic practices. Indeed, if Chestov's irrationalist approach could ultimately avoid identification with either pure solipsism or negative theology, this is partly thanks to its opening up to forms of artistic expression and the possible analogy with the creative potential of primitive mentalities, as suggested by Fondane's compelling essays on Lévy-Bruhl and ethnology.[15]

The comparative analysis carried out in this study has showed that one of the general, distinctive aspects of existential thought as outlined by Chestov and Fondane consists in an attempt to expose and undermine the limits of rational, philosophical discourse. The 'fight against self-evidence', whose significance I examined in the first chapter and whose full scope has been clarified in the following chapters, indicates that behind Chestov's and Fondane's revolt against rational limitations there is a meaningful attempt to point to something that exceeds the speculative criteria of truth and logical validation. This attempt corresponds to the disclosure of an 'irreducible residuum of being'—a realm of being that is irreducible to rational analysis. The contingent, temporal existence of particular individuals, as well as the transcendent existence of God, belongs to this realm of being, which Chestov and Fondane describe as 'the extreme regions of existence'. The concern with the limits of philosophical investigation, where human understanding runs into insoluble antinomies of thought, into contradiction and paradox, most adequately defines Chestov's and Fondane's project. Their contradictory, paradoxical style of argument and their occasional defiant brandishing of 'irrationalism'[16] need to be considered in relation to the transgressive character of a philosophical inquiry pursued at the limits of rational understanding.

The more specific aims of the existential critique of rationality have been examined with reference to Chestov's and Fondane's approach to four main areas of philosophical investigation: consciousness, subjectivity, time and history, ethics and freedom. Considering the arguments that define Chestov's and Fondane's views of these four areas, it can be said that existential thought explicitly tried to distinguish itself from emerging forms of atheist Existentialism. This affirmation is supported not only by my previous analysis of the existential critique of Husserlian phenomenology, which distinguishes Chestov's and Fondane's thought from all strands of phenomenological Existentialism, but also by the prominent existential concern with the obliterated relationship between the 'living man' and the 'living God', which finds no equivalent in Heidegger's ontology. However, existential thought does not perfectly overlap with later manifestations of religious Existentialism such as Gabriel Marcel or Martin Buber.

This is especially apparent in the existential interpretation of notions such as 'the fight against self-evidence', 'awakening' and 'anamnesis', 'creatio ex nihilo', 'the second dimension of thought', which this study has explored for the first time by corroborating Chestov's and Fondane's arguments relating to these notions. From the point of view of the proposed restoration of Chestov's and Fondane's understanding of existential thought, the elucidation of, and the consistent references to, such distinctive notions have proved crucial for the adequate presentation of the position of the two authors in the philosophical and cultural debates of the 1920s and 1930s. Clarifying the meaning of 'the fight against self-evidence' has been instrumental in at least two ways: on the one hand as part of a more accurate presentation of the existential critique of Husserl, on the other as an indispensable premiss for the further exploration of processes of 'awakening', of 'creatio ex nihilo' and of 'the second dimension of thought', which are all linked to the paradoxical, contradictory line of argument elaborated by Chestov and Fondane.

The analysis undertaken in the first chapter highlighted Chestov's and Fondane's idea of an opposition between the 'slumber' of rational, discursive knowledge and the sudden awareness of an alternative, anti-rational type of knowledge. As I have demonstrated, the notion of 'awakening' (which Chestov and Fondane trace back to Plotinus) is closely connected to the fight against self-evident, necessary and eternal truths, which constitute the foundation of rational knowledge. The awakening to the contingent, temporal, yet irreducible truth of individual existence uncovers a non-unitary configuration of consciousness, insofar as consciousness itself becomes the site of a confrontation between discursive reasoning and 'awakening', between self-evident, timeless truths and the contingent experience of one's temporal existence.

The contrastive investigation of existential and Surrealist interpretations of consciousness in the first chapter brought out two different views of 'revolt' directly relevant to the understanding of the fight against self-evidence and of the process of awakening to one's self. Whereas the mainstream Surrealist apology for dream and reverie led on the one hand to an increasing concern with more practical social and political determinations of revolt (inspired by Marxist ideology) and on the other to a Hegelian, idealistic search for a unifying, dialectical reconciliation of opposites, writers working on the boundaries of Surrealism developed an understanding of revolt that converged with the existential 'fight against self-evidence' and the existential process of 'awakening'. Daumal's and Gilbert-Lecomte's polemical emphasis on 'the revolt of the individual against itself', which involved the idea of an inwardly disrupted consciousness as well as the possibility of an 'awakening' to an 'absurd evidence', paralleled Artaud's similarly polemical arguments, which situated revolt at the level of processes of thought and consciousness, leading to the affirmation of an alternative order of things described in terms of 'foi', 'volonté de croyance' and 'volonté de sens'.

The wider scope of this interpretation of revolt and of the non-unitary configuration of consciousness associated with it was investigated in the second chapter. As I have argued, the inner struggle to undermine and suspend the limitation posed by self-evident truths and rational knowledge appears at first as a purely negative, self-destructive project. In fighting against established principles of thought, the individual actually fights against itself; in other words, it strives to dissolve or annihilate its rational self, insofar as the principles that it seeks to undermine inhabit its own consciousness and determine its understanding of self-consciousness and subjectivity. The comparison between the existential critique of the rational construal of the subject and the attempted 'dissolution of the rational subject' undertaken by Daumal, Gilbert-Lecomte and Artaud has shown that the initial, destructive stage is part of a process of negative reconstruction, which opens up a new configuration of the subject. The existential idea of 'creatio ex nihilo' leads to the emergence of a notion of subject defined by the relationship between the living man and the 'living God', which existential thought attempts to restore through the reinterpretation of tragedy as personal, lived experience.

In contrast to the Surrealist immanentist preoccupation with the social and political empowerment of the individual, the initial, negative stage of the existential approach to subjectivity placed a special emphasis on powerlessness, disengagement, renunciation (amply illustrated in *Le Grand Jeu* and *Discontinuité* and in Artaud's writings). However, the paradoxical movement of negative reconstruction transforms this powerlessness and disengagement (powerlessness in the face of rational necessity, disengagement from the necessary limits of rational understanding) into a willed engagement with issues that exceed rational comprehension and into a source of unlimited power corresponding to the omnipotence of the living God. The analysis of the notion of 'creatio ex nihilo' in the second chapter already signals the prominent role that the notion of the will plays in the existential attempt to recover the obliterated link between the living man and the living God through the 'fight against self-evidence' and the process of 'awakening'. The actual meaning that Chestov and Fondane attach to human and divine will has been further explored in relation to their understanding of questions of time, history, ethics and freedom.

As I have argued in the third chapter, the non-unitary model of consciousness that existential thought associates with a new configuration of the subject, focused on the encounter between the living man and the living God, has profound implications for the interpretation of time. Chestov's and Fondane's positive evaluation of 'the unhappy consciousness', as part of their explicit critique of the Hegelian doctrine of the history of Spirit, brings out two fundamental aims of the existential critique of rationality: (1) the destruction of the intertwined speculative concepts of truth and being, which involves the disclosure of their common grounding in a fallacious, homogeneous interpretation of time, which in turn obscures the discontinuity between contingent experience and conceptual analysis; (2) the uncovering of paradoxical processes of consciousness ('awakening', 'anamnesis') that make possible the reconstruction of notions of truth and being bound neither by the causality and irreversibility of historical unfolding nor by the timeless, abstract principles of pure logical analysis.

Chestov's and Fondane's affirmation of an 'irreducible residuum of being' has been examined in relation to the existential critique of Husserlian and Hegelian phenomenologies. In rejecting on the one hand Husserl's concepts of self-evident truth and self-evident being and on the other Hegel's dialectical superseding of the 'unhappy consciousness' and his doctrine of history, Fondane like Chestov developed two different yet interconnected strategies. The first consisted in foregrounding notions of temporal discontinuity and heterogeneity in order to recover the distinction between the real, temporal being of living individuals and the ideal, timeless being of abstract entities of thought. The second emphasized the irreconcilable contradiction of the 'unhappy consciousness' in order to open up the temporal, contingent existence of the living individual to the paradoxical timeless being of the 'living God'. The simultaneous attribution of temporality and timelessness to the living man as well as to the living God most adequately defines the scope of the twofold existential strategy of redefining being.

In opposition to the eternal, 'uncreated' concepts of truth and being, Chestov and Fondane revive the Scholastic argument on the divine origin of 'created truth' and 'created being'. The idea of divine 'creation' exceeds the limits of logical derivation and is no longer subject to the rules of logical validation. The epistemological grounding of speculative truth and being is replaced by the relationship between the human and the divine will, by the power of creating 'out of nothingness' (over and above the principles of rational thought), which subtends the horizon of faith, qualified by Chestov and Fondane as 'the second dimension of thought'. Insofar as the second dimension of thought actually relates the fight against rational limitations to the creative power of the divine will, the notion of 'created being' (unlike the speculative concept of being) supports man's aspiration to overcome his temporally determined condition by restoring the link between the living individual and the paradoxical existence of the 'living God'.

The simultaneous attribution of temporality and timelessness to contingent, real individuals in existential thought is coherent with the radical redefinition of truth, which involves the suspension of the principle of non-contradiction. If adequately grasped, the internal coherence of the existential type of argumentation can be said to resist the attempts to realign it with a measure of logical consistency and legitimacy, which it deliberately sets out to undermine. As Leszek Kolakowski has observed:

> Rationalists normally shrug off the idea of 'mystery' (as distinct from something not yet known) as a verbal cover for simple illogicality. However, when people think of ultimate realities, the experience of mystery, which often includes a logical helplessness, may be intellectually more fruitful than rationalist self-confidence that simply cancels metaphysical questions, relying on doctrinal dogmas.[17]

Chestov's and Fondane's critique of rational knowledge actually attempts to provoke a thorough reconsideration of the object and the aims of philosophy, not only by changing the understanding of such fundamental concepts as 'truth' and 'being' or by resetting the priorities of philosophical investigation (in starting from the limits and the antinomies of thought) but also and more significantly by establishing alternative methods of investigation as well as an alternative, paradoxical style of argument.

In the first two chapters, I examined Chestov's and Fondane's contention that the dispassionate, objective inquiry of the speculative philosopher (most often illustrated with reference to Spinoza's 'non ridere, non lugere, neque destestari, sed intelligere (do not laugh, do not mourn or curse, but understand)') can and should be replaced by non-discursive, alternative modes of inquiry, if one is setting out to change the established perspective on 'ultimate questions' and 'ultimate realities'. The methods advanced by existential thought range from the Psalmist's cry *De profundis clamavi ad te, Domine*, Pascal's approval of those only 'qui cherchent en gémissant', Kierkegaard's affirmation of truth as 'subjectivity', Dostoevsky's outrage at the rule of '2 × 2 = 4', to the liberating power of laughter, equally prominent in Fondane's, Daumal's and Gilbert-Lecomte's writings.

What distinguishes these methods from those conventionally used throughout the history of systematic philosophy is their explicit grounding in human, subjective passions, desires, inclinations—in the laughter, the crying or mourning, and the cursing that Spinoza's dictum banned from rational philosophical inquiry. The second dimension of thought mobilizes these discarded methods of investigation in order to recapture the residue, or more accurately the surplus, of an incommensurable dimension of being. According to Chestov's and Fondane's understanding, existential thought is defined precisely by this non-systematic, non-discursive approach, which is intimately related to the condition of the temporal, contingent being of the living individual and to its communication with the transcendent alterity of God. In contrast to Hegel's speculative elevation towards God or the Surrealist outright dismissal of any notion of transcendence, existential thought as well as the dissident projects pursued on the boundaries of Surrealism adopt highly unconventional methods of inquiry, capable of restoring the meaningful relationship between the living man and the living God.

This methodological emphasis on individual desires, passions and inclinations becomes especially relevant in the context of the existential views of ethics and freedom, which I have examined in the fourth chapter. The question of freedom is of paramount importance to the existential attempt to redefine the object and aims of philosophical inquiry. Two recurrent major themes of reflection emerge from the analysis carried out throughout the present study. The interconnected problems of truth and being reappear at all levels of the existential critique of rational knowledge. But the possibility of changing the conditions under which these two concepts have been traditionally defined ultimately depends on a re-evaluation and a redefinition of freedom. It is the freedom to adopt a completely different understanding of philosophy, the freedom to elaborate or revive different, marginalized and unconventional methods of investigation, that Chestov and Fondane seek to release. If philosophy can be defined in terms of 'the most important' (τὸ τιμιώτατον), as Fondane and Chestov insist, (recalling Plotinus's definition), then the search for the 'most important', ultimate realities of human existence should be guided by man's aspirations, by his desire to explore even those areas that lie beyond the limits set by his rationally-determined cognitive capacities.

As I argued in the final chapter of this book, existential thought foregrounds the idea of choice and the notion of human and divine will in the attempt to recapture an understanding of freedom that transcends the twofold—logical and ethical—foundation of rational knowledge. The freedom of the divine *fiat*, which exceeds the limits of logical affirmation, as well as the freedom of the divine *valde bonum*, which exceeds the dichotomous reasoning of good and evil, is thus recalled in support of a type of thinking that aims to re-establish the communication between the living man and the living God, beyond good and evil, beyond truth and error. Chestov ended his meditation on rational necessity and freedom, which constitutes the first part of his *Athènes et Jérusalem*, with a reference to the obliterated link between divine and human will:

Et ce τῆς ἐμῆς βουλήσεως primordial (libre volonté illimitée) que nulle connaissance ne peut contenir, est l'unique source de la vérité métaphysique. Que se réalise la promesse: οὐδὲν ἀδυνατήσει ὑμῖν (il n'y aura rien d'impossible pour vous)![18]

In opening up the space of this anticipatory waiting, beyond the limits of rational philosophical investigation, existential thought traces the link between the recollection of the divine promise and the human affirmation of the possibility of its fulfilment, as the ground of an unlimited aspiration towards freedom. Within 'the general economy of man's spiritual life',[19] it may be difficult to estimate the significance of any attempt to abandon 'rationalist self-confidence' and to admit a certain 'logical helplessness' that arises from the consideration of 'ultimate realities' and ultimate questions of human existence. However, the undeniable value of the existential project consists in creating and maintaining a space of reflection in which questions concerning 'elementary facts of experience—"I", existence, freedom' can be legitimately posed, 'all philosophers' condemnations notwithstanding'.[20]

Notes to Conclusions

1. It is true that among some of the main representatives of French Existentialism who explicitly thematized the absurd, Camus no less than Sartre became deeply concerned with precisely the kind of social and political commitments that the preceding generation of Surrealist dissident writers and existential philosophers had polemically discarded. However, the increasing difficulties that both Camus and Sartre faced in trying (and ultimately failing) to articulate a systematic ethical doctrine plainly illustrate the undeniable rift between the individualistic, trans-

historical understanding of revolt (commonly associated with the absurd) and the demands for social integration and social action. The strenuous attempt at reconciling revolt and revolution, the absurd and the ethical dimensions of existence is, after all, what most clearly separates Existentialism (and indeed mainstream Surrealism) from existential thought, whose critique of reason leads to the 'suspension of the ethical', to an understanding of freedom and faith 'beyond good and evil'.

2. Chestov's two articles, 'Memento mori: A propos de la théorie de la connaissance d'Edmond Husserl' and 'Qu'est-ce que la vérité? Ontologie et Ethique', appeared in *La Revue philosophique de la France et de l'étranger* in 1926 and 1927. They predate Emmanuel Lévinas, *Théorie de l'intuition dans la phénoménologie de Husserl* (Paris: Vrin, 1930), as well as the less well known earlier study by Georges Gurvitch, *Les Tendances actuelles de la philosophie allemande* (Paris: Vrin, 1930), to which Husserl's reception in France has most often been traced back.
3. See Roger Quilliot's comments on *Le Mythe de Sisyphe* in Albert Camus, *Essais* (Paris: Gallimard and Calmann-Lévy, 1965), 1411 ff.
4. I am greatly indebted to Olivier Salazar-Ferrer for bringing this to my attention and for letting me have a copy of his chapter on Fondane and Camus from a forthcoming volume on Fondane's existential thought.
5. Fondane, 'Le Lundi existentiel', 25–53. The volume opens with Camus's 'Remarque sur la révolte', immediately followed by Fondane's article. An unpublished letter from Fondane to Camus in Sept. 1943 further documents their relationship (my thanks to the Albert Camus Archives at the IMEC). It is worth mentioning that the letter was sent only a few months before Fondane was arrested by the Gestapo in Feb. 1944. He died at Auschwitz-Birkenau on 3 Oct. 1944.
6. Fondane, 'Le Lundi existentiel', 38.
7. Camus, *Le Mythe de Sisyphe*, 124.
8. R. M. Albérès, *La Révolte des écrivains d'aujourd'hui* (Paris: Corrêa, 1949), 69–70.
9. Fondane, 'Le Lundi existentiel', 37.
10. Fondane, *Faux Traité d'ésthetique*, 34–5; *Rimbaud le Voyou*, 22–3. For comments on Fondane's polemic with Breton, see Chap. 1 above. Albérès (*La Révolte des écrivains d'aujourd'hui*, 72) is again one of the first critics to have pointed out the possible parallel between Camus's conception of revolt and the Surrealist project, while discussing the ethical interpretation of the human condition which sets Camus's thought in opposition to Chestov's: 'Par la cruauté, la démesure et une logique sadique qui paraît illogique aux autres, il arrache aux hommes les illusions qui leur permettaient de donner faussement un sens à la vie. Ce que les surréalistes tentaient dans l'ordre de la connaissance, il veut le faire dans l'ordre de l'éthique. Au lieu d'accepter la condition d'esclave qui est faite à l'homme et d'y prendre son bien, il veut la transformer. [...] Alors la vie sera exempte d'illusions sur l'ordre du monde, la bonne volonté d'une Providence quelconque, et les espoirs de l'au-delà. C'est reprendre sous une forme nouvelle les thèmes de Kafka, et des réflexions de Chestov, sans suivre ce dernier dans cet acte de foi en un Dieu transcendant qui escamote le problème en en faisant attendre une explication. C'est le "Non" du vieux serviteur sourd, dans *Le Malentendu*, qui sépare Camus de Chestov.'

11. Fondane published several volumes of poems during his lifetime. A collected edition including previously unpublished texts and the French translation of his Romanian poems, *Paysages*, has been recently published: *Le Mal des fantômes; Paysages* (Paris: Paris-Méditerranée; Toulouse: L'Éther Vague, 1996). Influenced by Jacques Copeau, Fondane created in 1922 a theatre group 'Insula' (The Island) in Bucharest. His writings for the theatre have never been collected and remain, in great part, unpublished. An English translation of his play *Philoctetes* was published in a special issue of *Cardozo Studies in Law and Literature* 6/1 (Spring–Summer 1994), 2–49. Fondane's articles on cinema and his scenarios were published in *Écrits pour le cinéma* (Paris: Plasma, 1984).
12. Benjamin Fondane, *Trois Scenarii: Paupières, Barrefixe, Mtasipoj, cinépoèmes* (Paris: R. Baze, 1928), including two photographs of the author by Man Ray. The volume was reprinted with other writings on cinema in *Écrits pour le cinéma*.
13. Ibid., 17: 'Le cinéma [...] charrie la réalité énorme de son gros plan, accouche de l'arbitraire: il introduit la notion de *quantité lyrique*, le point de vue du discontinu, le jeu du simultané; il étaye ses jugements de l'homme sur la dimension-durée. Nulle réalité ne saurait lui dérober sa figure — sommes-nous encore à tes vérités, Physique? La sur-impression permet à deux corps d'occuper au même instant le même point de l'espace.'
14. Benjamin Fondane, 'Lettre ouverte à Antonin Artaud sur le Théâtre Alfred Jarry', *Europe* 667–8 (Nov.–Dec. 1984), 87–93. For a comparative analysis of the two authors' conceptions of cinema and theatrical representation, see my articles, 'Pictures of the Mind: Artaud's and Fondane's Silent Cinema', *Surrealist Visuality* (Keele: Keele University Press, 1996), 109–24; 'Fondane-Artaud: Une Pensée au-delà des catégories', *Europe* 827 (Mar. 1998), 143–50.
15. Benjamin Fondane, 'Lévy-Bruhl et la métaphysique de la connaissance', *Revue philosophique de la France et de l'étranger* 65/5–6 (May–June 1940), 289–316, 65/7 (July 1940), 29–54.
16. In 'Edmund Husserl et l'œuf de Colomb du réel', 339, revised and reprinted in *La Conscience malheureuse*, Fondane goes so far as to give a four-point definition of the nature of 'l'irrationnel': '1. de ne pas être raisonnable; 2. de représenter exactement toute la portion du réel, avec ses actions inconnues et sa logique de hasard; 3. de ne pas s'offrir justement sous les espèces du clair et du distinct; 4. de repousser le principe de non-contradiction.'
17. Leszek Kolakowski, *God Owes Us Nothing: A Brief Remark on Pascal's Religion and on the Spirit of Jansenism* (Chicago: University of Chicago Press, 1995), 43.
18. Chestov, *Athènes et Jérusalem*, 106.
19. In the concluding passage of 'A la mémoire d'un grand philosophe: Edmund Husserl', 32, written shortly after Husserl's death and only weeks before his own death, Chestov remarked: 'Dans l'économie générale de l'activité spirituelle humaine, les tentatives pour surmonter les évidences ont une signification immense bien que cachée, nullement appréciée.' The other quotations are from Kolakowski, *God Owes Us Nothing*, 43.
20. Ibid.

BIBLIOGRAPHY

I. Existential Thought

Primary Sources

CHESTOV, LEON, *Anton Tchekhov and Other Essays*, trans. S. Koteliansky and J. M. Murry (Dublin: Maunsel, 1916).

—— *All Things are Possible*, trans. S. S. Koteliansky (London: Martin Secker, 1920).

—— *Qu'est-ce que le bolchevisme?* (Geneva, 1920; repr. in *Mercure de France* 533 (1 Sept. 1920), 257–90).

—— 'Dostoievsky et la lutte contre les évidences', *La Nouvelle Revue française* 101 (Feb. 1922), 134–58.

—— *La Nuit de Gethsémani: Essai sur la philosophie de Pascal*, Les Cahiers verts, (Paris: Grasset, 1923).

—— *Les Révélations de la mort: Dostoievsky—Tolstoi*, trans. Boris de Schloezer (Paris: Plon, 1923).

—— 'Les Favoris et les deshérités de l'histoire: Descartes et Spinoza', *Le Mercure de France* 600 (15 June 1923), 640–74.

—— 'Dernier salut (A la mémoire de Jacques Rivière)', *La Nouvelle Revue française* 139 (Apr. 1925), 674–78.

—— *L'Idée de bien chez Tolstoi et Nietzsche*, trans. T. Beresowski-Chestov and Georges Bataille (Paris: Éditions du Siècle, 1925).

—— *La Philosophie de la tragédie: Dostoiewsky et Nietzsche*, trans. Boris de Schloezer (Paris: Éditions de la Pléiade), 1926.

—— 'Memento Mori (A propos de la théorie de la connaissance d'Edmund Husserl)', *Revue philosophique de la France et de l'étranger* 51/1–2 (Jan.–Feb. 1926), 5–62.

—— *Sur les confins de la vie (L'Apothéose du déracinement)*, trans. Boris de Schloezer (Paris: Schiffrin, 1927).

—— 'Qu-est-ce que la vérité? (Ontologie et Éthique)', *Revue philosophique de la France et de l'étranger* 51/1–2 (Jan.–Feb. 1927), 36–74.

—— 'Regarder en arrière et lutter / Look Back and Struggle', *Forum philosophicum* 1 (1930), 89–117.

—— 'Des sources des vérités métaphysiques', *Revue philosophique de la France et de l'étranger* 55/7–8 (July–Aug. 1930), 13–85.

—— *Pages choisies*, trans. B. de Schloezer (Paris: Gallimard, 1931).

—— 'Richard Kroner: Von Kant bis Hegel', *Revue philosophique de la France et de l'étranger* 56/3–4 (Mar.–Apr. 1931), 299–304.

—— *In Job's Balances: On the Sources of the Eternal Truths*, trans. Camilla Coventry and C. A. Macartney (London: J. M. Dent & Sons, 1932).

—— 'La Seconde dimension de la pensée', *La Nouvelle Revue française* 228 (1 Sept. 1932), 344–56; 229 (1 Oct. 1932), 544–55.

—— 'Dans le taureau de Phalaris', *Revue philosophique de la France et de l'étranger* 58/1–2 (Jan.–Feb. 1933), 18–60; 58/3–4 (Mar.–Apr. 1933), 252–308.

—— 'Martin Buber', *Revue philosophique de la France et de l'étranger* 58/11–12 (Nov.–Dec. 1933), 430–42.

—— 'Job ou Hegel? (A propos de la philosophie existentielle de Kierkegaard)', *La Nouvelle Revue française* 240 (May 1935), 755–62.

—— 'Kierkegaard et Dostoievsky: Les Voix qui clament dans le désert', *Cahiers du Sud* 181 (Mar. 1936), 179–200.

—— 'Iasnaia Poliana et Astapovo (A l'occasion du 25ème anniversaire de la mort de Tolstoi)', *Revue philosophique de la France et de l'étranger* 61/11–12 (Nov.–Dec. 1936), 281–95.

—— 'Sine effusione sanguinis: De la probité philosophique (A propos de Karl Jaspers)', *Hermès* 1 (Jan. 1938), 5–36.

—— 'Le Mythe et la vérité (A propos de la métaphysique de la connaissance', *Philosophia* 3/1 (1938), 60–71.

—— 'A la mémoire d'un grand philosophe: Edmund Husserl', *Revue philosophique de la France et de l'étranger* 65/1–6 (Jan.–June 1940), 5–32.

—— *Kierkegaard et la philosophie existentielle* (Paris: J. Vrin, 1948; repr. 1972).

—— 'Nicolas Berdiaeff: La Gnose et la philosophie existentielle', *Revue philosophique de la France et de l'étranger* 73/1–3 (Jan.–Mar. 1948), 2–35.

—— 'Les explications et la réalité', *84: Nouvelle Revue littéraire* 18 (May–June 1951), 12–16.

—— 'La Logique de la création réligieuse: A la mémoire de William James', *Synthèses* 93–4 (Feb.–Mar. 1954), 382–92.

—— 'Conclusions', *Cahiers du Sud* 321 (Feb. 1954), 223–37.

—— 'Discours exaspérés: Les extases de Plotin', *Revue philosophique de la France et de l'étranger* 81–2/4–6 (Apr.–June 1956), 178–216.

—— *Sola Fide: Luther et l'Église*, trans. Sophie Sève (Paris: P.U.F., 1957).

—— *La Philosophie de la tragédie: Sur les confins de la vie* (Paris: Flammarion, 1966).

—— *L'Homme pris au piège: Pouchkine, Tolstoï, Tchékhov* (Paris: Union Générale d'Editions, 1966).

—— *Le Pouvoir des clefs/Potestas clavium*, trans. Boris de Schloezer (Paris: Flammarion, 1967; 1st edn Paris: La Pléiade, 1928).

—— *A Shestov Anthology*, ed. Bernard Martin (Athens: University of Ohio Press, 1970).

—— *Sur la Balance de Job: Pérégrinations à travers les âmes*, trans. Boris de Schloezer (Paris: Flammarion, 1971; 1st French edn Paris: YMCA-Press, 1929).
—— *Spéculation et Révélation*, trans. Sylvie Luneau (Lausanne: L'Age d'Homme, 1981).
—— *Les Grandes Veilles*, trans. Sylvie Luneau and Nathalie Sretovitch (Lausanne: L'Age d'Homme, 1985).
—— *Les Commencements et le fins*, trans. Boris de Schloezer and Sylvie Luneau (Lausanne: L'Age d'Homme, 1987).
—— *Athènes et Jerusalem*, trans. Boris de Schloezer, (Paris: Flammarion, 1967; Paris: Aubier, 1993) [incl. Yves Bonnefoy, 'L'Obstination de Chestov'].
FONDANE, BENJAMIN, *Trois scénarii: Paupières, Barrefixe, Mtasipoj, cinépoèmes* (Brussels: Documents Internationaux de l'Esprit Nouveau, 1928).
—— 'Un philosophe tragique: Léon Chestov', *Europe* 19 (15 Jan. 1929), 142–50.
—— 'Edmond Husserl et l'œuf de Colomb du réel', *Europe* 20 (15 June 1929), 331–44.
—— 'Réflexions sur le spectacle', *Cahiers de l'Etoile* 2 (1929), 256–67.
—— 'Léon Chestov, temoin à charge', *Cahiers de l'Etoile* 2 (1929), 344–64.
—— 'Du muet au parlant: Grandeur et décadence du cinéma', *Bifur* 5 (April 1930), 137–50.
—— 'Sur la route de Dostoievsky: Martin Heidegger', *Cahiers du Sud* 8/141 (June 1932), 378–92.
—— 'Rimbaud le Voyou', *Cahiers du Sud* 10/149 (Mar. 1933), 196–209.
—— *Rimbaud le Voyou* (Paris: Editions Denoël et Steele, 1933; repr. Paris: Plasma, 1979; Brussels: Complexe, 1990).
—— 'Léon Chestov, Sœren Kierkegaard et le Serpent', *Cahiers du Sud* 11/164 (Sept. 1934), 534–54.
—— 'Une Politique de l'esprit: Le Premier Congrès des écrivains de l'URSS', *Cahiers du Sud* 11/166 (1934), 718–24.
—— 'Héraclite le pauvre, ou la nécessité de Kierkegaard', *Cahiers du Sud* 13/177 (Nov. 1935), 757–70.
—— 'L'Esprit et le temps: La Conscience malheureuse', *Cahiers du Sud* 12/171 (Apr. 1935), 304–17.
—— 'Léon Chestov à la recherche du judaïsme perdu', *Revue juive de Genève* 4 (1936), 326–8.
—— 'Lettre de Benjamin Fondane à David Gascoyne' [July 1937], London, British Library, Add. MS 56060, typed copy of original manuscript (David Gascoyne Archives).
—— *La Conscience malheureuse* (Paris: Denoël & Steele, 1936; repr. Paris: Plasma, 1979).
—— 'A propos du livre de Léon Chestov: Kierkegaard et la philosophie existentielle', *Revue de philosophie* 37 (1937), 381–414.

—— 'Léon Chestov et la lutte contre les évidences', *La Revue de la France et de l'étranger* (July–Aug. 1938), 13–50.
—— *Baudelaire et l'expérience du gouffre* (Paris: Seghers, 1972; Brussels: Complexe, 1994).
—— *Faux Traite d'esthétique* (Paris: Plasma, 1980).
—— *Rencontres avec Léon Chestov* (Paris: Plasma, 1982).
—— *Écrits pour le cinéma; Le Muet et le parlant* (Paris: Plasma, 1984).
—— 'Lettre ouverte à Antonin Artaud sur le théâtre Alfred Jarry', *Europe* 667–8 (Nov.–Dec. 1984), 87–93.
—— *Le Festin de Balthazar: Auto-sacramental*, ed. Eric A. Freedman (Saint-Nazaire: Arcane 17, 1985).
—— 'Interview avec moi-même et autres textes', *Le Beffroi* [Quebec] 2 (April 1987), 131–44.
—— *Le Lundi existentiel et le dimanche de l'histoire, suivi de La Philosophie vivante* (Brussels: Éditions du Rocher, 1990).
—— 'Philoctète' [extract], ed. Éric Freedman, *Le Mâche-Laurier* 2 (June 1994), 33–37.
FUNDOIANU, B. [= FONDANE, BENJAMIN], 'Judaism si Helenism', *Mintuirea* [Bucharest] 171–230 (1919).
—— *Imagini si carti din Franta* (Bucharest: Socec, 1922).
—— *Privelisti* (Bucharest: Cultura nationala, 1930).
—— *Privelisti si inedite* (Bucharest: Cartea Romaneasca, 1974).
—— *Poezii*, i (Bucharest: Minerva, 1983).
KIERKEGAARD, SØREN, *Le Concept de l'angoisse*, trans. Knud Ferlov and Jean J. Gateau (Paris: NRF and Gallimard, 1935).
—— *Training in Christianity*, trans. Walter Lowrie (Princeton: Princeton University Press, 1944).
—— *Kierkegaard's Concluding Unscientific Postscript*, trans. David F. Swenson (London: Humphrey Milford, Oxford University Press, 1945).
—— *L'Existence*, trans. P.-H. Tisseau, ed. Jean Brun (Paris: P.U.F., 1972).
—— *The Concept of Anxiety*, ed. and trans. Reidar Thomte and Albert B. Anderson (Princeton: Princeton University Press, 1980).
—— *Fear and Trembling; Repetition*, ed. and trans. Howard V. Hong and Edna H. Hong (Princeton: Princeton University Press, 1983).
—— *Philosophical Fragments; Johannes Climacus*, ed. and trans. Howard V. Hong and Edna H. Hong (Princeton: Princeton University Press, 1985).
—— *Either/Or*, ed. and trans. Howard V. Hong and Edna H. Hong (Princeton: Princeton University Press, 1987).
—— *The Concept of Irony*, ed. and trans. Howard V. Hong and Edna H. Hong (Princeton: Princeton University Press, 1989).
—— *Papers and Journals: A Selection*, trans. Alastair Hannay (London: Penguin, 1996).
PASCAL, BLAISE, *Œuvres complètes*, ed. Jacques Chevalier (Paris: NRF and Gallimard, 1954).

Secondary sources

ALBÉRÈS, R. M., *La Révolte des écrivains d'aujourd'hui* (Paris: Corrêa, 1949).

Approches: Cahiers israéliens de poésie et de critique 3 (1985), special issue 'B. Fondane'.

BARANOFF, NATALIE, *Bibliographie des œuvres de Léon Chestov* (Paris: Institut d'Études Slaves, 1975).

—— *Bibliographie des études sur Léon Chestov* (Paris: Institut d'Études Slaves, 1978).

BARANOFF-CHESTOV, NATALIE, *La vie de Léon Chestov*, i: *L'Homme de Souterrain, 1866–1929*; ii: *Les Derniers Années, 1928–1938*, trans. Blanche Bronstein-Vinaver (Paris: Éditions de la Difference, 1991–3).

BAYLE, JEAN-LOUIS LOUBET DEL, *Les Non-conformistes des années 30: Une tentative de renouvellement de la pensée politique française* (Paris: Éditions du Seuil, 1969).

BÉDARD, ANDRÉ, *La Nuit libératrice: Liberté, raison et foi selon L. Chestov* (Tournai: Desclée; Montreal: Bellarmin, 1973).

BERDYAEV, N. A., 'L'Idée fondamentale de la philosophie de Chestov', Léon Chestov, *Spéculation et révélation* (Lausanne: L'Age d'Homme, 1981).

BESPALOFF, RACHEL, *Cheminements et carrefours (Julien Green, André Malraux, Gabriel Marcel, Kierkegaard, Chestov devant Niezsche)* (Paris: J. Vrin, 1938).

BOWMAN, FRANK, 'Irredentist Existentialism: Fondane and Shestov', *Yale French Studies* 16 (Winter 1955–6), 111–17.

BRUN, JEAN, 'Le Livre scellé', *L'Europe Philosophe: 25 siècles de pensée occidentale* (Paris: Stock, 1988), 357–60.

BUCUR, MARIN, *B. Fundoianu* (Bucharest: Albatros, 1985).

Cahiers du Sud 26/283 (1947), special issue 'B. Fondane'.

CARASSOU, MICHEL, 'Benjamin Fondane (1898–1944)', *Sens: Juifs et chrétiens dans le monde aujourd'hui* 6 (1981), 125–8.

—— 'Fondane et le christianisme', ibid., 139–43.

—— 'Artaud, Fondane, même combat!', *Europe* 667–8 (Nov.–Dec. 1984), 84–6.

—— 'Benjamin Fondane, du surréalisme à l'existentialisme', Anne Roche and Christian Tarting (eds.), *Des Années trente: groupes et ruptures* (Paris: CNRS, 1986), 247–58.

—— 'Benjamin Fondane et la conscience honteuse du surréalisme', *Mélusine* 3 (1983), 181–89.

—— 'Benjamin Fondane entre le cri et le poème', *Jungle* 7 (15 Mar. 1984), 5–7.

—— 'Du côté de l'utopie avec Fondane et Janover', *Mélusine* 10 (1988), 267–70.

CASTILHO, LAURA AYERZA DE, and FELGINE, ODILE, *Victoria Ocampo* (Paris: Criterion, 1991).

CHOURAQUI, BERNARD, 'Le dialogue de l'urgence (Chestov-Fondane)', *Le Scandale juif ou la subversion de la mort* (Hallier: Éditions Libres, 1979), 193–251.

COPLESTON, FREDERICK S. J., 'L. Shestov: Rationalism, History and Religion', *Philosophy in Russia from Herzen to Lenin and Berdyaev* (Tunbridge Wells: Search; Notre Dame: University of Notre Dame Press, 1986), 389–99.

DECHET, FERUCCIO, *L'itinerario filosofico di Leone Chestov* (Milan: Marzorati, 1964).

DÉSILETS, ANDRÉ, *Léon Chestov: Des paradoxes de la philosophie* (Quebec: Éditions du Beffroi, 1984).

DOSTOEVSKY, FEODOR, *Notes from the Underground; The Gambler*, trans. Jane Kentish (Oxford: Oxford University Press, 1991).

EDIE, JAMES M., SCANLAN, JAMES P., and ZELDIN, MARY-BARBARA (eds.), with KLINE, GEORGE L., *Russian Philosophy*, iii (Chicago: Quadrangle, 1965).

Essays in Russian Literature: Leontiev, Rozanov, Shestov, trans. Spencer E. Roberts (Athens: University of Ohio Press, 1968).

FOTIADE, RAMONA, 'Évidence et conscience: Léon Chestov et la critique existentielle de la théorie de l'évidence chez Husserl', *Cahiers de l'émigration russe* 3 (1996), special issue 'Léon Chestov: Un philosophe pas comme les autres?', 111–25.

GASCOYNE, DAVID, *Rencontres avec Benjamin Fondane* (Saint-Nazaire: Arcane 17, 1984).

—— *Journal 1936–1937: Death of an Explorer: Leon Chestov* (London: Enitharmon Press, 1980).

GAULTIER, JULES DE, Introduction to Léon Chestov, *L'Idée de bien chez Tolstoi et Nietzsche: Philosophie et prédication* (Paris: Éditions du Siècle, 1925).

—— 'De l'éthique à l'esthétique à travers la mystique', *Revue philosophique de la France et de l'étranger* 52/5–6 (May–June 1928), 385–427.

—— 'Léon Chestov: *Le pouvoir des clefs/Potestas clavium*', *Revue philosophique de la France et de l'étranger* 53/5–6 (May–June 1929), 462–3.

GLOUBERMAN, EMANUEL, *Feodor Dostoevsky, Vladimir Soloviev, Vasilii Rozanov and Lev Shestov on Jewish and Old Testament Themes* (Ph.D. dissertation, University of Michigan, 1974).

Great Twentieth Century Jewish Philosophers: Shestov, Rozenzweig, Buber (New York: Macmillan, 1970).

GRENIER, JEAN, 'Kierkegaard et la philosophie existentielle, par *Léon Chestov*, traduit du russe par *T. Rageot* et *B. de Schlœzer* (Les amis de Léon Chestov)', *La Nouvelle Revue française* (Nov. 1936), 906–8.

HALÉVY, DANIEL, Preface to Léon Chestov, *La Nuit de Gethsémani* (Paris: Grasset, 1923).

HEURGON-DESJARDINS, ANNE, *Paul Desjardins et les Décades de Pontigny* (Paris: P.U.F., 1964).

HILL, RICHMOND KENT, *On the Threshold of Faith: An Intellectual Biography of Lev Shestov 1901–1920* (Ph.D. dissertation, University of Washington, 1980).

HYDE, JOHN K., *Benjamin Fondane: A Presentation of His Life and Work* (Geneva: Droz, 1971).

JUTRIN, MONIQUE, *Benjamin Fondane, ou Le Périple d'Ulysse* (Paris: A.-G. Nizet, 1989)

—— 'Benjamin Fondane et le surréalisme: Art poétique et langage poétique', *Mélusine* 12 (1991), 257–66.

LAZAREV, ADOLF M., 'La Philosophie de Léon Chestov', *Vie et connaissance*, trans. B. de Schloezer (Paris: J. Vrin, 1948).

LAWRENCE, D. H., Foreword to Leo Shestov, *All Things Are Possible*, trans. S. S. Koteliansky (London: Martin Secker, 1920).

LE RIDER, JACQUES, *Nietzsche en France: De la fin du XIXe siècle au temps présent* (Paris: P.U.F., 1999).

LOSSKY, N. O., 'Shestov's Irrationalism', *History of Russian Philosophy* (London: George Allen and Unwin, 1952), 325–6.

MAGNY, CLAUDE-EDMONDE, *Les Sandales d'Empédocle* (Neuchâtel: Éditions de la Baconnière, 1945).

MARITAIN, JACQUES, *Moral Philosophy* (London: Geoffrey Bles, 1964).

MARTIN, BERNARD, Introduction to Lev Shestov, *Dostoevky, Tolstoy and Nietzsche* (Athens: University of Ohio Press, 1969).

—— Introduction to *A Shestov Anthology* (Athens: University of Ohio Press, 1970).

MARTIN, MIRCEA, *Introducere in opera lui B. Fundoianu* (Bucharest: Minerva, 1984).

—— 'B. Fundoianu et Benjamin Fondane', *Cahiers roumains d'études littéraires* 1 (1991).

MONAS, SIDNEY, Introduction to Lev Shestov, *Chekhov and Other Essays* (Ann Arbor: University of Michigan Press, 1966).

MURRY, JOHN MIDDLETON, Introduction to Lev Shestov, *Anton Tchekhov and Other Essays* (Dublin: Maunsel, 1916).

NETO, JOSE MARIA, *The Christianization of Pyrrhonism: Scepticism and Faith in Pascal, Kierkegaard, and Shestov* (Dordrecht: Kluwer, 1995).

Non lieu (1978), special issue 'Benjamin Fondane: Études et témoignages, textes de Benjamin Fondane, *Au Temps du poème* et *Poèmes épars*'.

ROONEY, VICTORIA, *Shestov's Religious Existentialism: A Critique* (D.Phil. thesis, Oxford University, 1990).

ROSTENNE, PAUL, *Léon Chestov*, trans. N. Vilela (Buenos Aires: Columba, 1967).

SALAZAR-FERRER, OLIVIER, 'Benjamin Fondane le révolté', *Agone* 10 (1993), 45–69.

SCHLOEZER, BORIS DE, 'Un penseur russe: Léon Chestov', *Mercure de France* (1 Oct. 1922), 82–115.

—— 'Lecture de Chestov', Léon Chestov, *La Philosophie de la tragédie: Sur les confins de la vie* (Paris: Flammarion, 1966), 7–20.
SCHWARTZ, LEONARD, 'The Forgotten as Contemporary: Benjamin Fondane and Roger Gilbert-Lecomte', *The Literary Review* (Spring 1987), 465–7.
—— 'Introduction to Benjamin Fondane', *Pequod* 34 (1992), 73–5.
Sens: Juifs et Chrétiens dans le monde aujourd'hui 6 (1981), special issue 'B. Fondane'.
SHEIN, LOUIS S., *The Philosophy of Lev Shestov (1866–1938): A Russian Religious Existentialist* (Lewiston, ME: Edwin Mellen Press, 1991).
SMITH, DOUGLAS, *Transvaluations: Nietzsche in France 1872–1972* (Oxford: Clarendon Press, 1996).
SURYA, MICHEL, *Georges Bataille: La Mort à l'œuvre* (Paris: Garamont and Frédéric Birr, 1987).
VALEVICIUS, ANDRIUS, *Lev Shestov and His Times: Encounters with Brandes, Tolstoy, Dostoevsky, Chekhov, Ibsen, Nietzsche and Husserl* (New York: Peter Lang, 1993).
VAN SEVENANT, ANN, *Il filosofo dei poeti: L'Estetica di Benjamin Fondane* (Milan: Mimesis, 1994).
WERNHAM, JAMES C. S., *Two Russian Thinkers: Berdyaev and Shestov* (Toronto: University of Toronto Press, 1968).

II. Surrealism and Other Avant-Garde Groups and Writers

Primary sources

ADAMOV, ARTHUR, *L'Homme et l'enfant: Souvenirs, Journal* (Paris: Gallimard, 1968).
ARAGON, LOUIS, *Le Paysan de Paris* (Paris: Gallimard, 1926; repr. 1976).
Archives du Surréalisme, i: *Bureau de recherches surréalistes; Cahiers de la permanence (octobre 1924 – avril 1925)*; ii: *Vers l'action politique*; iii: *Adhérer au Parti communiste? (septembre – décembre 1926)* (Paris: NRF and Gallimard, 1988–92).
ARTAUD, ANTONIN, *Vie et Mort de Satan le feu; Textes Mexicains pour un nouveau Mythe* (Paris: Arcanes, 1953).
—— *Œuvres complètes*, 25 vols. (Paris: NRF and Gallimard, 1956–90).
—— *Le Théâtre et son double; Le Théâtre de Séraphin* (Paris: Gallimard, 1964).
—— *Œuvres complètes*, i–ib (supplement), rev. edn (Paris: NRF and Gallimard, 1970).
—— *Nouveaux écrits de Rodez; Lettres au docteur Ferdière (1943–1946) et autres textes inédits suivis de six lettres à Marie Dubuc (1935–1937)* (Paris: NRF and Gallimard, 1977).
BRETON, ANDRÉ, *Entretiens* (Paris: Gallimard, 1952).
—— *Signe ascendant* (Paris: Gallimard, 1968).

—— *La Clé des champs* (Paris: U.G.E., 1973).
—— *Manifestes du surréalisme* (Paris: NRF and Gallimard, 1979).
—— *Œuvres complètes*, 3 vols. (Paris: NRF and Gallimard, 1988–99).
—— *Investigating Sex: Surrealist Discussions, 1928–1932*, ed. Jose Pierre, trans. Malcolm Imrie (London: Verso, 1992).
DAUMAL, RENÉ, *Le Contre-Ciel* (Paris: Éditions de l'Université, 1936; repr. Paris: Gallimard, 1970, 1988).
—— *La Grande Beuverie* (Paris: Gallimard, 1938).
—— *Chaque fois que l'aube paraît*, Essais et notes, i (Paris: NRF and Gallimard, 1953).
—— *Lettres à ses amis* (Paris: Gallimard, 1956).
—— *Tu t'es toujours trompé* (Paris: Mercure de France, 1970).
—— *Les Pouvoirs de la parole*, Essais et notes, ii (1935–43) (Paris: Gallimard, 1972).
—— *L'Évidence absurde* (Paris: Gallimard, 1972).
—— *Mugle* (Montpellier: Fata Morgana, 1978).
—— *Le Mont analogue* (Paris: Gallimard, 1981).
—— *Correspondance*, i. *(1915–1928)*; ii. *(1929–1932)* (Paris: NRF and Gallimard, 1992–3).
DAUMAL, RENÉ, VAILLAND, ROGER, and GILBERT-LECOMTE, ROGER, *Rimbaud* (Charleville-Mezières: Musée-Bibliothèque Arthur Rimbaud, 1984).
Discontinuité 1 (June 1928), ed. Arthur Adamov, Monny de Boully and Claude Sernet.
GILBERT-LECOMTE, ROGER, *La Vie, l'Amour, la Mort, le Vide et le Vent* (Paris: Éditions des Cahiers Libres, 1933).
—— 'Une lettre inédite de Roger Gilbert-Lecomte' [à Benjamin Fondane], *Cahiers du Sud* 377 (May–June 1964), 388–94.
—— *Correspondance* (Paris: Gallimard, 1971).
—— *Arthur Rimbaud* (Montpellier: Fata Morgana, 1972).
—— *L'Horrible révélation, la seule...* (Paris: Gallimard, 1974).
—— *Œuvres complètes*, i: *Proses*; ii: *Poésie* (Paris: Gallimard, 1977).
La Révolution surréaliste 1–12 (1 Dec. 1924 – 15 Dec. 1929) (collected repr. Paris: Jean-Michel Place, 1975).
Le Grand Jeu (collected repr. with additions, Paris: Éditions de l'Herne, 1968).
Le Grand Jeu (collected repr. Paris: Jean-Michel Place, 1977).
Le Surréalisme au service de la révolution 1–6 (July 1930–May 1933) (collected repr. Paris: Jean-Michel Place, 1976).
Littérature, 1st ser., ed. Louis Aragon, André Breton and Philippe Soupault, 1–20 (Mar. 1919 – Aug. 1921); 2nd ser., ed. André Breton, 1–13 (Mar. 1922 – June 1924) (collected repr. Paris: Jean-Michel Place, 1978).
Raison d'être 1–7 (Dec. 1928 – July 1930).
Zarathoustra: Revue de l'activité de l'esprit 1–6 (Jan.–Nov. 1929), ed. Jean Audard.

Secondary sources

ABASTADO, CLAUDE, *Introduction au surréalisme* (Paris: Bordas, 1986).

ABIRACHED, ROBERT, RUHE, ERNSTPETER, and SCHWADERER, RICHARD (eds.), *Lectures d'Adamov: Actes du colloque international Würzburg 1981* (Tübingen: Günter Narr; Paris: Jean-Michel Place, 1983)

André Breton: La Beauté convulsive [exhibition catalogue] (Paris: Centre George Pompidou, 1991).

ADES, DAWN, *Dada and Surrealism Reviewed* (London: Arts Council of Great Britain, 1978).

ADMUSSEN, RICHARD L., *Les Petites Revues littéraires 1914–1939: Répertoire descriptif* (St Louis: Washington University Press; Paris: A. G. Nizet, 1970).

ALEXANDRIAN, SARANE, *Surrealist Art* (London: Thames and Hudson, 1970).

—— *Le Surréalisme et le rêve* (Paris: Gallimard, 1974).

ALQUIÉ, FERDINAND, *La Philosophie du surréalisme* (Paris: Flammarion, 1977).

—— 'Humanisme surréaliste et humanisme existentialiste', *Cahiers du Collège philosophique* (1948), special issue 'L'Homme, le monde, l'histoire', 139–163.

ANDRÉ-CARAZ, DANIELE, *L'Expérience intérieure d'Antonin Artaud* (Paris: Saint-Germain-des-Prés, 1973).

BATAILLE, GEORGES, 'Le Surréalisme au jour le jour', *Le Groupe, la rupture* (Paris: Éditions du Seuil, 1970), 84–98.

BÉHAR, HENRI, *André Breton: Le Grand Indésirable* (Paris: Calmann-Levy, 1990).

BÉHAR, HENRI (ed.), *Les Pensées d'André Breton* (Lausanne: L'Age de l'Homme, 1988).

BÉHAR, HENRI, and CARASSOU, MICHEL, *Le Surréalisme: Textes et débats* (Paris: Livre de Poche, 1984).

BIRO, ADAM, and PASSERON, RENÉ, *Dictionnaire général du surréalisme et de ses environs* (Paris: P.U.F., 1982).

BRADBY, DAVID, *Adamov*, Research Bibliographies and Checklists (London: Grant & Cutler, 1975).

BRIDEL, YVES, *Miroirs du surréalisme: Essais sur la réception du surréalisme en France et en Suisse française (1919–1939)* (Lausanne: L'Age de l'Homme, 1988).

CAHIERS DE L'HERNE, 'Le Grand Jeu-Textes' (Paris: Editions de l'Herne, 1968).

CAILLOIS, ROGER, *Le Procès intellectuel de l'art: Exposé des motifs* (Marseilles: Cahiers du Sud, 1935).

CARROUGES, MICHEL, *André Breton et les données fondamentales du surréalisme* (Paris: Gallimard, 1950).

CHÉNIEUX-GENDRON, JACQUELINE, *Le Surréalisme* (Paris: P.U.F., 1984).

CHÉNIEUX-GENDRON, JAQUELINE, and DUMAS, MARIE-CLAIRE (eds.), *L'Objet au défi* (Paris: P.U.F., 1987).

DELEUZE, GILLES, and GUATTARI, FELIX, *L'Anti-Œdipe* (Paris: Minuit, 1972).

—— '28 novembre 1947: Comment se faire un corps sans organes', *Minuit* 10 (Sept. 1974), 56–84.

—— *Cinéma 2: L'Image-Temps* (Paris: Minuit, 1985).

DELONS, ANDRÉ, *Au Carrefour du Grand Jeu et du surréalisme*, ed. Odette Virmaux and Alain Virmaux (Paris: Rougerie, 1988).

DERRIDA, JACQUES, *L'Écriture et la différence* (Paris: Éditions du Seuil, 1967).

DUMAS, ROLAND, *Plaidoyer pour Roger Gilbert-Lecomte* (Paris: NRF and Gallimard, 1985).

DUMOULIÉ, CAMILLE, *Nietzsche et Artaud: Pour une éthique de la cruauté* (Paris: P.U.F., 1992).

Europe 475–6 (Nov.–Dec. 1968), special issue 'Surréalisme'.

Europe 667–8 (Nov.–Dec. 1984), special issue 'Antonin Artaud'.

Europe 782–3 (June–July 1994), special issue 'Le Grand Jeu'.

FOTIADE, RAMONA, 'Entretien avec David Gascoyne, 15 août 1994', *Bulletin de la Société d'Études Benjamin Fondane* 3 (Spring 1995), 4–7.

—— 'Benjamin Fondane et le Théâtre Alfred Jarry', *Revue roumaine* 1 (1996), 42–55.

GARELLI, JACQUES, *Artaud et la question du lieu: Essai sur le théâtre et la poésie d'Artaud* (Paris: José Corti, 1982).

GASCOYNE, DAVID, *Collected Journals (1932–1942)* (London: Skoob Books, 1991).

Hermes: Recherches sur l'expérience spirituelle 5 (1967–8), special issue 'La Voie de René Daumal du *Grand Jeu* au *Mont analogue*'.

JANOVER, LOUIS, *La Révolution surréaliste* (Paris: Plon, 1989).

JOUVE, PIERRE-JEAN, '*Les Cenci* d'Antonin Artaud', *La Nouvelle Revue française* 261 (1 June 1935), 910–15.

LEGRAND, GERARD, *André Breton en son temps* (Paris: Le Soleil noir, 1976).

Magazine litteraire 388 (June 2000), special issue 'La Pataphysique: L'Histoire d'une société très secrète'.

MAXWELL, H. J. (ed.), *René Daumal ou le retour à soi* (Paris: L'Originel, 1981).

MOURIER-CASILE, PASCALINE, *De la chimère à la merveille: Recherches sur l'imaginaire fin de siècle et de l'imaginaire surréaliste* (Lausanne: L'Age d'Homme, 1986).

NADEAU, MAURICE, *Histoire du surréalisme* (Paris: Éditions du Seuil, 1945).

—— *Histoire du surréalisme: Documents surréalistes* (Paris: Éditions du Seuil, 1948).

PONTALIS, J.-B., 'Les Vases non communicants', *La Nouvelle Revue française* 302 (1 March 1978), 26–45.

POWRIE, PHILIP PETER, *René Daumal: Étude d'une obsession* (Geneva: Droz, 1990).

—— 'Film—Form—Mind: The Hegelian Follies of Roger Gilbert-Lecomte', *Quarterly Review of Film and Video* 12/4 (1991), 19–32.

RANDOM, MICHEL, *Le Grand Jeu* (Paris: Denoël, 1970).

RISPAIL, JEAN-LUC, and BONNAUT-LAMOTTE, DANIELLE, *Politique, poétique, polémique: Le Surréalisme des Années Trente à l'épreuve de l'ordinateur* (Paris: Champion; Geneva: Slatkine, 1991).

ROBERT, BERNARD-PAUL, *Antécédents du Surréalisme* (Ottawa: Presses de l'Université d'Ottawa, 1988).

ROCHE, ANNE, and TARTING, CHRISTIAN (eds.), *Des Années Trentes: Groupes et ruptures: Actes du colloque organisé par l'antenne de l'U.R.L. no. 5 à l'Université de Provence I, 5–7 mai 1983* (Paris: CNRS, 1985).

Salvador Dali, 1980 [exhibition catalogue] (Paris: Centre Georges Pompidou, Musée National d'Art Moderne, 1979).

Sima [exhibition catalogue] (Paris: Musée d'art moderne de la ville de Paris, 1992).

TZARA, TRISTAN, *Œuvres complètes*, i: *(1912–1924)* (Paris: Flammarion, 1975).

VACHÉ, JACQUES, *Soixante-dix-neuf lettres de guerre*, ed. Georges Sebbag (Paris: Jean-Michel Place, 1989).

VAILLAND, ROGER, *Le Surréalisme contre la révolution* (Paris: Éditions Sociales, 1947).

VIRMAUX, ALAIN, and VIRMAUX, ODETTE, *Les Surréalistes et le cinéma* (Paris: Seghers, 1976).

—— *Artaud: Un Bilan critique* (Paris: Pierre Belfond, 1979).

—— *Artaud Vivant* (Nouvelles Éditions Oswald, 1980).

—— *Antonin Artaud: Qui êtes-vous?* (Paris: La Manufacture, 1986).

—— *Roger Gilbert-Lecomte et Le Grand Jeu* (Paris: Pierre Belfond, 1981).

III. Background Philosophical and Theoretical Writings

ADORNO, THEODOR, and HORKHEIMER, MAX, *Dialectic of Enlightenment*, trans. John Cumming (London: Verso, 1995).

ALLISON, HENRY E., *Kant's Theory of Freedom* (Cambridge: Cambridge University Press, 1995).

ARVON, HENRI, *L'Anarchisme* (Paris: P.U.F., 1951).

BARRETT, WILLIAM, *Irrational Man: A Study in Existential Philosophy* (Westport, CT: Greenwood Press, 1977).

BELL, DAVID, *Husserl* (London: Routledge, 1995).

BERGSON, HENRI, *Les Deux Sources de la morale et de la religion* (Paris: P.U.F., 1932).

—— *Essai sur les données immédiates de la conscience* (Geneva: Albert Skira, 1945).

—— *L'Évolution créatrice* (Geneva: Albert Skira, 1945).

—— *Matière et mémoire* (Geneva: Albert Skira, 1946).

BERLIN, ISAIAH, *Four Essays on Liberty* (London: Oxford University Press, 1969).

BLANCHOT, MAURICE, *La Part du feu* (Paris: Gallimard, 1949).

—— *L'Espace littéraire* (Paris: Gallimard, 1955).
BOUVERESSE, JACQUES, *Wittgenstein Reads Freud: The Myth of the Unconscious*, trans. Carol Cosman (Princeton: Princeton University Press, 1995).
BREAZEALE, DANIEL (ed. and trans.), *Philosophy and Truth: Selections from Nietzsche's Notebooks of the Early 1870s*, D. Breazeale (New Jersey: Humanities Press, 1995).
BRENTANO, FRANZ, *Psychology from an Empirical Standpoint*, trans. Antos C. Rancuello, D. B. Terell and Linda L. McAlister (London: Routledge & Kegan Paul: New York: Humanities Press, 1973).
CADAVA, EDUARDO, CONNOR, PETER, and NANCY, JEAN-LUC (eds.), *Who Comes After the Subject?* (London: Routledge, 1991).
CAMUS, ALBERT, *L'Homme révolté* (Paris: Gallimard, 1963).
—— *Essais* (Paris: NRF/Gallimard, 1965).
CLARK, MAUDEMARIE, *Nietzsche on Truth and Philosophy* (Cambridge: Cambridge University Press, 1990).
DELEUZE, GILLES, *Différence et répétition* (Paris: P.U.F., 1968).
—— *Logique du sens* (Paris: Minuit, 1969).
DESCARTES, RENÉ, *Meditations on First Philosophy; with Selections from the Objections and Replies*, trans. John Cottingham (Cambridge: Cambridge University Press, 1993).
DORÉ, JOSEPH, *Introduction à l'étude de la théologie* (Paris: Desclée, 1991).
FARRELL KRELL, DAVID, 'Paradoxes of the Pineal: From Descartes to Georges Batailles', A. Phillips Griffiths (ed.), *Contemporary French Philosophy* (Cambridge: Cambridge University Press, 1987), 215–28.
FOUCAULT, MICHEL, *L'Histoire de la folie* (Paris: Plon, 1961).
FREUD, SIGMUND, *Civilization and Its Discontents*, trans. James Strachey (New York: Penguin, 1961).
—— *Civilization, Society and Religion*, trans. James Strachey (New York: Penguin, 1991).
GILSON, ÉTIENNE, *The Philosophy of St. Thomas Aquinas*, trans. Edward Bullough (New York: Dorset Press, 1948).
GRENIER, JEAN (ed.), *L'Existence: essais par Albert Camus, Benjamin Fondane, M. de Gandillac, Étienne Gilson, J. Grenier, Louis Lavelle, René le Senne, Brice Parain, A. de Waelhens* (Paris: NRF and Gallimard, 1945).
GRIEDER, ALFONS, 'Husserl in the Thirties: The Hegelian Connection', *Journal of the British Society for Phenomenology* 11/3 (Oct. 1980), 255–70.
—— 'What did Heidegger mean by "Essence"?', *Journal of the British Society for Phenomenology* 19/1 (Jan. 1988), 64–89.
HEGEL, G. W. F., *Hegel's Logic: Being Part One of the Encyclopaedia of the Philosophical Sciences (1830)*, trans. William Wallace (Oxford: Clarendon Press, 1975).
—— *Phenomenology of Spirit*, trans. A. V. Miller (Oxford: Clarendon Press, 1977).

HEIDEGGER, MARTIN, 'Qu'est-ce que la métaphysique?', trans. H. Corbin-Petithenry, introd. A. Koyré, *Bifur* 8 (1931), 5–27.

—— *History of the Concept of Time: Prolegomena*, trans. Theodore Kissel (Bloomington: Indiana University Press, 1985).

—— *The Basic Problems of Phenomenology*, trans. Albert Hofstadter, rev. edn (Bloomington: Indiana University Press, 1988).

—— *Being and Time*, trans. John Macquarrie and Edward Robinson (Oxford: Blackwell, 1993).

—— *Basic Questions of Philosophy: Selected "Problems" of "Logic"*, trans. Richard Rojcewicz and André Schuwer (Bloomington: Indiana University Press, 1994).

HINGLEY, RONALD, *Nihilists: Russian Radicals and Revolutionaries in the Reign of Alexander II (1855–81)* (London: Weidenfeld & Nicolson, 1967).

HUSSERL, EDMUND, *La Philosophie comme science rigoureuse*, trans. Quentin Lauer (Paris: P.U.F., 1955).

—— *Logical Investigations*, trans. J. N. Findlay (London: Routledge & Kegan Paul; New York: Humanities Press, 1970).

—— *Ideas: General Introduction to Pure Phenomenology*, trans. W. R. Boyce Gibson (New York: Collier, 1962; 1st publ. London: Allen & Unwin; New York: Macmillan, 1931).

—— *On the Phenomenology of the Consciousness of Internal Time (1893–1917)*, trans. John Barnett Brough (Dordrecht: Kluwer, 1991).

—— *Cartesian Meditations: An Introduction to Phenomenology*, trans. Dorion Cairns (Dordrecht: Kluwer, 1993).

HYPPOLITE, JEAN, *Genesis and Structure in Hegel's Phenomenology of Spirit*, trans. Samuel Cherniak and John Heckman (Evanston, IL: Northwestern University Press, 1974).

IZENBERG, GERALD N., *The Existential Critique of Freud: The Crisis of Autonomy* (Princeton: Princeton University Press, 1976).

JAY, MARTIN, *Downcast Eyes: The Denigration of Vision in Twentieth Century French Thought* (Berkeley and Los Angeles: University of California Press, 1994).

KANT, IMMANUEL, *Critique of Pure Reason*, trans. Norman Kemp Smith (London: Macmillan, 1993).

—— *Critique of Practical Reason*, trans. Lewis White Beck (New York: Macmillan, 1993).

—— *Foundations of the Metaphysics of Morals*, trans. Lewis White Beck (Englewood Cliffs, NJ: Prentice Hall, 1995).

—— *The Metaphysics of Morals*, trans. and ed. Mary Gregor (Cambridge: Cambridge University Press, 1996).

KOLAKOWSKI, LESZEK, *Husserl and the Search for Certitude* (New Haven: Yale University Press, 1975).

—— *God Owes Us Nothing: A Brief Remark on Pascal's Religion and on the Spirit of Jansenism* (Chicago: University of Chicago Press, 1995).

LAUER, QUENTIN, Introduction to Edmund Husserl, *La Phénoménologie comme science rigoureuse* (Paris: P.U.F., 1955).

LEVINAS, EMMANUEL, *De l'existence à l'existant* (Paris: J. Vrin, 1993).

—— *En découvrant l'existence avec Husserl et Heidegger* (Paris: J. Vrin, 1994).

—— *Totalité et infini: Essai sur l'extériorité* (Dordrecht: Kluwer, 1994).

—— *Difficile liberté: Essai sur le judaïsme*, 3rd edn (Paris: Albin Michel, 1995).

—— *The Theory of Intuition in Husserl's Phenomenology*, 2nd edn, trans. André Orianne (Evanston, IL: Northwestern University Press, 1995).

LYOTARD, JEAN-FRANÇOIS, *La Phénoménologie* (Paris: P.U.F., 1954).

MARION, JEAN-LUC, *L'Idole et la distance* (Paris: Grasset, 1977).

—— *Sur la théologie blanche de Descartes: Analogie, création des vérités éternelles et fondement* (Paris: P.U.F., 1981).

—— *Réduction et donation: Recherches sur Husserl, Heidegger, et la phénoménologie* (Paris: P.U.F., 1989).

—— *God Without Being*, trans. Thomas A. Carlson (Chicago: University of Chicago Press, 1991).

MATUSTIK, MARTIN J., and WESTPHAL, MEROLD (eds.), *Kierkegaard in Post/Modernity* (Bloomington: Indiana University Press, 1995).

MOONEY, EDWARD, *Selves in Discord and Resolve: Kierkegaard's Moral-Religious Psychology, from Either/Or to Sickness unto Death* (London: Routledge, 1996).

NANCY, JEAN-LUC, *Des lieux divins* (Mauvezin: Trans-Europ-Repress, 1987).

—— *L'Expérience de la liberté* (Paris: Galilée, 1988).

NIETZSCHE, FRIEDRICH, *The Will to Power*, trans. Walter Kaufmann and R. J. Hollingdale (New York: Vintage, 1968).

—— *Thus Spoke Zarathoustra*, trans. R.J. Hollingdale (London: Penguin, 1969).

—— *The Gay Science, with a Prelude in Rhymes and an Appendix of Songs*, trans. Walter Kaufmann (New York: Vintage, 1974).

—— *Twilight of the Idols; The Anti-Christ*, trans. R. J. Hollingdale (London: Penguin, 1990).

—— *Beyond Good and Evil*, trans. R. J. Hollingdale (London: Penguin, 1990).

—— *Ecce Homo*, trans. R. J. Hollingdale (London: Penguin, 1992).

—— *The Birth of Tragedy*, trans. Shaun Whiteside (London: Penguin, 1993).

—— *On the Genealogy of Morality*, ed. Keith Ansell-Pearson, trans. Carol Diethe (Cambridge: Cambridge University Press, 1994).

—— *Philosophy and Truth: Selections from Nietzsche's Notebooks of the Early 1870's*, ed. and trans. Daniel Breazeale (Atlantic Highlands, NJ: Humanities Press, 1995).

RICOEUR, PAUL, *Freud and Philosophy: An Essay on Interpretation*, trans. Denis Savage (New Haven: Yale University Press, 1970).

ROUDINESCO, ELISABETH, *La Bataille de cents ans: L'Histoire de la psychanalise en France*, ii: *(1925–1985)* (Paris: Éditions du Seuil, 1986).

SARTRE, JEAN-PAUL, *L'Existentialisme est un humanisme* (Paris: Nagel, 1946).
—— 'Qu'est-ce que la littérature?', *Situations* ii. (Paris: Gallimard, 1948).
SCRUTON, ROGER, *Kant* (Oxford: Oxford University Press, 1996).
SPIEGELBERG, H., *The Phenomenological Movement: A Historical Introduction*, ii (The Hague: Martinus Nijhoff, 1965).
—— *The Context of the Phenomenological Movement* (The Hague: Martinus Nijhoff, 1981).
WAHL, JEAN, 'Kierkegaard: L'Angoisse et l'instant', *La Nouvelle Revue française*, 20/223 (1 Apr. 1932), 634–55.
—— *Études kierkegaardiennes* (Paris: Fernand Aubier, 1938).
WILLIAMS, BERNARD, *Ethics and the Limits of Philosophy* (London: Fontana, 1993).
WITTGENSTEIN, LUDWIG, *On Certainty*, trans. Denis Paul and G. E. M. Anscombe (Oxford: Basil Blackwell, 1969).

INDEX